PROMOTERS, PATRIOTS, AND PARTISANS
Historiography in Nineteenth-Century English Canada

During the nineteenth century, the writing of history in English-speaking Canada changed from promotional efforts by amateurs to an academically based discipline. Professor Taylor charts this transition in a comprehensive history.

The early historians – the promoters of the title – sought to further their own interests through exaggerated accounts of a particular colony to which they had developed a transient attachment. Eventually this group was replaced by patriots, whose writing was influenced by loyalty to the land of their birth and residence. This second generation of historians attempted both to defend their respective colonies by explaining away past disappointments and to fit events into a predictive pattern of progress and development. In the process they established distinctive identities for each of the British North American colonies.

Eventually a confrontation occurred between those who saw Canada as a nation and those whose traditions and vistas were provincial in emphasis. Ultimately the former prevailed, only to find the present and future too complex and too ominous to understand. Historians subsequently lost their sense of purpose and direction and fell into partisan disagreement or pessimistic nostalgia. This abandonment of their role paved the way for the new, professional breed of historian as the twentieth century opened.

In the course of his analysis, Taylor considers a number of key issues about the writing of history: the kind of people who undertake it and their motivation for doing so, the intended and actual effects of their work, its influence on subsequent historical writing, and the development of uniform and accepted standards of professional practice.

M. BROOK TAYLOR is a member of the Department of History, Mount St Vincent University.

M. BROOK TAYLOR

PROMOTERS, PATRIOTS, AND PARTISANS

Historiography in Nineteenth-Century English Canada

UNIVERSITY OF TORONTO PRESS
Toronto Buffalo London

© University of Toronto Press 1989
Toronto Buffalo London
Printed in Canada

ISBN 0-8020-2683-4 (cloth)
ISBN 0-8020-6716-6 (paper)

∞

Printed on acid-free paper

Canadian Cataloguing in Publication Data

Taylor, M. Brook (Martin Brook), 1951–
Promoters, patriots, and partisans: historiography
in nineteenth-century English Canada

Includes index.
ISBN 0-8020-2683-4 (bound)   ISBN 0-8020-6716-6 (pbk.)

1. Canada – Historiography. 2. Canada – History –
19th century. I. Title.

FC149.T38 1989   971'.007'2   C89-094731-7
F1024.T38 1989

This book has been published with the help of
a grant from the Canadian Federation for the
Humanities, using funds provided by the Social Sciences
and Humanities Research Council of Canada.

To Hilary, without whom ...

Contents

ABBREVIATIONS viii
PREFACE ix

Introduction 3

1 Promoters and the Decision to Write Canadian History 9

2 The Patriot Reaction in the Maritimes 41

3 The Anomaly of Quebec 84

4 Reform Challenge in Upper Canada 116

5 A National Consensus 152

6 The Maritimes Opt Out 181

7 Partisans and Pessimists 231

Conclusion 267

INDEX 273

Abbreviations

AO	Archives of Ontario (Toronto)
CHR	*Canadian Historical Review*
DCB	*Dictionary of Canadian Biography*
JCS	*Journal of Canadian Studies*
NA	National Archives of Canada (Ottawa)
NBM	New Brunswick Museum (Saint John)
PANS	Public Archives of Nova Scotia (Halifax)
PAPEI	Public Archives of Prince Edward Island (Charlottetown)
RHPRC	*Review of Historical Publications Relating to Canada*

Preface

My decision to study the writing of Canadian history in the pre-professional age sprang from two deep-seated compulsions. First, it was and is a source of puzzlement to me why I should find the past fascinating. The study of others who write history, especially when no one paid them to do so, had in it an element of self-exploration. Second, my father early instilled in me a love of books, preferably old, leather-bound, and slightly musty volumes, with what the antiquarian dealers call light foxing at the edges. The prospect of passing several years in the company of such books was irresistible. I can only hope that a work so selfishly conceived incidentally proves valuable to others.

Not the least among the satisfactions of completing this book is the opportunity thereby provided to thank those who assisted in its preparation. These include the knowledgeable and helpful staffs at the Archives nationale du Québec, the New Brunswick Museum, the National Archives of Canada, the Public Archives of New Brunswick, the Public Archives of Nova Scotia, the Archives of Ontario, the Public Archives of Prince Edward Island, and the University of Toronto Library. Robert Wuetherick was instrumental in obtaining permission for me to examine manuscript entries for the unpublished volumes of that essential work, the *Dictionary of Canadian Biography*. Several individuals also contributed valuable pieces of information or tracked down leads at the expense of their own research, among whom I must note Brian Cuthbertson, Elinor Kyte Senior, Alice R. Stewart, and Tom Vincent. Still others provided the intellectual fellowship necessary to maintain morale and a sense of proportion. In this regard, the members of Gilbert Ryle, especially Ben, Brad, and Carol, were invaluable.

Professor Carl Berger supervised the PH D thesis from which this study is derived: his patience made the task easier; his example made the result better. Professor Jack Bumsted read and commented upon the final manuscript. Although he may not be satisfied that this historian is yet entirely free from the prejudice of being born, raised, and educated in Toronto, he did his best to broaden my perspective.

Despite the support of these institutions and individuals, errors of fact and weaknesses of interpretation no doubt remain. I alone am accountable for such faults. There is, however, someone else who must bear a measure of responsibility, if not for this book then for my decision to become a historian. Many individuals make their choice to pursue an academic career because of a teacher: for me, Ian Ross Robertson was that teacher, now friend.

Finally, I would like to thank Gerry Hallowell, manuscript editor at the University of Toronto Press and seasonal neighbour on the South Shore, for his wise guidance. I would also like to thank copy editor Margaret Allen; it was an education. The manuscript was prepared with the aid of an internal grant from Mount Saint Vincent University and published with financial support from the Social Sciences and Humanities Research Council of Canada. Portions of this work previously appeared in slightly different form in the *Journal of Canadian Studies* ('The Poetry and Prose of History: *Evangeline* and the Historians of Nova Scotia,' vol. 23, nos 1, 2 (Spring/Summer 1988): 46–67) and *Acadiensis* ('Thomas Chandler Haliburton as a Historian,' vol. 13, no. 2 (Spring 1984): 50–68). Grateful acknowledgement is made for permission to reprint them here.

PROMOTERS, PATRIOTS, AND PARTISANS

*We do not imagine that any one except
the printers ever read these works
through, yet the true historical writer
might find in them useful materials for
his purpose.*

Anonymous reviewer, *Athenaeum*,
2 May 1857

Introduction

This book is about memory. Specifically, it is about the public memory that passes as history. Such memory is plural not singular. Theologians, natural scientists, and novelists, for example, will remember the past in different ways, use it to serve different purposes, and employ distinct methods to recall it. Each strand of memory will have its own anniversaries and cycles of events, and there is no *a priori* reason why these different strands should merge into a single image.[1] If one could identify all the diverse traditions of a nation through a given period of time, one would have something approaching a study of the historical consciousness of, say, English-Canadian society in the nineteenth century. That would be an ambitious project; this is a modest one. My purpose here is simply to examine one particular strand in the memory of English Canadians – that found in writings tracing the history of a colony, province, or the nation to the year 1896.

Authors were generally attracted to the history of British North America by prosaic contemporary conditions, not by a self-conscious desire to publish historical works. Few among them were academic scholars; none were professional historians; usually they did not write more than one book. The upper chronological limit falls in the decade in which, with the emergence of history as a major university subject and a profession, these characteristics changed. The year 1894 might well have served as the terminus, for in that year George MacKinnon Wrong (1860–1948) was appointed to a newly created chair of history at the University of Toronto; this event, along with the similar appointment of Charles William Colby (1867–1955) at McGill in 1895, marked the

1 J.G.A. Pocock, 'The Origins of Study of the Past: A Comparative Approach,' *Comparative Studies in Society and History: An International Quarterly* 4 (1961–2): 213

acceptance of history as a separate subject in English-Canadian academe.[2] It was Wrong himself, however, who selected 1896 as the traditional date to signify the beginning of a new era, for in that year he established the *Review of Historical Publications Relating to Canada*, the catalyst for the formation of the Canadian Historical Association and the precursor of the *Canadian Historical Review*.[3] Although many of the original reviewers were not themselves professional historians, most pridefully traced their intellectual ancestry to the new scholarly discipline of the German universities and, through the medium of the *Review of Historical Publications Relating to Canada*, sought to instil or impose their standards upon all historians operating in the country.

Questions naturally arise. Who would write history before universities were willing to pay them to do so, and why? Furthermore, in the absence of uniform and accepted standards of professional practice, how would they carry out their task? What effect did they hope to have? What effect did they have? Finally, what was their influence on the subsequent development of historical writing in Canada? These are the questions to which this study addresses itself.

A few simple generalizations can be made. Individuals moved to write about the course of development in their colony, province, or nation were naturally drawn from the initially small but rapidly expanding literate élite. Those most likely to take the time to publish their historical reflections were lawyers, journalists, office-holders, and others whose stock-in-trade was the written word. More significantly, almost all existed at the edges of, flirted with, or in some cases actively participated in political life and were invariably motivated to write by personal engagement in the concerns of the day. As the direction of public affairs changed, the purpose of writing history altered, audiences shifted, and methods were adjusted. Yet whatever transformations took place over time, all these writers were joined by the common desire to trace the historical pace and direction of development.

In asking the question, How did my colony, province, or nation evolve? individual authors became participants in an ongoing debate with presuppositions that they could influence but not escape. They may not have been bound by a professionally instilled code of conduct, but they were not free to set their own rules. To have an effect they must be believed; to be believed they must recognize conventions. While such

2 Carl Berger, *The Writing of Canadian History: Aspects of English-Canadian Historical Writing Since 1900*, 2nd ed. (1976; Toronto 1986) 8–9
3 George MacKinnon Wrong, 'The Beginnings of Historical Criticism in Canada: A Retrospect, 1896–1936,' *CHR* 17 (1936): 1–8

conventions were dynamic and changes did take place, especially in the reasons for asking the question and the manner of answering it, alterations in the terms of debate must be justified and explained. Viewed from this perspective, the most important histories were those that had the greatest effect on the shape and direction of continuing discussion.

By focusing on this single strand of memory, I have fastened on to what is known in the jargon of intellectual historians as a 'discourse.'[4] Long caught between the competing schools of idealism and positivism, between the treatment of ideas as causes or effects, many intellectual historians now bypass this dilemma and seek to determine why individuals used particular ideas in the way they did by asking how ideas work within the context of a specific debate. Such a debate, or discourse, is an interaction between minds and revolves around something possessed in common. Participants in a discourse share certain values, beliefs, concepts, presuppositions – 'ideas,' in short – which at the most functional and concrete level issue as a shared question. 'Questions,' writes American intellectual historian David A. Hollinger, 'are the points of contact between minds, where agreements are consolidated and where differences are acknowledged and dealt with; questions are the dynamism whereby membership in a community of discourse is established, renewed, and sometimes terminated.'[5] When ideas are viewed in their capacity as answers to a question shared with other persons – for example, How did Canada develop? – they become contributions to a discourse.

The purpose of this study, then, is to follow the discourse, the conversation of a community of intellects attempting to trace the historical ascent of the country. A premium is placed on the discovery of how questions first came to be asked of the past, who asked them, and how the questions were answered. As the debate grew, altered, and diversified, and as purposes, audiences, and methods changed, our focus remains on those who pushed the argument forward and fashioned definitive answers. Less attention is accorded to writers who merely repeated accepted interpretations or took idiosyncratic turnings. The discourse,

4 See the papers in two recent collections: John Higham and Paul K. Conkin, eds, *New Directions in American Intellectual History* (Baltimore, Md., 1979); Dominick LaCapra and Steven L. Kaplan, eds, *Modern European Intellectual History: Reappraisals and New Perspectives* (Ithaca, NY, and London 1982). The theoretical godfathers of the discourse are Thomas S. Kuhn, Quentin Skinner, and Clifford Geertz. See Thomas S. Kuhn, *The Structure of Scientific Revolutions*, rev. ed. (1962; Chicago 1970); Quentin Skinner, 'Meaning and Understanding in the History of Ideas,' *History and Theory* 8 (1969): 3–53; Clifford Geertz, *The Interpretation of Cultures* (New York 1973).
5 David A. Hollinger, 'Historians and the Discourse of Intellectuals,' in Higham and Conkin, eds, *New Directions*, 42–4

rather than an arbitrarily selected list of authors, ideas, or themes, is the focus of this study.

The decision to follow a particular discourse will not be taken as a licence to ignore parallel developments among other preoccupations. Authors fascinated by the question of how their colony, province, or nation evolved did not operate in an intellectual vacuum; neither were they monomaniacal. Individuals engaged in other quests made, whether on purpose or by accident, crucial interventions in the course of debate over the historical evolution of colonies. Politicians, government officials, and, in one extraordinary case, a poet, as well as others with little interest in historical questions, occasionally played a significant role in the way history was written. Archival institutions and historical societies also made important contributions to the direction of research and patterns of interpretation. Nevertheless, such influences will be regarded as just that, influences, rather than elements to be studied for their own sake; the criterion for consideration is the effect exerted on the mainstream historical debate.

What gives coherence, then, both to this study and to the discourse on which it is based, is consideration of the historical development of British North America. Whether the answers historians provided were accurate or persuasive is not so much the issue as why they thought the question – How did Canada develop? – worth asking. The reason they turned to the past, it quickly becomes clear, was because they were interested in the future. Some would excuse the past, others build on it, and a few see it as divinely ordained, but all sought a better future – for themselves, their colony, and the nation. Their faith was that the golden age would come; their motivation was that it would come sooner if history were understood aright.

Naturally no two individuals saw the future that determined their past exactly alike. Nevertheless debate over the past and future history of colonial development went through three general phases, for which 'Promoters, Patriots, and Partisans' is a convenient shorthand. Initially, with so few permanent English-speaking residents in the territory of the future Canada, there was little history of the area. In this phase a number of individuals sought to further their own self-interest through the promotion of a particular colony to which they had developed a transient attachment. Seeking the favour of the British government, which wielded economic, political, and military power, they explained away the inevitable setbacks of early colonization and extolled to exaggerated extent the future potential of the land. While they often succeeded in promoting their own careers before their predictions proved false, they left the reputation of many colonies in tatters.

The second phase effectively began with the emergence of the first generation of native-born colonists. With personal fortune now irrevocably linked to place, patriots attempted to undo the damage done to their respective colonies by promotional excesses; they were particularly concerned to correct earlier false impressions given to officials in London, in whom many fundamental powers still lay. Sights were lowered and more realistic goals established in order that faith in the future might be reaffirmed. Indeed, according to patriot historians, hardships created virtues of character necessary to wrest deserved success from modest resources; it was the quality of people rather than the quantity of opportunity that created stable and lasting progress. This shift in emphasis from the land to its people incidentally provided colonists with an identity of their own. This in turn became more important at mid-century as responsible government and free trade shifted the burden of decision-making power from Great Britain to British North America.

Now, for the first time, historians spoke primarily to their compatriots rather than a distant power. Forms, method, and subject matter shifted, but the purpose remained constant: to use the past to influence the present to shape the future. The question was, what shape should the future take? Were the sturdy identities patriots had built for their separate colonies ultimately harmonious or fundamentally incompatible? According to the historians of the Canadas, the future of British North America lay in unity; according to patriots in Nova Scotia, New Brunswick, and Prince Edward Island, colonial destinies were distinct. Confederation did not so much solve this problem as abolish it, making the patriotism of one colony that of all and rendering competitors parochial.

Much was sacrificed to achieve Confederation; much was expected of Confederation. The final phase of the discourse began when the new nation failed to deliver. Instead of producing the promised peace, order, and good government, the first years of Confederation were marked by economic stagnation, political scandal, and rebellion. Horizons receded and then disappeared from view altogether. Confidence in the future, the fuel that had animated historians since the first settlement, evaporated. It was replaced by partisan recrimination, the search for what went wrong degenerating into a counter-productive drive to fix blame. In despair, some historians turned to the past with nostalgia, finding there the golden age they no longer believed lay ahead. Few had the assurance to contend with the new professional historians, who, armed with science, promised to bring order out of confusion.

The three general phases represented by promoters, patriots, and partisans give shape to the historical discourse in much though not all of British North America. The phases are pronounced in those colonies whose pace and type of social and economic development were relatively congruent: Nova Scotia, New Brunswick, Prince Edward Island, and the two Canadas. The unifying effect of propinquity was reinforced by the common political experience of representative, responsible, and confederate government. Although these five colonies developed in their own particular, not to say peculiar, ways, many of their distinct responses were to shared questions. In short, the pattern of discourse examined in this book is theirs.

Newfoundland, the Arctic, the Northwest Territories, and the west coast colonies developed at a different, usually later, pace, and in ways relatively dissimilar to those that characterized the more mature colonies. Certainly some questions were common to the whole of British North America, if only that of mother country. Nevertheless, only in Nova Scotia, New Brunswick, Prince Edward Island, and the two Canadas were historic parallels sufficient to create a common pattern of discourse. Different though their responses were, historians in these five colonies saw many of their most important problems as mutual. For this reason they often considered, if only to dismiss, the answers arrived at by their colleagues in comparable situations, whereas they would have been insulted by the suggestion that they had anything to learn from one of the less developed territories or colonies. A discourse is a conversation of a community of intellects and, since the community in question excluded Newfoundland, the territories, and the west coast, so will this study.[6]

In summary, then, the purpose of this book is to examine how the central questions of early English-Canadian historiography were initially formulated and subsequently developed. There is, in the elaboration of this discourse, a built-in bias in favour of the exemplar over the extraordinary, the common over the unusual, and the enduring over the transient. However, it is only through the description of the presuppositions guiding any discourse that the extraordinary, unusual, and transient can be defined as such.

6 Fortunately, there are excellent analyses of historical writing in these regions, which somewhat excuses their exclusion here. See Patrick O'Flaherty, *The Rock Observed: Studies in the Literature of Newfoundland* (Toronto 1979); Doug Owram, *Promise of Eden: The Canadian Expansionist Movement and the Idea of the West, 1856–1900* (Toronto 1980); and Allan Smith, 'The Writing of British Columbia History,' *BC Studies* 45 (1980): 73–102.

1

Promoters
and the Decision
to Write Canadian History

When Christopher Columbus reached America, it had no past – at least none recognizable to European historians. The extraordinary consequence was that the written history of the New World would occur entirely within the memory of modern man. Voyages of discovery and exploration, however remarkable in their own right, were not fabulous. Native peoples were extraordinary but not phantoms. Colonies were founded by all-too-human adventurers and the immigration of ordinary men and women, not by the likes of Romulus and Remus. Nothing was irrecoverable; all was comprehended. The 'discovery' of America, then, offered Europeans the opportunity both to make and to watch themselves make history. Indeed, the task set historians by the age of discovery was nothing less than the consideration of an encounter with a new land. The result was a sudden and dramatic expansion of historiographical practice, from the selective recovery of moral and practical lessons of statecraft to the comprehensive recording of a process of exploitation and settlement. Abstract scholasticism gave way to empiricism. History was now active, not contemplative.[1]

It followed that to write the history of the New World one had to leave the Old. Participation was the only way to gain knowledge of the European conquest of America. There was no substitute for experience. Thus when histories came, they came from the pens of men (as they invariably were) who were actors in the events they observed. The past they chronicled was often in part their own. The result was a rough-and-tumble mixture of experience, explanation and rationalization. Canadian

---

1 Wayne Franklin, *Discoverers, Explorers, Settlers: The Diligent Writers of Early America* (Chicago 1979) 1–14

historiography began in an age of engaged observation and was written by individuals whose aims were rarely disinterested.

The first history in English relating to Canada is generally regarded to be an anonymous pamphlet published in 1749 at London under the title *A Geographical History of Nova Scotia.*[2] A modest tract of some 110 pages, it is devoted primarily to, in the words of the subtitle, 'An Accurate Description of the Bays, Harbours, Lakes, and Rivers, the Nature of the Soil, and the Produce of the Country.' The author also chose to allot approximately thirty pages to, again in the words of the subtitle (this being an age in which the title page really did tell you what was to be found inside a book), 'an Account ... of the various Struggles between the Two Crowns of *England* and *France* for the Possession of [Nova Scotia].' In the event, the 'Account' is little more than a précis of the relevant passages of the *Histoire et description générale de la Nouvelle France*, published at Paris five years earlier by Pierre-François-Xavier de Charlevoix (1682–1761).[3] There was, then, nothing new, nothing exceptional, about the tale told – except the fact that it was there in the pamphlet at all.

A Geographical History of Nova Scotia was, in fact, part of that genre commonly referred to as promotional literature, a genre that for obvious reasons was never entirely comfortable with chronicles of bloodshed, Indian raids, and instability. In order adequately to explain this anomaly – this first decision to write Canadian history in English – it is not enough simply to examine the thirty-odd pages of historical narrative to be found in *A Geographical History of Nova Scotia*, or even to analyse the pamphlet as a whole. One must begin instead with a study of the style and form of the genre of which *A Geographical History of Nova Scotia* is a part. In particular, the pamphlet should be studied as a contribution to Canadian promotional literature, which, in the first instance, emanated from the Maritime region. This broad approach not only accounts more convincingly for the presence of a narrative history in *A Geographical History of Nova Scotia*, it also clearly exhibits how early English-Canadian historical writing grew out of, and was conditioned by, the writing of promotional literature.

Considering its quantity, the promotional literature dealing with

2 Kenneth N. Windsor, 'Historical Writing in Canada to 1920,' in Carl F. Klinck, gen. ed., *Literary History of Canada: Canadian Literature in English* (Toronto 1965) 210

3 [Pierre-François-Xavier] de Charlevoix, *Histoire et description générale de la Nouvelle France, avec le journal historique d'un voyage fait par ordre du roi dans l'Amérique septentrionnale,* 3 vols and 6 vols (Paris 1744)

North America has received very little scholarly attention in either Canada or the United States.[4] In part this is due to the amorphous nature of the genre, for anything that was not derogatory was, to some degree, promotional. In a sense, 'all the descriptive writers of early America were promoting or advertising the new land.'[5] Promotional literature was, then, an often indistinguishable part of the extensive effort to answer what were for contemporary Europeans the profound epistemological problems posed by the New World: Where was it? What was there? Who was there? And, above all, why go there? The distinguishing feature of promotional literature was not how it answered these questions but why. Among the many men on the spot upon whom European governments, potential investors and settlers, and the simply curious relied for information, promoters were those who had tied their personal fortunes to the fate of the colony observed. In most cases this was why they were where they were. The result was a genre characterized by an uneasy alliance between descriptive method and questionable motive. The quality of the prose, the deadening lists of natural phenomena, and the prosaic descriptions of exploitable resources have subsequently drawn few literary critics. Historians, for their part, have naturally suspected the veracity of works so obviously the product of self-interest. Nevertheless, the fact remains that contemporary Europeans were to a disturbing extent dependent upon promoters for information about the New World during those crucial early years of acquisition and settlement.

In large measure the individual requirements of various colonies during comparable periods of growth produced a body of promotional literature of tactical variety and strategic uniformity. In the case of the Maritime region, promoters were most influential during the settlement-planting period of the mid-eighteenth century. During this time perhaps a dozen or more tracts, pamphlets, or broadsides relating to the region were published – to say nothing of the wealth of unpublished reports making their way back to England. Of those items published, six have been selected for study here, singled out because they were frequently

4 The secondary literature on promotional pamphlets and books is largely bibliographical. Exceptions are: Howard Mumford Jones, 'The Colonial Impulse: An Analysis of the "Promotion" Literature of Colonization,' American Philosophical Society, *Proceedings* 90 (1946): 131–61; Hugh T. Lefler, 'Promotional Literature of the Southern Colonies,' *Journal of Southern History* 33 (1967): 3–25; Richard Beale Davis, *Intellectual Life in the Colonial South, 1585–1763*, 3 vols (Knoxville, Tenn., 1978) vol. 1, 1–102.
5 Jarvis Means Morse quoted in Lefler, 'Promotional Literature,' 24

referred to, copied, or imitated in the subsequent historiography of their respective colonies.[6]

Who wrote Maritime promotional literature? For the most part we do not know. Like the author of *A Geographical History of Nova Scotia*, Maritime promoters wished to remain anonymous, perhaps in the hope that their motives would be hidden with their identity. Of the six promotional works examined below, two were signed,[7] the author of another has been subsequently identified,[8] and three will in all likelihood remain unattributed.[9] Generalizations must therefore be advanced with caution. To begin with the obvious, all six authors were literate men of some education. All of them were socially pretentious: anonymity was never intended as a renunciation of an author's claim to the status of

6 In 1749 the boundaries of Nova Scotia were still those set by the Treaty of Utrecht in 1713, that is to say the peninsula and indefinite portions of the north shore and the mainland. In 1763 Cape Breton Island (Île Royale) and the Island of St John (Île Saint-Jean) were surrendered by France in the Treaty of Paris and annexed to Nova Scotia by the Proclamation of 1763. That same proclamation annexed to Nova Scotia those portions of the mainland south of the Restigouche and east of the St Croix rivers. In 1769 the Island of St John was separated from Nova Scotia and in 1798 was renamed Prince Edward Island. New Brunswick and Cape Breton Island were likewise separated in 1784. In 1820 Cape Breton Island was reannexed to Nova Scotia. This study will adhere to contemporary usage.

7 [Otis Little (he signed the Preface),] *The State of Trade in the Northern Colonies Considered; With an Account of Their Produce, and a Particular Description of Nova Scotia* (London 1748); John Wilson, Late Inspector of the Stores, *A Genuine Narrative of the Transactions in Nova Scotia, since the Settlement, June 1749, till August the 5th, 1751; In which the Nature, Soil, and Produce of the Country Are Related, with the Particular Attempts of the Indians to Disturb the Colony* (London [c. 1751])

8 [William Bollan,] *The Importance and Advantage of Cape-Breton, Truly Stated, and Impartially Considered* (London 1746). For the generally accepted attribution see Justin Winsor, 'Authorities on the French and Indian Wars of New England and Acadia, 1688–1763,' in Justin Winsor, ed., *Narrative and Critical History of America*, 8 vols (Boston 1884–9) vol. 5 (1887) 434.

9 *A Geographical History of Nova Scotia. Containing an Account of the Situation, Extent and Limits Thereof. As Also of the Various Struggles between the Two Crowns of England and France for the Possession of that Province. Wherein Is Shewn, the Importance of It, as Well with Regard to Our Trade, as to the Securing of Our Other Settlements in North America. To Which Is Added, an Accurate Description of the Bays, Harbours, Lakes, and Rivers, the Nature of the Soil, and the Produce of the Country. Together with the Manners and Customs of the Indian Inhabitants* (London 1749); *The Importance of Settling and Fortifying Nova Scotia: With a Particular Account of the Climate, Soil, and Native Inhabitants of the Country*, by a Gentleman lately arrived from that Colony (London 1751); *An Account of the Present State of Nova-Scotia: In Two Letters to a Noble Lord: One from a Gentleman in the Navy Lately Arrived from Thence. The Other from a Gentleman Who Long Resided There. Made Public by His Lordship's Desire* (London 1756)

'Gentleman.' Specifically, from internal evidence we know that John Wilson was inspector of the stores at Halifax some time between 1749 and 1751, and that another author was a 'Gentleman in the Navy.' Subsequent scholarship tells us that *The Importance and Advantage of Cape-Breton* was by William Bollan, the agent for Massachusetts in London and son-in-law of Governor William Shirley.[10] In short, the six authors all seem to have been either military or civil officers who observed their respective subjects at first hand in the line of duty. Such was likely to be the case in the freshly conquered Maritime region, where so little English development had yet occurred beyond that directly initiated by the governments of Great Britain or the New England colonies.

The general picture of the six promoters is given particular colour by Otis Little, the one confirmed author for whom there exists an excellent biography.[11] Little was born into an important Massachusetts family in 1712. He received a degree from Harvard, was called to the provincial bar, and for a time was active in politics as an ally of Governor Shirley. Despite such advantages, Little did not prosper in any of his endeavours. Too ambitious, too greedy, 'he was clearly a man out to make his living from public life and connections.'[12] With the outbreak of the War of the Austrian Succession in 1744, Little saw his main chance for advancement and gain. He raised his own company of volunteers but was captured on his way to Annapolis Royal in Nova Scotia. Released on parole too late to take part in the first siege of Louisbourg, Little was stationed for a time at Annapolis Royal. In May of 1746 he was sent to London with official papers from Governor Shirley and with letters of introduction to important people in England. Once in London Little occasionally lobbied for a group of New England merchants, more often for himself. It was during this period that he wrote *The State of Trade in the Northern Colonies Considered*, in part to please Governor Shirley, but largely with the thought, as he later admitted, that Nova Scotia might yet provide a 'chance to get some Employment.'[13]

Otis Little certainly received his reward. Having established his credentials as one knowledgeable about Nova Scotia, he was selected to accompany Governor Edward Cornwallis and the Halifax colonization

10 Winsor, 'Authorities on the French and Indian Wars,' 438–9; J.S. McLennan, *Louisbourg from Its Foundation to Its Fall* (London 1918) 167; Bernard Bailyn, *The Ordeal of Thomas Hutchinson* (Cambridge, Mass., 1974) 42, 58
11 J.M. Bumsted, 'Otis Little,' *DCB*, vol. 3 (Toronto 1974) 403–5
12 Ibid., 403
13 Quoted in ibid., 404

fleet of 1749. Over the next two years he acquired positions as captain in an independent company, commissary of stores and provisions in Halifax, advocate-general in the Vice-Admiralty Court of Nova Scotia, and king's attorney. Unhappily his venality and pretentious manner unwound his web of success. In 1751 he was suspended from his position as commissary for 'irregularities in the books,' and in 1753 was found guilty as king's attorney of taking a bribe. Unable to support himself, in 1754 he disappeared into the West Indies. He died there or on the way.

A self-interested office seeker, Little is the epitome of the image scholars have developed to characterize writers of promotional literature, and what is known of the other five authors under examination here tends to confirm academic prejudice.[14] The predominant image is of a minor office-holder, a 'Gentleman in the Navy,' a 'Late Inspector of the Stores,' hoping to receive the 'Thanks and Applause of all his Fellow Citizens.' In addition there is a rootless quality to Maritime promoters that the life and career of Otis Little exemplifies. Born in New England or Britain, Maritime promoters were gentlemen who spent 'several years' in Nova Scotia, 'Long Resided There,' and now were 'lately arrived from that Colony.'[15] They were mid-Atlantic men with no fixed abode and no inherent attachment to the interests of Nova Scotia. Little wrote to promote the colony in the hope of gaining employment there. Others wrote to promote Nova Scotia in order to defend the position of a patron or employer. William Bollan, for instance, as agent for Massachusetts, was elaborating the position of Governor Shirley in arguing for the retention of Cape Breton.[16] John Wilson was a separate case. Perhaps for reasons relating to the fact that he was the *late* inspector of the stores, Wilson wrote a scathing 'demotional' pamphlet with an animus that clearly had its roots in events having little to do with the intrinsic merits of the colony itself. Each pamphlet message sent back to England was at least potentially a play for favour; the facts could be arranged so as to increase the expected grant of favour, and circulation need not be wide to have the desired

14 Jarvis Means Morse, *American Beginnings: Highlights and Sidelights of the Birth of the New World* (Washington, DC, 1952) 23; Richard S. Dunn, 'Seventeenth-Century English Historians of America,' in James Morton Smith, ed., *Seventeenth-Century America: Essays in Colonial History* (Chapel Hill, NC, 1959) 206

15 *Importance of Settling and Fortifying Nova Scotia*, Title Page, 37; *Account of the Present State of Nova-Scotia*, Title Page

16 [Bollan,] *Importance and Advantage of Cape-Breton*, 117; Winsor, 'Authorities on the French and Indian Wars,' 438–9; George A. Rawlyk, *Nova Scotia's Massachusetts: A Study of Massachusetts–Nova Scotia Relations, 1630 to 1784* (Montreal 1973) 200–1; Francis Jennings, *Empire of Fortune: Crowns, Colonies, and Tribes in the Seven Years War in America* (New York 1988) 305–10

effect. To the reader of promotional literature this group portrait, such as it is, would suggest that the genre had an acute problem of credibility.

In the first instance, however, promoters gained influence according to the power of the patron or faction for whom they wrote. The pamphlets of Otis Little and William Bollan on their own were unlikely to convince imperial authorities to retain and develop either Nova Scotia or Cape Breton, but Governor Shirley and the government of Massachusetts might use them to achieve these ends. Whether their works had this effect or not, as long as their sponsors were pleased Little and Bollan would personally benefit.[17] Nevertheless, in order for a patron or faction to use a pamphlet, and consequently in order for its author to benefit, it must be reasonable and persuasive. Suspicious and preoccupied officials in London must be convinced. Pamphlets still had to be plausible.

Maritime promoters were not defenceless before the sceptic, for they had one crucial advantage – possession of firsthand information of Nova Scotia. For a time this asset permitted promoters to control the language and the very forms of expression employed in the composition of early reports from the colony. The scope of their knowledge should not, however, be exaggerated. All six promoters wrote in the decade between 1746 and 1756, and the ground that any one of them had covered in Nova Scotia was probably quite restricted. To say this is not to belittle their achievement, which was in some ways remarkable. It simply reflects the dislocated, scattered, extensive, and inaccessible character of Maritime geography. Prior to the founding of Halifax in 1749, English establishments in Nova Scotia were limited to a miscellany of forts, the headquarters of which were to be found at Annapolis Royal. The English had been 'masters of this extensive country for forty years, without ten *English* families (except those of the garrison) in the whole country.'[18] The lands of the future provinces of New Brunswick and Prince Edward Island were largely a closed book to the English.[19] The settlement at Halifax began a

17 For a superb analysis of a contemporary example of how a patron used a promotional pamphlet, see the account of Pennsylvania proprietor Thomas Penn's sponsorship of William Smith's *A Brief State of the Province of Pennsylvania* (London 1755) in ibid., 224–43.
18 *Importance of Settling and Fortifying Nova Scotia*, 8
19 For a description of the lands that would one day form New Brunswick and Prince Edward Island, the English reading public of the mid-eighteenth century had to rely upon a work by French spy Thomas Pichon (1700–81), which was published anonymously and translated as *Genuine Letters and Memoirs, Relating to the Natural, Civil, and Commercial History of the Islands of Cape Breton, and Saint John, from the First Settlement There, to the Taking of Louisbourg by the English, in 1758 ...* (London 1760). See T.A. Crowley, 'Thomas Pichon,' *DCB*, vol. 4 (Toronto 1979) 630–2.

process of expansion but at a pace insufficient to change the rudimentary nature of English settlement prior to 1756. Those Maritime promoters who wrote before 1749 displayed scant knowledge of geography beyond Annapolis Royal and Cape Breton; those after 1749 were familiar with little outside Halifax. Otis Little said he made an 'appeal to the most intelligent Persons' who had resided in Nova Scotia 'long enough to make proper Observations,'[20] and we may presume other authors widened their knowledge in a similar fashion. These inquiries do not change the fact that the true extent of a promoter's knowledge did not match the compass so often implied on the title page.

What Maritime promoters required was, first, a forum in which they could unselfconsciously present their case, a debate in which their motives would not immediately be called into question, and, second, a literary strategy for deploying their knowledge in a way that exaggerated its scope. To solve the first problem, promoters simply posed as disinterested contributors to the ongoing debate in Britain over the merits of an expanding empire. In common with the authors of official reports, topographical surveyors, and other visitors to the colonies, they supplied the facts necessary to sustain arguments over the advantages and disadvantages attending the foundation and maintenance of colonies. Invariably promoters wrote to recommend the utility of colonies in general and of one colony in particular – that colony to which their individual ambition was tied. Their ability to hide behind the patriotic assumptions of debate in England should not obscure the fact that, unlike British colonial theorists, Maritime promoters were generally more interested in what happened to themselves than to the empire.

When Maritime promoters began to write in the late 1740s the strategic debate over the empire was beginning to show signs of running against procolonial assumptions. Traditional mercantilist economic theory, which had held sway in Britain since the sixteenth century, assumed a world of finite capacity: no single country could achieve a material advantage without at the same time disadvantaging another; self-sufficiency in all things was considered the only guarantee of a nation's independence. In this scheme of things colonial acquisitions were almost always seen as beneficial. Colonies generally contributed to self-sufficiency by providing commodities not indigenous to the mother country. A colony that lacked such assets might still be useful in so far as it hindered an enemy by, for instance, straddling a trade route. The one fact inhibiting unlimited

20 [Little,] *State of Trade in the Northern Colonies Considered*, vii

colonial growth was the knowledge that the mother country must never deplete its own supply of men, resources, and money if a concomitant gain was not assured.[21] As the eighteenth century progressed, and as the cost of maintaining civil and military establishments in a far-flung empire continued to rise, each proposed new colony received increasing scrutiny.

Maritime promoters naturally fell into line with the mercantilist position, and typically began pamphlets with a series of arguments justifying the utility of colonial acquisition. According to Otis Little, the fact that 'the Riches and Strength' of Britain depended principally on its commerce was 'a Fact that need[ed] no Illustration';[22] and, according to another promoter, among 'the various Methods that have been at any time thought of for enlarging this great Source of Power and Opulence, the settling of new Colonies has in the general always been marked out as one of the principal and most desirable.'[23] The more trade that could be carried on within Britain's own colonial network, the more self-sufficient and independent the nation would be. Similarly, any lessening of the necessity to trade with a rival had 'the same effect as if this Kingdom had enlarged the Sources of its own Wealth.'[24] That said, the anonymous author of *A Geographical History of Nova Scotia* acknowledged that each colonial undertaking was 'no trifling matter,' as each acquisition was necessarily 'attended with great Expence.' 'The Question will occur,' he continued, 'What Returns may be expected? What Advantages are there in Prospect to balance the Risque[?]'[25] The attempt to answer this question was the explicit purpose of all Maritime promoters.

Maritime promoters focused their attention on the question they were best prepared to answer. Their arguments would be based upon personal observation, for the moment as difficult to verify as to confute. As Dr Johnson put it, 'he who tells nothing exceeding the bounds of probability, has a right to demand that they should believe him who cannot contradict him.'[26] From this position of strength Maritime promoters could bring their intelligence to bear on the issues that English theorists had established as central to the colonial debate.[27] These issues fell into three categories. The first concentrated on the question of the ability of any

21 Klaus E. Knorr, *British Colonial Theories, 1570–1850* (Toronto 1944) 3–6
22 [Little,] *State of Trade in the Northern Colonies Considered*, 10–11
23 *Geographical History of Nova Scotia*, 10
24 [Little,] *State of Trade in the Northern Colonies Considered*, 10–11
25 *Geographical History of Nova Scotia*, 10.
26 Samuel Johnson as quoted in James Boswell, *Life of Johnson* (1791), ed. R.W. Chapman, rev. J. D. Freeman, with a new introduction by Pat Rogers (Oxford 1980) 63
27 Knorr, *Colonial Theories*, chs 1–4

given colony to support settlers. Soil, climate, and types of produce had to be established. Ancillary debates took place over the safety of the settlers from native attack, over what kinds of settlers should be sent, and generally over the speed with which a colony could be brought within the realm of European civilization. The second category of questions dealt with how a colony would fit into the general economic pattern of the empire: were its raw materials needed by England? what kind of market would the settled colony provide? would there be a net economic advantage for the mother country? The third category centred on questions of strategic military significance. These questions were to be of particular importance in the debate over Nova Scotia. 'Upon the Whole, nothing can be more obvious, than that no just Estimation can be had, nor any clear Resolution be given to all, or any of these Points, without a sufficient Knowledge of the Country in question.'[28]

The unquenchable thirst of Europeans for knowledge determined the very form and style of reports from the New World. In order to meet the demand for a comprehensive array of facts, the aim of the factual travel account was to spread graphically before the reader a great range of exact information, the function not so much to narrate as to exhibit the natural scene. In works of this type, as Germaine Warkentin observes, 'there is a definite displacement of the mythic values of the quest into a scientific and mercantile ethos that insists on the primary value of the strictly factual account.'[29] The development of this scientific vision went hand in hand with an increasingly utilitarian prose style. Indeed, it was the age of discovery that elevated truth-telling to an aesthetic status. Metaphorical extravagance, irony, and idiosyncrasy were banished, and a masculine, plain language cultivated. Descriptions tended

> whenever possible to rely on a group of presentational means in which time plays no crucial role – catalogs, tables, descriptions, discourses, expositions – forms which by their own static, even iconographic, nature convey writer and reader alike into a state of existence beyond the limits and confusions of a historical moment.[30]

The literary strategy of the patriotic debate into which Maritime promoters inserted themselves had the happy consequences of both

28 *Geographical History of Nova Scotia*, 12
29 Germaine Warkentin, 'Exploration Literature in English,' in William Toye, gen. ed., *The Oxford Companion to Canadian Literature* (Toronto 1983) 243. See also Barbara Maria Stafford, *Voyage into Substance: Art, Science, Nature, and the Illustrated Travel Account, 1760–1840* (Cambridge, Mass., 1984) ch. 1.
30 Franklin, *Discoverers, Explorers, Settlers*, 21

exaggerating the scope of their knowledge and also further submerging their motives from view. Lists, charts, maps, and so forth, by their very nature implied the comprehensive if not omniscient intelligence of the compiler. Who was to know that, for instance, a catalogue of animals was based on observations from within sight of the walls of Annapolis Royal, on rumour, or on pure invention? Taxonomic principles of ordering, whether of natural phenomena or civil institutions, were deceptive. Information so marshalled was then presented in a style whose seeming transparency avoided drawing attention to the writer's personality or feelings or, in the promoter's case, motives. Few cracks in the façade of objectivity were ever permitted.

If language and form presented Maritime promoters as all-knowing and unprejudiced, they also conspired to bring Nova Scotia into the realm of the knowable, to make Nova Scotia appear as ordered and civilized as the promotional tracts themselves. What formerly had been dispersed and unlimited was now codified and limited. For instance, when the author of *A Geographical History of Nova Scotia* began his account by outlining the boundaries of Nova Scotia, the colony's longitude and latitude, and the distances from Halifax to Boston and St John's, he was by the process of description turning several thousand square miles of wilderness into another civilized British colony. On a smaller scale, the author of *The Importance of Settling and Fortifying Nova Scotia* was doing the same thing when he outlined the first two years of growth at Halifax. Here the descriptions of both the speed and the kind of development were calculated to impress. Six hundred homes within the palisades and another five hundred without certainly represented a rapid advance, and included in those totals were a 'handsome church,' a hospital, and an orphan house.[31] The military, religious, and civil institutions of the Old World had, as it were, already planted their first seeds in Nova Scotia. The disastrous Indian attack on Dartmouth in 1750 was not mentioned. When it came time to organize information, not just about the size and extent of the colony, but also about its climate, soil, produce, and raw materials, long lists of advantages, or later the graphic device of the chart, as well as the general descriptive approach, were employed by promoters to fit colonial life within the quite literal boundaries of European control.

In summary, for a variety of reasons our six authors connected their self-interest to the promotion of Nova Scotia. Should the nature of their motives be exposed it might irrevocably damage the credibility of their works. The debate in England over the value of colonial possessions

31 *Importance of Settling and Fortifying Nova Scotia*, 18–19

offered Maritime promoters a forum in which to introduce their works as patriotic contributions to a national question. With firsthand information momentarily at a premium, promoters could deploy their valuable but limited knowledge so as to disguise both its inadequacies and their motives. The descriptive response they made to questions concerning the ability of Nova Scotia to support settlers and to complement imperial trade patterns established a detached context into which any information could be placed. At the same time, by posing as neutral, omniscient observers, Maritime promoters freed themselves from time and extent and from awkward questions of motivation and reliability. In this way their declaratory assertions achieved a measure of credibility.

There was no reason for Maritime promoters to introduce a narrative history of past events into their discussion of raw materials or the advantages of Nova Scotia for settlers. Indeed, the corrosive influence of time could easily undermine the façade of comprehensive impartiality promoters had worked so diligently to achieve. Unhappily the decisive issue that carried the debate in Britain in favour of first retaining and then settling Nova Scotia was that of strategic location, not economic potential. If all Nova Scotia's physical attributes proved illusory, Little for one believed,

> the Advantages the *French* might otherwise make of this Province, and the Want of an effectual Barrier for securing the Possession, Trade, and Fishery of the Northern Colonies against their Efforts in a future War, sufficiently demonstrate the Necessity of keeping it out of their Hands, without being diverted by the Consideration of the Expence.[32]

It was the unanimous contention of Maritime promoters that the preservation of all British colonies in North America depended 'upon the security of that one, which is a barrier to all the others.'[33] One could best prove this point by an appeal to history. The trick for promoters was to reconcile their introduction of time, and of tales of violence and uncertainty, with their larger static picture of a civil wilderness ripe for exploitation.

The ease with which history as a chronicle of recent events could be used to the detriment of Nova Scotia's reputation was amply illustrated by John Wilson's *A Genuine Narrative of the Transactions in Nova Scotia, since the Settlement, June 1749, till August the 5th, 1751.* Not content to detail Nova

32 [Little,] *State of Trade in the Northern Colonies Considered,* vi
33 *Importance of Settling and Fortifying Nova Scotia,* 31

Scotia's physical inadequacies, Wilson added 'that the Poor Inhabitants are under continual Alarms from the *Indians*, who are spirited by the *French*.' Pages were devoted to lurid descriptions of the techniques of native torture, and the pamphlet culminated with an account of the sacking of Dartmouth in June 1750. Clearly, if not controlled, such history threatened to strike fear into any potential immigrant or investor. Perhaps for this reason Maritime promoters were generally content to assert Nova Scotia's strategic significance as self-evident. Otis Little, for example, did not give a detailed historical account of events on the peninsula.

The strength of *A Geographical History of Nova Scotia* as a promotional pamphlet was its handling of history. The anonymous author of this work faced up to the fact that in order to set Nova Scotia's strategic importance 'in a clear Light,' it would be necessary to give a 'short Narrative of the *Affairs of this Province*, from the first Discovery to the present Time.' Nor did this author flinch from accepting as his organizational theme the perfidy of '*that* Nation [the French] which set no Bounds to their Ambition,' a nation that had 'during a Course of near a hundred and fifty Years, continually [made] use of both the Methods of *Arms* and *Artifice*, to wrest this Country out of the Hands of the *English*.' Nova Scotia was, according to the author, England's by right of discovery, but this right had been consistently neglected due to the 'impolitic' ignorance of the British government. While France was constantly defeated militarily in the field, it always regained its Maritime possession at the conference table. The New Englanders, alternately harassed by the French and betrayed by the British, finally won the peninsula of Nova Scotia in 1710, and now, at mid-century, threatened Cape Breton. All that was required to end the battle for control of all Nova Scotia was the enlightened determination of the British government to keep what rightly belonged to it: 'by establishing a Civil Government, and raising Forts and Garrisons in proper Parts of the Country, ... there is all the Reason in the World to expect, that in a few Years *Nova Scotia* will become a flourishing and opulent Colony.'[34]

The historical lesson drawn by the author of *A Geographical History of Nova Scotia* was that the irresolution of the English, not the strength of the French, was all that stood in the way of the successful, peaceful settlement of Nova Scotia. Two years later, in 1751, the anonymous author of *The Importance of Settling and Fortifying Nova Scotia* was able to give a brief elaboration of this lesson. 'The improvements that have been made in

34 *Geographical History of Nova Scotia*, 35, 110

[Nova Scotia] within these last two years are surprizing to every one that has seen it.' Four thousand five hundred new settlers had been brought over, a city founded, and institutions established. Forts had been constructed at the top of Bedford Basin, at Piziquid, and at Minas. 'The last two are placed just in the centre of our *French* settlements, which effectively keeps the inhabitants in awe.' The garrison on the isthmus at Chignecto likewise deterred the native people to the extent 'that there has been scarce an instance of any *Indians* being seen on the peninsula.'[35] The implication of both these anonymous pamphlets was that the history of Nova Scotia started in 1749 and had yet to be made. What went before was a bellicose, feudal-like regime; what was to come was the development of an enlightened, prosperous, and peaceful British colony.

The notion that the history of Nova Scotia began anew in 1749 (*anno* Halifax), was reinforced by the contrast promoters drew between British development and that of the Acadians and the native inhabitants. One promoter, for instance, found the native people 'a lazy Set of People without any Forecast,' who did not take the pains to provide any store against a bad season, 'so that in case the Crop comes to any Mischance, they live miserably, and suffer great Want, even in the Midst of Plenty.'[36] The Acadians were described by another writer as little better than the native people with whom they intermarried: the 'indolent *French*, who don't work scarce above half the year, on account of their superstitious holidays,' were able, because of the natural richness of the land, to produce a surplus of grain and cattle; but this only demonstrated what the country could have produced 'had it been in any other hands.'[37] Now the country was in other hands, and the 'spectacular' progress made in the short space of two years was 'proof' of the superiority of English settlement and justified the British government's expropriation of the squandered resource that was Nova Scotia. To the nervous settler the clear suggestion was that the once dangerous Acadians and native people were now more to be pitied than feared.

Nova Scotia's change in historical direction was accompanied by a shift in historical method. Promoters preferred to portray the French regime as a semi-feudal era of internecine warfare between the fur lords Charles de Menou d'Aulnay and Charles de Saint-Étienne de La Tour, of French fraternization with the native people, and of depredations against English settlements. Nova Scotia itself was merely the scene of man's troubled activities. The consequent emphasis on things military, diplomatic, and

35 *Importance of Settling and Fortifying Nova Scotia*, 17–23
36 *Geographical History of Nova Scotia*, 47
37 *Importance of Settling and Fortifying Nova Scotia*, 13

political could best be handled in a chronicle or narrative form. The main sources were literary, and such authors as Charlevoix were repeatedly quoted or condensed by the promoter-historian so as to imitate factual truth and deflect intimations of bias. The author of *The Importance and Advantage of Cape-Breton* created almost his entire work by marshalling verbatim extracts from sources as diverse as travel narratives and international treaties, saying that he 'chose to use the very Words of ... his Authorities, lest it might be objected that I had represented Places and Things more favourably than they are in Reality.' Accordingly, his ambition was less to be original than it was simply to bear 'Testimony to the Truth.'[38]

The adherence to truth was avowed no less in accounts of the first few years of British rule, but the type of truth aimed at, and the sources required to establish it, had altered. Tales of derring-do gave way within the same work to more stolid, and more reassuring, descriptions of the methodical development of land through enlightened British policy. The most appropriate historical method for the new age was that of the antiquarian, not the chronicler, for the former traditionally put systematic description before chronological illustration. The antiquarian studied all aspects of life, not just military and political but also social, economic, and cultural. As a corollary, the sources antiquarians consulted were far more diverse than those of the chronicler and included virtually any human artifact or record.[39] But unlike European antiquarians, whose history was based on the idea of civilization recovered by systematic collection of all the relics of the past, the antiquarians of the New World collected signs of potential for the future. When the systematic descriptive history of the antiquarian met the promoter's systematic descriptive geography, one had the co-ordinates to permit Europeans to orient themselves in the New World.

The history of Nova Scotia as recounted by several Maritime promoters had, then, squared the circle. Time had been introduced into the promotional pamphlet and a credible argument made for the strategic retention and settlement of Nova Scotia. At the same time, all that had gone before was rendered irrelevant to the present task of building an English colony. The Acadians and native people had been brought under the civilizing control of British power in much the same fashion as the wilderness itself. The conquest had wiped the slate clean; progress was now assured; a new and quite different historical process had begun.

38 [Bollan,] *Importance and Advantage of Cape-Breton*, iv, vi
39 Arnaldo Momigliano, 'Ancient History and the Antiquarian,' in his *Studies in Historiography* (New York 1966) 3–5

Time and static description were accommodated together in promotional literature by making the future, not the past, the focus of history. No matter how distant it might be from his own day, the promoter's future always served as the time of final resolution. The first reports of English progress in Nova Scotia were the promoter's fragile hints of future expansion. Unfortunately, the historical terrain between the present and the future was to provide a source of potentially disruptive events. For with time came change and, unless the writer was in a position to control events and the flow of information, his static ideal would soon be exposed to the critical contrast of real achievement. Indeed, from the beginning of colonial enterprise human and natural insubordination placed a good deal of strain on the promotional image: the relationship between prediction and accomplishment could only become more complex. Time was for the promoter a sand-glass of diminishing credibility.

In the event, the royal colony established at Halifax by the British government as a conscious act of public policy fell from the promotional ideal very quickly. The settlers brought out by Cornwallis in 1749 turned out to be, like Otis Little, 'the King's bad bargains': discharged soldiers and sailors, Irish labourers, and idle adventurers were not qualified for clearing the wilderness. The author of *The Importance of Settling and Fortifying Nova Scotia* to the contrary, the French and native people were not in awe of British power and initially denied much of the agricultural hinterland to the new settlers. In 1750 the population of Halifax approached five thousand; by 1755 it had shrunk to fifteen hundred. Industry languished and then disappeared, and Halifax became a community without support save the bounty of the British treasury – a fact Edmund Burke noticed in a speech (infamous to Nova Scotians) of 11 February 1780:

> The province of Nova Scotia was the youngest and the favorite child of the Board [of Trade and Plantations]. Good God! what sums the nursing of that ill-thriven, hard-visaged, and ill-favored brat has cost to this wittol nation! Sir, this colony has stood us in a sum of not less than seven hundred thousand pounds. To this day it has made no repayment, – it does not even support those offices of expense which are miscalled its government; the whole of that job still lies upon the patient, callous, shoulders of the people of England.[40]

40 'Speech on Presenting to the House of Commons a Plan for the Better Security of the Independence of Parliament, and the Economical Reformation of the Civil and Other Establishments, February 11, 1780,' in *The Writings and Speeches of Edmund Burke*, 12 vols (Toronto 1901) vol. 2, 345

The traditional Maritime promoter was hard pressed to repel such attacks, which were in any case part of a broader reassessment of British colonial policy in the wake of the economy of Adam Smith and the apostasy of the thirteen colonies.[41] Promoters could not hide the fact that problems of colonial development did not end with the conquest. Their ability to manage the flow of information was lost, and with it their ability to reassure an increasingly well informed and sceptical British audience. The era of unrestrained Maritime promotion was over. Recent history stood in the way of a ready acceptance of an optimistic rendering of Nova Scotia's destiny; to re-establish the colony's reputation, the frustrations and failures of the British regime, too, must be accounted for. It was up to those who followed to restore faith in the future by renewing confidence in the past.

In the event, the task was not easy. For instance, John Day (d. 1775), a member of the Assembly of Nova Scotia, traced the source of the colony's frustrations to the pre-emption of the public good by the private scheming of the local merchant oligarchy. To prove his point, Day wrote a short historical essay outlining how a variety of merchants had been attracted to the new colony by the lavish expenditure of public money. These merchants took control of the government and economy of Nova Scotia 'as a Junto of cunning and wicked Men' whose views extended no further 'than their own private Emolument,' and who added to 'the Distresses of the Community in order to promote a slavish Dependence on themselves.' As a consequence, Nova Scotia now offered a 'dreary and melancholly ... Prospect,' of 'illcultivated' lands, 'dispirited' husbandmen, and a general 'Depravity of Manners.' Day's solution might have been anticipated: set up a clear method of reviewing expenditures by increasing the power of the elected assembly.[42] In short, Day's pamphlet was as much a political tract as it was a history.

John Day's *Essay* may have been an effective attack on the merchants of Halifax; it was less successful as a defence of Nova Scotia. Ostensibly written to clear barriers to future prosperity, this short history read more like a chronicle of a colony's fall from grand beginnings to a small conclusion. Because of Day's emphasis on the problem of the oligarchy, the effect of his pamphlet turned out, unintentionally, to be similar to that of John Wilson's demotional tract. The detailing of short-term difficul-

41 Knorr, *Colonial Theories*, 155–74
42 [John Day,] *An Essay on the Present State of the Province of Nova-Scotia, with Some Strictures on the Measures Pursued by Government from Its First Settlement by the English in the Year, 1749* (np [*c.* 1774]) 5, 20; Wendy L. Thorpe, 'John Day,' *DCB*, vol. 4, 199

ties, if not sufficiently controlled by an author, could fatally compromise the credibility of hope for long-term advancement.[43] The first and greatest lesson of Maritime promoters was just this: history must be at all times subordinate to a belief in progress. How to do this in the light of continuing events was a very difficult question. In fact, when the answer came, it did not come from Nova Scotia at all.

If any Maritime colony was sunk in a controversy that threatened to destroy its reputation, it was the Island of St John. Like Nova Scotia before it, the future colony of Prince Edward Island initially received favourable notice. As the French Île Saint-Jean, it had fallen to the British in July 1758 with the second capitulation of Louisbourg. An expedition under Colonel Andrew Rollo, fifth Baron Rollo, occupied the renamed Island of St John later that summer, and British officers accompanying Rollo were impressed by French reports of the island's agricultural productivity.[44] This impression was reinforced by the published account of Thomas Pichon, a French spy in British employ.[45] While 'it could hardly be maintained that the Island of St. John had a high profile in Britain in the early 1760s,' a small group of Anglo-American merchants, and a larger number of military officers who had served in the area, took note of the island's potential.[46] When the colony was confirmed as British territory by the Treaty of Paris in 1763 and annexed to Nova Scotia, memorialists already were busy formulating requests for grants of land on the island, the most famous of which were those of John Perceval, second earl of Egmont.[47]

In order to facilitate the disposition of the Island of St John, the British government dispatched Captain Samuel Johannes Holland there in 1764 to begin his survey of the northern district of North America. If the captain's report of 1766 avoided the lyrical prose of Pichon, it neverthe-

43 A similarly destructive debate took place in Cape Breton, see William Smith (fl. 1784–1803), *A Caveat against Emigration to America; With the State of the Island of Cape Breton, from the Year 1784 to the Present Year; and Suggestions for the Benefit of the British Settlements in North America* (London 1803); [Joseph Frederick Wallet DesBarres (1721–1824),] *Letters to Lord ***** on 'A Caveat Against Emigration to America ...'. Lately Published by William Smith, Esq., formerly Surgeon Physical on the Military Establishment of that Island, and Late Chief Justice Thereof* (London 1804).
44 Admiral Edward Boscawen to William Pitt, 13 Sept. 1758, quoted in D.C. Harvey, *The French Régime in Prince Edward Island* (New Haven, Conn., 1926) 194–5
45 [Pichon], *Genuine Letters*, 64–5
46 J.M. Bumsted, *Land, Settlement, and Politics on Eighteenth-Century Prince Edward Island* (Kingston and Montreal 1987) 12–14
47 Great Britain, Public Record Office, Colonial Records, *Journal of the Commissioners for Trade and Plantations*, vol. 11, *January 1759 to December 1763* (London 1935) 369–424; vol. 12, *January 1764 to December 1767* (1936) *passim*

less highlighted the agricultural and fishing potential of the island and certainly did nothing to diminish the ardour of memorialists.[48] In 1767 the British government used Holland's division of the island into sixty-seven lots of approximately twenty thousand acres each to grant all the land, with only a few reserves for the Crown, to private proprietors. The proprietors were in turn obliged to settle and develop the island and to pay a quit rent, which was tied in 1769 to the maintenance of a local government independent of Nova Scotia. The British government optimistically hoped that the proprietors would move with their tenants to the island and within a few years create a stable, hierarchical, and financially self-sufficient colony – thereby avoiding the twin evils of American democracy and reliance upon the British treasury. Disappointment was immediate.[49]

Few proprietors had any intention of going to the island or of meeting their obligations to provide settlers and pay quit rents. Most proprietors were content to let the initiative of others increase the value of their land as a prelude to a speculative sale. Those few proprietors who did try to fulfil their obligations found, as had so many developers in the New World before them, that establishing a settlement was not a profitable business proposition. Rebel incursions on the island during the American Revolution simply worsened an already bad situation.[50] In 1775 the island's population was estimated to be thirteen hundred; it was half that by 1779.[51]

The failure of the proprietorial system was a heavy blow to the resident élite of the Island of St John. The members of this élite, composed of lower-level military officers, second sons of gentry, and professional men with cloudy pasts, often from outlying, marginal areas of the United Kingdom, were all drawn by the expectation of a place in the island government. The competition for the limited number of offices available inevitably spawned a fierce factionalism that would only be rivalled in intensity by the emergent oligarchy's collective hatred of the absentee proprietors. As long as the proprietors failed to pay quit rents, even those individuals lucky enough to obtain a post on the island would have no revenue from which to draw their salary. The proprietors' monopoly over

48 Duncan Campbell, *History of Prince Edward Island* (Charlottetown 1875) 3–10
49 Bumsted, *Land, Settlement, and Politics*, ch. 1
50 Ibid., chs 3–4; J.M. Bumsted, 'The Origins of the Land Question on Prince Edward Island, 1767–1805,' *Acadiensis* 11 (1981): 43–4; and his 'The Patterson Regime and the Impact of the American Revolution on the Island of St. John, 1775–1786,' ibid. 13 (1983): 47–67
51 J.M. Bumsted, 'Sir James Montgomery and Prince Edward Island, 1767–1803,' ibid. 7 (1978): 84

land simultaneously blocked the local élite's access to the only alternative source of income and status on the island. By 1777 the British government had recognized the reality of the situation and henceforth made provision for a civil list. Unfortunately by that date the local oligarchy already was committed to a full assault on the prerogatives of the absentee landowners, often characterized by the 'asset-stripping' of proprietorial holdings. In short, the island's officials and leading citizens bitterly resented the proprietors for their failure to fulfil the terms of the original grants, while at the same time they rapaciously devoured such capital as those few landowners who sought to meet their obligations invested. A vicious circle was thus established that virtually guaranteed a slow and painful period of development on the island.[52]

The local élite thought the circle of mutual recrimination and distrust could best be broken if its own members obtained control over the land. To this end a series of investigations were undertaken by the assembly in order to document the persistent failure of proprietors to meet the terms of their grants. Subsequently the provincial government took steps to initiate judicial distraint (the seizure of land to compel payment of money due) and escheat (revocation of original title for non-fulfilment of terms). For their part, truant proprietors responded with an effective series of pamphlets excusing their conduct on grounds of the impracticability of the original terms, the interruption caused by the American Revolution, and latterly the nefarious conduct of island officials. The proprietors argued that measures taken against them for non-fulfilment were not the judicious acts of local officers of the Crown but the schemes of individuals intent upon seizing control of the land for personal use. According to one proprietor, Captain John MacDonald of Glenaladale (1742–1810):

> The principal remaining proprietors of this island are under painful apprehensions that it may not be eligible for them to proceed farther in expenditures for settling their lots, if ... neither the best efforts to comply dutifully with the laws, nor the most meritorious exertions for the settlement of the island, are sufficient to protect occasionally from the utmost rigor, or unnecessary severity.[53]

52 Bumsted, *Land, Settlement, and Politics*, chs 2–4; and his 'Origins of the Land Question,' 43–53
53 [John MacDonald,] *Narrative of Transactions Relative to St. John's Island, in the Gulf of St. Lawrence, from the Year 1769; And Observations on the Purchases of Lands, Belonging to the Proprietors, Made by the Officers of that Government in 1781* ([London 1783?]) 16; J.M. Bumsted, 'Captain John MacDonald and the Island,' *Island Magazine* 6 (1979): 15–20. A summary of this pamphlet debate can be found in Bumsted, 'Patterson Regime,' 60–7.

The British government generally found the proprietors' arguments convincing, with consequent damage not only to the credibility of the local oligarchy, but to the reputation of the island as a whole. Thus, by the turn of the century it was becoming increasingly apparent that a continuation of the struggle between absentee proprietors and the local oligarchy was inimical to the long-term interests of both parties.

In 1806 John Stewart (c. 1758–1834) published *An Account of Prince Edward Island* in London.[54] This work, through a subtle blend of partisan comment, colonial promotion, and self-interested rationalization, moved toward effecting a reconciliation between the oligarchy and certain of the absentee proprietors, as well as toward re-establishing the reputation of Prince Edward Island. Stewart was himself a member of what was 'probably the most extensive and influential Island family in the first half-century of British settlement' – and certainly the most notorious.[55] As a Scottish youth of sixteen, John Stewart came to the Island of St John in November of 1775 in the company of his father, Peter, the colony's chief justice from 1775 to 1800. The heavy sea that caused their ship to founder within sight of the north coast was but the first of many island tempests the family would weather.[56] John, or 'Hellfire Jack' as he was known to those most familiar with him, set out to garner as many public offices as possible – after the fashion of both the numerous members of his family and a generation of mid-Atlantic men on the make. His efforts culminated with an appointment in 1790 to the office of receiver-general of quit rents for the Island of St John, a post he obtained only after guaranteeing a rival applicant an annuity of £85 in lieu of what it was possible to milk from the collection.[57] Although Stewart was absent from

54 John Stewart, *An Account of Prince Edward Island, in the Gulf of St. Lawrence, North America. Containing Its Geography, a Description of Its Different Divisions, Soil, Climate, Seasons, Natural Productions, Cultivation, Discovery, Conquest, Progress and Present State of the Settlement, Government, Constitution, Laws, and Religion* (London 1806)

55 J.M. Bumsted, 'The Stewart Family and the Origins of Political Conflict on Prince Edward Island,' *Island Magazine* 9 (1981): 12. F.L. Pigot, 'John Stewart,' *DCB*, vol. 6 (Toronto 1987) 735–8, is the disappointing standard biography.

56 Thos. Curtis, 'A Narative of the Voyage of Thos Curtis to the Island of St. John's in the Gulf of St. Lawrence in North America, in the year 1775. Giving an acct of the Ship-wreck, and many other hardships, which my Self and many Others endured 'till my return to England, having been gone about 18 months,' in D.C. Harvey, ed., *Journeys to the Island of St. John or Prince Edward Island, 1775–1832* (Toronto 1955) 17, 24–9

57 PAPEI, Jean and Colin MacDonald Papers, Acc. 2664, item 18, John MacDonald to Nelly [Helen] MacDonald, 7 July 1790; Public Record Office [PRO], Colonial Office Series [CO], 226/18/433, John Hill, 'A Detail of Various Transactions at Prince Edward Island,' appendix 'John Stewart'

Prince Edward Island during most of his term as paymaster of His Majesty's forces in Newfoundland (1804–17), he continued to champion his own and the colony's affairs in London.[58]

'Being much interested' in the prosperity of Prince Edward Island, Stewart began his account by admitting and regretting the 'disappointment which has been experienced in regard to its colonization and settlement.' One should not, however, attribute past setbacks to 'any defect in the climate or soil'; rather, blame was 'fairly to be charged to the neglect of many of those into whose hands the property of the lands unfortunately fell.' Indeed, from the moment the original grants were made in 1767 the island's fate was, in Stewart's opinion, sealed:

> The accounts of the Island which were published soon after its conquest, were so favourable, both in regard to its fertility, and the natural beauty of the country, that a great part of the proprietors (who never saw the Island) seem to have expected, that it was to be settled by a resort of people in consequence of its natural advantages, without any exertion on their part, and that their large grants of forest lands were to be converted into valuable estates, by the labour and exertions of people, who they expected would be tempted to resort to, and settle in the Island, as their tenants, without any expence or exertion on their part.[59]

Tenants similarly arrived with expectations coloured by the too-favourable reports of the conquest period. Their subsequent disappointment, expressed in 'dismal letters' to their families and friends at home, was a sad corollary to proprietorial inaction.[60]

The informed contemporary reader might now have expected the account to continue its assault upon the absentee proprietors in the tradition of the island's frustrated oligarchy. Instead, Stewart wrote that in his estimation the damage done to the island's prospects, though grave, was not beyond repair. The principal difficulty was at that moment being surmounted by the expedient retirement of those original proprietors and subsequent speculators who were disappointed at the discovery that they could not make money without first spending it. In their place came 'others who have more activity, and juster views of their own interest, and the value of the country.' A co-requisite for the success of the active breed of proprietor now appearing was a more mature understanding of the

58 Bumsted, 'Stewart Family,' 16–17
59 Stewart, *Account of Prince Edward Island*, iii–iv
60 Ibid., ix

nature of Prince Edward Island on the part of potential settlers. Stewart flatly declared that 'any man that emigrates, under an idea that he is going to a country where he is to live without labour is most grossly deceived: on the contrary every man who expects to thrive in a new country must work and be industrious.' If both proprietors and tenants came to Prince Edward Island with a full knowledge of what to expect, they would find 'that the natural and moral state of things in the colonies is such, as promises to every industrious man an ample reward for his labour, with a certainty of leaving his family if not wealthy, still with such prospects as will divest his mind of all anxiety on their account.'[61]

Stewart saw as his first task the need to clear away confusion as to the real nature of Prince Edward Island's advantages and possibilities. He began with a disavowal of the exaggerated claims made for the colony by the likes of Pichon. By rejecting too-enthusiastic views, Stewart postured as a man of candour. His doubts allay those of the reader, and he appears as a man of detachment and wise caution. The sceptic may suspect Stewart of partisan motives, but initially such fears are eased by the straightforward account of the island's physical attributes – an account the author has done his utmost to dispose the reader to believe.

Stewart was in a better position than the earlier promoters to speak authoritatively on his subject, and not simply because of its more manageable size. In common with all students of Prince Edward Island, Stewart was able to build upon the complete and accurate survey that Samuel Holland carried out between 1764 and 1766. The pattern of counties, lots, and royalties devised by Holland left a permanent cartographic imprint on the imagery as well as the physical shape of the colony. Subsequent inquiries by the island assembly into proprietorial inaction, notably that carried out by a special committee in 1797, provided lot-by-lot analyses of population growth, buildings constructed, and agricultural improvement.[62] As receiver-general of quit rents and as speaker of the assembly in 1797, it was Stewart's business to be familiar with island development and any inquiries relating thereto. In addition Stewart could himself bring the experience of upwards of thirty years' residence on the island to any examination of the colony's progress.

Almost half of Stewart's account of the island was devoted to a description of geography, topography, and resources. In this expansive setting, Stewart opened with an outline of the island's longitude and

61 Ibid., v–vii
62 Andrew Hill Clark, *Three Centuries and the Island: A Historical Geography of Settlement and Agriculture in Prince Edward Island, Canada* (Toronto 1959) 42–8

latitude, counties, towns, rivers, and coastline. The colony was literally dissected and exposed to the civilizing air of British development. There followed a leisurely depiction of the landscape that blended fine illustration with hints of future possibilities: 'Though some parts of the coast have a low flat look, the greatest part of the face of the country is much waived and often rises into beautiful swells, and being much intersected with arms of the sea, creeks, and rivulets, presents every where a vast variety of fine situations for building and improvements.'[63] In quick succession Stewart backed up his rhetoric with comprehensive lists of soil types, trees, vegetable productions, and native birds, animals, fishes, reptiles, and insects ('arranged in the order of Linnaeus'), all with a view to demonstrating the utility to which these various resources might be put. He rounded out his description with a chapter on the salubrious climate of the colony and concluded that all these advantages 'must finally enable [Prince Edward Island] to maintain a much greater population than most other countries of the same extent.'[64]

Stewart's Prince Edward Island was not an Elysium. It was an environment favourable to the success only of those willing to work hard at clearing and cultivating the land. Past failures were directly attributable to high initial expectations and an unwillingness on the part of tenants to engage in work with the sobriety and industry that alone might have brought success. Eschewing the slow but steady rewards of clearing the land, too many farmer-landlords and tenants sought quick returns in the fisheries and the timber trade. Subsequent vagaries in the markets for these products illustrated the folly of such short-sightedness. Stewart was convinced that 'agriculture is, and must long continue to be the chief pursuit of the inhabitants of this Island.' Unhappily, he continued, 'the conduct of our rural affairs in most respects is extremely defective, there are few cultivators among us who theorize, and still fewer who read.' If only tenants attended to their true interest, they would realize that 'every tree which is cut down in the forest opens to the sun a new spot of earth, which, with cultivation, will produce food for man and beast.'[65]

Promotional literature traditionally assessed the fitness of land for Europeans: Stewart assessed the fitness of Europeans for the land. The potential of Prince Edward Island, once accurately established in a comprehensive, almost encyclopaedic, fashion, became the criterion by which to judge tenants, farmers, landlords, governments, even races.

63 Stewart, *Account of Prince Edward Island*, 24
64 Ibid., 26
65 Ibid., 122–3, 145–6

Those with a willingness to work, those with the foresight to see what was realistically possible, and those who were interested in more than the quick profit of the moment were to be pointed out and praised. Those hoping for an easy life, those chasing chimeras, and those intent on plunder were to be pilloried and condemned. Having established the nature of the resources of Prince Edward Island, Stewart was in a position to embark on a history of man's failure there, passing out judgments that appear less his own than those of the land itself. This was the key John Day sought, a method to explain and explain away continuing difficulties in the colonies. Once discovered, it accounted for a wide range of historical insubordination and put the train to progress back on track.

In any event, the French regime simply did not measure up to Stewart's agrarian ideal. The French government had 'never encouraged ... settlement,' and the 'adventurers' who did come to Île Saint-Jean 'assimilated in manners and customs' with the 'savage practice of their Indian neighbours.' For Stewart the expulsion was an issue of little moment: 'It having been found after fifty years experience, that no dependance could be placed in the Accadians [sic] ever becoming good subjects to Great-Britain.' The only evidence that remained of the French presence were the ruins of their slight improvements, and the memories of a few old Acadians. Given the failure of the French to use the resources at hand, the demise of their regime was, in Stewart's view, not only inevitable, but just.[66]

Prince Edward Island's counterpart to Nova Scotia's year of Halifax, 1749, was the year of the lottery, 1767. In the case of the island, however, we have already seen that disappointment was immediate, and that Stewart proposed to use the land itself to judge those who mistreated it. Relieved of personal responsibility for any criticism he levelled, Stewart avoided the pitfalls of an overtly partisan narrative. This façade of objectivity was complemented by Stewart's historical method, which was documentary. Using a series of key letters and memorials issued by the governments of Prince Edward Island and Great Britain, to which he had access as speaker of the assembly and as an officer of the Crown, Stewart constructed a legal case rather than a historical narrative. For instance, in opening the account of the British regime Stewart provided a précis of the earl of Egmont's memorials to the British government. Egmont had proposed that the island be divided into 'Baronies,' with 'Men at Arms,' according to the 'ancient feudal' customs of Europe, all under Egmont as

66 Ibid., 148–53

'Lord Paramount of the Island.' This memorial was permitted to condemn itself as obviously ridiculous. Stewart only needed to alter quietly a few phrases in order to emphasize the point.[67]

The key document in the case against the proprietors was that containing the terms and conditions of settlement under which the land was to be held. No sleight-of-hand was required here, and the conditions were given verbatim. The optimism about the colony's advantages engendered by 'Military and Naval Officers' had seduced both the proprietors and the British government into the belief that without any exertion 'little less than the immediate and complete settlement of the Island [could be] looked for.' Without effort and realistic expectations, the results were predictable. Stewart provided a lot-by-lot survey from 1779 demonstrating that after twelve years only ten lots out of sixty-seven could be said to have fulfilled the requirements of their grants; forty-eight lots had been totally neglected.[68] The use of a survey was ideal for Stewart's historical method, for it provided irrefutable documentary evidence detailing the failure of individual proprietors, while at the same time it once again illustrated, lot by lot, the potential of the island. The short-term vagaries of man were thus never allowed to overshadow the predominant notion that the island's resources made progress inevitable.

The Quit Rent Act passed by the assembly in 1773 (13 Geo. III, c. 13) and a British treasury minute dated 7 August 1776 – both given verbatim – should have provided the legislative tools needed to dispose of proprietors in default. Governor Walter Patterson at first failed to act out of fear of the power of the proprietors in London. When he did act in 1781, the lands distrained ended up in the hands of Patterson himself, his relatives, and his friends. Presented by the British government with a draft bill overturning the proceedings of 1781, Patterson neglected to convey it to the island assembly for passage. When the slow workings of the British colonial administration finally realized in 1786 that its wishes were being thwarted, Patterson was replaced as lieutenant-governor by Edmund Fanning. Patterson did not turn over the reins of power until 1787 and even then continued to abuse the new Fanning administration until at least 1791.[69]

67 Ibid., 155–7. The term 'Lord Paramount of the Island,' for instance, was an invention of Stewart's but has entered island mythology as a delusion of the earl's; see Bumsted, Land, Settlement, and Politics, 16.

68 Stewart, Account of Prince Edward Island, 157–73

69 Ibid., 176–81, 189–203, 233–42. For a modern account of these complex proceedings see Harry Baglole, 'Walter Patterson,' DCB, vol. 4, 605–11; J.M. Bumsted, 'Edmund Fanning,' ibid., vol. 5, 308–12; Bumsted, Land, Settlement, and Politics.

The confusion caused by Patterson's self-interested factionalism sapped the will of the island government for more than twenty years and permitted absentee proprietors to neglect their duties. As proof Stewart presented yet another survey, this time dated 1799, which he compiled from the investigations of a committee of the assembly in 1797 and from his own personal observations as receiver-general of quit rents. From this survey Stewart concluded 'that the exertions of the proprietors were feeble in proportion to their obligations, and the length of time the period embraces, and the opportunities it afforded.'[70] The survey proved the justness of the 1797 petition of the assembly, which had rated the proprietors according to their efforts, suggested that a court of escheat dispossess those proprietors in complete default, and proposed that such confiscated lands be 'regranted in small tracts to actual settlers.' Stewart issued a brief caveat to the petition's solution by noting that giving tenants freehold grants of confiscated lands would penalize those proprietors who had exerted themselves – such individuals as James William Montgomery, lord chief baron of His Majesty's Court of Exchequer in Scotland, and Thomas Douglas, fifth Earl of Selkirk.[71]

Fanning was 'a prudent and steadily moderate' lieutenant-governor, unlikely either to pursue personal interest or to be swayed by the mob's desire for full escheat. He instructed Stewart, his receiver-general of quit rents, to use the investigations of 1797 to establish five classes of proprietorial conduct, with a rated composition of past quit rents due – a document that Stewart provided.[72] In 1804, Stewart obtained judgments against the worst offenders, and ten lots, five half-lots, and one-third of a lot were returned to the Crown. Stewart suggested that these lands could either be regranted 'in small tracts to actual settlers, or in order not to interfere with the other proprietors, they may be divided into tracts of a thousand acres, *and sold*, subject to the same rate of quit rents to which they were originally liable, by which means they will not interfere with the plan of the colony, or in any respect injure the other proprietors.'[73] Within two years another one-third of the lots changed hands without government interference, as inactive proprietors blanched at the size of their compositions. The new owners, most notably Lord Selkirk, were far more active and added fully one-third to the population of the island. When Fanning turned over the reins of office in 1805 to J.F.W. DesBarres, he

70 Stewart, *Account of Prince Edward Island*, 203–19
71 Ibid., 219–26, 229–30
72 Ibid., 239–54
73 Ibid., 256

left the colony 'in perfect peace and harmony, and in a rapid state of improvement.'[74]

So immediate and healthful had the effect of the disburthening of the lands of their heavy arrears of quit rents been that Stewart had only two substantial recommendations to make to those in the British government 'on whose Judgment and determination [Prince Edward Island's] future progress and prospects must depend': first, that the strictures of the Passenger Vessel Act of 1803 (43 Geo. III, c. 56) be eased to permit greater emigration from the Scottish highlands; second, that Lieutenant-Governor DesBarres's proposed tax on uncultivated lands be vetoed as detrimental to the continued progress of active proprietors.[75]

Coming as it did after the constant battles between the island élite and the absentee proprietors, Stewart's *Account of Prince Edward Island* appeared judicious and reasonable. He provided a more comprehensive and moderate (and hence more believable) description of the colony's resources and potential than hitherto had been available. He suggested that the real blame for previous failures rested upon a too-optimistic appraisal of the island's capabilities and therefore did not feel the need to condemn the proprietorial system as a whole. Instead he seemed quite sensibly to draw a distinction between active and inactive proprietors and demonstrated how the 'prudent' policy of quit rent compositions introduced by Fanning had punished the latter and encouraged the former. This was in stark contrast to the failures of the self-interested actions of Patterson and his administration.

The reality of Stewart's position was not, however, nearly so reasonable and objective. The *Account of Prince Edward Island*, for instance, made no mention of the fact that the Stewart family first broke with Governor Patterson when it received none of the lands distrained in 1781. This rivalry was consummated when Chief Justice Peter Stewart's wife was seduced by Patterson. As for Lieutenant-Governor Fanning, his policies marked a change in form rather than substance. Captain John MacDonald described the transition as being from an 'audacious open tyranny' to a 'deep far fetched despicable Yankey cunning.'[76] According to J.M. Bumsted:

Fanning and his adherents, led by the interlocking Stewart and Desbrisay clans, had trod a tightrope, whipping up public support for an Island Court of

74 Ibid., 252–3, 263–5
75 Ibid., x–xiii; PRO, CO 226/22/140-1, John Stewart to Robert Stewart, 1st Viscount Castlereagh and 2nd Marquess of Londonderry, 3 May 1807
76 John MacDonald to Nelly MacDonald, 7 July 1790

Escheat to depress land values at the same time that they sought to persuade the absentee landholders of their whole-hearted support for proprietors who would actively engage in capital investment on the Island. Land about to be seized for non-fulfillment of obligations obviously had little value upon the property market in London, and the Fanningites could either buy Island townships at bargain prices from their proprietor holders in advance of legal action or from the Crown after escheat proceedings had been completed.[77]

Those proprietors who were too powerful to antagonize – for instance, Sir James Montgomery and Lord Selkirk – were appeased and praised for their efforts. By dividing the proprietors into classes, Fanning's policy split his opponents, and in the confusion the lieutenant-governor and his allies took what they could. Fanning ultimately came away with sixty thousand acres of Governor Patterson's land for a purchase price of less than £100.[78]

The *Account of Prince Edward Island* walked the same tightrope as the Fanning regime. Stewart held out escheat leading to small freehold farms as a possibility in order to keep pressure on inactive proprietors, while at the same time he supported proposals for the Crown to regrant land in one thousand-acre blocks so as to mollify the active (that is powerful) absentee proprietors. In fact it was more likely that Stewart privately intended that land should change hands in larger blocks and that he and his allies would receive their fair share of the crumbs falling from Fanning's table of compositions. When in London in 1802 and 1803, Stewart used the stick and the carrot not as a judicious government official but as a 'land broker' bridging the interests of the local island oligarchy and certain powerful landholders resident in Great Britain.[79] He had no intention of seriously compromising the proprietorial system from which he hoped to benefit, and he viewed with alarm DesBarres's proposed tax on uncultivated lands. A champion of escheat to the tenants on the island, a moderate island ally to the powerful proprietors in Great Britain, an informed public official to the British government, Stewart played all three of these roles with aplomb. He may even have entertained the idea that his central position on the land question, when buttressed by his

77 J.M. Bumsted, 'The Loyal Electors of Prince Edward Island,' *Island Magazine* 8 (1980): 9; see also [Joseph Robinson (*c.* 1742–1807),] *To the Farmers in the Island of St. John, In the Gulf of St. Lawrence* (np [*c.* 1796])
78 Bumsted, 'Origins of the Land Question,' 53
79 PAPEI, Palmer Family Papers, Acc. 2849, item 82, James Bardin Palmer to Lawrence Sulivan, 1 Sept. 1818

information book, would recommend his elevation to the post of lieutenant-governor.[80]

Stewart's *Account of Prince Edward Island* was a book of nuances, many of which were to be understood only by a select few in the island oligarchy. Stewart was especially coy about his objections to granting distrained or escheated land in freehold to small tenant farmers. To many islanders he appeared to support the ambitions of the popular party of tenants; a party that he had on more than one occasion whipped up for his own electoral benefit. It was as a text in favour of the 'Country' party that his book came to be remembered, and it was this seminal interpretation that so heavily influenced subsequent historical writing in the colony.[81] In this view Stewart's thesis represented the history of Prince Edward Island as one of conflict between absentee proprietors (generally backed by the British government) and the resident tenants (generally backed by the local assembly). It was a conflict pitting islanders against outsiders, working farmers against negligent landlords, progress against reaction.[82]

Whatever the influence of the *Account of Prince Edward Island* on later historiography, it was clearly an advance on the naïve promotion of the mid-eighteenth century. For a colony ruled, or more often misruled, by an élite composed almost entirely of self-interested office seekers of the most predatory sort (the smaller the pit, the fiercer the rats, is J.M. Bumsted's laconic assessment), promotion was an extraordinarily difficult task. Yet Stewart, by providing a multiplicity of readings, managed to satisfy tenants, absentee and resident landlords, and officials of the imperial government as to the island's worth. In so doing, he also advanced the career of himself, his family, and his faction. He did so by inverting the traditional promotional assumption that the land must prove its fitness for Europeans. Stewart's formula, that Europeans must prove their fitness for the land, explained away problems of the immediate past and provided assurance of future progress. It also gave the first hints of a distinctive colonial identity. In short, Stewart's work left promoters behind and looked forward to the patriots to come.

Profoundly self-interested promoters were bound to be superseded in any event. They were the product of a special set of circumstances, foremost among which was their ability to control the flow of information

80 John Stewart to Lord Castlereagh, 3 May 1807
81 See below, pages 78–82.
82 J.M. Bumsted, '"The Only Island There Is:" The Writing of Prince Edward Island History,' in Verner Smitheram, David Milne, and Satadal Dasgupta, eds, *The Garden Transformed: Prince Edward Island, 1945–1980* (Charlottetown 1982) 16–19

between the New World and the Old. This permitted them to deceive audiences through a mixture of exaggeration, distortion, and outright falsehood. For a brief period they were useful to a variety of sponsors, who were in turn responsible for whatever influence their works may have had. While in the short run promoters advanced their own careers, in the long run they did great harm to the stature of the region. When they could no longer control the flow of information to Europe, they were undone. When their predictions proved false, the reputation of colonies suffered. Promotion's immediate legacy to native-born colonial historians was shattered credibility.

Paradoxically, promoters also bequeathed methods for re-establishing colonial reputations. First among these was the use of description to tame the environment. To name, define, and depict was to civilize. Promoters also taught that it was even more important to keep events under control than to control the wilderness. Indeed, the historian's artifice consisted of his ability to chronicle the follies of man without doing irreparable damage to his optimistic description of the potential for eventual prosperity. In this context history should not be regarded merely as a preface or appendix to reports on resources but as an integral part of the promotional argument. History was a process of removing roadblocks in the way of future prosperity.

Various expedients were required to ease the tension between a historical past characterized by human ignorance and failure and the fulfilment of potential in the future. Promoters commonly used narratives of national rivalry, Indian raids, and individual bravery as a contrast to the progressive present. A shift in method reinforced the contrast, as narrative of the past gave way to description of the present and prediction for the future. Unfortunately, narratives of the frustrations and failures of the British era could not be hidden indefinitely and were much more difficult to assimilate. John Stewart's solution was to use the supposedly fixed criterion of the potential of the land to judge the actions of men. This deft means of handling a thorny problem stood up to the scrutiny of a better informed and more critical British audience. It permitted Stewart to look once again with confidence to the future.

It was in the future that the true focus of early Maritime historiography was to be found; a future that left behind narratives of warfare and rationalizations of partisans. This future was to be one of material achievement best analysed not as a narrative but as a broad description of human progress. In the tense of the historical future one did not find a tangled forest of hostile Indians and wild animals, but rather a civil wilderness of untapped resources waiting for those deserving of its potential wealth to begin exploitation. It was not the individual adventurer or speculator who deserved the land; it was the hard-working yeoman farmer who did. The new colonies by the sea were publicly declaring that they had no room for unproductive lords and gentry, for self-interested officials and partisan politicians, or for lazy and unscientific farmers. It was in the notion that man must prove his fitness for the land that one finds the first glimmerings of a distinctive Maritime identity, an identity based on an ideal of what Maritimers hoped to become, not on what they were. Ironically, by the end of the nineteenth century Maritime historians would see this ideal as something people had been and were no longer.

2

The Patriot Reaction
in the Maritimes

The first histories in English relating to the Maritime colonies were written by authors who thought of themselves primarily as British subjects living abroad. The patriotism averred by promoters and early colonists, no matter how hedged about it might be by personal concerns, was fundamentally British. Only with the growth of a generation of native Maritimers, particularly in Nova Scotia, was the nature of patriotism in the colonies altered. According to Joseph Howe (1804–73), the most famous member of this generation, it was the 'unerring law of nature' that the first-born of the colonies should transfer a priority in their hearts to the land of their birth and replace their parents' transitory motives of exploitation with a permanent sentiment of attachment.[1] Ancestral loyalties would not be forgotten, imperial duties could not be avoided, but by the late 1820s many Nova Scotians were giving precedence to the bias of a motto drawn from the poetry of Sir Walter Scott: 'This is my own my native land.'[2] It was this reorientation of local and imperial patriotism that Daniel Cobb Harvey labelled 'the intellectual awakening of Nova Scotia.'[3]

Prior to this acclimation, English-language accounts of Nova Scotia, written by men in pursuit of individual goals and uninhibited by native

1 'Love of Country a Stimulus to Enterprise,' an address delivered before the Halifax Mechanics' Institute, 5 Nov. 1834, and partially reprinted in *The Heart of Howe: Selections from the Letters and Speeches of Joseph Howe*, ed. D.C. Harvey (Toronto 1939) 49–66
2 Walter Scott, *The Lay of the Last Minstrel*, canto vi, st. i. The line was adopted as the motto for a series of articles entitled 'Characteristics of Nova Scotia,' which ran in the *Acadian Magazine; or Literary Mirror* (Halifax) in 1826. The motto was prefixed to Thomas C. Haliburton, *An Historical and Statistical Account of Nova-Scotia*, 2 vols (Halifax 1829).
3 D.C. Harvey, 'The Intellectual Awakening of Nova Scotia,' *Dalhousie Review* 13 (1933): 1–22

loyalty, had run to extremes of praise and condemnation. 'It has been,' wrote one observer, 'the peculiar misfortune of Nova-Scotia, to have suffered alike from its enemies and friends. By the former it has been represented as the abode of perpetual fog and unrelenting sterility, and by the latter as the land of the olive and grape.'[4] The observer was Thomas Chandler Haliburton (1796–1865), the future creator of the satirical *Clockmaker* series and of its hero, Sam Slick. In Haliburton's eyes, and in the eyes of his generation, the exaggerations of promoters and over-zealous Nova Scotians were an irresponsible legacy that could only compromise the reputation of the province. Determined to do something to correct this situation, in 1823 he published anonymously *A General Description of Nova Scotia*,[5] and in 1829, under his signature, the two-volume *Historical and Statistical Account of Nova-Scotia*.

Haliburton wrote because he recognized that reputation was important to a young colony. Nova Scotia depended on the tolerance of the British government to carry the expense of civil administration and military defence and on the goodwill of the British people for capital and settlers. Furthermore, many Nova Scotians were eager to see the young colony become a credible alternative to the New England states in the Atlantic carrying trade through the maintenance of a system of colonial preferences. Unfortunately, British domestic needs usually combined with the pressures of international rivalries to withhold from Nova Scotia the privileged status its inhabitants coveted. Only on occasion, as during the War of 1812–15, did events coalesce in a way that propelled the colony to the forefront of the imperial economy. Unhappily, this prosperity proved momentary and simply made the post-war recession and Nova Scotia's return to a peripheral economic position all the harder to bear.[6]

The first generation of Nova Scotians thus came of age at a time when their compatriots, not just the British public, were beginning to question provincial conceits. 'There is,' wrote one of Haliburton's friends, 'a difference between being inspired and being puffed up – The latter is as injurious to weak heads as it is often distressing to weak bowels.' It was, this writer contended, 'impossible to push on a colony advantageously beyond the course of nature.'[7] Such was the mature patriotism of

---

4 Haliburton, *Statistical Account*, vol. 2, 358
5 (Halifax)
6 David Sutherland, 'Halifax Merchants and the Pursuit of Development, 1783–1850,' *CHR* 59 (1978): 1–17
7 PANS, Peleg Wiswall Papers, MG 1, vol. 980, item 1, Peleg Wiswall to Samuel George William Archibald, 14 Mar. 1818; reprinted as 'A Blue Print for Nova Scotia in 1818,' ed. D.C. Harvey, *CHR* 24 (1943): 397–409

awakened Nova Scotians, of individuals aroused to the strengths and weaknesses of their birthright: defending themselves from insult and trying to understand their predicament, they sought to fashion a responsible, realistic image for their homeland.

Haliburton was in sympathy with his generation, but in speaking for it he also spoke for himself. One must not lose sight of the fact that the young man who wrote the *General Description* and the *Statistical Account* was not yet famous, although by all reports he had a desire so to be.[8] Briefly, Haliburton was born 17 December 1796 at Windsor, a descendant on his father's side of a successful Tory family of lawyers, and on his mother's of Loyalist refugees. He was educated locally and well at King's College, graduating in 1815. Called to the provincial bar in 1820, he settled at Annapolis Royal and represented that town and its constituency in the assembly of Nova Scotia from 1826 until his elevation to the bench in 1829. Unhappily, Haliburton lacked the patience and humility necessary to accept an assured, slow passage through life as a member of the local Anglican élite. His was an ambitious and restless intelligence, rendered all the more piquant by its expression in bold oratory and satirical wit.[9] Colonial society offered many targets for his talents but could only whet, not satisfy, his appetite.

The decade prior to the appearance of Sam Slick was a frustrating time for Haliburton. Harbouring aspirations that could only be fulfilled on a larger stage, he tended to be at once both defensive and contemptuous of his colonial upbringing. From his second trip to England, in 1816 he brought back a bride and also an abiding sense of grievance:

> in early life I twice visited Great Britain, and was strongly, and I may say painfully, impressed with a conviction that has forced itself upon the mind of every man who has gone to Europe from this country – namely, that this valuable and important Colony was not merely wholly unknown, but mis-understood and misrepresented.[10]

The distinct impression left with the reader is that slander of Nova Scotia

8 NA, Henry James Morgan Papers, MG 29, D 61, vol. 47, Beamish Murdoch to Henry James Morgan, 28 Sept. 1865; Beamish Murdoch, *A History of Nova-Scotia, or Acadie*, 3 vols (Halifax 1865–7) vol. 3 (1867) 577–8; V.L.O. Chittick, *Thomas Chandler Haliburton ('Sam Slick'): A Study in Provincial Toryism* (New York 1924) 122–3

9 Ibid., 15–42; Fred Cogswell, 'Thomas Chandler Haliburton,' *DCB*, vol. 9 (Toronto 1976) 348–9

10 From a speech reported in the *Novascotian* (Halifax) 12 June 1839; partially reprinted in D.C. Harvey, 'History and Its Uses in Pre-Confederation Nova Scotia,' Canadian Historical Association, *Annual Report* (1938) 8–9

was one thing, but that Haliburton himself should be considered inferior by association was quite another. Fred Cogswell places the resulting conflict at the heart of Haliburton's literary character: 'say, do, or write what he would, Haliburton knew himself to be a colonial and that on this account all his achievement would be patronized in the very places that he considered to be his own true spiritual home.'[11] It was this potent combination of personal and provincial pride that made Haliburton such a determined historian. As he wrote of the *Statistical Account* to his friend Judge Peleg Wiswall (1763–1836), a Loyalist living in Digby, 'I feel great ambition to have this book do justice to our country, and some little credit to myself.'[12]

The writing of a comprehensive account of Nova Scotia was, in the 1820s, a difficult and time-consuming undertaking. Haliburton began his collection of material in 1821, but was pre-empted in 1823 when Walter Bromley of Halifax heard of his endeavours, and, having an unemployed press, convinced Haliburton to throw together such information as he had in hand. The result, the *General Description*, was a disappointment to Haliburton, who never acknowledged its authorship publicly, and privately complained of the 'hasty manner' of its composition and the 'inconsiderate alteration' of his plan from a wide-ranging account to a simple emigrants' guide.[13] Haliburton resumed his efforts to write the more comprehensive *Statistical Account* almost immediately. Originally he thought of it as a second edition of the *General Description*, and on this basis hoped to complete the project within two years.[14] Imperceptibly Haliburton found the work growing in size and scope into something far more ambitious. At one point he even hoped to include studies of New Brunswick and Prince Edward Island in order to increase the *Statistical Account*'s potential interest for a British audience.[15] But, as Samuel Johnson said, 'He who calls for much information will advance his work

11 Cogswell, 'Haliburton,' 355
12 T.C. Haliburton to Peleg Wiswall, 1 Dec. 1824, in *The Letters of Thomas Chandler Haliburton*, ed. Richard A. Davies (Toronto 1988) 23
13 Haliburton to Wiswall, 31 Dec. 1823, ibid., 12–13. The most significant difference between the *General Description* and the *Statistical Account* is the inclusion in the fifth chapter of the former of a large amount of information on the Micmacs. This material was certainly supplied and probably written by Bromley. That Haliburton did not see fit to include it in the second work may indicate his lack of interest in the subject. See Chittick, *Haliburton*, 68–9; and Patrick D. Clarke, 'The Makers of Acadian History in the Nineteenth Century' (PH D Diss., Université Laval 1988) 130–55.
14 Haliburton to Wiswall, 31 Dec. 1823, in *Letters of Thomas Chandler Haliburton*, 12–13; Haliburton to Abbé Jean-Mandé Sigogne, 5 Sept. 1825, ibid., 33
15 Haliburton to Wiswall, 1 Dec. 1824, ibid., 21–3

but slowly.'[16] In Haliburton's case intentions outpaced stamina, his interest began to flag, and before 1824 was out he wrote to Wiswall, 'I feel like the man who walked by land to the East Indies (Capn. Campbell), got half way, and find the other half appearing a great deal longer, than the whole did at first.'[17] Under pressure from Wiswall, as well as from his own ambition, Haliburton did complete the task, but not until 1829.

The *Statistical Account* was divided into two volumes. The first comprised a narrative history of Nova Scotia down to the British conquest, with a chronology of subsequent events – whose significance for Nova Scotians is often difficult to ascertain – appended. The so-called statistical second volume was not in fact statistical in any real sense at all; it was a chorography, a form that fused topographical description with an assessment of the material achievement of human settlement. It was upon this, the second volume, that Haliburton desired to 'bestow the most labour.' Anxious to correct slanders and exaggerations, he considered the description of the province's true situation 'by far the most important part' of his work.[18]

What distinguished Haliburton from a plague of earlier promoters? He aimed to establish his credentials as a responsible patriot first by the quality of the information he provided. In this regard he had a distinct advantage over the promoters of the mid-eighteenth century, who had feigned a comprehensive knowledge of the colony and enthused over fictitious assets. English settlement was now no longer restricted to isolated footholds established by a few families; by 1800 up to 50,000 settlers were spread around the peninsula seaboard and up fertile valleys; by 1827 this number had swollen to 120,000.[19] Those areas of Nova Scotia not populated had been professionally surveyed by agents of a provincial government impatient to 'be put in possession of facts.'[20] The counties Haliburton described were not the fictions of a topographer; they were populated civil divisions containing mills, churches, and schools, and sending elected representatives to the assembly in Halifax. In writing the descriptive second volume, Haliburton did not have to rely entirely on the

16 Samuel Johnson as quoted in James Boswell, *Life of Johnson* (1791), ed. R.W. Chapman, rev. J.D. Freeman, with a new introduction by Pat Rogers (Oxford 1980) 558

17 Haliburton to Wiswall, 1 Dec. 1824, in *Letters of Thomas Chandler Haliburton*, 23

18 Haliburton to Wiswall, 7 Jan. 1824, ibid., 14–15

19 Andrew Hill Clark, 'Titus Smith, Junior, and the Geography of Nova Scotia in 1801 and 1802,' Association of American Geographers, *Annals* 44 (1954): 295–7; Harvey, 'Intellectual Awakening of Nova Scotia,' 14–16

20 Report of the Council Committee on Hemp Culture, 5 May 1801, quoted in Clark, 'Titus Smith,' 296n. This committee was directly responsible for Titus Smith's commission to survey the peninsula interior in 1801–2.

observations of his travels or the hearsay of a few adventurers; he could harvest a mass of information from the public records, surveys, and charts of the document-generating local government, 'and also from an extensive correspondence with respectable and intelligent people in all parts of Nova-Scotia.'[21] Many of his inquiries (which took the form of a general appeal for information rather than of a questionnaire) could be answered by his fellow MHAS, by duty drawn from every county to the capital each winter.[22] Writing in 1968, Gerald T. Rimmington admired the sweep of Haliburton's knowledge, faulting only his unfamiliarity with a portion of the Minas basin shoreline.[23]

Determined to be reliable, Haliburton did not inflate or meddle with his information once gathered. The purpose he avowed was simply to compile and fit the material 'in *the stocks*.'[24] The work of the surveyors Titus Smith, Charles Morris, III, and Henry William Crawley, the reports of the Central Board of Agriculture, census returns, and the responses from dozens of individuals named in the preface, were all arranged and displayed.[25] Haliburton felt no inhibition about giving over entire sections of the second volume to the submissions of others[26] while himself often compiling from the whole cloth of his sources.[27] He hoped that the British

21 Haliburton, *Statistical Account*, vol. 1, vii
22 T.C. Haliburton to John George Marshall, 7 Dec. 1826, in *Letters of Thomas Chandler Haliburton*, 34–5; Haliburton to John A. Barry, 20 Oct. 1828, ibid., 45
23 Gerald T. Rimmington, 'The Geography of Haliburton's Nova Scotia,' *Dalhousie Review* 48 (1968–9): 494
24 Haliburton to Wiswall, 10 May 1825, in *Letters of Thomas Chandler Haliburton*, 30
25 PANS, RG 1, vols 380–380A, Titus Smith, Surveys of Nova Scotia; PRO, CO 384/17, 'Copy of the Report Laid before the Colonial Department by Lieut. Colonel Cockburn, on the Subject of Emigration, together with the Instructions Received from that Department on 26 January 1827, Printed by Order of the House of Commons, 10 March 1828,' appendix A, no. 1, 'Extracts from the Letter and General Information Book of Charles Morris Esq. Surveyor General of Nova Scotia'; PANS, RG 1, vol. 234/39, Charles Morris, III to Lt.-Col. Cockburn, 15 June 1827; Haliburton, *Statistical Account*, vol. 2, 201n; J.S. Martell, 'The Achievements of Agricola and the Agricultural Societies, 1818–25,' Public Archives of Nova Scotia, *Bulletin*, vol. 2, no. 2 (Halifax 1940) 14
26 For example, 'the whole of the information contained in the geological sketch of the Eastern District of Nova-Scotia, and of the Island of Cape-Breton' (Haliburton, *Statistical Account*, vol. 2, 414–53) came from Richard Brown and Richard Smith, Haliburton, *Statistical Account*, vol. 1, viii.
27 It has been recognized for some time that large sections of Haliburton's second volume were copied from the 'General Information Book' of Charles Morris, III; see Victor H. Palsitts's review of *Builders of Nova Scotia*, by John G. Bourinot, *American Historical Review* 5 (1900): 801–2. Other portions of the volume were taken from the now lost replies to Haliburton's inquiries, see John Roy Campbell, *A History of the County of Yarmouth, Nova Scotia* (Saint John 1876) ix.

public would accept the verbatim provision of state documents as 'a true picture of the posture of affairs at their respective dates.'[28] Indeed, the very absence of a personal voice in such a composition was a kind of guarantee of authenticity. When Haliburton did occasionally insert his own prejudices, they were so clearly demarcated that the reader could easily come to terms with them without compromising the objectivity of the whole.[29] All this was done with scarcely a footnote or quotation mark, but it drew no criticism from the individuals involved. Haliburton was defending a community, and the community was only too glad to help. Together they served up a comprehensive and dependable array of facts meant to convince the sceptic.

The first 273 pages of the second volume's total of 453 pages provided an appraisal of the boundaries, physical and natural characteristics, and human settlement of the whole of Nova Scotia, county by county. Subsequent chapters examined the size and composition of the population, religious denominations, institutional forms of government and justice, climate, soil and agriculture, trade, natural history, and geology and mineralogy. Haliburton's usual approach was to lay down the boundaries and extent of a county to establish units of political and judicial control, and then to introduce local topography by following the various routes of access. The land was drawn and quartered; resources were catalogued and human achievements noted. Like a phrenologist feeling his way across a cranium, Haliburton probed for the potential of his province. The land was a commodity waiting for human development: trees were cut, rivers dammed, minerals extracted, and land ploughed. The topical form enhanced the objective and comprehensive appearance of the volume; the very process of description assimilated and then civilized the terrain; and by division were the vagaries of time mastered.

Because the second volume was predominantly descriptive and the information it contained quickly dated, its reputation has subsided. It is now rarely read in conjunction with the first volume's narrative account of Nova Scotia's history prior to 1763. This partition was reinforced by Haliburton's scattered comments on the nature of history, which reiterated the promoters' distinction between events before and after the conquest. To Wiswall he wrote that after 1763 'the "short & simple annals of the poor" afoard no materials for a continuation, and a history of the province subsequent to that epoch would be about as interesting as one of Dalhousie Settlement.' However, in the same letter Haliburton also

28 [Haliburton,] *General Description*, 179
29 For example, Haliburton supported the claims of Pictou Academy and questioned the need for Dalhousie College, Haliburton, *Statistical Account*, vol. 2, 17–18, 54–6.

indicated, 'when I ... called the work I had in hand the history of the country I did not mean to apply it in its usual acceptation as a narrative of political events, but in a more enlarged sense as an account of whatever of interest might be found in the colony.' Climate, population, trade, towns, mines, government institutions, agriculture, natural advantages, were all for Haliburton worthy of historical consideration, because, as he said, they showed 'the manner in which our little colonial machine is put into motion, the objects that attract the attention of its government, the mode of conducting public business and the gradual and progressive improvement of the colony.'[30] The second volume was not, then, a description of an isolated moment in the development of Nova Scotia; it was a rendering of the dynamic accretion of colonial settlement. This was a significant innovation, for it permitted Haliburton to merge topographical description with the notion, first floated by John Stewart, that men should prove themselves worthy of the land.

Thus, despite the static appearance of the second volume's catalogues, tables, and reports, the sketches Haliburton drew of each county were in his mind historical. They were not so much accounts of raw materials as descriptions of human achievement. Each unit outlined the sufferings the early settlers experienced, the difficulties they surmounted, and, in combination, the rise and progress of a young nation. The process by which the wilderness is converted into a fruitful country was, Haliburton admitted, slow, but 'time, that crumbles into dust the exquisite monuments of art,' eventually fostered colonial improvements, 'until at length hills, vales, groves, streams and rivers, previously concealed by the interminable forest, delight the eye of the beholder in their diversified succession.'[31] To a British audience Haliburton was suggesting that the frustrations and difficulties of the past were the natural and unavoidable consequences of pioneer life. He was proud rather than ashamed of this heritage of struggle, for it linked inextricably Nova Scotia's future prospects to the proven quality and achievements of the founding settlers. This became in Haliburton's mind the central theme of Nova Scotia's history.

Haliburton's theme of historical progress was also a potent weapon when turned on Nova Scotians. The scattered lessons of each settlement were that true progress came only with hard work and agricultural self-sufficiency. Colonization was a weaning process in which 'idle and profligate' disbanded soldiers, inexperienced Loyalists, and would-be

30 Haliburton to Wiswall, 7 Jan. 1824, in *Letters of Thomas Chandler Haliburton*, 14–15
31 Haliburton, *Statistical Account*, vol. 2, 126

aristocratic landlords, failed and 'soon removed to other places.' Of the native people there was no word at all. Highland Scots and the Acadians of Clare, although industrious and frugal, were found to be held back by their antiquated agricultural habits. The real progenitors of Nova Scotia were the energetic agriculturalists from the Scottish Lowlands, Germany, and the United States. The moral Haliburton drew was that those who dabbled in the fisheries and the lumber industry and neglected their farms from the 'prospect of support, with less labour and fatigue' inevitably suffered economic loss and moral decay. In this regard the profit seeking of the late war had been particularly debilitating.[32] Continued progress, while still inevitable, would be greatly speeded if Nova Scotians demonstrated the moral and mental vitality of their forefathers. In the temper of compatriots John Young (Agricola), Thomas McCulloch, and Joseph Howe, and often in the face of economic common sense, Haliburton promoted the virtues of a staunch agrarianism, unweakened by the vices of luxury and idleness.

The characteristic Nova Scotian, as pictured by Haliburton, was a yeoman of the middle class, one who accepted the challenge of clearing the wilderness. The selective process of emigration and the initial hardships of colonial settlement forged the Nova Scotian patriot from an 'Anglo American' alloy.[33] This sophisticated environmental approach provided Haliburton with a useful tool for generalizing the Nova Scotian experience. It also served another purpose: for a people who thought of themselves as Nova Scotians but could not reject their British heritage, environmentalism offered a formula for explaining why they were at once British yet distinctly Nova Scotian. Here we have the ambiguous nexus of Haliburton's patriotism. Within the sharply demarcated environment of Nova Scotia's peninsula the best of the British character emerged without the concomitant extremism of the limitless, lawless American frontier.

In the opinion of the young Haliburton, Nova Scotia should, in its relations with Britain, imitate the independent yeoman, stand on its own two feet, and not rely on imperial patronage. Such an emancipation would be invigorating for colonials and would deflect the animosity of the British taxpayer and consumer. He therefore welcomed the liberation of the colonies from the mercantilist 'spirit of jealous exclusion' brought about by William Huskisson's reform of the Navigation Laws, for he was confident that freer trade would prove more profitable for both Nova

32 Ibid., 52, 67, 85–6, 101, 171, 179, 196, 278–80, 366
33 Ibid., 293

Scotia and Great Britain. Haliburton was eager to strike a similar balance between colonial and imperial political power. He rejected the doctrine of virtual representation in the British Parliament, preferring to build on the maturity of the provincial government with its lieutenant-governor, council, and assembly – the constitutional rather than the social equivalents of the British Crown, Lords, and Commons.[34] The overriding message was that the association could go forward only if Nova Scotians lived up to their potential and the British adequately recognized colonial contributions.

Joseph Howe recognized the dual nature of Haliburton's work when recommending the *General Description* to a friend:

> Everything which tends to make our country better known in Great Britain – does it a positive advantage – because the more these Colonies are known on that side of the water – the greater value must be placed upon them by the Mother Country, which will have the effect of strengthening the ties which bind them to each other – There is also another advantage which may in some degree flow from this work – that it tends to make the Nova Scotian himself better acquainted with the value and usefulness of the soil he inhabits and to turn his attention to the many advantages he enjoys under the present state of things.[35]

Likewise, as Peleg Wiswall wrote to Haliburton, 'I feel a great desire that, your [*Statistical Account*] should afford pleasant reading, together with a comprehensive view of our Province, to foreigners, – and at the same time become a standard book of reference for ourselves.'[36]

A history of Nova Scotia before the British conquest was not immediately relevant to Haliburton's descriptive task. He, like early promoters, realized that the introduction of the French and Indian wars would clearly be incompatible with his carefully fashioned picture of British progress in a civil wilderness. For this reason, the opening chapter of the *General Description* was designed simply 'as a sketch of the political changes of the country' prior to the conquest,[37] and Haliburton maintained this

---

34 Ibid., 326–8, 377–89
35 PANS, Burgess Family Papers, MG 1, vol. 162A, Joseph Howe to Agnes Wallace, 9 Apr. 1826; partially reprinted in *Heart of Howe*, ed. Harvey, xxvi. This reference was drawn to the author's attention by Tom Vincent.
36 Wiswall Papers, vol. 979, folder 1, Notes for a History of Nova Scotia, 5a [enclosure], Wiswall to Haliburton [1826?]; reprinted in Chittick, *Haliburton*, 133–4
37 [Haliburton,] *General Description*, 8

limited view when he first contemplated the structure of the *Statistical Account*. As he explained to Wiswall in 1824:

> there is in fact no history of Nova Scotia to relate, and that the few military events which might have happened here have as little bearing on the true history of the country as the Battle of Trafalga[r] of which it can only be said that it was fought in a particular latitude & longitude and of which the sole remaining trace is a point on the general chart of the world – These occurrences resemble duels, for which the parties for political purposes sought our wilderness as the most convenient place of rendezvous.[38]

Wiswall, contemporaneously working on his own manuscript history of the province, agreed:

> The numerous strange adventures, intrigues, petty wars, and revolutions which occurred amidst the wild scenery and wilder savages of Nova Scotia from the time of Demonts' attempt to colonize in the year 1602 up to the expulsion of the french neutrals in 1755 may afford material for american poets and novelists to work upon, but the history of that period is otherwise of little general interest, saving that it accounts for the small progress made by the colonists in population and improvement during so great a space of time.[39]

Wiswall's letter did provide Haliburton with one important reason for not dissociating his own generation from its distant past entirely: that past and its bloody wars explained the failure of settlement to take hold in Nova Scotia for almost two centuries. 'It must be admitted,' Wiswall added, 'that Nova Scotia is not that naturally rich country which can bear up against plunder, oppression or mismanagement. Its inhabitants require both present protection and prospective security in order to [develop].'[40] Since at least the time of the conquest, Britain had provided such security, with results now obvious to all. As early promoters had already discovered, if properly handled the conflict of the past might act as a foil against which present achievements could be measured. The new sense of Nova Scotia maturity could in part, then, be articulated by contrasting the civil present with the rude past. The implication was that time and society had grown beyond their semi-feudal roots. Or, as Joseph Howe put it:

38 Haliburton to Wiswall, 7 Jan. 1824, in *Letters of Thomas Chandler Haliburton*, 14
39 Wiswall Papers, vol. 979, folder 1, Notes for a History of Nova Scotia, 15
40 Ibid.

> Go seek the records of a fearful age
> In dark Tradition's stores, or History's page,
> Of scenes like these you now shall find no trace
> On fair Acadia's calm and smiling face.[41]

The presentation of early Nova Scotia history as a foil for the modern era had a nice corollary too. Haliburton's generation believed that the critical period in the history of their colony ran from the decision of the British government to build Halifax in 1749 to the Treaty of Paris in 1763. Economic progress did not follow immediately – the land and the Acadians had still to be cleared, speculators discouraged, and representative institutions established. Nonetheless, imperial resolve had finally ended two centuries of frustration for British interests in the region. Haliburton thought this a moral with a contemporary ring. What better way to catch the attention of officials in London than with a portrayal of the high cost of ignorance and inattention?

The sources for a narrative history of early Nova Scotia were to be found 'in an infinite variety of old Colonial books, in which the country [had] been incidentally mentioned, and in the public records.'[42] The town in which Haliburton resided, Annapolis Royal, contained neither public nor private libraries, and thus he was forced to procure books of reference from Halifax, Boston, and London, and from an assortment of friends. Under the best of circumstances this would have been a laborious process, and it was rendered still more tedious by the demands of his fledgling law practice and political career. It has subsequently become traditional to speak of his 'almost complete dearth of materials for the work he had in mind.'[43] However, such difficulties were a matter of degree, and Haliburton's were incomparably less than those faced by earlier promoters. He often spent portions of the year in Halifax, which had a public library and a commercial reading room, and where the collections of a number of scientific and literary associations were located (the Provincial Agricultural Society alone had more than three hundred catalogued volumes in 1825).[44] The legislative journals had been ordered

41 Joseph Howe, 'Acadia,' in his *Poems and Essays* (1874), ed. M.G. Parks (Toronto 1973) 31
42 Haliburton, *Statistical Account*, vol. 1, vi
43 Archibald MacMechan, *The Centenary of Haliburton's 'Nova-Scotia'* (Halifax 1930) 1
44 Haliburton to Wiswall, in *Letters of Thomas Chandler Haliburton, passim*; Robert Cooney, *A Compendious History of the Northern Part of the Province of New Brunswick, and of the District of Gaspé, in Lower Canada* (Halifax 1832) vii; Martell, 'Achievements of Agricola,' 15; D. C. Harvey, 'Early Public Libraries in Nova Scotia,' *Dalhousie Review* 14 (1934): 436–7

organized and bound in 1809, and £150 had been voted in 1811 to put other public documents in order. These papers, which included among other items the governors' letter-books and the original minutes of His Majesty's Council at Annapolis Royal, were in the custody of the provincial secretary, Sir Rupert George, who in 1828 gave Haliburton unique permission 'to take them to his lodgings for more convenient reference.'[45] The city also offered Haliburton the supportive companionship of 'The Club,' a convivial literary association inhabited by the likes of Joseph Howe, the lawyer-historians Beamish Murdoch (1800–76) and Thomas Beamish Akins (1809–91), poet Andrew Shiels, and the historian of New Brunswick's north shore, Robert Cooney (of whom more in due course).[46] Finally, Haliburton could obtain transcripts from repositories in England and America, especially from the library and collections of the Massachusetts Historical Society.[47]

The information Haliburton presented was carefully controlled. The narrative of Nova Scotia's early history would lose all credibility, even as a foil, if it descended to a fanciful or romantic level. Thus Haliburton's object was, according to the Preface, to collect 'scattered notices' of Nova Scotia from the writings of Marc Lescarbot, Pierre-François-Xavier de Charlevoix, Thomas Hutchinson, George Richards Minot, Jeremy Belknap, John Huddlestone Wynne, William Douglass, Abiel Holmes, Tobias George Smollett, and Abbé Guillaume-Thomas-François Raynal, 'and form them into a connected narrative.' These prefatory acknowledgments were rarely repeated in the footnotes 'from a wish to avoid ... pedantry.' All matter was 'collated with great care' before being 'compiled,' and Haliburton apologized for 'the irregularity in the style' his method necessitated.[48]

Today Haliburton would be called a plagiarist, and it is a charge that has often been laid at his door. John George Bourinot in particular drew

45 Thomas Beamish Akins, letter to the editor, *Boston Evening Transcript*, 19 Mar. 1885; PANS, William Cochran Papers, MG 1, vol. 223, items 3–4, Memoranda ... with a View to a History of Nova Scotia; C. Bruce Fergusson, 'The Public Archives of Nova Scotia,' *Acadiensis* 2 (1972): 73–4
46 Gwendolyn Davies, 'The Club Papers: Haliburton's Literary Apprenticeship,' in Frank M. Tierney, ed., *The Thomas Chandler Haliburton Symposium*, Reappraisals, Canadian Writers, No. 11, gen. ed. Lorraine McMullen (Ottawa 1985) 65–82; Carrie MacMillan, 'Colonial Gleanings: 'The Club" Papers (1828–31),' *Essays in Canadian Writing* 31 (1985): 51–64
47 Haliburton, *Statistical Account*, vol. 1, vi
48 Ibid., vi–vii; Haliburton to Wiswall, 19 Feb. 1824, in *Letters of Thomas Chandler Haliburton*, 19

attention to Haliburton's version of the Seven Years' War, which Bourinot claimed was drawn verbatim from Smollett's *History of England*.[49] The problem was, in fact, somewhat more complex. There are few passages in the first volume where Haliburton openly copied from one source for pages on end. The longest of these was taken from Minot (143–8),[50] while Smollett's longest continuous run was only a little more than two pages (206–8).[51] Far more often Haliburton followed the method adopted in chapter one: he selected the best single source as the backbone of his narrative, in this case Belknap's *American Biography*, and then mixed in additional material from such subsidiary sources as Lescarbot and Charlevoix, with an occasional extra point supplied from the likes of the Reverend Thomas Prince.[52] A still better example of Haliburton's method of gluing sources together was his account of the first siege of the fortress at Louisbourg (111–34): almost every word in the section was copied from another work, but so finely were his four main sources (Belknap, Douglass, Hutchinson, and Minot) woven together, that rarely did one run uninterrupted for more than a paragraph at a time.[53]

49 John George Bourinot (1837–1902), 'Builders of Nova Scotia: A Historical Review; With an Appendix Containing Copies of Rare Documents Relating to the Early Days of the Province,' Royal Society of Canada, *Proceedings and Transactions*, ser. 2, vol. 5 (1899) sec. ii, 63

50 George Richards Minot (1758–1802), *Continuation of the History of the Province of Massachusetts Bay from the Year 1748. With an Introductory Sketch of Events from Its Original Settlement*, 2 vols (Boston 1798–1803) vol. 1 (1798) 122–30

51 Tobias George Smollett (1721–71), *Continuation of the Complete History of England*, 4 vols (London 1760–1) vol. 2 (1760) 284–6

52 Jeremy Belknap (1744–98), *American Biography: Or an Historical Account of Those Persons Who Have Been Distinguished in America, as Adventurers, Statesmen, Philosophers, Divines, Warriors, Authors, or Other Remarkable Characters, Comprehending a Recital of the Events Connected with Their Lives and Actions*, 2 vols (Boston 1794–8); Marc Lescarbot (c. 1570–1642), *Histoire de la Nouvelle France: contenant les navigations, découvertes, & habitations faites par les François és Indes Occidentales & Nouvelle-France souz l'avoeu & authorité de noz rois tres-chrétiens, & les diverses fortunes d'iceux en l'execution de ces choses, depuis cent ans jusques à hui. En quoy est comprise l'histoire morale, naturele, & geographique de ladite province: avec les tables & figures d'icelle* (Paris 1609); [Pierre-François-Xavier] de Charlevoix, *Histoire et description générale de la Nouvelle France, avec le Journal historique d'un voyage fait part ordre du roi dans l'Amérique septentrionnale*, 3 vols and 6 vols (Paris 1744); Thomas Prince (1687–1758), *A Chronological History of New England in the Form of Annals* (Boston 1736)

53 Jeremy Belknap, *The History of New Hampshire. Comprehending the Events of One Complete Century and Seventy-Five Years from the Discovery of the River Pascataqua to the Year One Thousand Seven Hundred and Ninety. Containing also, a Geographical Description of the State, with Sketches of Its Natural History, Productions, Improvements, and Present State of Society and Manners, Laws, and Government*, 3 vols (1784–92) 2nd ed. (Boston 1813); William Douglass (d. 1752), *A Summary, Historical and Political, of the First Planting, Progressive*

When Haliburton interfered with a source the motive was not style but length. He spoke out only if there was an open disagreement among his sources over a fact, usually a date. Otherwise he remained uncritical of his material, ignoring changes in style and even of approach. This did of course raise a few anomalies: in the fourth chapter, for instance, Haliburton's discussion of the expulsion of the Acadians shifted from such anti-Acadian sources as Smollett and Douglass to the more sympathetic Minot to the pastoral Raynal, with ambiguous results. Thus, although the arrangement of material took time, once the books were collected most of Haliburton's creative task was over. A comparison of the sources listed in the preface with Haliburton's actual text reveals that approximately 70 per cent of the narrative in volume one was copied.[54]

One obvious reason for Haliburton's slavish adherence to sources was that this was the accepted practice of the writers whom he admired. Belknap's *History of New Hampshire*, for example, paraphrased and copied from many of the same sources Haliburton used. Indeed, virtually all the works available to Haliburton were by historians who had, according to a recent student, 'merely rephrased or copied the best or most recent secondary works at hand, achieving, as a result, little more in much of their prose than crudely spliced editions of large blocks of material copied from prior histories.'[55] It is true that earlier historians tended to footnote more than Haliburton, but when the Reverend William Cochran (*c.* 1757–1833) criticized Haliburton for not following their practice, he did so only because the failure to footnote made it difficult for readers to go back to the sources themselves, not because it was dishonest.[56] A remarkable freedom from scholarly rivalry and a strong sense of being part of a co-operative venture meant that most historians were flattered to have their writings borrowed by others.[57] At a time when basic facts were not as near as the closest library or textbook, when many of the relevant

---

Improvements, and Present State of the British Settlements in North America, 2 vols [2nd ed.] (Boston and London 1755); Thomas Hutchinson (1711–80), *The History of the Colony and Province of Massachusetts-Bay*, 3 vols (1764–1828) ed. Lawrence Shaw Mayo (Cambridge, Mass., 1936); Minot, *Continuation of the History of the Province of Massachusetts Bay*

54 For an exhaustive reconstruction of Haliburton's use of sources see Clarke, 'Makers of Acadian History,' ch. 1.

55 Richard C. Vitzthum, *The American Compromise: Theme and Method in the Histories of Bancroft, Parkman, and Adams* (Norman, Okla., 1974) 45

56 Cochran Papers, Memoranda ... with a View to a History of Nova Scotia, item 4, enclosure inside the front cover

57 Arthur H. Shaffer, *The Politics of History: Writing the History of the American Revolution, 1783–1815* (Chicago 1975) 181–2

books were almost unobtainable, creativity lay in bringing a story together for the first time in a convenient form. Originality of expression was a secondary consideration and one that opened the door to prejudice and bias; far better to leave sources untouched, really uncorrupted. The Anglo-Irish author Oliver Goldsmith made this point when reviewing the very work Haliburton was so often accused of plagiarizing, Smollett's *History of England*:

> in proportion as History removes from the first witnesses, it may recede also from truth, – as, by passing thro' the prejudices, or the mistakes of subsequent Compilers, it will be apt to imbibe what tincture they may chance to give it. The *later* Historian's only way, therefore, to prevent the ill effects of that decrease of evidence which the lapse of years necessarily brings with it, must be, by punctually referring to the spring-head from whence the stream of his narration flows; which will at once cut off all appearance of partiality, or misrepresentation.[58]

And if credibility was a tricky philosophical issue in Europe, it was a harsh pragmatic reality when writing of colonial British North America.

In so far as Haliburton could be said to have disappointed his contemporaries, it was because he failed to take full advantage of the government records thrown open to him. Although 'directions were given by the provincial secretary to afford every facility to Mr. Haliburton in his inquiries,' and the ante-room of the council chamber was made over to his use, Haliburton's researches through the public papers were, to judge by the results, irregular and fitful.[59] The pressure of time seems to have dictated Haliburton's policy, for he came to the documents only in 1828, well after he had already composed much of his narrative. William Cochran, one-time president of King's College, contemporaneously worked through the public papers in order to compile his own manuscript history of the province and gave a much fuller account of events on the peninsula between 1713 and 1755. Cochran inserted in his manuscript a list of criticisms he had of the *Statistical Account*, prominent among which was the young Haliburton's failure to consult these same sources.[60] T.B. Akins, Nova Scotia's first archivist and one of Haliburton's research

58 *Collected Works of Oliver Goldsmith*, ed. Arthur Friedman, 5 vols (Oxford 1966) vol. 1, 44
59 William H. Keating to Thomas Beamish Akins, 11 Mar. 1885, quoted in Akins, letter to the editor, *Boston Evening Transcript*, 19 Mar. 1885
60 Cochran Papers, Memoranda ... with a View to a History of Nova Scotia, item 4, enclosure inside the front cover

assistants, also later complained that his friend had not made effective use of the papers in the office of the provincial secretary and had instead relied for the most part on the publications of others.[61] In summary, despite Haliburton's claim to have made 'numerous searches' of the public records, he barely scratched the surface of the manuscript collections available to him in Halifax.[62]

Haliburton used the narrative of the first volume to demonstrate how little could be gained in Nova Scotia so long as imperial inattention permitted desultory conflict and ignorance hindered development. His cautionary tale began with the French, who were so determined to discover riches of gold and silver that they ignored the more prosaic agricultural potential of their colony on the Bay of Fundy. Acadia fell into disrepute and neglect, and this 'spirit of inconstancy contributed to the loss of the country to France, and operated as an insuperable barrier to the acquisition of any solid advantage from it.' The British acted little better. They often found themselves in possession of Acadia (more through accident than design), but until 1713 they were repeatedly to bargain the area away at the conference table. Indeed, according to Haliburton, it was the New Englanders who, appreciating Acadia's strategic position and perceiving a threat to their vital interests, finally forced Britain's hand and secured the peninsula by the Treaty of Utrecht.[63]

Haliburton was disappointed that British possession did not bring about immediate change. By 1713 the peninsula's existing inhabitants, the Acadians, 'had become so discouraged by the repeated attacks of the

61 PANS, Thomas Beamish Akins Papers, MG 1, vol. 8, T.B. Akins to S.G. Lajoie, 12 Jan. 1860; T.B. Akins to Francis Parkman, nd, quoted in Francis Parkman, 'The Acadians Again,' *Nation* (New York) 22 Jan. 1885, 73; Akins, letter to the editor, *Boston Evening Transcript*, 19 Mar. 1885; F. Blake Crofton, 'Haliburton: The Man and the Writer,' in [A.B. DeMille, ed.,] *Haliburton: A Centenary Chaplet, with a Bibliography by John Parker Anderson* (Toronto 1897) 57; Archibald MacMechan, 'A Gentleman of the Old School,' *Halifax Herald*, 31 Dec. 1932

62 Haliburton, *Statistical Account*, vol. 1, viii. Haliburton's habits of research later became a matter of controversy (see below 200-2) because he suggested in a footnote in the *Statistical Account* (vol. 1, 196n) that his failure to provide fuller documentation regarding the expulsion of the Acadians was due to a conspiracy among the perpetrators to suppress all incriminating evidence relating to that event. According to Akins, Haliburton had an exaggerated idea of what kinds of documents should have survived and furthermore missed many of the documents that did survive. Certainly nothing was withheld from Haliburton at the time. See Akins, letter to the editor, *Boston Evening Transcript*, 19 Mar. 1885.

63 Haliburton, *Statistical Account*, vol. 1, 46, 68, 80–5

English that they made but little progress in settling the country.' After 1713 matters were no different: 'the English did not display the same zeal in the settlement of the Country which they had manifested in its conquest'; and the French, now realizing the value of what they had lost and what they could still lose, started a new round of violence that eventually led to the expulsion of 1755. Once again it was the New Englanders who, in the face of French incursions from Louisbourg, forced the British government to wrest control of the whole of the Maritime region from their enemies.[64] In the meantime, the political changes and insecurity of property caused by recurrent conflict 'had a tendency to divert the attention of the settlers from agriculture' and operated powerfully to check the progress of the region.[65]

Significant British development in Nova Scotia commenced only in 1749 with the decision to build at Halifax. Born of military necessity, according to Haliburton Halifax was a symbol of the arrival of the permanent civilization that would finally break patterns of neglect and violence. A fortress for 'confirming and extending the dominion of the Crown of Great Britain,' Halifax also constituted 'Communities, diffusing the benefits of population and agriculture.' The settlers on board ships resting in Chebucto harbour, surveying the beautiful wooded coastline, 'reflected that it was to be removed by their hands,' and 'they were appalled at the magnitude of their undertaking.' But the wilderness did not frighten them, much less assimilate them. Of this British authorities made sure: before any settlers 'were allowed to reside on shore, it was necessary to convince them that crimes could not be committed with impunity, and that as much of the Law of England had followed them to the wilderness of Nova-Scotia, as was necessary for their government and protection.'[66] In contrast, the Indians and French had acted in defiance of civilized law, oaths, and treaties, and had squandered their legitimate opportunities.

The fourth chapter was organized around the conflict between the nascent settlement at Halifax and the Indians, Acadians, and French – a conflict that was resolved only by the expulsion of 1755. Haliburton's presentation of the expulsion was to play an important role in the development of Maritime historiography in the late nineteenth century and has a retrospective fascination. His position was purposely ambiguous. On the one hand, as the legislative representative for the constituency

64 Ibid., 65–6, 92–111
65 Ibid., vol. 2, 274
66 Ibid., vol. 1, 136, 139

harbouring the largest number of Acadians in the province, Haliburton was disposed to be sympathetic to their predicament in 1755.[67] Relying on Minot, Raynal, and a partial transcript of the journal of Colonel John Winslow (which he obtained from the Massachusetts Historical Society), Haliburton labelled the expulsion 'cruel,' 'unnecessary,' and 'totally irreconcileable with the idea, as *at this day* entertained of justice.' (Emphasis added.) On the other hand, he used Smollett and Douglass to establish a clear picture of the immediate pressures of war. What other course could a governor have adopted, Haliburton asked rhetorically, which 'while it ensured the tranquility of the Colony, should temper justice with mercy to those misguided people?' 'Seduced' by the French government, the Acadians 'would neither submit to the English Government themselves, nor allow others to enjoy it with tranquility.'[68] In Haliburton's eyes the crime of the Acadians was just this, their failure to let British agricultural settlement grow in peace. If he was content to obscure the harsh implications of this judgment by the use of contradictory sources, there can be no doubt that in the broad sweep of history the foundation of Halifax, not the expulsion, was for Haliburton the central fact of Nova Scotia's past.

The last chapter and concluding chronology rounded off Haliburton's tale of the arrival of civilization in Nova Scotia. Using council minutes and the legislative journals, he described the decision in 1758 to establish an assembly: as an event in Nova Scotia history this ranked only slightly behind the founding of Halifax. In 1760, 'while the settlement of the Province was advanced by these liberal and judicious proposals, its tranquility was secured by the operations of the army [in Canada].'[69] The volume came to a satisfying and natural conclusion with the peace of 1763.

Taken together, Haliburton's two volumes composed a single drama in four acts: two in the past, one in the present, and one in the future. The

67 Adams George Archibald, 'The Expulsion of the Acadians, part 1,' Nova Scotia Historical Society, *Collections* 5 (1886–7): 12; Archibald MacMechan, 'Evangeline and the Real Acadians,' in his *The Life of a Little College and Other Papers* (Boston and New York 1914) 209–10; Rimmington, 'Haliburton's Nova Scotia,' 497–8

68 Haliburton, *Statistical Account*, vol. 1, 159, 196–7. Abbé [Guillaume-Thomas-François] Raynal (1713–96), *A Philosophical and Political History of the Settlements and Trade of the Europeans in the East and West Indies*, trans. J. Justamond, 3rd ed., 5 vols (London 1777) vol. 5, 164–75. The journals of John Winslow (1703–74) have been published as 'Journal of Colonel John Winslow ...' part 1, Nova Scotia Historical Society, *Collections* 3 (1882–3): 71–196; part 2, ibid., 4 (1884): 113–246.

69 Haliburton, *Statistical Account*, vol. 1, 223

first act, a moral tale in narrative form, detailed the feudal era of the French and Indian wars, the purpose of which was to act as a foil for subsequent plot development and as a lesson for British officials on the penalties imposed for ignorance. The crucial role New England played as prime mover was itself an implied threat that Nova Scotians had other avenues for evolution.[70] The second act, which began as a narrative of institution building in volume one and then dispersed into a series of descriptive accounts in volume two, portrayed an age of valiant pioneers around whose memory a golden glow was already beginning to descend. The third act highlighted contemporary development and catalogued the material progress of Nova Scotia society. This was the crisis of the play, in which the characters could either derive inspiration from their own and their forefathers' achievements or mark time living off the family patrimony. The climactic fourth act took place off-stage in the future. It was Haliburton's hope that Nova Scotians had the moral and intellectual qualities necessary to exploit, in conjunction with an understanding and supportive imperial government, the natural advantages of their colonial environment. In this respect, whatever one's pride or natural interest in the past might have been, history was subordinate to the future of Nova Scotia.

Haliburton's optimism took the form of a mature patriotism rather than a selfish promotionalism. His concern for the long-term reputation of Nova Scotia and the moral instruction of its people instilled in him a restraint, the methodological consequences of which were a dependence on documents and previous historical writings. This meant that as a historian Haliburton laboured under a certain tension: he was conscious of the demands of critical method, but working against this were his own desire and the insistence of his society that history strengthen local loyalties, confirm provincial pride, and teach moral lessons.

While it is to Haliburton's credit that his scholarship rarely degenerated into propaganda, his patriotic assumptions were not without their cost. He demonstrated a distinct lack of sympathy for those who did not contribute to his notion of what was best for progress in Nova Scotia: natives, lumbermen, fishermen, merchants, soldiers, and most government officials were given short shrift; the French era was condemned out of hand for its short-sighted approach to development. Haliburton also

70 For a time Haliburton viewed annexation to the New England states as the natural course of development for Nova Scotia, see Haliburton to Wiswall, 7 Jan. 1824, in *Letters of Thomas Chandler Haliburton*, 16–17.

created a false impression of contemporary Nova Scotia by shunning any discussion of internal political, religious, or personal animosities. Yet under the necessity of describing Nova Scotia and promoting its image, Haliburton avoided excessive concentration on the constitutional issues that so engrossed European historians. In common with most other early Maritime reports and apologias, Haliburton's *Statistical Account* reflected a wider desire to provide a systematic description of both human activity and physical geography, co-ordinated by the unifying theme of progress.

Haliburton's history was patriotic because it met the needs of Nova Scotians. Specifically, he fashioned a comprehensive descriptive and narrative account that fitted the conception his fellows had of themselves, their partnership with Great Britain, and their future together. At least three other Nova Scotians were contemporaneously engaged in the production of a manuscript history of the province, none of which, if published, would have been so satisfactory. Peleg Wiswall's 'Notes for a History of Nova Scotia' were too obviously polemical in tone, impressionistic rather than documentary, and would have offended without convincing.[71] William Cochran's 'Memoranda ... with a View to a History of Nova Scotia' offered a chronology that surpassed Haliburton's first volume in research and detail but lacked a unifying form as history, and commented neither on the present nor the future concerns of Nova Scotians.[72] Beamish Murdoch, in open imitation of the various 'memoirs' of Lower Canada by Robert Christie, used real scissors and real paste to manufacture from newspaper clippings 'Historical Memoirs of the British North American Provinces since His Present Majesty's Accession.' His purpose was to defend the right of colonial assemblies to control the public purse, but in so doing he exposed debilitating conflicts not only between colonists and the imperial government but also among the colonists themselves.[73] Only Haliburton struck the right balance. Indeed, in defending the honour of his native land and defining the characteristics of its people, Haliburton was a source, not merely an echo, of the commonplace attitudes of his time.

Haliburton was weary of the *Statistical Account* long before it was published, and its immediate reception did little to revive his historical curiosity. His hope of appearing before the British public was effectively dashed by his failure to attract a publisher in London, and although the

---

71 Wiswall Papers, vol. 979, folder 1
72 Cochran Papers, vol. 223, items 3–4
73 PANS, Beamish Murdoch Papers, MG 1, vol. 726

work was initially honoured in Nova Scotia,[74] it did not generate much in the way of sales. Joseph Howe, the eventual publisher, found the work a 'ruinous speculation':

> It cumbered my office for two years, involved me in heavy expenses for wages, and in debts for paper, materials, binding and engraving ... None sold abroad. The Book, though fairly printed, was wretchedly bound, the engravings were poor, and I was left with about 1000 copies, scattered about, unsaleable on my hands.[75]

A problem of equal if not greater concern to Haliburton was the constraint historical method imposed on his natural wit and flair for the satirical. Certainly what he called his 'resort to a more popular style' in the *Clockmaker* series better suited his talents.[76] In 1839 he thought of updating the statistics and descriptions in the second volume of the *Statistical Account*, but failed to do so when he was unable to obtain a guarantee of £250 from either the provincial government or his publisher.[77] As for Haliburton's two-volume *Rule and Misrule of the English in America*, published in New York in 1851, it was less a formal history than an outgrowth of his polemical, political writing, and was more single-mindedly plagiarized in an era when the practice was viewed more critically. It did not enhance his stature either at home or abroad, and it justified his natural instinct to concentrate on his humorous sketches.[78] Of

74 On 27 Mar. 1829 the House of Assembly of Nova Scotia unanimously resolved to thank Haliburton 'for the very laudable and laborious effort which he has made,' see Haliburton, *Statistical Account*, vol. 2, Frontispiece. The *Statistical Account* was also favourably received in New England, where it was responsible for Haliburton's being elected an honorary member of the Massachusetts Historical Society, see the *Novascotian*, 1 Apr. 1830.

75 Quoted in Chittick, *Haliburton*, 144; see also J. Murray Beck, *Joseph Howe*, vol. 1, *Conservative Reformer, 1804–1848* (Kingston and Montreal 1982) 98–9; and George L. Parker, *The Beginnings of the Book Trade in Canada* (Toronto 1985) 61–2

76 Quoted in Tom Marshall, 'Haliburton's Canada,' *Canadian Literature* 68–9 (1976): 134

77 *Letters of Thomas Chandler Haliburton*, T.C. Haliburton to Richard Bentley, 19 Dec. 1839, 111–12; 1 Sept. 1840, 118–20; Haliburton to Sir Rupert D. George, 18 Nov. 1840, 120–1; Haliburton to Bentley, 1 Dec. 1840, 122–3

78 Published in London that same year under the less contentious title of *The English in America*, it was a blatant plagiarism of *History of the United States in America* by Richard Hildreth (1807–65) 6 vols (New York 1849–52); see Chittick, *Haliburton*, 509–10. For a more sympathetic discussion of Haliburton's later historical work see Stanley E. McMullin, 'In Search of the Tory Mind: Thomas Chandler Haliburton and Egerton Ryerson,' in Tierney, ed., *Haliburton Symposium*, 43–8.

all his non-fiction writing, only the *Statistical Account* left a lasting legacy. Everyone who wrote on Nova Scotia in the next generation used his work, either directly or indirectly, as a source-book and an inspiration.[79]

In summary, the historical elements to be found in both the *General Description* and the *Statistical Account* cannot be separated from the patriotic purpose that determined their arrangement and interpretation. Together historical narrative and topographical description merged in Haliburton's hands to give substance to Nova Scotia patriotism – a patriotism that suggested the colony represented the best and most vital qualities of British civilization. The qualities Haliburton admired most were those of the intelligent, hard-working, progressive yeoman farmer. More to the point, Haliburton implied that the typical Nova Scotian exhibited these qualities and that he was himself proud to be associated with his compatriots. By the time he came to write the Sam Slick stories in the 1830s, Haliburton delighted in demonstrating how far Nova Scotians fell short of this ideal, and by extension how far he was himself drifting from identity with them.

The fading of Haliburton's patriotism, from which Nova Scotians generally did not suffer, coincided with the gradual emergence in New Brunswick of similar provincial loyalties reflected in like histories. Despite the enthusiasm of its Loyalist founders, the younger colony initially lagged behind Nova Scotia in social, economic, and political maturity, and its settlers were naturally slower to develop a cohesive sense of themselves as the basis for provincial patriotism. But in time New Brunswick historians attempted to narrow the definition of their provincial identity. They did so in the face of greater practical difficulties than beset Haliburton.

New Brunswick was and is a province notoriously difficult to characterize. In an age reliant on water-borne communication, its continental geography was a persistent barrier to internal cohesion, and, long after the colony was given a separate existence in 1784, the north shore remained isolated from the south, the upper Saint John River valley from the lower, and the valley as a whole from the Bay of Fundy. The bulk of the provincial land mass consisted of a tree-covered extension of the Appalachian mountains, which, with the exception of a few fertile pockets, was overlaid with thin acidic soils whose agricultural potential was low. In the absence of any alternative employment, the perhaps 25,000 settlers resident in the colony by 1800 farmed where they could,

79 Harvey, 'History and Its Uses,' 9; see also Haliburton's own observations in the *Novascotian*, 12 June 1839.

their small communities separated one from the other. The advent of a vibrant trade in timber following Napoleon's embargo of Britain's traditional Baltic sources in 1806 injected vitality into the provincial economy and was attended by a significant increase in population (to 74,000 in 1824; 120,000 in 1834; 200,000 in 1850), but the extensive nature of the new industry served only to accentuate centrifugal tendencies. The dispersal of rural communities was matched by a municipal parochialism, which saw the likes of Saint John, Fredericton, Saint Andrews, and Newcastle each grasp for its own small area of influence. Diffusion of knowledge from the outside was limited and interaction among districts poor, with the result that as late as mid-century 'most New Brunswick lives were lived in relative isolation.'[80]

It was only with some difficulty that thoughtful New Brunswickers were able to comprehend their province and present an articulate picture of its predicament to outsiders. A migratory population, scattered settlements, insubstantial towns, ephemeral boundaries, and tenuous political and judicial control did not offer discrete building blocks to the would-be chorographer. Especially debilitating was the lack of a cosmopolitan centre with libraries and supportive intellectual companionship. Despite such handicaps, in the three decades following 1825 at least a dozen descriptive and historical accounts of the province made their way into print. With one interesting exception, each of these works was in the first instance published to defend New Brunswick's general reputation and place in the empire, and in the second specifically to counter the arguments of those British liberals whose fulminations against the protective structure of imperial tariffs threatened with abrupt extinction New Brunswick's critical trade in timber.

Given the rude and amorphous nature of the colony, New Brunswick's pioneer historians were thrown back upon the methods of extensive personal observation employed by eighteenth-century Maritime promoters, their descriptions limited by the range of their experience. The very number of works published was a sign of weakness rather than strength. The one major advantage patriot writers had over their promotional predecessors was the existence of a local government producing, however imperfectly, journals, statistics, and reports. It is indicative of the first generation of New Brunswick historians that most were themselves

80 Graeme Wynn, *Timber Colony: A Historical Geography of Early Nineteenth Century New Brunswick* (Toronto 1981) 9. This paragraph relies heavily on the first chapter of the *Timber Colony* and on Wynn's 'Population Patterns in Pre-Confederation New Brunswick,' *Acadiensis* 10 (1981): 124–38.

employed in some public capacity. Alexander Wedderburn (1796?–1843), for instance, was the emigration officer; Moses Henry Perley (1804–62) was commissioner of Indian affairs and Wedderburn's successor as emigration officer; Thomas Baillie (1796–1863) was commissioner of Crown lands and surveyor-general; Calvin Luther Hatheway (1786–1866) held various posts as a land surveyor, and Abraham Gesner (1797–1864) was provincial geologist.[81] Peter Fisher (1782–1848) and Robert Cooney (1800–70) held no such posts but used their respective careers as lumber merchant and journalist to gather information.[82] Only William Christopher Atkinson (fl. 1835–45), a sedentary missionary to New Brunswick for less than five years, had no occupational advantage, and, in spite of his scavenging from the work of others, his three pamphlets were distinctly inferior.[83]

The problem Peter Fisher encountered in gathering information may be taken as typical of those faced by New Brunswick historians. He was, by virtue of his *Sketches of New-Brunswick* (published anonymously in Saint John in 1825), the first historian of the province.[84] Born in a Loyalist camp on Staten Island, New York, Fisher was only sixteen months old when he arrived in New Brunswick with his refugee parents in 1783. He resided at Fredericton, was educated at a local school, developed an extensive

81 Alexander Wedderburn, *Statistical and Practical Observations, Relative to the Province of New-Brunswick, Published for the Information of Emigrants* (Saint John 1835), Title Page; W.A Spray, 'Alexander Wedderburn,' *DCB*, vol. 7 (Toronto 1988) 899, and 'Moses Henry Perley,' ibid., vol. 9, 628–32; W.S. MacNutt, 'Thomas Baillie,' ibid., 21–4; J.M. Whalen, 'Calvin Luther Hatheway,' ibid., 374–5; Loris S. Russell, 'Abraham Gesner,' ibid., 308–12

82 Ann Gorman Condon, 'Peter Fisher,' *DCB*, vol. 7, 288–91; William Odber Raymond, 'Peter Fisher. The First Historian of New Brunswick,' New Brunswick Historical Society, *Collections* 4 (1919): 5–56; 'Robert Cooney. First Historian of Northern and Eastern New Brunswick,' ibid., 67–85; [Robert Cooney,] *The Autobiography of a Wesleyan Methodist Missionary, (Formerly a Roman Catholic,) Containing an Account of His Conversion from Romanism, and His Reception into the Wesleyan Ministry; Also, Reminiscences of Nearly Twenty-Five Years' Itinerancy in the North American Provinces, &c.* (Montreal 1856) 72–8

83 William Christopher Atkinson, *The Emigrants' Guide to New Brunswick, British North America* (Berwick-upon-Tweed, England, 1842) 23, 49; 2nd ed., *A Guide to New Brunswick, British North America, &c.* (Edinburgh 1843) iii; 3rd ed., *A Historical and Statistical Account of New-Brunswick, B.N.A., with Advice to Emigrants* (Edinburgh 1844) 49

84 [Peter Fisher,] *Sketches of New-Brunswick; Containing an Account of the First Settlement of the Province, with a Brief Description of the Country, Climate, Productions, Inhabitants, Government, Rivers, Towns, Settlements, Public Institutions, Trade, Revenue, Population, &c.*, By an Inhabitant of the Province (Saint John 1825); reprinted as *The First History of New Brunswick*, with notes by William Odber Raymond (Saint John 1921; reprinted Woodstock, NB, 1980)

lumber business, and was known as 'a tireless pedestrian.'[85] He wrote the *Sketches of New-Brunswick* 'to diffuse a general knowledge of the Country, its productions, sources of wealth, &c.' among ignorant outsiders and in the hope that it would be 'interesting to every person who possesses a feeling of interest for his own fireside.'[86] Being the first historian, Fisher had little to work with, and he relied primarily on his mother's memory of early hardships and on his own considerable perambulations.[87] It was his continual complaint that no register or survey had yet been made of the province's crops, plants, animals, birds, minerals, and climate – information he knew he should be providing. Of greater concern to Fisher was his lack of sufficient knowledge to furnish a comprehensive description of the physical geography of each county in its turn. Normally the core of any colonial account, Fisher's county outline was uneven; entire areas with which he was unfamiliar were neglected; and the 1824 census appeared too late for him to make full use of its findings. A 'Compiler' with little to compile, he warned his readers that 'FRACTIONAL accuracy' was not to be expected in his brief outline.[88]

Within his limitations, Fisher did his best to provide a survey of the history, present state, and future prospects of his adopted homeland. It was by now axiomatic that progress should be the unifying theme, and Fisher oriented his material on this axis. Without secondary works covering the French period in New Brunswick, Fisher simply relegated the whole to a misty realm in two short paragraphs. The pre-Loyalist Maugerville settlement and its apostasy during the American Revolution were also disposed of in short order – obviously not a suitable foundation on which to build. The pivotal date, the New Brunswick equivalent to Nova Scotia's *anno* Halifax, was 1783, the year of the arrival of the Loyalists – although 1784, the year New Brunswick was established as a separate province, 1785, the year of the first election, and 1786, the year the first assembly met, tended to be thought of as a related unit. 'From this period the Province slowly improved'; and it was a matter of sweet filial pride as well as of thematic convenience to portray the Loyalist era as one of heroic struggle to establish civilization in a hostile environment, 'the country all round being a continued wilderness – uninhabited and untrodden, except by the savage and wild animals.' Here was the yardstick by which to measure present achievement: 'Many ... Loyalists were in the prime of life when they came to this country; and most of them had young

85 Condon, 'Peter Fisher,' 288–9; Raymond, 'Peter Fisher,' 5–11, 17–19
86 [Fisher,] *First History of New Brunswick* (1980), 7, 100
87 Ibid., 7, 12; Raymond, 'Peter Fisher,' 11–16

families. To establish these they wore out their lives in toil and poverty, and by their unremitting exertions subdued the wilderness, and covered the face of the country with habitations, villages, and towns.' Indeed, matters had so changed that Fisher feared 'some readers looking only at the present state of the country may smile at this account as wildly exaggerated.' He assured them it was not and exhorted them 'to use their own exertions to improve the country, and duly to appreciate the many blessings and privileges they enjoy.'[89]

Passing from narrative history to the description of the present state and potential of each county, Fisher, like Haliburton, retained a historical perspective to give substance to colonial achievements and to his affirmation of a prosperous future. Whenever his knowledge permitted he gave the names of founding settlers and an outline of the slow and steady growth of civilization and its institutions. Still, the main function of the body of the work was to catalogue the potential of the country, and it was here that the uneven nature of Fisher's observations became evident and the unruly character of New Brunswick troublesome. Fisher, unlike Haliburton, could not rely on documentary surveys, could not avoid the use of a personal voice, and could not pretend to have provided a comprehensive overview. In fact the very amiability with which Fisher related his experiences itself undermined the objectivity of the schematic organization of the *Sketches of New-Brunswick* and his ability to impose a coherent order on his subject.

Whatever the shortcomings of Fisher's county survey, the association of time, man, and geography was sufficient to pull him into a discussion of New Brunswick character:

The genius of these people differ greatly from Europeans – the human mind in new countries left to itself exerts its full energy; hence in America where man has in most cases to look to himself for the supply of his wants, his mind expands, and possesses resources within itself unknown to the inhabitants of old settled countries, or populous cities.[90]

Ideally colonists should establish self-sufficient farms, in equality with their neighbours, independently of patronage, corruption, and faction, and free from oppression. 'Indeed,' Fisher would later write, 'a strict

88 [Fisher,] *First History of New Brunswick*, 7–8, 18, 29, 32, 39, 52
89 Ibid., 9–13
90 Ibid., 21

attention to the cultivation of the soil is essential to the political freedom of a people. No country can be independent without it.'[91]

Those who did not fit the image Fisher had fashioned of the ideal New Brunswicker were either dismissed or condemned. The native people were said to be declining fast and, in their destitution, harmless. Acadians were similarly portrayed as living in quiet, 'slovenly' isolation. Fisher's position on his own ancestors, the Loyalists, was more ambiguous. When it served his purpose, he emphasized that the Loyalist heritage provided a much-needed element of restraint in the often unbridled provincial society; or he appealed to it as a touchstone to reassure British officials, potential settlers, and those New Brunswickers uncomfortable with an equivocal patriotism.[92] Yet Fisher also hinted on more than one occasion that too many Loyalists had been 'gentlemen' unsuitable to meet the demands of the wilderness – a reservation he repeated with greater emphasis in a later work, the *Notitia of New-Brunswick*, published in 1838.[93] What is clear is that, for Fisher, New Brunswick was a yeoman before it was a Loyalist society.

All things considered, Fisher found the failings of native people, Acadians, and the few aristocratic Loyalists minor matters compared to the problems posed by the timber trade with Great Britain, a wartime expedient preserved by an imperial tariff wall for strategic reasons following the cessation of hostilities. His concern was a product of the anomaly that, although the majority of New Brunswickers were farmers, wood products dominated the provincial economy throughout the first half of the nineteenth century, often accounting for 75 per cent or more of export revenues. The very success of the timber trade bred an anxiety in New Brunswickers, first over the stability of markets, and second over what it was doing to colonial society. Heavy reliance on a single export commodity, with only one significant market and dependent on external tariff decisions, produced conditions of chronic economic instability.[94] The internal corollary of dependency on a single staple was that diversification had much to recommend it. Specifically, agriculture must be taken more seriously. The New Brunswick pattern – 'that of a society in

91 [Peter Fisher,] *Notitia of New-Brunswick, for 1836, and Extending into 1837; Comprising Historical, Geographical, Statistical, and Commercial Notices of the Province*, By an Inhabitant (Saint John 1838) 30

92 [Fisher,] *First History of New Brunswick*, 20–2, 52–3, 93–4

93 Murray Barkley, 'The Loyalist Tradition in New Brunswick: The Growth and Evolution of an Historical Myth, 1825–1914,' *Acadiensis* 4 (1975): 8–9

94 Wynn, *Timber Colony*, ch. 2

which agriculture offered rewards only after many years of unremitting toil and in which the timber trade, by the seductions of quick profits, tempted the more feckless and less patient' – must be broken.[95]

Fisher's criticism of the timber trade was sophisticated and not unequivocal, as befitted a man who was himself involved in it. He saw the timber industry as a helpmate to struggling pioneers, generating a vital supplement to farm incomes in the lean early years. 'By this method, as the pine disappears, houses and barns will rise in its place.' All too often, unfortunately, lumber was cut off by selfish 'monopolists' and 'speculators,' men who 'wantonly destroyed' the forest, and thereby created vast tracts of 'uncultivated waste,' which settlers 'neither have the inclination or ability to occupy.' Indeed, in many instances the timber industry drew settlers from domestic habit 'to a dissipated mode of living, to the loss of their morals and property.'[96] Saint John was home to many of these monopolists and associated 'transient persons,' all eager 'to make as much as they can, in as short a time as possible, with the intention of soon returning to enjoy their gains in their native country.' No local attachment was to be expected from this class. 'Such persons, ... who are to be found in all the ports of the Province[,] add nothing to the wealth of the country, but rather act as drains to it.' It was up to the patriots of New Brunswick, those who had the best interests of the colony at heart, to act quickly to conserve the essential forest resource and rationally plan subsequent exploitation for the benefit of all.[97] If they did so, Fisher could see nothing to prevent the continued, steady progress of the province.

Although Fisher's *Sketches of New-Brunswick* was inferior in execution, it resembled Haliburton's *General Description* and *Statistical Account* in many ways. Like Haliburton, Fisher wrote as a responsible patriot. He sought to correct misinformation about his province through the presentation of a clear, factual picture of its present condition and future potential rather than by promotional exaggeration. Fisher deployed a combination of history and description to reassure the British public that New Brunswick was a loyal colony under civilized control, a suitable destination for British emigrants, and deserving of the continued patronage of the imperial government, particularly in matters relating to the preferential tariff on timber. Similarly, as Fisher fashioned a history of the progress of his

95 W.S. MacNutt, *New Brunswick: A History, 1784–1867* (Toronto 1963) 163; Graeme Wynn, '"Deplorably Dark and Demoralized Lumberers"? Rhetoric and Reality in Early Nineteenth-Century New Brunswick,' *Journal of Forest History* 24 (1980): 168–76
96 [Fisher,] *First History of New Brunswick*, 55, 87; Wynn, '"Demoralized Lumberers,"' 176–7
97 [Fisher,] *First History of New Brunswick*, 45, 85

adoptive country he gave definition to the New Brunswick character — ideally that of a hard-working, independent, yeoman farmer. However, Fisher also had to contend with the unique fact that the engine of economic growth in New Brunswick was located in an uneasy alliance between timber and agriculture, and to some extent this tarnished the purity of the yeoman image he was trying to create. It was his opinion that the long-term primacy of the farmer would win out, and in the meantime he exhorted his fellow citizens to keep agricultural needs constantly in mind when planning short-term development.

Those patriot historians who came after Fisher did not so much fill in the gaps in his knowledge as tell what they knew, show off New Brunswick from another angle, and call on different expertise. Thomas Baillie, the English-born commissioner of Crown lands, despite a reputation for arrogant condescension, brought his considerable experience of the topography of the backwoods to the defence of the province, using as an innovation the natural boundaries of geography in preference to county lines, which were 'merely drawn on paper.'[98] Alexander Wedderburn, the Scottish-born emigration officer, could not match the firsthand knowledge of Fisher or Baillie but was in a position to compile whatever 'accurate statistical records' the provincial government was then capable of producing. When he received an inquisitive circular letter in April of 1835 from the Limerick Emigrants' Friend Society, he assembled information on the specific points raised and published it in 'catechical form' both as an answer to the society and as a public work.[99] The Reverend Christopher Atkinson was something of a separate case. He 'humbly' hoped to 'promote the Public Welfare' by draining England of her surplus population for the mutual advantage of both the mother country and New Brunswick, and the three editions of his guide were written to establish the colony's reputation among potential British emigrants as a site offering significant scope for greater agricultural development. However, his experience of the colony was limited in both time and extent, and he exhibited a disquieting tendency toward promotional exaggeration.[100]

Baillie's, Wedderburn's, and Atkinson's descriptions of New Brunswick were, like Fisher's, permeated with a sense of the progress made

---

98 MacNutt, 'Thomas Baillie,' 23; Thomas Baillie, *An Account of the Province of New Brunswick; Including a Description of the Settlements, Institutions, Soil, and Climate of that Important Province: With Advice to Emigrants* (London 1832) v–vii
99 Alexander Wedderburn, *Statistical and Practical Observations*, 5–6
100 Atkinson, *Emigrants' Guide*, iii, 1–3

since the colony was established in 1783–4, and they too found themselves speculating on the character of the society thereby created and on the qualities individuals required to survive and flourish in a wilderness environment. There was little variation in the conclusions they reached. Baillie could well have been speaking for them all when he wrote of New Brunswick, 'If it is not a land flowing with milk and honey, it is at all events a land of promise, and will not deceive the exertions and labour of the agriculturalist.'[101] And of the life of the agriculturalist, the ideal New Brunswicker, he observed (with the patronizing wonder of a man who has never been behind a plough):

> Here there are no seasons of rest or recreation, but the darkness of the night or the sabbath-day. At early dawn our sturdy native rises from a hard and thinly-clad bed, and proceeds to his labour before the rising of the sun. He requires no more time for his frugal repast than that which suffices for him to eat it; and he cheerfully resumes his work, which he will pursue incessantly, and exert for the whole day his utmost degree of strength. This practice is universal, and to which an emigrant must conform; for until he has acquired the same habit, he will be the butt and the ridicule of the native.[102]

That the future of the province lay with the 'intelligent agriculturalist' was held to be indisputable, but ambiguity still surrounded the nature of his relationship to the timber trade. Baillie, like Fisher, argued that a winter spent in a lumber camp provided the newly arrived settler with a vital supplement to his farm income and that the industry was of incalculable benefit to the province as a whole.[103] Atkinson, however, spoke for a growing number of New Brunswick writers when he described lumbering as a 'toilsome and semi-savage life,' demeaning to man and subversive of the long-term progress of the colony.[104] Indeed, a major purpose of New Brunswick writers in the first half of the nineteenth century – Fisher and Baillie included – was to attract agricultural settlers in order to reduce provincial dependence on a single staple.

Although Baillie and Wedderburn, and to a lesser extent Atkinson,

---

101 Baillie, *Account of the Province of New Brunswick*, 3; see also Wedderburn, *Statistical and Practical Observations*, 8–10; Atkinson, *Emigrants' Guide*, 2–5; *Historical and Statistical Account of New-Brunswick*, iii
102 Baillie, *Account of the Province of New Brunswick*, 26
103 Ibid., 2–3
104 Atkinson, *Guide to New Brunswick*, 66; quoted in Wynn, '"Demoralized Lumberers,"' 170

increased contemporary awareness of the degree to which New Brunswick had developed since the arrival of the Loyalists in 1783, they added nothing to Fisher's cursory narrative of earlier transactions in the colony. In part this was due to a lack of readily available sources, but primarily it was because they thought pre-Loyalist events had nothing to do with them. The preceding two hundred years of Anglo-French rivalry properly belonged to the history of Nova Scotia, and it was up to the historians of that province to explain matters away. As far as the likes of Fisher and Baillie were concerned, the first ships of the Loyalist Spring Fleet arrived to find a clean slate: 'no previous vestiges of the labours of civilized man were presented to view to diversify the gloomy prospect.'[105]

There were, however, exceptions to this rule, and foremost among these was north shore eccentric Robert Cooney. An Irish Roman Catholic from Dublin, in 1824 Cooney abandoned his studies for the priesthood and immigrated to Newcastle, New Brunswick, where he took up a position as clerk first in a mercantile firm and then in a barrister's office, and where he witnessed the 'Great Fire' of 1825.[106] Between 1829 and 1831 he was employed as a writer for the *Northumberland Gleaner* at Chatham. According to his own evidence, his connection with that journal led to an 'intimate acquaintance with the principal merchants and the professional classes, and through them to a general knowledge of the entire community.'[107] In addition, on foot he criss-crossed the largely unexplored interior of the north shore counties: 'And, although I had sometimes to "camp out," I suffered very little inconvenience from this nomadic way of spending the night. I availed myself of many opportunities to converse with the Indians in their wigwams – with lumberers in their camps – and with Acadian habitans, and with the old settlers.'[108] Along the way Cooney fell in love with the people and the land of the north shore and determined to defend them from the slander of unnamed 'scribblers.' He therefore gathered his notes together and travelled to Halifax, where his publisher, Joseph Howe, guided him through local libraries and presented him to 'The Club.'[109] Finally, after he had incorporated the results of his research at Halifax in his manuscript, in 1832 *A Compendious History of the Northern Part of the*

105 Atkinson, *Emigrants' Guide*, 36–8; see also Baillie, *Account of the Province of New Brunswick*, 1–2
106 P.M. Toner, 'Robert Cooney,' *DCB*, vol. 9, 154–5
107 [Cooney,] *Autobiography*, 73
108 Ibid., 78
109 Cooney, *Compendious History*, vii, 57

Province of New Brunswick, and of the District of Gaspé, in Lower Canada went to press.

Apart from the fact that it dealt with a clearly circumscribed and limited area, there was nothing in basic form to distinguish Cooney's *Compendious History* from the numerous contemporary accounts of the province as a whole. There were sections on animals, soils, trees, mineral productions, and climate; and as usual the book's core was composed of a county-by-county description of the present state and future prospects of the area – all of which was given in a detail provincial compilers could only envy. However, unlike Fisher, Baillie, and the rest, Cooney lacked a firm chronological starting point. No hordes of Loyalist refugees had washed up on the north shore in 1783 or at any later date, nor did the earlier conquest of New France herald any major new initiatives in the region. In short, all the epoch-making events of the eighteenth century seemed to have passed the north shore by. With no base line from which to measure subsequent development, and unwilling to manufacture one, Cooney plotted the region's history as a seamless web of transient exploitation stretching back as far as recorded activity.

Cooney drew on Haliburton and Fisher to provide a brief summary of the general historical context in which the north shore found itself, but then quickly moved on to give a detailed account of local events that was almost entirely the fruit of his own researches. According to Cooney, 'although the object of the French Court was dominion, that of the people was gain.' Early explorers and traders naturally sought out the shortest avenues to profit and found them in fishing, hunting and bartering for furs. Their attitude, the hostility of the native population, 'and, above all, the oscillating proprietorship, which occasionally shifted the country to a different owner, every ten or twelve years,' all combined to inhibit the growth of long-term agricultural settlements.[110] In time population thickened around some trading posts, and after the Treaty of Utrecht the French government actually promoted permanent settlements on the north shore as a counterweight to Nova Scotia, but it was all too little too late. After the conquest 'the French totally abandoned Miramichi, and dispersed themselves through the Counties of Westmorland and Cumberland; and thus, in the brief space of three years, did the whole Northern part of this Province relapse into almost original solitude.' A few scattered ruins were the only tangible signs remaining of this transitory regime.[111]

110 Ibid., 28–9
111 Ibid., 32–8

If the French were quick to depart, the English were slow to arrive. When the latter did put in an appearance, they fell into the same pattern as their Gallic predecessors: they did a little trading, cut down a few trees, and sank very shallow roots. As late as 1793 their settlements were still subject to native incursions. Then suddenly, 'in the pressing exigencies of the British Nation,' the colonial timber trade originated. 'Villages and settlements, Churches and Schools, with other corresponding features of improvement,' abruptly shot up from the wilderness. Unhappily, the industry responsible for this growth was tainted: it fostered an unhealthy dependence on a single source of income; it introduced a system of credit buying in the local economy that was much abused; and it drew settlers away from the more salutary pursuit of agriculture.[112] Then, at the very moment all were joined 'in a general crusade against the forests,' the Great Fire of October 1825 struck down the vain ambitions of man:

> That calamity, associated with other incidents, forced a reformation upon us; and the general stagnation which prevailed in Great Britain, during the years 1826, and 1827, communicating itself to us, it became both unavoidable and necessary that credit should be restricted. This course, was followed by a diminution of business, which effectively cut off the superabundant Lumberers, as well as many other excrescences that had so long disfigured and encumbered our industry.[113]

As a result:

> A salutary variety has invigorated our commerce; and the sphere of our manufacture has been enlarged by the erection of Saw Mills. Agriculture is rapidly advancing; every day extends the diffusion of its benignity; and while, by the exercise of its embellishing and provident genius, it labors to reclaim the wilderness, clothe the soil with verdure, and provide a granary for future exigency, it also mildly reproves us for our former negligence.[114]

The *Compendious History* of the north shore was almost entirely the product of Cooney's own research, of his interviews with native people, Acadians, and old settlers, and of his rooting through the physical remains left behind by early explorers and traders. His interpretation of events was unique, for he put at the centre of his account not the arrival of

112 Ibid., 53, 58–9, 97–8
113 Ibid., 98–9
114 Ibid., 87–8

the Loyalists or the conquest of New France but the region's own Great Fire. Although later New Brunswick historians pillaged Cooney's work for its story of the fire and its topographical descriptions, they found it difficult to assimilate his narrative history into that of the province as a whole. In short, Cooney gave the people of the north shore a history of their own.

Another work that broke in an even more dramatic way with the general pattern of patriot histories was Calvin Luther Hatheway's *History of New Brunswick*, published in 1846.[115] A native of Sunbury County, New Brunswick, the son of a Loyalist, and a professional land surveyor, Hatheway thought to produce a school manual of both the history and geography of New Brunswick, with special emphasis on the former.[116] His brief topographical descriptions were unexceptional, as were his perfunctory lists of animals, birds, minerals, and so forth. More unusual was his insistence that New Brunswickers were typically 'men ready to shift from one pursuit to another, and generally acquainted with all.' He gave no special status to the farmer, and instead praised those who were 'awake to every opportunity which may present itself.'[117] Nor was this an end to his unexpected stands: although his history was based on little more than prejudice, he dated the foundation of the province from the arrival of pre-Loyalist traders at the mouth of the Saint John River in 1764; and his opinion of his own Loyalist ancestors was less than enthusiastic. Strangely, this account was not preface to a declaration by Hatheway of support for democratic principles. In fact his brief three-page summary of recent political events dealt sarcastically with the pretensions of reformers and called their motives into question.[118] It is difficult to know now what Hatheway's contemporaries thought of his puzzling production, which provided neither a clear provincial identity nor credible support for the colony's future.

In any event, thanks to the considerable effort expended by several patriot authors, New Brunswickers found themselves approaching mid-century with a tolerable understanding of who they were and of the

115 Calvin Luther Hatheway, *The History of New Brunswick, from Its First Settlement, Containing a Geographical Description of the Province; Its Boundaries, Rivers, Lakes, Streams, and Division into Counties and Parishes; Also, Its Climate, Soil, Fisheries, Mines and Minerals, Animals, Birds, &c.; Government, and Effects of Emigration, Capabilities for Further Settlement, Trade and Exports, Internal Communications, Character of Inhabitants, and of the Aborigines, Religion, &c.* (Fredericton 1846)
116 Whalen, 'Calvin Luther Hatheway,' 374–5; Hatheway, *History of New Brunswick*, iii–iv
117 Ibid., 23–67, 76
118 Ibid., 7–8, 13–14, 19–22

special circumstances of the timber trade. What they did not have was a clear narrative of their past. Indeed, had it not been for the publication in 1847 of Abraham Gesner's *New Brunswick*, they would not have possessed a truly comprehensive description of the land.[119] Gesner, the future inventor of kerosene, was born in Cornwallis Township, Nova Scotia, in 1797. He studied medicine, mineralogy, and geology in London, and returned to Nova Scotia as a farmer-physician and amateur geologist.[120] In 1836 he published at Halifax *Remarks on the Geology and Mineralogy of Nova Scotia*, on the strength of which he was hired as New Brunswick's provincial geologist. From 1838 to 1843 he lived and worked in New Brunswick, systematically travelling its length and breadth, often with native guides as his only companions. 'The objects of a Geological Survey,' according to Gesner, were 'to discover and examine, and thereby bring into operation, so far as may be practicable, the mineral resources of a country.'[121] Had he stuck to this narrow aim, his work would now be of little interest. However, in his official reports he took it upon himself to go further, cataloguing the potential of the country for agricultural development and commenting on the full range of human activities and achievements he observed. In short, Gesner's enthusiasm overwhelmed the constraints of profession and office; and while this would eventually lead to his dismissal, it also induced him to set his observations in print.

It is clear from the evidence of Gesner's book that there were no corners of the province he had not seen for himself, and the result was a comprehensive description of New Brunswick, county by county, which superseded all precursors. Yet, although Gesner's *New Brunswick* rivalled Haliburton's *Statistical Account of Nova-Scotia* in thoroughness, it is the differences between them that are most instructive. Haliburton was able to construct his second, 'statistical' volume from behind his desk, relying on government surveys and information provided by local worthies. Gesner was his own government survey and had no comparable infrastructure of educated observers scattered throughout the country to call upon. He gathered his facts from the back of a horse or from a canoe when he was lucky, by foot when he was not. This difference in method

119 Abraham Gesner, *New Brunswick; With Notes for Emigrants. Comprehending the Early History, an Account of the Indians, Settlement, Topography, Statistics, Commerce, Timber, Manufactures, Agriculture, Fisheries, Geology, Natural History, Social and Political State, Immigrants, and Contemplated Railways of that Province* (London 1847)
120 Russell, 'Abraham Gesner,' 308; G.W. Gesner, 'Dr. Abraham Gesner – A Biographical Sketch,' Natural History Society of New Brunswick, *Bulletin* 14 (1896): 3–11
121 Abraham Gesner, 'Report on the Geological Survey of Prince Edward Island,' *Journal of the House of Assembly* (1841) appendix 4 [1]

caused a corresponding change in style. Unlike Haliburton's pretended omniscient view, Gesner's survey more closely resembled a travelogue, in which topographical description was occasionally abandoned in order to relate tales of the journey or contemplate arresting scenes of natural beauty. Gesner was exhilarated by the wilderness and gloried in what he planned to tame and in some cases destroy.

Gesner preceded his topographical description with fifty pages of historical narrative. Although he relied almost exclusively on the first volume of Haliburton's *Statistical Account* for his information, Gesner was selective in what he chose to use. Rather than provide a précis of the history of Nova Scotia, he highlighted those events that had special relevance to New Brunswick. He was the first, for instance, to claim as New Brunswick's particular heritage the story of the struggle between the de La Tour family and Charles de Menou d'Aulnay – a tale of romance and intrigue worth telling in its own right and providing a natural foil against which to contrast later British development.[122] Gesner dated the new progressive era from the arrival of the Loyalists in 1783, at which point his narrative ended. Henceforth, the rival fur lords and the Loyalists were New Brunswick's particular heritage.

Gesner's subsequent description of the accretion of human settlement was unexceptional apart from its detail and scope. However, from the vantage point of mid-century he was able to see that those Jeremiahs who had predicted that the timber trade would irretrievably corrupt colonial society had overreacted to a passing phase in the development of New Brunswick. Soon timber resources would run out, and, he reasoned, the turn to agriculture would be inevitable. In the meantime lumbering was not to be denigrated: it had opened up new areas to the plough, given farmers an extra margin of comfort, and brought the province a large revenue. It would be counterproductive to try and turn people to other activities. Settlers would, Gesner believed, 'direct their labours into channels that seem to them most inviting and profitable.' Every country, he continued, 'has its epochs of industry: the present, in New Brunswick, is the timber period, which will be followed by the agricultural, fishing, and, finally, the manufacturing eras.'[123]

In Gesner's open-eyed observations one can sense a less self-conscious patriotism; a patriotism less reliant upon, and consequently less defensive toward, the British connection; one consonant with a new era of free trade and incipient responsible government. Within the context of loyalty to

122 Gesner, *New Brunswick*, 23–8
123 Ibid., 237–8

Great Britain –which he never directly questioned – Gesner felt free to criticize the ignorance of British officials and the damage they had done to New Brunswick interests, specifically their appeasement of the Americans with portions of provincial territory.[124] Within New Brunswick, Gesner ridiculed the aristocratic pretensions of the official civil and military élite in Fredericton and saw their hierarchical structure as a source of conflict rather than stability. Personally, Gesner preferred the go-ahead mercantile society of Saint John. The dichotomy between the two cities reflected deeper antagonisms in New Brunswick society. According to Gesner,

> There is a constant struggle between the aristocratic principle and the spirit of freedom and equality characteristic of the Americans. Persons who have risen from the lower ranks, and have arrived at affluence, are apt to overrate their importance; and such as have the advantages of birth and education are frequently supercilious. It is to be regretted that, from these causes, endless jealousies and bickerings arise, and society is divided into small circles and parties.[125]

Gesner believed that this antagonism, like the era of the timber trade, would pass with time. 'It is a common remark,' he wrote, 'that the customs and manners of the inhabitants of New Brunswick are more similar to those of the people of the United States than to those of any other British Province.'[126] Just as New Brunswick would soon be ready to move into an agricultural and manufacturing era, so too would it soon be ready to slip the political bonds of empire. New Brunswickers knew who they were and where they were going. Gesner prepared provincial patriotism for independence.

Despite such innovations, when Gesner provided a modest and accurate description of New Brunswick, when he suggested that Europeans must prove themselves fit for the land, and when he held up the independent yeoman farmer as the ideal citizen of the New World, he was using a formula common to almost all patriot historians in the Maritimes, key elements of which had been employed earlier by John Stewart. In his *Account of Prince Edward Island*, Stewart blamed that colony's lack of progress on the first generation of proprietors and tenants, who had been deluded by too-optimistic appraisals of the island's capabilities and had

124 Ibid., 57–65
125 Ibid., 161, 329
126 Ibid., 330

consequently fallen into idle habits. Individuals, not the colony's unique land-tenure scheme, were at fault. According to Stewart, the administration of Lieutenant-Governor Edmund Fanning marked a turning point in the affairs of the province. 'A prudent and steadily moderate' man, Fanning had instructed Stewart, his receiver-general of quit rents, to force the retirement of inactive absentee landlords. Stewart also took it upon himself to produce a book that would end any misconceptions prospective settlers or investors might have had with regard to the island's potential. The land, fertile, salubrious, and fair though it was, would respond only to patient hard work and support only a population steeped in such virtues.[127]

The patriots of Prince Edward Island inherited, then, a usable past and a serviceable identity that put them much in advance of their fellows in Nova Scotia and New Brunswick. Stewart's account was comprehensive, convincing, and durable, giving no cause for patriot rebuttal. Those few individuals who subsequently felt compelled to write their own description of the colony amplified, updated, and called attention to the essentials of Stewart's argument, particularly his emphasis on the need for hard work and thrift. Unfortunately they also followed him in turning a blind eye to the fact that many potential settlers, especially settlers of the better sort, avoided the colony because of its system of tenancy. Prince Edward Island patriots thus did not face up to their colony's central problem, the land question. The myopia of such writers may be due to the fact that invariably they, like Stewart, were members of the local élite, which still depended on the tenancy system for wealth and employment.

One example will suffice. In 1832 John Lewellin Lewellin (c. 1781–1857) published a pamphlet entitled *Emigration. Prince Edward Island.*[128] Born in Wales, Lewellin farmed for sixteen years in England before emigrating to Prince Edward Island in 1824. There he acted as land agent for two large absentee proprietors and at the same time established his own farm and experimented with the latest and most scientific methods of agriculture and animal husbandry.[129] Motivated by both job and convic-

127 See above 29–38.
128 John Lewellin Lewellin, *Emigration. Prince Edward Island: A Brief but Faithful Account of This Fine Colony; Shewing Some of Its Advantages as a Place of Settlement; Addressed to Those British Farmers, and Others, Who Are Determined to Emigrate, and Try Their Fortune in a New Country: With Directions How to Proceed, What to Provide, and What Steps to Take on Arriving in the Colony* (Charlottetown 1832); reprinted in D.C. Harvey, ed., *Journeys to the Island of St. John or Prince Edward Island, 1775–1832* (Toronto 1955) 181–213. All references are to the reprinted edition.
129 D.C. Harvey, Introduction to Lewellin, 'Emigration,' 175–9; H.T. Holman and Basil Greenhill, 'John Lewellin Lewellin,' *DCB*, vol. 8 (Toronto 1985) 505–6

tion to attract more and better settlers to the island, Lewellin spent six years compiling material for his pamphlet. Although the avowed purpose of his work was 'to redeem a beautiful island from the most unaccountable neglect' in Great Britain, it also served to recall island colonists to the virtues of their forefathers. In fact, the two purposes were connected. Prince Edward Island was, according to Lewellin, 'inundated with the dregs of the poor houses of England, the lowest description of Irish, and the scum of Newfoundland.' As a result, 'the general mode of conducting a Farm is slovenly, often wretched.'[130] Whether qualified immigrants or reformed residents, better farmers were required. Once again a descriptive account of future potential is in reality a historical account of improvements made and prescription for change.

Lewellin's findings, both as to the nature of the land and of the colonists, were supported by the writings of another, more prominent observer, John MacGregor (1797–1857).[131] The Scottish-born MacGregor, privy councillor and member of Parliament for Glasgow, was the author of more than thirty works of political economy specializing in Britain's American colonies. In his early volumes, particularly *Historical and Descriptive Sketches of the Maritime Colonies of British America*, MacGregor devoted inordinate space to Prince Edward Island, extolling the virtues of island resources and urging on immigrants and settlers alike a moderate stock of industry and sobriety.[132]

The prominence given to the island is undoubtedly due to the fact that MacGregor resided there from 1806 to 1827, employed as a merchant and land agent. He was also high sheriff of Prince Edward Island during the controversial final months of the administration of Lieutenant-Governor Charles Douglass Smith. Indeed, MacGregor was instrumental in furthering the local élite's successful campaign to have the meddlesome Smith removed in 1824. Although elected to the local assembly that same year, MacGregor resigned within a few months and then left the island altogether, probably because of his straitened personal financial situation. Whatever the reason for his departure, MacGregor retained faith and optimism about the future prospects of the colony and said so in many of his publications.

130 Lewellin, 'Emigration,' 181, 193; John Lewellin Lewellin, letter to the editor, *Royal Gazette* (Charlottetown), 29 Jan. 1833
131 J.M. Bumsted, 'John MacGregor,' *DCB*, vol. 8, 547–9
132 John MacGregor, *Historical and Descriptive Sketches of the Maritime Colonies of British America* (London 1828); see also his *Observations on Emigration to British America* (London 1829)

Apart from the later prominence he achieved as a political economist, and hence the wider circulation his judgments received, what makes MacGregor's comments on Prince Edward Island in the *Sketches* special is the extent to which he not only described material potential but also narrated political events. Unlike Lewellin and other patriots, MacGregor seriously questioned whether the problems posed by corrupt administration had ended, as Stewart would have it, with the arrival of Edmund Fanning. Freed from the inhibitions permanent residence imposed on patriot writers, MacGregor criticized Fanning, Fanning's successor, Joseph Frederick Wallet DesBarres, and, of course, DesBarres's successor, Smith.[133] MacGregor's political narrative, brief though it was, reopened questions Stewart, Lewellin, and other residents would have preferred to keep closed.

In the autumn of 1828 excerpts from MacGregor's book ran serially in the *Register* of Charlottetown. The early chapters, which dealt with the potential of the colony, were lavishly praised by the newspaper's editor. When printing MacGregor's political commentary, however, the editor not only condemned the author for hasty judgment, he also appended a variety of documents intended to establish the good character of the Loyalist Edmund Fanning. The editor was subsequently supported by many letters.[134]

Moralizing about the general character of the people was an acceptable, even indispensable, means of furthering improvement and sharpening the definition of colonial patriotism. Indiscriminate criticism of political institutions was, on the contrary, demoralizing, divisive, and degenerate – unpatriotic, in short. Most Maritime historians of the period understood this basic principle. For his part, MacGregor understood that Prince Edward Island suffered from an intractable problem for which the patriot formula provided no solution. To suggest, as island patriots continued to do, that the poor quality of settlers, participation in the timber trade and shipbuilding, or misleading reports were the cause of halting development was incredible and stood in the way of progress.[135] This was not patriotism at all but self-interest of the kind that had motivated the mercenary Stewart. In short, alone among the Maritime

133 MacGregor, *Historical and Descriptive Sketches*, 82–95
134 *P.E.I. Register* (Charlottetown), 7, 14 Oct.; 11 Nov. 1828; 20 Jan. 1829
135 See for example [S.S. Hill,] *A Short Account of Prince Edward Island Designed Chiefly for the Information of Agriculturalist and Other Emigrants of Small Capital, by the Author of 'The Emigrant's Introduction to an Acquaintance with the British American Colonies, &c.'* (London 1839).

colonies, Prince Edward Island suffered from internal problems such that there could be no patriotism that did not involve their resolution.

Whatever the particular problems of Prince Edward Island, the fact remains that historical writing in the Maritimes grew out of the larger campaign to defend a homeland – for reasons of filial pride and economic self-interest – before a British audience. The key to a successful defence was to convey an image of civilized control over a tamed wilderness, to instil a sense of progress in a new environment. Thus 'present state' accounts were rarely that. Almost always they were thematic or topical descriptions of human accomplishments over time, having a view to a better future. The progressive stages of colonial development explained initial hardships, justified current pride, and guaranteed a prosperous destiny. Historical narratives of presettlement events were a subordinate arm of the progressive theme and not always necessary or convenient. Their main function was to act as a contrast to the civilized present state, with suitable object lessons clearly drawn. The irony was that although patriot histories were primarily written to bend British opinion, it seems likely that they were most influential at home, where they played a significant role in developing colonial self-awareness and self-confidence.

The fact is that individual settlers were often as unfamiliar with the general geography and present state of their colonies as the outsiders for whom topographical descriptions and statistical accounts were ostensibly intended. Orientation alone was a valuable means for colonists to get their bearings and so establish a measure of identity with and control over their surroundings. Furthermore, given a measure of their own achievement, colonists found a basis not only for optimism in the future but also for pride in their past. History taught that they had met the challenge of the wilderness and were the best guarantee of continued success. Their attributed qualities of hard work, thrift, and self-sufficiency made them distinctive, exemplars of the best qualities of British civilization.

That the image of the sturdy, independent yeoman farmer should become the representative ideal in all three Maritime provinces suggests that patriot historians were giving voice to a profound community of perception. Yet patriot historians were doing more than simply reflecting popular sentiment. When they traced the historical development of a people and described present achievement, they gave the ideal clarity and credibility. Certainly Howe, Wiswall, and others recognized Haliburton's contribution to fashioning the Nova Scotia identity that lay behind the intellectual awakening. Similar claims could be made on behalf of the likes of Fisher, Gesner, and Stewart in their respective colonies. It was the patriot historians who invested settlers with a yeoman identity and charged the future to it.

All identities are, however, by nature exclusionary. The yeoman ideal developed by patriot historians in three provincial variants, as a matter of course excluded native people and Acadians. And because there was a discrepancy between the ideal and the reality of colonial society, many groups within that society were overlooked or, worse, shut out. Fishermen, shipbuilders, lumbermen, merchants, professionals, and the like did not fit easily into the images fashioned by the patriots. Above all, in defence of their colonies and in promoting a distinctive provincial identity, patriot historians ignored internal divisions of a partisan, religious, class, or other nature. They did not so much weld society together into a homogeneous whole as disregard its heterogeneity. This was generally acceptable so long as the desire to defend a colony before an external audience was greater than concern over internal problems.

3

The Anomaly
of Quebec

The signing of the Treaty of Paris in 1763 ratified the military conquest by Great Britain in 1760 of the extensive French possession in North America known as New France. A new colony called Quebec was created along the banks of the St Lawrence River when the ceded territory was reorganized by royal proclamation that same year. This new acquisition to the British empire already contained some 70,000 colonists, almost all of whom were French in language, culture, and law, and Roman Catholic in religion. The Proclamation of 1763 imposed upon these people English forms of government and law and was 'conceived solely in the expectation of a great influx of Protestant settlers whose assimilating wave would obliterate the *historical past* of New France.'[1] This hope went largely unfulfilled: the colony exerted no greater attraction on emigrants under English domination than it had under French.

The unrealistic assumption that a wave of settlement from an overcrowded Atlantic coast would surge into the country stemmed largely from ignorance of North American geography and of the difficult living conditions in the St. Lawrence valley. Americans were attracted by the luxuriance of the west, not the cold of Quebec. Two years after the Royal Proclamation, [Governor James] Murray's census showed that only a couple of hundred British settlers had answered the call of the north, choosing to live for the most part in the towns of Quebec and Montreal ... The limited numbers of British settlers, as opposed to the astonishing population growth of the Canadians [as the French-speaking

1 Pierre Tousignant, 'The Integration of the Province of Quebec into the British Empire, 1763–91, Part I: From the Royal Proclamation to the Quebec Act,' *DCB*, vol. 4 (Toronto 1979) xl. Emphasis added.

colonists were then called], made the assimilation hoped for by [the British government] highly problematical.[2]

For English-speaking colonists, then, the conquest was not the hoped-for new beginning; it was not an unambiguous break with a foreign past; it was not the historical equivalent to the Holland survey in Prince Edward Island, the founding of Halifax in Nova Scotia, or the arrival of the Loyalists in New Brunswick. The passage of the Quebec Act in 1774 (14 Geo. III, c. 83) marked a partial return to French law and custom and a recognition of the colony's racial duality. The division of Quebec by the Constitutional Act of 1791 (31 Geo. III, c. 31) only added to the English-speaking community's sense of besieged isolation in the new lower province.

The fact that English-speaking residents in Quebec did not achieve unequivocal domination over provincial society had a profound effect on the way their history came to be written. It was difficult to promote the potential of the land if it was still in the hands of seigneur and habitant; it was ludicrous to make a foil of a French past that was still present; and it was impossible to focus on future achievement based on the quality of non-existent British yeomen. The primary source of English anxiety was the persistence of French culture, not the reputation of the land.[3] As one contemporary wrote:

> Were any of us desirous to persuade a friend in Britain to emigrate to Canada, how should we best recommend such a step? Should we not immediately after those most common topics of the cheapness and variety of land and the extensive field of enterprise and industry which it affords, tell him that we have enjoyed a free Constitution, formed upon the model of that of Britain; that our lives and our liberties were here equally secure as in that favored Country; that, in fine, tho' to a stranger, it might still have a foreign appearance, it was clearly assuming new features more congenial to those of his native land?[4]

It was precisely this claim of a correspondence to British law, politics, culture, and religion that the English-speaking people of Quebec could

2 Ibid., xli
3 Carl F. Klinck, 'Literary Activity in the Canadas 1812–1841,' Carl F. Klinck, gen. ed., *Literary History of Canada: Canadian Literature in English* (Toronto 1965) 125–6
4 [John Fleming,] *Some Considerations on This Question; Whether the British Government Acted Wisely in Granting to Canada Her Present Constitution? With an Appendix; Containing Documents, &c*, by a British Settler (Montreal 1810) 15

not make. The first order of business, therefore, was not to defend the colony from slander before a British audience, but to establish control over internal affairs.

Thus it was that when Francis Maseres (1731–1824) wrote in 1772 'with a view to facilitate and expedite the settlement of the province of Quebec,' he did not consider it necessary to provide a chorography of the colony. Instead, he believed that the British government could not properly face the issue of immigration 'without a careful perusal and examination of the several instruments of government' that were responsible for the maintenance of French culture in Quebec.[5] Consequently, his numerous works were compilations of laws, regulations, and reports, with appropriate commentaries on each. Maseres, as provincial attorney-general from 1766 to 1769, and thereafter as an occasional representative in London of the colony's merchant community, advocated the absorption of French by English colonists through the penetration of British law and language, and the Protestant religion.[6] His books were the published tip of a paper iceberg composed of reports, petitions, and letters by officials, associations, and individuals, all variously intended to help the British government settle the growing antagonism between the French and English in Quebec.[7] Little of this material was explicitly historical, but it was based on an acknowledgment that two historically distinct cultures were now in conflict on the banks of the St Lawrence. A resolution of this conflict must, it was commonly believed, precede discussion of all other issues.

English opinion was divided on how to handle the problem of the French in Quebec: governors Murray and Sir Guy Carleton wished to indulge and appease the empire's new subjects; the small and vigorous communities of merchants in Quebec City and Montreal (including a surprising number of French speakers) hoped to eradicate the 'unprogressive' and 'illiberal' legacy of the *ancien régime*. Despite their differences, both sides drew on a common stereotype, one that saw New France

5 [Francis Maseres,] *A Collection of Several Commissions, and Other Public Instruments, Proceeding from His Majesty's Royal Authority, and Other Papers, Relating to the State of the Province in Quebec in North America, Since the Conquest of It by the British Arms in 1760* (London 1772) v

6 W. Stewart Wallace, Introduction to *The Maseres Letters, 1766–1768*, ed. W. Stewart Wallace (Toronto 1919) 21–32; Elizabeth Arthur, 'Francis Maseres,' *DCB*, vol. 6 (Toronto 1987) 491–6

7 Tousignant, 'Integration of the Province of Quebec'; Fernand Ouellet, *Lower Canada, 1791–1840: Social Change and Nationalism*, trans. Patricia Claxton (Toronto 1980) 11–27

as a quasi-feudal society ruled by military discipline and inhibited by the Roman Catholic Church. Whereas Carleton embraced this legacy as a buttress for a new conservatism in North America, most English-speaking colonists tended to deplore the political tyranny and religious obscurantism that they believed had proved fatal to New France and continued to hinder the political and economic development of the colony under British rule.[8] In either case, while the conventional British picture of New France certainly contained elements of national and religious prejudice, it could also lay claim to a certain degree of historical authenticity.

It may well be that the majority of the population of New France had been happy and content; it is clear, however, that many of the writers who described the state of New France were critical of its institutions. Local French officials, as well as visiting metropolitan observers, often wrote to protest the political power of the intendant and the governor and occasionally the influence of the church. Their aim in doing so was probably to increase their own political power, but read years later they would often appear as popular spokesmen against tyranny. Indeed, in the works of Claude-Charles Le Roy de La Potherie (1663–1736), Louis-Armand de Lom d'Arce de Lahontan (1666–1715), and Louis-Antoine de Bougainville (1729–1811), British authors found the first stirrings of later enlightenment criticism of the divine right of kings, revealed religion, and economic monopoly;[9] and in *A Philosophical and Political History of the Settlements and Trade of the Europeans in the East and West Indies*, by Abbé Guillaume-Thomas-François Raynal, the assault of an Encyclopaedist on the evils of the *ancien régime* provided a French endorsement of the benefits of the British conquest.[10]

The foremost historian of North American affairs, Pierre-François-Xavier de Charlevoix, cannot be so easily classified as a typical enlightenment historian. Having visited New France as a teacher between 1705 and 1708, and then again as a Jesuit missionary and explorer between 1720 and 1722, Charlevoix published in 1744 a journal of his second voyage and a general history of the colony. His main purpose in writing these volumes was to chronicle the efforts of Catholic missionaries among the native people, and he often antagonized English-speaking readers by drawing unfavourable comparisons with the activities of British Protest-

8 Tousignant, 'Integration of the Province of Quebec,' xl–xlviii
9 Yves F. Zoltvany, *The Government of New France: Royal, Clerical, or Class Rule?* (Scarborough, Ont., 1971) ch. 1
10 5 vols, trans. J. Justamond, 3rd ed. (London 1777) vol. 5, 95–6

ants.[11] On the other hand, Charlevoix was 'immersed in the humanistic and philological tradition of one of the most renowned Jesuit colleges of Europe,' Collège Louis-le-Grand in Paris.[12] His history of New France was not a simple hagiology but part of a grand 'Project of a series of histories of the New World' (for which he also completed volumes on Japan, Saint-Domingue, and Paraguay); and his method exhibited less the credulity of the devout than it did the most modern techniques of the philologist and historian, critically evaluating all secondary sources and collating oral evidence and written documents in the light of personal experience.[13] Thus, despite Charlevoix's evident and freely acknowledged concern with missionary activities, his relative impartiality within the context of the eighteenth century cannot be questioned. He was willing to criticize government neglect, gubernatorial corruption, and monopolistic greed. On the whole, then, British liberal Protestants found much in Charlevoix's work to confirm their prejudices about New France, especially after exercising their inevitable inclination to disregard his Catholic bias.

George Heriot (1759–1839) and William Smith, Junior (1769–1847), were the historians who condensed the work of French writers, particularly Charlevoix, and fixed the image of New France that survived among English-speaking colonists in the Canadas until well past the middle of the nineteenth century. Heriot, a Scot, was educated at the Royal High School in Edinburgh and, after a four-year sojourn in the West Indies, briefly attended the Royal Military Academy at Woolwich. Although he obtained neither a degree nor a commission, Heriot did take advantage of the presence at the military academy of famed topographical artist Paul Sandby to become an accomplished artist in his own right. In 1783 he was appointed a civilian clerk in the arsenal at Woolwich and nine years later turned up as clerk of cheque for the ordnance department at Quebec. Through his brother's friendship with William Pitt, in 1799 Heriot was catapulted into the position of deputy postmaster-general of British North America. Unfortunately, Heriot demonstrated little aptitude as an administrator: the independence of his imperial office and the obstinacy

11 Pierre-François-Xavier de Charlevoix, *History and General Description of New France*, trans. John Gilmary Shea, 6 vols (New York 1866–72; reprinted Chicago 1966) vol. 1, 103–4; vol. 3, 259–60, 307–8; vol. 5, 265, 304

12 David M. Hayne, 'Pierre-François-Xavier de Charlevoix,' *DCB*, vol. 3 (Toronto 1974), 109

13 Charlevoix, *History and General Description*, vol. 1, 5–12, 104

of his character slowly alienated many of the provincial élite in Quebec City, and he was virtually forced to resign and return home in 1816.[14]

In the meantime, Heriot's duties provided an opportunity to travel throughout the British colonies, an opportunity he put to good use as a painter and writer. In 1804 he published *The History of Canada* and in 1807 a two-volume work, *Travels through the Canadas*.[15] Both were written explicitly to enlighten and entertain a British audience with a 'disquisition' on the habits of native people, an exciting account of the French and Indian wars, and descriptions of 'the picturesque scenery on the Saint Lawrence.'[16] While these were not the facets of the province most English-speaking colonists wanted featured in Britain, Heriot's *History of Canada* did at least give settlers their first English translation of substantial portions of Charlevoix's work.

Heriot made no pretence to the rank of creative scholar. He did not offer his *History of Canada* to the public 'as composing an original work,' and simply admitted that the 'greatest part' of its contents was taken from Charlevoix's *Histoire et description générale de la Nouvelle France*.[17] Heriot did nevertheless make the *History of Canada* his own, for as he condensed, he cleansed the text of Charlevoix's Gallic bias and long martyrology, exposed the secular aspects of Charlevoix's interpretation of New France, and discarded the broader providential tone of the Jesuit's work. As a result, Heriot's history has a particularly Anglo-Saxon understanding of the misfortunes of New France. Once again an alleged French desire for the quick profits of gold, silver, furs, and fish was blamed for impeding the more stolid progress of agricultural settlement. The French government, 'dazzled' by the riches of Peru and Mexico, let their North American possession fall into disrepute as the want of precious metals became obvious. Thereafter, the colony 'never received from France the

14 Gerald Finley, *George Heriot: Postmaster-Painter of the Canadas* (Toronto 1983) 15–83; 'George Heriot,' *DCB*, vol. 7 (Toronto 1988) 400–3; Mary Sparling, *Great Expectations: The European Vision in Nova Scotia, 1749–1848*, ed. Scott Robson (Halifax 1980) 21–3

15 George Heriot, *The History of Canada, from Its First Discovery, Comprehending an Account of the Original Establishment of the Colony of Louisiana* (London 1804); *Travels through the Canadas, Containing a Description of the Picturesque Scenery on Some of the Rivers and Lakes; With an Account of the Productions, Commerce, and Inhabitants of Those Provinces. To Which is Subjoined a Comparative View of the Manners and Customs of Several of the Indian Nations of North and South America, Illustrated with a Map and Numerous Engravings, from Drawings Made at Several Places by the Author*, 2 vols (London 1807)

16 Heriot, *History of Canada*, vii; *Travels*, vol. 1, iii

17 Heriot, *History of Canada*, v

assistance which was requisite for its advancement and prosperity.' The court took no further role in Canada's affairs, which were left to various monopolies 'whose views were solely directed to the fur trade.' According to Heriot the imposition in 1663 of royal government, headed by a military governor and civilian intendant, did little to alter the state of the colony. Unrestrained by any representative element, unsupported and underfunded by Paris, a succession of local officials abused the trust of their offices to seek personal gain in the fur trade and through military adventurism. Not only did they fail to support settlement, their expansionist policies endangered it by antagonizing first the native people and then the neighbouring British.[18] A series of appalling wars therefore dominated the history of New France, and Heriot detailed their course by examining and judging the efforts of each governor in turn.

If the broad outline of Heriot's *History of Canada* is blunt and rude, the discussion of the various governors gave him an opportunity to demonstrate his subtle understanding of human nature and his eye for irony in the affairs of men. Three individuals in particular engaged his attention, and his interpretation of each pulled together and clarified Charlevoix's original portraits. Heriot first singled out Samuel de Champlain as a governor of extraordinary talent, whose 'sentiments were liberal and directed to the public welfare,' and who provided for the spiritual and material needs of the settlers of New France. Yet, as the ally of the Hurons on an expedition against the Iroquois, it was Champlain who unwittingly set in motion the conflict that would eventually bring about the colony's fall. Heriot next turned to Louis de Buade de Frontenac's two terms as governor and observed how the Frenchman's imperious character damaged the reputation of his first administration and then supplied the courage necessary to face the military challenges of the second. Finally, Heriot repeated Charlevoix's approach to René-Robert Cavelier de La Salle, an explorer of energy and resolve, whose very dedication offended his subordinates and rendered his efforts futile and his life forfeit.[19]

Heriot's *History of Canada* concluded in 1731, as did that of Charlevoix. The *Travels* added little more to the narrative, although a good deal more on native culture. On the whole, Heriot regarded the *ancien régime* as one in which the natural advantages of the land were overlooked through the folly of men and the impolicy of government:

18 Ibid., 30–1, 275, 303–4, 334; *Travels*, vol. 1, 223–4
19 Heriot, *History of Canada*, 13–15, 22, 31, 51–2, 140–4, 227–8, 274–5, 345–6, 430–1

Considerable fortunes were made with rapidity; but they were almost as quickly dissipated as they had been acquired; like those moving hills, which in the sandy deserts of Asia or of Africa, are drifted and deposited by whirlwinds, and which possessing no consistency or solidity, are by the same cause again as suddenly dispersed ... [Hence] it may easily be conceived, that when the English took possession of Canada, they found its inhabitants to have made but little progress in commerce or in agriculture. The long continuance of warfare might have tended to depress the former, but the latter had never attained to any stage of improvement.[20]

If the *Travels'* concluding remarks on the period of British rule were relatively short and innocuous, this was probably due not so much to a desire to hide unpleasant realities as it was to a recognition that for many Europeans the subject would have been of little interest.

William Smith, Junior, was born in New York State, the son of a prominent lawyer, councillor, and historian. The elder Smith shifted to the Loyalist cause late in the day, suffered exile in London, and came to Quebec in 1786 as chief justice.[21] Dependent on his father for preferment, the young Smith accompanied him to Quebec. In 1792 the junior Smith was appointed clerk of the Legislative Council, in 1803 made a master-in-chancery, and in 1823 (after considerable lobbying) selected for a seat on the Executive Council of Lower Canada. Although an *anglais*, a Loyalist, a plural office holder, and a *bona fide* member of Lower Canada's ruling oligarchy, the 'Château Clique,' he was rarely attacked directly by the largely French-speaking and reform-minded *parti canadien* – surviving even the Rebellions of 1837–8 with his pension intact. According to a recent biographer, Smith emerged unscathed because his anxiety to gain and retain office was such that he avoided giving offence to anyone. Perhaps in recognition of his obsequious skills, he was made chairman of the executive council upon his appointment to that body, 'a position from which he could not debate and seldom had to vote.'[22] Smith brought the same politic reticence to the writing of his *History of Canada*.

20 Heriot, *Travels*, vol. 1, 211, 225
21 In Canada the author of the *History of Canada*, vol. 1, *From Its First Discovery to the Peace of 1763*; vol. 2, *... to the Year 1791* (Quebec 1815), is known as William Smith, Junior. To avoid confusion it must be noted that he was the third in his family line to be so named, and American historians commonly refer to his father as junior.
22 John M. Bumsted, 'William Smith, Jr., and *The History of Canada*,' in Lawrence H. Leder, ed., *The Colonial Legacy*, vol. 1, *Loyalist Historians* (New York 1971) 192; 'William Smith,' *DCB*, vol. 7, 816–19

Certainly he did everything he could to rid his book of controversy, delayed its publication for almost a decade and its release, after publication in 1815, for a decade more. Indeed, if he had not had the example and incentive of his father's celebrated history of New York State before him, he might not have risked the endeavour at all.[23]

As it was, Smith made few claims for his work – and justifiably so. It was, as he said, 'serviceable to the public' only because it offered 'a true and faithful account of a colony daily augmenting in Wealth, Prosperity and Happiness.'[24] Wedded to his sources, the timid author hugged them so tightly that he squeezed out all contentious judgments, indeed almost any interpretations at all. Where Heriot's editing simplified and clarified, Smith atomized material into unrelated units. When covering the same ground as Heriot, Smith lost Charlevoix's sense of the relationship between the fur trade and settlement, between the expansion of New France and the conflict with the native people and the British, as well as any understanding of the complexities of Frontenac's career. Only Champlain's status as a hero survived unimpaired, confirming his adoption by English-speaking historians as the one Frenchman to have approached colonial development in the correct (that is, British) settlement-first fashion.[25]

Smith's narrative of the pre-conquest era is worthy of note only for what it relates about the period following 1731, when Charlevoix and Heriot both came to a halt. The core of Smith's account of this chapter of the *ancien régime* was an unacknowledged transposition from a manuscript history now known to be the work of Louis-Léonard Aumasson de

23 NA, John Neilson Papers, MG 24, B 1, vol. 2; 515–16, W. Smith to J. Neilson [26 Aug. 1815]; vol. 3; 117–18, 27 Sept. 1817; 234–7 [5 June 1818]; vol. 7; 20–1, 4 Feb. 1830; 510–12, Nov. 1830; vol. 11; 132–3, 20 Oct. 1833; vol. 12; 65–6, Neilson to Smith, 9 Mar. 1805; 71–5, Nov. 1809; 83–4, Smith to Neilson [10 Aug. 1815]; 85–8, 26 Aug. 1815; 91, nd; 104, 7 Aug. 1817; 106–8, Neilson to Smith, 26 Sept. 1817; 266, Smith to Neilson, 17 July 1824; 267–8, Neilson to Smith, 9 Sept. 1824; 295–9, 12 May 1826; 350–4, 9 May 1830; 508–9, 4 Nov. 1835. This correspondence is the most complete we have between a nineteenth-century English-Canadian historian and his publisher. It has been carefully summarized in Bumsted, 'William Smith, Jr.,' 196–201.
24 Smith, *History of Canada*, vol. 1, i–iii
25 Smith, ibid., 1–189. Michael Kammen observed how Smith edited his father's history of New York State with similarly unhappy results, see M. Kammen, A Note on the Text of *The History of the Province of New-York*, by William Smith [Sr.], ed. William Smith [Jr.] (1826) ed. M. Kammen, 2 vols (Cambridge, Mass., 1972) vol. 1, lxxviii–lxxix. I cannot agree with Bumsted's remark that 'Smith succeeded in making a good deal of sense out of his sources,' see Bumsted, 'William Smith, Jr.,' 201–2.

Courville (1722?–82?). Secretary to Governor Jacques-Pierre de Taffanel de La Jonquière, present at the fall of Fort Beauséjour and the surrender of New France, Aumasson de Courville vociferously attacked the debilitating corruption of French colonial officials and the malevolence of such priests as Abbé Jean-Louis Le Loutre, while at the same time he appeared sycophantic toward his new British masters.[26] This relation of events fitted neatly into Smith's inherited suspicion of priests and his notion that New France had been ruled by a corrupt government whose alternately neglectful and dictatorial methods were inimical to prospects for both long-term economic development and short-term military survival. Effective use of land being the test of a claim to possession, France's loss was merited and inevitable.[27]

In Smith's opinion Quebec was, or should have been, happy to become a British colony in 1763. A dispassionate review of the system established in Canada while under the dominion of France clearly indicated, so he thought, that the people were ruled in an arbitrary and despotic manner. 'The powers exercised by the several Governors and Intendants knew no bounds, and unrestrained by law, their decisions were dictated by the caprice of the moment' and often by personal avarice. 'How happy, then, ought the Canadians to be, that God in his Providence, has severed them from the ancient stock to which they belonged, and committed them to the care of a Monarch, who, by making the success of his arms the means of extending his beneficence, has an incontestible right to their affectionate fidelity.'[28] This, the 'salvation theory' of the conquest, implicit in Heriot's *History of Canada*, was first enunciated – so it is said – by Smith's father at the opening of a court of King's Bench in November 1789.[29] It would subsequently become a commonplace of nineteenth-century Canadian historiography.

The more controversial corollary to the salvation theory was that British immigration and French assimilation would dispose of the legacy of the *ancien régime* and the colony of Quebec would embark on a new era

26 Aegidius Fauteaux, 'Le S ... de C ... enfin démasqué,' *Les Cahiers des Dix* 5 (1940): 261–3, 283–92; François Rousseau, 'Louis-Léonard Aumasson de Courville,' *DCB*, vol. 4, 35–6

27 Smith, *History of Canada*, vol. 1, 217–22, 235–6, 245–51. For his father's views on the Roman Catholic clergy, see L.F.S. Upton, *The Loyal Whig: William Smith of New York & Quebec* (Toronto 1969) 161–2.

28 Smith, *History of Canada*, vol. 1, 382–3

29 Upton, *Loyal Whig*, 192

of commercial prosperity and political liberty. Such had been the pattern in the Maritimes, where the Acadian period provided novelists and poets with the raw material of romance and adventure and historians with a foil by which to measure modern, British achievement. Unhappily for Smith and men of like mind, in Quebec the continued presence and then resurgence of the French-speaking population kept the past alive, deterred British immigration, and obstructed plans for commercial exploitation. The province's English-speaking historians had to deal with the consequences of continuity with the past: they had to explain how French settlers and their culture had managed to survive and how this was detrimental to the long-term interests of the colony. When they did so, historical explanation slipped into an overtly political campaign to control and assimilate French-speaking Canadians. The result was internally divisive and externally humiliating.

The second volume of Smith's *History of Canada* was a significant contribution to the discussion of the frustrating inability of the British regime to establish a clear political and economic hegemony over the conquered colony. On the surface Smith 'did little more than abstract public papers and reproduce documents *in extenso*,' avoiding narrative comment in order to protect himself from charges of political and racial bias.[30] Nonetheless, implicit in his account of the post-conquest period was the understanding that progress could not come to the colony until French Canadians had assimilated English law and custom. The tyranny of the French regime may have been removed, but according to Smith it left behind a habitant population susceptible to the dictates of their clergy and the blandishments of new demagogues and as yet unsuited to the political and economic function of an independent yeomanry.[31]

Assimilation being liberation, the British government did the habitant no favour by postponing the introduction of English practices, and the failure to move slowly and deliberately toward eventual assimilation was folly. Specifically, Smith directed the reader toward the course promoted by his father when chief justice: impose English criminal law and limit the use of French civil law to those cases arising from pre-conquest disputes between French settlers; restrict the seigneurial system to its existing boundaries and allow voluntary adoption of the English form of common soccage by seigneurs and tenants; and finally, establish a system of free schools and a non-denominational college. With these or like engines of assimilation in place, the glory of the English constitution, including free

30 Bumsted, 'William Smith, Jr.,' 204
31 Smith, *History of Canada*, vol. 2, 167

elections and an assembly, could be conferred as a just and deserved reward for a people capable of responsible participation.[32] Progressive institutions had to be in the hands of progressive people.

Smith believed that the Royal Proclamation of 1763 was on the whole meant 'to assimilate the laws and government of [Quebec] to those of the other American colonies and provinces which were under His Majesty's immediate government'; it therefore had his full support, provided its implementation was in the humane hands of the likes of governors Murray and Carleton. Unfortunately, certain self-interested French-speaking leaders played on the anxieties the proclamation raised in the minds of the habitants, and under the threat of revolution in America the British government gave in to those fears. The Quebec Act of 1774 revived French custom and denied to English-speaking settlers their basic rights as British subjects, including political representation and universal access to trial by jury. This course was folly: first because when the Americans invaded in 1775 'no persuasion could induce [the habitants] to stand forth in the hour of danger'; second, because it saddled Quebec with political tyranny (albeit in a benign form), judicial anarchy, and economic uncertainty. Smith deemed it only natural that British settlers should call for a return to British law entirely and the creation of an elected assembly. Furthermore, he was sanguine that they would not use this power to harm their French-speaking neighbours, for the British settlers 'were possessed of nearly one half in value of all the Seigniories, and had besides the whole mercantile and floating property of the Province, and were too much interested in the welfare and prosperity of the Province for any danger to be apprehended from their possessing a large share in the Legislative power.'[33]

Smith ended on a positive note somewhat at odds with the concerns he had earlier expressed, writing that he believed the Constitutional Act of 1791 established the political framework by which Lower Canada 'was assimilated, (as near as the condition of the Country would permit) to that Constitution which has made England the admiration of the world.'[34] In search of a seat on the executive council, Smith obviously removed the sting from his gloss and did not broach subsequent constitutional problems in Lower Canada. The resulting history was so gratifyingly innocuous that when it was finally released for sale in 1826 most French Canadians chose to ignore it. The only spirited response came from Abbé

32 Ibid., 35, 174–214; Upton, *Loyal Whig*, 162, 187–97
33 Smith, *History of Canada*, vol. 2, 2–7, 30–7, 61–76, 164–7
34 Ibid., 221

Thomas Maguire (1776–1854), who thought he discerned through Smith's opaque prose 'the conspiracy surreptitiously set afoot at the Conquest ... to place the Canadian people's loyalty in question and to annihilate its religion.'[35] Still, this criticism was sufficient to cow Smith into silence.

William Smith was surrounded by other English-speaking writers who were not so reticent in bringing their narratives up to date and engaging in contemporary controversies. At the heart of their concerns was the unexpected success the French Canadians had in taking control of the assembly and using that body to obstruct commercial expansion and to investigate the administration of government in Quebec City. Rather than accept British leadership and imitate the models offered, French Canadians retrenched in those areas they already controlled, most notably the professions and agriculture. Indeed, they in turn stereotyped British settlers as a bourgeoisie, 'which thought of the development of the country in terms of capitalist economic expansion, revolutionized transportation, massive immigration, and institutional reforms.' The racial dimension of what was essentially a class contest among merchants, bureaucrats, and professionals came increasingly to the fore, and by 1810 the racial division in Lower Canada was almost complete.[36] Clearly this was not what Smith or any other spokesman for the English Canadians had in mind when petitioning for an assembly. Subsequently numerous contemporary pamphlets and books devoted to explaining the social, economic, and racial origins of the conflict were published, and many solutions to the crisis vetted. Regrettably, these works tended to be long on racial prejudice and short on historical analysis.[37]

Worthy exceptions to this general rule were the works of John Fleming

35 Bumsted, 'William Smith,' 818; [Thomas Maguire,] 'Observations d'un catholique sur l'*Histoire du Canada* par l'honorable William Smith,' by Vindex, *La Gazette de Québec*, 11 Jan. 1827; quoted by Serge Gagnon, *Quebec and Its Historians, 1840 to 1920*, trans. Yves Brunelle (Montreal 1982) 44. On Maguire see James H. Lambert, 'Thomas Maguire,' *DCB*, vol. 8 (Toronto 1985) 591–6.
36 Clearly this potted version of the pre-Rebellion crisis in Lower Canada skates over a large debate on the origin and nature of French-English tensions in the province. The general interpretation here presented is from Ouellet's *Lower Canada*, especially 52–76.
37 For summaries of a representative selection, see John Hare and Jean-Pierre Wallot, comps, *Les Imprimés dans le Bas Canada, 1801–1840: bibliographie analytique*, vol. 1, 1801–1810 (Montreal 1967), especially 205–11; and M. Brook Taylor, 'The Writing of English-Canadian History in the Nineteenth Century' (PH D Diss., University of Toronto 1984) vol. 1, 146–58.

(*c.* 1786–1832), a Scottish-born Montreal bourgeois and president of the Bank of Montreal from 1830 to his death. In a pamphlet published in 1810, and then again in a much longer and more thoroughly researched book published in 1828, Fleming established as a first principle that the basic rights of the British constitution could not be denied to any British citizen.[38] Not only was this essential to maintain the loyalty of English Canadians, it was also the only way, short of a 'ruinous' confrontation, to win over the French-Canadian population. Example, not force, was the key to Fleming's program. In his opinion the British constitution had 'only to be known, that it may be admired.' Unless it was preserved 'in its purity,' it would not attract, nor merit, French-Canadian support. As a bourgeois he reached out to the habitant in order to make common cause against their mutual enemies, the bureaucrats and the seigneurs. The primary difficulty was to breach the walls of racial animosity built up by history and maintained by self-interested oligarchs, so that British forms could be coolly and rationally judged and undoubtedly accepted by French Canadians.[39]

A bibliophile who amassed one of the largest personal libraries in Lower Canada, nearly 10,000 volumes, Fleming read most contemporary histories of New France for himself.[40] His findings were not, however, dissimilar to those of Heriot and Smith: New France had been misgoverned by a tyrannical and rapacious élite to the extent that 'the half-famished remains of the plundered Colony' were said to have hailed the conquest as the most auspicious event in their short history.[41] In 1760, then, the British found themselves in possession of a colony that was, after more than a century of French rule, filled by 'an agricultural and military people, distinguished by habits of implicit submission to their spiritual and temporal leaders.'[42]

Abetted by the expected influx of British settlers, the assimilating measures of the Royal Proclamation of 1763 were intended to begin the

38 [Fleming,] *Some Considerations*; [John Fleming,] *Political Annals of Lower Canada; Being a Review of the Political and Legislative History of That Province, under the Act of the Imperial Parliament, 31, Geo. III., Cap. 31, Which Established a House of Assembly and Legislative Council; Showing the Defects of this Constitutional Act, and Particularly Its Practical Discouragement of British Colonization. With an Introductory Chapter on the Previous History of Canada, and an Appendix of Documents, &c.*, by a British Settler (Montreal 1828). Peter Deslauriers, 'John Fleming,' *DCB*, vol. 6, 259–61
39 [Fleming,] *Some Considerations*, Advertisement, 5
40 Deslauriers, 'John Fleming,' 261
41 [Fleming,] *Some Considerations*, 7–8
42 [Fleming,] *Political Annals*, xl

slow process of liberating the political and economic life of the habitant.[43] Unhappily, according to Fleming, a repressive new ministry came to power in England in 1760 that attempted to usurp constitutional power by controlling the king. As 'the forerunner of tyranny at home,' it struck at the freedom of British colonies in America. The Quebec Act was passed as part of this program, 'a Statute expressly calculated to keep this Province as distinct and as different as possible from the other Colonies, with respect to the essentials of Government, Laws, Religion, Manners and Language.' The Roman Catholic clergy and French *noblesse* were 'indulged,' and the 'common People of Canada were left entirely at the mercy of those higher orders.' The Quebec Act 'rivetted on the necks of the lower classes the chains of ignorance, superstition and vassalage.'[44]

In the short term the Quebec Act was a failure: it did not inspire habitant militancy on behalf of British forces during the American Revolution; and it frightened off potential British settlers with its foreign laws. In the long term the Quebec Act was a tragedy: it placed in power a French-Canadian clerical and professional élite that subsequently strove to maintain its position by making all things English the 'legitimate objects of jealousy to the Nation Canadienne.' English settlers, now 'intruders' in a British colony, fought for a return to English law and custom and had their case strengthened by the growth of Loyalist settlements to the west.[45] It was the cruellest legacy of the Quebec Act that, when representative institutions came, they were accompanied by a division of the province that isolated the English-Canadian community in Lower Canada under a mongrel system of law. 'Government seem to have thought that they had conceded too much to Popery, prejudice and feudal pride, to be able now to stop with a good grace; and they finally abandoned the Lower Province to divisions, parties, rivalships, the end of which it is hard to conjecture.'[46] In 1774 the British government had injudiciously given over power to the French-Canadian élite; in 1791, by dividing the province, the government gave over power to the untutored mass of French Canadians. It was Fleming's unavoidable conclusion that the Quebec Act remained 'the principal basis of the existing pretension on the part of the French Canadians to be a separate people, or as they shortly express it, "*la Nation Canadienne.*"'[47]

43 Ibid., lxxiii–lxxv; [Fleming,] *Some Considerations*, 8
44 [Fleming,] *Some Considerations*, 8–10
45 [Fleming,] *Political Annals*, v–vi, lxxvii, 7–10
46 [Fleming,] *Some Considerations*, 11
47 [Fleming,] *Political Annals*, 7

The Constitutional Act of 1791, '*like other paper Constitutions,*' contained 'the forms and theory without the substance and practice of that of England.' The habitant was not an independent yeoman; he was a peasant in the unbroken habit of obeying his leaders; and these leaders (anxious to secure their own position) blinded the habitant to his true interests, which lay with the economic and political liberty offered by British custom. Meanwhile, the English minority in Lower Canada was 'to be domineered over by a faction, armed by the British Parliament, with an authority which has gradually been turned against the views and interests of the Empire.'[48] The remainder of Fleming's *Political Annals* was a chronology of legislative affairs from 1791 to 1811, a review 'of the most remarkable steps evincing the ambition in the Leaders of the House of Assembly,' and how they had consistently '*neglected to provide for the immediate wants of a new Country [by] making provision for the characteristic vanities of an old Society.*' Within this chronology certain governors were praised for standing up for British rights (for example, Sir James Craig) and others condemned for appeasing the French Canadians (for example, Sir Robert Shore Milnes); but it was clear that regardless of individuals an oligarchy composed of bureaucrats, seigneurs, and wealthy merchants was incapable of thwarting the French-Canadian party in control of the assembly. That party of professionals, by its obstruction of all progressive measures in the areas of transportation, landholding, and taxation, made a mockery of the notion that the assembly was an institution of liberal reform. Its failure to vote supplies, the proximate cause of the crisis of 1828, was also the penultimate step in the total alienation of the colony.[49]

Fleming advocated the reunification of the Canadas as a 'means of redressing those grievances of His Majesty's Subjects of British descent,' giving English-speaking settlers the numerical ability to gain control of their own destiny and easing the task of liberating the mass of French Canadians through assimilation. The 'extensive measure of a Legislative Union of Lower Canada with Upper Canada, would place a skilful Executive in a favourable position for holding the balance and compromising the disputes between the two parties of French and English origin, in the new House of Assembly.' Above all, it would finally permit the British to lead by example, for Fleming wrote that he still hoped a 'spirit of enquiry, leading to attention to education, will gradually open the minds of the Canadians, and render them truly worthy of legislating for themselves, and contributing along with us to the internal peace and

48 Ibid., xiii, 7, 11, 134
49 Ibid., 2, 10–13, 17, 68–9, 87

prosperity of the Colony.'[50] Fleming worked hard to have the Union Bill of 1822 passed and was deeply disturbed when it did not. He was even more disturbed that the British government professed to see executive corruption rather than the constitutional impasse as the source of the crisis in Lower Canada. The *Political Annals* were intended to correct that misconception and impress upon officials in London that no improvements could be expected in Lower Canada until the British Parliament acted to investigate and reform the constitution of 1791 in such a way as to ensure that the 'variegated' nature of the Canadian population was represented in the assembly.[51]

While it was certainly an exaggeration to call Fleming 'le père de l'historiographie canadienne-anglaise,' his work did provide in summary form what Yves Zoltvany terms 'the liberal critique' of New France.[52] This critique began with the assumption that maladministration was responsible for the sluggish development of New France, the colony's hostile relations with native and British neighbours, and the enervation of its defensive military capacity. Remove the Bourbon tyranny, so the theory went, and the colony would be liberated. In retrospect, the salvation theory of the conquest neither appreciated the deep-rooted attachment of the common habitant to traditional practices nor anticipated the reluctance of English-speaking colonists to populate so northern a colony. The Quebec Act, for whatever reason introduced, revived French-Canadian leadership and seriously reduced the likelihood that an assimilating wave of English-speaking settlers would ever arrive. The resultant alleged hegemony of a French-Canadian élite did, however, provide English-Canadian historians with a convenient conspiracy theory with which to explain the habitants' rejection of Britain's liberating embrace. It followed that the Constitutional Act of 1791's gift of representative institutions to the now-circumscribed province of Lower Canada was worse than no remedy at all. The British constitution was fit for responsible citizens, not an ignorant peasantry.

By this very different route the English-speaking historians of Lower Canada arrived at the same conclusion as their Maritime brethren, namely that the independent yeoman was the basic building block of a

50 Ibid., iii, vi; [Fleming,] *Some Considerations*, 16–17
51 [Fleming,] *Political Annals*, iii–iv, 121
52 Jean-Pierre Wallot, 'La crise sous Craig (1807–1811): nature des conflits et historiographie,' in his *Un Québec qui bougeait: trame socio-politique du Québec au tournant du XIXe siècle* (Montreal 1973) 144; Zoltvany, *Government of New France*, 35

sound, progressive, political and economic system in North America. The distinction was that Maritime historians confidently asserted that their respective colonies lived up to the yeoman ideal and looked forward to a bright future, while English-speaking historians of Quebec despaired of assimilating the French-Canadian majority and saw nothing but turbulence ahead. Indeed, what was unifying and patriotic in one region was perceived as divisive and racist in the other. Haliburton clarified and articulated a distinctive identity for his fellow Nova Scotians and received their thanks. In attempting the same feat, Fleming was excoriated by those he sought to liberate.

The reaction of the French-Canadian community was brought directly before the English-speaking audience in the *Political and Historical Account of Lower Canada* published in 1830 by the urbane Pierre-Jean de Sales Laterrière (1789–1834).[53] Son of an apothecary, Laterrière was educated at the Petit Séminaire de Québec and then trained as a physician, first under his father at Quebec and then under famous surgeon Astley Paston Cooper at St Thomas's Hospital, London. Laterrière was admitted to membership in the Royal College of Surgeons in 1809, succeeded to his father's practice in 1810, and was appointed surgeon to the Voltigeurs Canadiens in 1812. When visiting London in 1815, he married the only daughter of Sir Fenwick Bulmer. Her dowry, an inheritance from his father, and professional competence made Laterrière an extremely wealthy man. Upon the death of his father-in-law in 1824, Laterrière received an additional annuity of £3,000 and subsequently purchased a property in Middlesex, taking up permanent residence there with his family. In England Laterrière acted as a voice for his French-Canadian compatriots, and wrote the *Political and Historical Account* primarily as a refutation of the arguments of John Fleming, whose book Laterrière described as being 'full of information as it is of prejudice against the French Canadians.'[54]

Laterrière's argument, the obverse of Fleming's, began at the same point: 'To those ... who believe that a divided people must be an unhappy

53 [Pierre-Jean de Sales Laterrière,] *A Political and Historical Account of Lower Canada: With Remarks on the Present Situation of the People, as Regards Their Manners, Character, Religion, &c. &c.*, by a Canadian (London 1830). Laterrière wrote the manuscript in French but published in English specifically to reach a wider audience in London's governing councils.

54 Pierre Dufour, 'Pierre-Jean de Sales Laterrière,' *DCB*, vol. 6, 680–2; [Laterrière,] *Political and Historical Account*, v–xii

people; who consider that internal discord is a fruitful source of misery and crime, the subject of a remedy must be an interesting topic.' In Lower Canada the division of society was between French and English,

> meaning, by French, all such as were originally, or have, by long dwelling in the country or otherwise, become attached to the French Canadian habits and language; meaning, by English, such as are really English, or have, in spite of their continuance in the country, retained a decided predilection for what they believe to be English manners, language, tastes, &c.[55]

The remedy for this conflict was, as Laterrière intimated, not the assimilation of the French but the acculturation of the English. It was the French who had settled the land, accepted Canadian nationality, and tied their fortunes to the province's development. The English, in contrast, were either administrators, 'persons drawn from a distant country, ignorant of the manners and situation of the people they are destined to rule, and careless of those interests with which they are but temporarily connected,' or merchants by whom 'Canada is never considered ... other than a place of momentary sojourn.' In short, the English were self-interested 'birds of passage,' unattached to the soil, and therefore to be considered, in the best British constitutional tradition, unfit to rule. It was Laterrière's complaint that it was such parasites as these who were selected to rule and that the history of Quebec and then Lower Canada was the story of 'how a whole people have been checked in the progress of improvement, enthralled, ill-treated, abused, and then misrepresented, by the evil influence of a handful of grasping functionnaires.'[56]

Nevertheless, Laterrière saw cause to rejoice, for the French-Canadian people, through their independent elected representatives, 'determined to resist, step by step, every encroachment on their rights.' 'Thus,' he continued, 'attempts to establish a despotic sway, and to beat down the spirit of the people, served to establish a free government, and create sturdy independence.'[57] The more successfully the French-Canadian people defended themselves, Laterrière found, the more desperate the English Canadians became in their efforts to discredit both the assembly and the race it represented. For some considerable period the bureaucrats' most effective libel was to denounce all assertions of popular will as Jacobin. Such a charge was effectively deflated by the support French

55 Ibid., 114, 150
56 Ibid., 4–5, 21
57 Ibid., 32–6

Canadians gave to British forces throughout the War of 1812. With their lies no longer credible, the bureaucrats fastened on any expedient that might cut the rights of the assembly, limit the franchise of French Canadians, and otherwise reduce the power of the majority. The remedy most often proposed by the English-speaking community in Lower Canada was union with Upper Canada. The whole object of the Union Bill of 1822 was 'to destroy the political influence of the French Canadians; to overturn their laws, their religion, and their language; and to make the people quickly forget, by a lapse of years, that they ever had been French Canadians.'[58] Laterrière returned the history of Lower Canada to the point where, for the French Canadians' own good, Fleming would have said 'Amen.'

In 1828 Lower Canada was in a state of social and political crisis. The French-dominated assembly was withholding supplies, and the English were using this latest example of obstruction to renew calls for union with Upper Canada. With the power between local antagonists in balance, 'it was at last deemed advisable by the colony to have recourse to the Imperial Government, in order to settle the differences existing.' As a result a committee of the British Parliament was established to inquire into the civil government of the Canadas. Fleming, Laterrière, and a host of less memorable authors all wrote to 'enable the British Legislature to adjuge between contending parties.'[59] But as Laterrière himself admitted, the tone of their work only demonstrated the height to which party feeling had by then arrived. Argued from alleged principles of political economy (for the most part read prejudice) rather than historical fact, debate degenerated to a point where it discredited all protagonists and dishonoured the colony. Everyone lost.

Largely discounted in Great Britain, Quebec's English-speaking historians' only service at home was to sharpen and confirm racial division. Indeed, so long as the key to historiographic debate in Lower Canada was the emotionally charged and politically volatile issue of assimilation, it was virtually impossible to write a history of the province acceptable to both races. In this environment even topographical descriptions and settlers' guides were controversial. For instance, because immigration – by which everyone meant English-speaking immigration – was such a critical element in the further assimilation of French Canadians, to describe the land and attract settlers affected the racial contest. Thus the surveyor-

58 Ibid., 36, 75
59 Ibid., vi

general of Lower Canada, Joseph Bouchette (1774–1841), executed the most comprehensive surveys of the province only to find his motives and person subject to attack from the French-Canadian majority in the assembly.[60] No one was immune.

By the end of the 1820s, then, political and racial conflict in Lower Canada had become a vortex that swallowed almost any statement made concerning the colony. This was the training ground of Robert Christie (1787–1856). Christie was born in Windsor, Nova Scotia, the son of a shoemaker and farmer. He was educated at King's College School, and then, after the fashion of such classmates as Andrew Cochran and James Stuart, he drifted to Lower Canada in search of a career. There he was indentured in 1805 to study law in the office of Attorney-General Edward Bowen; he was called to the bar in 1810 and helped to defend the province as a militiaman during the War of 1812. After the war he established and edited the *Quebec Telegraph*, which, while it lasted less than two years, secured Christie's credentials as a journalist and political observer.[61]

In the meantime Christie's friend Cochran also had made good, becoming civil secretary to a succession of governors, beginning with Sir George Prevost. It was perhaps no accident that in 1818 Christie was appointed law clerk to the assembly, or that he should be dismissed eight years later on suspicion of furnishing the office of the then governor, George Ramsay, ninth earl of Dalhousie, with confidential legislative information.[62] Whatever the truth of the charges, Christie's political career soon became even more contentious. Dalhousie appointed him chairman of the Court of Quarter Sessions for Quebec City, in which capacity Christie deleted from the roll of magistrates such enemies of the

60 Joseph Bouchette, *A Topographical Description of the Province of Lower Canada, with Remarks upon Upper Canada, and on the Relative Connexion of Both Provinces with the United States of America* (London 1815); *The British Dominions in North America; Or a Topographical and Statistical Description of the Provinces of Lower and Upper Canada, New Brunswick, Nova Scotia, the Islands of Newfoundland, Prince Edward, and Cape Breton. Including Considerations on Land-Granting and Emigration. To Which Are Annexed, Statistical Tables and Tables of Distances, &c.* 2 vols (London 1831)

Biographical details are available in several sources, the most comprehensive of which are: John E. Hare, 'Présentation,' in Joseph Bouchette, *Description topographique* ..., ed. John E. Hare (Montreal 1978) 5–22; Claude Baudreau and Pierre Lépine, 'Joseph Bouchette,' *DCB*, vol. 7, 95–8. See also Taylor, 'Writing of English-Canadian History,' vol. 1, 166–73.

61 NA, Commission of Advocates, RG 6, B 8, vol. 18, 6659–63; Shirley C. Spragge, 'Robert Christie,' *DCB*, vol. 8, 154–6

62 Joseph-Guillaume Barthe (1818–93), *Souvenirs d'un demi-siècle ou mémoires pour servir à l'histoire contemporaine* (Montreal 1885) 126–31

governor as John Neilson and Dr François-Xavier Blanchet. In 1829 a special committee of the assembly denounced Christie's actions as a gross interference in the judicial system and dropped his salary from the provincial budget. What is more, Christie, as of October 1827 the member for the recently organized and predominantly English-speaking constituency of Gaspé, was expelled from his seat in the assembly. In all he was expelled and re-elected five times over the next three years, and he agitated for the annexation of Gaspé to New Brunswick before giving up the struggle.[63] Yet in the midst of his partisan career, Christie produced a series of *Memoirs* that his political opponent Pierre de Sales Laterrière described as 'very interesting, and although intended to please the ruling power, impartially written.'[64]

How did a such a renowned partisan as Christie win the respect of a political opponent like Laterrière where Fleming and others had drawn only the ire of French Canadians? Primarily because Christie admitted his bias in favour of Lord Dalhousie and realized that 'our testimony of itself may carry but little weight.' Furthermore, Christie accepted the methodological consequences of this admission and adopted a rigorously documentary approach to the past in order to avoid relying upon his personal observations and words. He gathered 'official or authentic documents, and where these were not to be had, from such other sources as seemed fully entitled to credit,' and he reproduced them 'in a clear and intelligible order, *sans fard*, and ... *sans fiel*, fear, favor, affection, or resentment towards any political party, partisan, or person whomsoever, living or dead.' In short, historical actors were 'allowed to tell their own tale, lest the writer should misunderstand and unintentionally do them injustice'; the reader was permitted to judge for himself 'of their pretensions and of their doctrines, by their own shewing and the fruits they have produced.'[65] It was this comprehensive documentary method that recommended Christie even to his political opponents.

Between 1818 and 1829 Christie produced five volumes of variously titled *Memoirs* and then at leisure merged and enlarged these works as

63 *Journal de la Chambre d'Assemblée du Bas-Canada* (1829) 93; (1830) 11; (1831) 43; (1831–2) 13; (1832–3) 25, 50ff; Robert Christie, *A History of the Late Province of Lower Canada, Parliamentary and Political, from the Late Commencement to the Close of Its Existence as a Separate Province ...*, 6 vols (vols 1–5, Quebec 1848–54; vol. 6, Montreal 1855) vol. 3 (1850) 150–1, 240–51, 436; Henri Brun, *La Formation des institutions parlementaires québécoises, 1791–1838* (Quebec 1970) 109–10
64 [Laterrière,] *Political and Historical Account*, 214
65 Christie, *History of the Late Province of Lower Canada*, vol. 1 (1848) iv; vol. 3, 180; vol. 5 (1850) iii

part of his six-volume *History of the Late Province of Lower Canada*, published between 1848 and 1855.[66] Although documentary, these volumes were not dull. Christie actually heightened the reader's awareness of different personalities by permitting a succession of interesting political characters to come into view – individuals who had been lumped by previous historians into such anonymous categories as 'demagogues,' 'bureaucrats,' or 'bourgeoisie.' Christie did, of course, present his own views too, but as just that, his own views. And the most surprising aspect of Christie's work is the way in which his political views changed over time. While it is true he cannibalized his early *Memoirs* to produce his later history, in the interval he changed his mind on fundamental historical interpretations.

The conservative defender of Lord Dalhousie actually began life as a liberal champion of the rights and privileges of the assembly. Undoubtedly schooled at King's College in the niceties of the English constitution, Christie initially was a supporter of the Canadian party in Lower Canada: a party he preferred to see as a liberal or radical organization intent on increasing the power of the assembly rather than as a nationalist party defending the rights of the French-Canadian race. Christie was not alone in this perception. James Stuart, who took over the leadership of the Canadian party upon the downfall of his friend Pierre-Stanislas Bédard during Governor Craig's administration, 'gave it credibility as a liberal

---

66 Robert Christie, *Memoirs of the Administration of the Colonial Government of Lower-Canada, by Sir James Henry Craig, and Sir George Prevost; From the Year 1807 until the Year 1815, Comprehending the Military and Naval Operations in the Canadas, during the Late War with the United States of America* (Quebec 1818), also published under the title *The Military and Naval Operations in the Canadas during the Late War with the United States, Including Also the Political History of Lower Canada during the Administration of Sir James Henry Craig and Sir George Prevost, from 1807 until 1815* (Quebec 1818; reprinted New York 1818); *A Brief Review of the Political State of Lower Canada, since the Conquest of the Colony, to the Present Day. To Which Are Added, Memoirs of the Administrations of the Colonial Government of Lower Canada, by Sir Gordon Drummond, and Sir John Coape Sherbrooke* (New York 1818); *Memoirs of the Administration of the Government of Lower-Canada, by Sir Gordon Drummond, Sir John Coape Sherbrooke, the Late Duke of Richmond, James Monk, Esquire, and Sir Peregrine Maitland; Continued from the 3rd April, 1815, until the 18th June, 1820* (Quebec 1820); *Memoirs of the Administration of the Government of Lower Canada, by the Right Honourable the Earl of Dalhousie, G.C.B., Comprehending a Period of Eight Years, vizt: – from June, 1820 till September, 1828* (Quebec 1829), Christie issued an unsigned continuation with consecutive pagination entitled *Administration of the Honourable Sir Francis N. Burton, G.C.H.* (np, nd).

On Christie's relationship with his publishers see George L. Parker, *The Beginnings of the Book Trade in Canada* (Toronto 1985) 86.

party in the eyes of the English-speaking.' The party was to retain this credibility until Louis-Joseph Papineau eased Stuart out in the years 1817–18, and even then the implications of this change were not as clear to contemporaries as to later historians.[67]

In a *Review of the Political State of Lower Canada*, published in 1818, Christie gave a liberal interpretation of provincial history that bore many similarities to the one later found in the work of Laterrière. The main purpose of the work, published in New York, was 'to explain ... those internal difficulties which strangers have mistaken for evidences of a seditious spirit.' Simply stated, false accusations that the constitutional opposition in the Assembly of Lower Canada was disloyal misled Americans into assuming they could take Canada and the British government into backing a scandalous oligarchy. The lessons of the recent war should be taken to heart, especially by the government in London when evaluating conflicting reports from the colony.[68]

According to Christie the history of Quebec, and then of Lower Canada, could be seen as a battle between two political factions, which, modifying the terminology of eighteenth-century constitutional conflict in England, he called 'the Party' and 'the Country.' The former was an oligarchy composed of those 'commercial adventurers' who had accompanied the British army of occupation in 1760, augmented by American Loyalists bemoaning their 'pretended' losses. Having no attachment to the land, the Party 'thwarted the beneficent views of the mother country, and checked the improvement of the internal state of the province,' all the while draining government coffers to fill the pockets of its members. 'The position which had been gained by artifice, was maintained by fraud, and frequently by violence.' The Country faction was composed primarily of French Canadians. This was the real landed interest, but its voice, speaking in a foreign tongue and uncertain of the workings of the constitution, was rarely heard. Generally patient, when the Country faction did raise a cry in self-defence it was labelled seditious by the local oligarchy and dealt with harshly.[69] In short, Christie preferred to see the dispute in Lower Canada as a constitutional struggle between the historic forces of oligarchy and yeomanry, with the racial component a complicating, secondary factor.

Within this framework, Governor Craig was portrayed as an honourable soldier who was misled by the oligarchy, which he trusted. Under the

67 Ouellet, *Lower Canada*, 191–3
68 Christie, *Brief Review of the Political State of Lower Canada*, 3–4
69 Ibid., 6–11

burden of his oppression the French-Canadian people spoke up through the pages of *Le Canadien*, which on occasion was 'perhaps licentious' but never treasonable. The War of 1812 gave the Country faction an opportunity to prove its loyalty, and, with the understanding and sympathetic guidance of Governor Prevost, Lower Canadians were more than equal to the task. The Party, its slander of the Country disproved, gained a short respite when Prevost was recalled after the humiliating military defeat at Plattsburg. However, the Party's optimism was short-lived, and Lower Canada's history reached a climax with the appointment of Sir John Coape Sherbrooke as governor in 1816. Sherbrooke, according to Christie, refused to be the tool of any faction, restored the balance between the two bodies of the legislature, and remained an impartial arbiter. Above all, Sherbrooke placed the assembly on an equal footing with the legislative and executive councils by accepting the elected body's offer to vote supplies for the provincial civil list.[70] With political conflict now at an end, Christie closed with a flourish of praise for the colony's physical resources, climate, and people. Peace assured and prospects bright, Lower Canada was now Great Britain's most valuable colony.

The next instalment of the *Memoirs* carried the history of the province up to June in the year of its publication, 1820. The intervening two years had not seen the end of animosity between the assembly and the councils, largely because the civil list question remained unaccountably a contentious issue. Governor Sherbrooke's successor, Charles Lennox, fourth duke of Richmond and Lennox, presented a large budget (including a round sum of £8,000 for various pensions), which the assembly proposed to reduce through an item-by-item examination. Richmond, backed by the legislative council's veto, rejected the assembly's course of action as an unconstitutional expansion of that body's role and an infringement of royal prerogative. A middle group wanted to compromise by passing the budget in 'chapters.' 'The proposal,' to which Christie was attracted, 'came too late, and from the excitement already created by the debates on the two main questions, was not listened to.'[71] Slightly confused and uneasy, Christie provided no reason for the continuance of factional strife, save perhaps a residue of past resentment.

It was almost a decade before the next volume of Christie's historical *Memoirs* appeared, during which time Christie was forced to re-evaluate the actions of the Canadian party, just as we know its members were

70 Ibid., 26–33, 52, 63–70
71 [Christie,] *Memoirs of the Administration of ... Sir Gordon Drummond*, 183–4

re-evaluating him. Christie was neither the first nor the last to confuse the Canadian and Patriote movements with a liberal party. Fernand Ouellet observes that, for English-speaking liberal politicians in Lower Canada in the 1820s, the revelation that the Canadian party was not liberal was particularly discouraging: 'these men must either accept the French implications of the party's goals or eventually find their way back to the British party, no matter what their theoretical political animosity might be toward the government.'[72] In Christie's case the patronage of Lord Dalhousie eased the transition, but the internal consistency of his own professions, as well as the testimony of friend and foe alike, suggest that his course was also one of principle.[73]

The *Memoirs of the Administration of ... the Right Honourable the Earl of Dalhousie*, the last of Christie's preliminary volumes, was a work of frustration.[74] A man of liberal sentiments, Christie wanted the voice of the people, be they French or English, to carry weight in the balance of government. He also wanted to see the entire population benefit from agricultural and commercial growth. In the early years of the nineteenth century Christie opposed the self-interested oligarchy for hoarding political power and appropriating the fruits of the economy. When, in the early 1820s, the balance of political power tipped toward the assembly, Christie was shocked to discover that its members were just as obstinate and selfish as the bureaucrats they replaced. Dalhousie arrived as governor, for instance, with an array of enlightened plans to promote immigration, agriculture, transportation, and education, all of which died for want of funds – funds denied by an assembly claiming a constitutional right to a detailed annual examination of public expenditure. Christie labelled the assembly's position 'presumptuous,' and went on to criticize the 'spirit of intolerance and tyranny' with which the elected body rejected all executive legislative proposals, regardless of merit. Nonetheless, Christie did not make an open accusation of racial prejudice against the Canadian party and thought the English-speaking community's push for union in 1822 dangerous.[75] Despite signs to the contrary, he was not yet willing to admit that his political and economic hopes for Lower Canada were inherently anathema to the French-Canadian people and their leaders.

72 Ouellet, *Lower Canada*, 192
73 'Obituary Notice of the Late Robert Christie, Esq. [reprinted from the *Quebec Mercury*, 16 Oct. 1856],' *Le Bulletin des recherches historiques* 44 (1938): 9–12
74 Neilson Papers, vol. 6, 431, Christie to Neilson, 4 May 1829
75 [Christie,] *Memoirs of the Administration of ... the Right Honourable the Earl of Dalhousie*, 212–21, 228–35, 252–5

Christie had the succeeding volume of his *Memoirs* ready for publication by the time of the Rebellions of 1837–8, but in light of those events decided to withhold it and embark on a large-scale revision of all his previous work.[76] Only in 1848 was the first volume of Christie's new six-volume *A History of the Late Province of Lower Canada* published, by which time he had reformulated his approach to the colony's past. The new volumes were devoted to the discovery of why the British constitution granted to both Upper and Lower Canada in 1791 worked comparatively well in the former, which was populated exclusively by English-speaking settlers, and failed in the latter, where the majority of settlers were of the French race.

> Whether it were that one race had more aptitude and were better qualified for the appreciation and use of it than the other, it is not with us to say; but, from whatsoever cause, the fact always is patent and irrefutable, that, in the hands of the one it throve, answered the intended purpose, and was appreciated by the people as a blessing, the palladium of their privileges, and made available accordingly. Whereas, in those of the other, notwithstanding that during the first twenty-five years of its existence it worked to admiration, it signally failed, turning out, unhappily, something worse than a mere failure.[77]

On the other side of the rebellions, Christie was at last willing to accept that race animated 'the spirit that rendered the constitution abortive.'[78]

This time round Christie decided that it was the British colonists who wanted an assembly and the French who were opposed; and he praised London's procrastination in granting such an institution, as 'few in the mass were then qualified to partake of it, if established.' The Quebec Act was a sound compromise, which, while it did not gain short-term French-Canadian constancy in 1775, did ensure long-term loyalty by guaranteeing them 'almost a national existence.' The granting of the constitution of 1791 was natural and timely and marred only by a division that impeded intrinsic economic channels and weakened the political influence of the English-speaking population of Lower Canada.[79]

Christie thought the constitution operated well for a time, permitting the two races to work in political harmony for their mutual economic

76 NA, Sir John Harvey Papers, MG 24, A 17, vol. 1, 140, Sir John Harvey to Christie, 3 Sept. 1839
77 Christie, *History of the Late Province of Lower Canada*, vol. 1, ii
78 Ibid., iii
79 Ibid., 5–6, 9–14, 66–115

benefit. In retrospect, however, Christie admitted that this tranquil period was deceptive. French-Canadian politicians used it to learn the intricacies of strange legislative procedures, which, once mastered, allowed them to renew their aggressive struggle for racial supremacy in Lower Canada. No sooner were they confident of their power, than they turned every conflict into a test of racial will. Innocent differences of economic interest were transformed by them into contests between French and English, especially in the pages of *Le Canadien*, which was 'from the outset, anti-executive in politics, anti-commercial in its doctrines, and, indeed, anti-british in spirit, treating as anti-canadian every thing british in the colony, and the british immigrants and population as "*étrangers et intrus*," strangers and intruders.'[80] Governor Craig had no choice but to close the newspaper. The subsequent outrage of the French-Canadian community was almost entirely the product of 'political intriguers ... mischievously working upon the prejudices of national origin in the people.'[81] In Christie's revised version, ambitious French-Canadian politicians, not the English-speaking oligarchy, were primarily responsible for the breakdown of racial harmony.

The explosive racial animosities of Governor Craig's last years were for the moment diffused, according to Christie, by the 'equitable, wise, successful' policies of the succeeding governor, Sir George Prevost. The clash over *nationalité* was then submerged in 1812 by that between nations. And as racial conflict subsided, the political struggle between an irresponsible oligarchy and the elected assembly was free to resume its natural course. In volumes two and three, therefore, Christie returned to the interpretation of events given in his earlier *Memoirs* and once again portrayed Governor Sherbrooke's acceptance of the assembly's offer to pay the civil list as the climax to the political crisis in the province. Christie now believed, however, that the resolution of the political problem only served to unleash dormant racial antagonisms. It soon became apparent, for instance, that the matter of the civil list 'was not contemplated in the same point of view by all who looked towards it.' Thus, 'instead of tranquilising it helped, as the sequel will shew, to bring on, after some years of agitation on that and other subjects, still greater difficulties than before, ending unhappily, in disaster and blood.'[82]

It was now clear to Christie that whereas most English-speaking liberals, like himself, saw in the civil list question 'the means of giving

80 Ibid., 243, 252
81 Ibid., 310–11
82 Ibid., vol. 2, 10, 265–93

efficiency to the government' by the provision of a 'constitutional check upon the executive,' others, mostly French Canadians, viewed it as a means of establishing 'an undue sway on the part of the commons of the province over the government, at variance with the form and spirit of the british constitution and subversive of it.'[83] The English faction, Christie wrote in a key passage,

> were quite disposed to go with [the French] in all just reforms in the legislative bodies, as well as in the executive and judicial departments, consistent with the constitution, and conducive to the public good and permanent connexion of the colony with Great Britain, and to respect their religion, their laws and even their prejudices; but were far from entertaining a desire to part with their national character for that which it was now proposed to set up and invest them with, or to repudiate their own honest english prepossessions or prejudices in mere complacency to, much less adopt in their stead those of frenchmen, (as seemed to be expected of them,) and as indeed, some few, of british origin, from motives best known to themselves really have done, or at least feigned to do, and, in certain instances, to profit.[84]

Self-interested French-Canadian agitators, consisting 'chiefly of country notaries, doctors, surveyors, briefless lawyers, and small fry of that description,' resorted to 'absurd tales, improbable, palpable untruths,' in order to excite the habitants, 'for whom, in their credulity and implicit faith in their leaders, nothing could be too gross.' The British government mistakenly met this agitation with the same generosity of spirit that had marked its rule from the start: it removed Governor Dalhousie, whom the Canadian party disliked, and replaced him with Sir James Kempt, who courted the leading demagogues of the day 'with an assiduity approaching to obsequiousness.'[85] This policy demoralized loyal British subjects and incited opposition leaders to ever greater demands. Before long the very arm of civil power in the province was in disaffection, the very source of justice poisoned, and the executive rendered powerless. 'In fact, it was now but too evident that the races, of british and french origin, in the province, were at issue, the former for maintaining the constitution inviolate, ... the latter for subverting it.'[86]

Christie's interpretation of events was now fixed. The closer he moved

83 Ibid., 293–4
84 Ibid., vol. 3, 4–5
85 Ibid., 132–5, 216
86 Ibid., 514

in volumes four and five to the rebellions themselves (the sixth volume being a collection of documents), the more completely he withdrew his narrative voice, refraining from any further commentary. Henceforth he relied on the momentum of events to carry the story along tracks of his construction to its inevitable destination.[87]

Christie's account of the history of Lower Canada was controversial. Like Fleming, he proposed a course of economic and political development that many French Canadians viewed with concern; yet he failed to recognize their concern as legitimate. But Christie gained acceptance as a historian because his methods were as conservative as his principles. In order to rise above the consuming morass of partisan debate in Lower Canada and establish a measure of credibility, he was willing to permit contending individuals to speak for themselves, uninterrupted and at length. As a result, even so partisan an enemy as William Lyon Mackenzie was moved to write that Christie's fifth volume was 'filled with useful accounts of the days of 1837–38–39.'[88] This was, given the time and place, a remarkable achievement.

Still, there were limits to what Christie could and did accomplish. It was beyond his power, for instance, to banish or resolve the profound racial tensions existing in Lower Canada. As a consequence, it was impossible to establish an acceptable common interpretation of the past, a plan for the future, or a perception of provincial identity. There was no reason for the British government to find Christie's interpretation of events persuasive, and there is no proof that it did in fact influence the direction of imperial policy. At home, Christie's histories at best created tolerance of differences. This at least was something, for in the face of the responsible government and free trade initiatives of the 1840s Lower Canadians increasingly would have to solve their problems on their own. As Christie wrote in the preface to his sixth and final volume, 'We have literally the entire government of our own local affairs, and if we allow or connive at misgovernment on the part of those we entrust with our interests, whom but ourselves have we to blame?'[89]

87 Christie solicited funds from the Library Committee of the Legislature of the United Canadas (which had given him £250 to defray the costs incurred in the production of volume six) for a '7th and final volume' covering events in Upper Canada leading up to and including the rebellion. Apparently no money was granted. NA, Alpheus Todd Papers, MG 24, K 23, vol. 1, Christie to Alpheus Todd, 11 Feb. 1856

88 NA, William Lyon Mackenzie Papers, MG 24, B 18, vol. 9, 1640–3, William Lyon Mackenzie to James Mackenzie, 2 Sept. 1854

89 Christie, [History of the Late Province of Lower Canada,] Interesting Public Documents, and Official Correspondence, Illustrative of, and Supplementary to the History of Lower Canada, vol. 6 (1855) x

Perhaps Christie also became more acceptable to Canadians of all political stripes because he no longer knew what he wanted. As a young liberal he promoted the rights of the assembly; later, as a conservative convert, he took a firm line against the presumption of that same body. In the wake of the rebellions, the union of the Canadas, and the coming of responsible government, Christie was at sea. As member for Gaspé in the Parliament of the United Province of Canada from 1841 to 1854, Christie dealt with realities he found uncongenial, namely, union with Upper Canada and then, later, responsible government. It had been his hope that Lower Canadians would solve their own problems and avoid union with the growing province to the west.[90] As for responsible government, he objected to a system that shifted the control of patronage from the Crown to the assembly. He believed this change made corruption more insidious and intractable, for department heads, sitting in the assembly and protected by a majority, were far less vulnerable to instant dismissal and far better positioned to see to their own interests than royal appointees ever had been.[91] Not surprisingly, Christie developed the reputation of being an irascible gadfly, a loner with an opinion on every issue and a solution for none.

Christie did not try to write a history of this later period. For whom would he write? And what would he tell them? Still, he continued to make lasting contributions to historical endeavour. From his seat in the legislature he urged several administrations to take responsibility for the collection, preservation, and publication of historical documents. In 1844 and 1845 he moved the establishment of, and chaired, the committee appointed to inquire into the state of the papers and public records of New France, the province of Quebec, and Lower Canada. It was largely due to the efforts of Christie and this committee that some semblance of order was brought to the papers of many government departments. He also played a role in the decision taken by the government to have documents of New France copied in Albany, New York, and France. Such efforts brought Christie into contact with many of his old Patriote foes, for whom he subsequently developed a certain respect. Indeed, it seems fitting that one of Christie's last steps was to introduce Louis-Joseph Papineau to the young American historian Francis Parkman.[92]

90 Ibid., vol. 1, xiv; *Debates of the Legislative Assembly of United Canada*, vol. 1, ,1841, ed. Elizabeth Nish (Montreal 1970) 106; vol. 2, ,1842 (Montreal 1971) 329; Neilson Papers, vol. 10, 364–7, Christie to Neilson, 27 Mar. 1842
91 Christie, *History of the Late Province of Lower Canada*, vol. 1, 350–2; *Debates of the Legislative Assembly*, vol. 2, 375
92 *Appendix to the ... Journals of the Legislative Assembly of the Province of Canada*, 1844–5, appendix HH; 1846, appendix KK; Spragge, 'Robert Christie,' 155–6

Christie's relative success among English-speaking historians of Lower Canada should not disguise his and their mutual inability to function in the manner of the patriot historians of the Maritimes. It was the anomaly of Quebec that alone among the colonies of British North America it did not shed its past. As long as the French fact persisted, there was simply too much from the past in the present to permit historians to focus on the future. From their point of view, it was futile to describe the potential of the land as long as human affairs were out of control. As a result, their works were an appeal to the commanding external authority of London for confidence-building sanction to assimilate or suppress French Canada. This the home authorities would not, probably could not, provide. In the event, neither the imposition of union nor the coming of responsible government resolved this dilemma. 'Who was to say when and in what circumstances [the French Canadians] would seek to turn back the page of history?'[93]

The tenacity of French Canadians defied all attempts by the likes of Fleming and Christie to impose a unifying identity based on the yeoman ideal. Indeed, rather than reducing differences, the English-speaking historians of Quebec actually clarified and thereby hardened racial distinctions in the province. Frustrated and defensive, they achieved precisely the opposite affect of the patriot historians of the Maritime colonies. Nevertheless, their very failure led to an uneasy recognition if not acceptance of another identity. Bent on assimilation, they ultimately introduced the perception of duality into Canadian historiography. However grudgingly conceded, this was of major importance.

---

93 Nicholas Mansergh, *The Commonwealth Experience*, vol. 1, *The Durham Report to the Anglo-Irish Treaty*, 2nd ed. (Toronto 1982) 35

4
Reform Challenge in Upper Canada

Prior to 1780 the peninsula that was shortly to become Upper Canada remained a wilderness inhabited by a few white and not many more native people. Within the short span of sixty years the same area was settled by several hundred thousand people, who brought with them the tensions of the social, technological, and ideological upheaval of the early and mid-nineteenth century. The first to arrive were the approximately six to ten thousand Loyalists dislocated by the American Revolution. After an indiscernible pause, many more thousands of apolitical American land seekers swamped the original Loyalists, before their immigration was curtailed in the aftermath of the War of 1812. Following them came still larger numbers of immigrants from the British Isles, *les déplacées* of agricultural, industrial, and demographic change. Most of Upper Canada's resultant population – more than four hundred thousand by the time of the 1840 union with Lower Canada – came as individuals or as part of single, independent households; and, apart from the Loyalists and a few small religious communities, most came primarily to better their economic condition. The typical immigrant, whatever his origin, had, according to geographer R. Cole Harris,

> come to a place in motion, and in adapting to a new setting he adapted to change itself. He came to expect new faces, new accents, new clearings, new machines. He had little difficulty, as a clearing became a farm or a track a road, in coming to expect progress, which he defined in material terms. His sense of time, weakened by the dislocation that had led to immigration, by the pace of change in [Upper Canada], and simply his new setting, was not strong.[1]

1 R. Cole Harris and John Warkentin, *Canada before Confederation: A Study in Historical Geography* (Toronto 1974) 112

With only the most inchoate sense of its own identity, this new, shifting, and otherwise preoccupied pioneer population had little time or inclination for literary pursuits. (The novelist John Frederick Richardson [1796-1852] was the exception to prove the rule.)² Upper Canada's reputation was established initially therefore in works published by outsiders and transients, usually from Great Britain. While many travellers to the province were sympathetic to the settlers and a few actually wished to promote emigration from Great Britain, they suffered the same disadvantages as their fellows the empire over: brevity of visit, a propensity to focus on the unfamiliar and picturesque, a shallow knowledge of colonial society, and a tendency to patronize their hosts.³ In any event, judgments of Upper Canadian society were made, often using the neighbouring American states as a basis for comparison. The most common reproach was that Upper Canadians were not developing quickly enough, that they lacked the American spirit of enterprise.⁴ In this, as in so much else, visitors had a different conception of relative progress in the backwoods from the settlers themselves.

Upper Canadians, while sharing the British desire to foster emigration, were less likely to regard criticism as constructive or very helpful. This patriot reaction was typical of colonists and similar to that engendered by promoters in the Maritimes. However, it would take some time for the younger colony of Upper Canada to develop a literary culture capable of defending itself. In the meantime the task fell to those local officials with the leisure and inclination to make it part of their duty to champion the province. In 1799, for instance, Surveyor-General David William Smith (1764–1837), at the behest of Lieutenant-Governor John Graves Simcoe,

2 Desmond Pacey writes that 'Richardson is an isolated figure in the early history of the literature of Ontario. He had no literary acquaintances in this country, very few readers and no disciples. He was the product of a raw provincial society which at his birth was only itself five years old and even at his death was only just emerging from the frontier stage. There was no current of ideas to sustain him, no depth to the cultural soil in which his roots were set.' Desmond Pacey, *Creative Writing in Canada: A Short History of English-Canadian Literature*, 2nd ed. (Toronto 1961) 31; see also Carl F. Klinck, 'Literary Activity in the Canadas, 1812–1841,' in Carl F. Klinck, gen. ed., *Literary History of Canada: Canadian History in English* (Toronto 1965) 137–9

3 Gerald M. Craig, ed., *Early Travellers in the Canadas, 1791–1867* (Toronto 1955); Daniel John Keon, 'The "New World" Idea in British North America: An Analysis of Some British Promotional, Travel and Settler Writings, 1784 to 1860' (PH D Diss., Queen's University 1984)

4 See for example John Howison, *Sketches of Upper Canada, Domestic, Local, and Characteristic: To Which Are Added, Practical Details for the Information of Emigrants of Every Class; And Some Recollections of the United States of America* (Edinburgh 1821).

compiled and published a comprehensive topographical description and gazetteer of Upper Canada. Fourteen years later the then lieutenant-governor, Francis Gore, considered the work important enough to revise and republish it himself.[5] Both editions, in common with like works, stressed the possibilities of Upper Canada, gave evidence of improvements already completed, and presented history as something yet to be made by the hardy yeoman and the application of British capital. Upper Canada was an accessible, safe, and loyal province of the empire, ripe for development. But these works were inevitably something more than a vindication of the province. To say that Upper Canada flourished was to say that local officials were competent and successful. In defending the colony, Smith and Gore were implicitly defending themselves. In this sense they used patriot history for their own political and ultimately partisan ends.

This appropriation of patriot history by the ruling élite placed the largely inarticulate mass of settlers in an awkward position. As good patriots themselves, they were pleased to see misrepresentations of Upper Canada corrected. At the same time they were not entirely happy with the corollary that all was well with the administration of the province. In fact settlers had grievances, especially over the way land was granted and the government directed. The Constitutional Act of 1791 reserved one-seventh of the township lots for the Protestant clergy (that is, for the clergy of the Church of England), and in 1792 another one-seventh was reserved for the Crown. The imperial government was apparently more concerned to retain land until it had increased in value, in order to subsidize colonial administration, than it was to foster immediate settlement. This pattern of paternal control extended to the constitutional structure, which was often accused of giving disproportionate power to the appointed executive and legislative councils. These arrangements were commonly held to be an impediment to economic development, a cause of sectarian conflict, and a hindrance to the full exercise of British liberties.[6] All was not well.

As a result, there were those who questioned the likelihood that

5 David William Smith, *A Short Topographical Description of His Majesty's Province of Upper Canada, in North America. To Which Is Annexed a Provincial Gazetteer* (London 1799, 2nd ed. 1813); Jane Errington, *The Lion, the Eagle, and Upper Canada: A Developing Colonial Ideology* (Kingston and Montreal 1987) 161–2

6 Gerald M. Craig, *Upper Canada: The Formative Years, 1784–1841* (Toronto 1963) ch. 3; Colin Read, *The Rising in Western Upper Canada, 1837–8: The Duncombe Revolt and After* (Toronto 1982) 3–6

material progress could be made under contemporary constitutional arrangements. A series of political 'smoke-makers' – who included Joseph Willcocks, William Weekes, Charles Burton Wyatt, and Robert Thorpe – were able to touch raw nerves of resentment and irritation. In time this sporadic movement spawned a literature of grievance and reform paralleling that of the patriot histories. In 1809, for example, John Mills Jackson (1764–1836) wrote a pamphlet that charged Upper Canada's appointed administrators with forming a self-enriching and perpetuating oligarchy that was subverting the good intentions of the home government and the wishes of the province's elected assembly.[7] The reception of Jackson's pamphlet is instructive. Naturally, government officials reacted strongly to his accusations,[8] but so too did colonists generally. In the patriot tradition, the majority of Upper Canadians accepted that as long as their prosperity depended on attracting settlers from abroad, efforts should be made to avoid vehemently airing the admittedly real controversies of the day. Criticism must be kept within bounds. Jackson went too far and found himself reproved by a majority vote of the assembly. One assemblyman put the matter succinctly: if 'oppositionists' there must be, 'let them not be such as to expose us to the contempt and ridicule of our neighbours.'[9]

The tension between grievance and patriotism, between legitimate protest and the overriding façade of optimism and confidence, was severely strained following the conclusion of the War of 1812. Great Britain's return to its traditional neglect of the colony, the first stirrings of free trade, and the general reaction to the slower peace-time economy were all a source of unease for the Upper Canadian population. The colonists had demonstrated that they could defend the land, but not yet that they could exploit its resources. However, the restlessness caused by

7 John Mills Jackson, A View of the Political Situation of the Province of Upper Canada, in North America. In Which Her Physical Capacity is Stated; The Means of Diminishing Her Burden, Encreasing Her Value, and Securing Her Connection to Great Britain, are Fully Considered. With Notes and an Appendix (London 1809) 19–20; Robert L. Fraser, 'John Mills Jackson,' DCB, vol. 7 (Toronto 1988) 438–40

8 See for example the pamphlet of legislative councillor Richard Cartwright (1759–1815) Letters, from an American Loyalist in Upper Canada, to His Friend in England; On a Pamphlet Published by John Mills Jackson, Esquire: Entitled, 'A View of the Province of Upper Canada' (Halifax [1810]); George Rawlyk and Janice Potter, 'Richard Cartwright,' DCB, vol. 5 (Toronto 1983) 167–72.

9 Quoted in Hartwell Bowsfield, 'Upper Canada in the 1820's: The Development of a Political Consciousness' (PH D Diss., University of Toronto 1976) 21; Craig, Upper Canada, 63; Errington, The Lion, the Eagle, and Upper Canada, 64–7

the pace of economic development had now to be placed within the context of the solidified position of the administration that had preserved the province for the empire. The Upper Canadian élite, as well as imperial officials in London, had been alarmed at the extent of disaffection in Upper Canada during the early months of the war. This discovery heightened awareness of possible democratic and opportunistic strains in their own society and led to the effectual halt of emigration from the American states. Indeed, it imposed a duty to stifle all American tendencies and offered the opportunity to define these broadly enough to cover almost any form of opposition to the *status quo*.[10] Vocal protest was henceforth inhibited both by patriotic considerations and by the bounds of allegiance. The question of loyalty gave to Upper Canadian politics what Robert Fraser calls a 'razor's edge,' similar in form and effect to the question of race in the neighbouring province to the east.[11] An acceptable provincial identity could not be fashioned until the larger question of loyalty was resolved.

The line was now drawn. On the one (for the moment predominant) side was a historical tradition of loyal patriotism. It pictured Upper Canada as an extension of British civilization, both progressive and distinct from the United States. In the cause of promoting this happy image, the governing élite ignored, stifled, or libelled internal dissent. On the other side were those now tentatively fashioning a reform challenge. Believing that current constitutional arrangements hindered progress and fostered disaffection, reformers of several stripes determined to chronicle their grievances, recommend changes, and at the same time expose the élite's patriotism for what in their opinion it was, self-serving partisanship. Because this contest between loyal patriotism and reform was at base political, the strength of the contending parties ultimately decided the influence of their respective historians. In the wake of the War of 1812, reform began at a distinct disadvantage.

It was fitting that both the personality and the work of Upper Canada's first significant historian, Robert Fleming Gourlay (1778–1863), exemplified the contradictions and tensions of colonial society in Upper Canada. Born at Craigrothie, Fifeshire, Scotland, Gourlay was the son of a substantial farmer and took a gentleman's education at St Andrews and

10 Bowsfield, 'Upper Canada in the 1820's,' 107–18; Robert L. Fraser, 'Like Eden in Her Summer Dress: Gentry, Economy, and Society: Upper Canada, 1812–1840' (PH D Diss., University of Toronto 1979) 15–31
11 Ibid., 31

the University of Edinburgh. He became greatly interested in 'scientific' approaches to agricultural improvement and in 1799 undertook a study of farm labourers in two English shires for Arthur Young, then secretary of the Board of Agriculture. Gourlay put his improving methods to the test as manager of his father's estate from 1800 to 1809, and from 1809 to 1817 at Deptford Farm, Wiltshire, as tenant to Edward Adolphus Seymour, eleventh duke of Somerset.[12] Unfortunately this superficial sketch of personal determination and application was shaded by physical illness and mental disequilibrium, which manifested themselves in the form of a neurotic and headstrong temper, 'wilfully blind' to its own flaws and the good sense of others. Gourlay's life can easily be plotted by a succession of personal disputes, commencing in an argument with Arthur Young, and continuing in quarrels with Thomas Erskine, ninth earl of Kellie, Lord Somerset, and ultimately with his own father. By 1817 Gourlay had produced a large number of intemperate pamphlets and tracts, fought consequent lawsuits, and arrived on the brink of financial ruin.[13]

Gourlay was always able to give substance to his quarrels, for he had developed theories of social organization and reform that, if not pressed too hard, maintained a degree of coherence. A radical by temperament, and an agrarian radical by conviction, he believed that widespread – indeed universal – private ownership of land was the basis of healthy moral, economic, and political relationships. He regarded the country-side less as the natural home of a squirearchy than as a crucible in which to forge a rough equality among yeomen farmers. Consequently he undertook to fight the banishment of tenants and small farmers caused by the contemporary trend toward enclosure and tacitly encouraged by the

12 The personal details of Robert Gourlay's life are scattered throughout his written works, but see especially his *Statistical Account of Upper Canada, Compiled with a View to a Grand System of Emigration*, 2 vols (London 1822) vol. 1, 458–66, 552–8, 566–83; vol. 2, i–xviii, 421–5, 452–704; *General Introduction to Statistical Account of Upper Canada, Compiled with a View to a Grand System of Emigration, in Connexion with a Reform of the Poor Laws* (London 1822); *The Banished Briton and Neptunian: Being a Record of the Life, Writings, Principles and Projects of Robert Gourlay, Esquire* (Boston 1843). These details have been drawn together in Lois Darroch Milani, *Robert Gourlay, Gadfly: The Biography of Robert (Fleming) Gourlay, 1778–1863, Forerunner of the Rebellion in Upper Canada, 1837* ([Thornhill, Ont., 1971]); and with more economy and insight in S.F. Wise, 'Robert Fleming Gourlay,' *DCB*, vol. 9 (Toronto 1976) 330–6.

13 William Renwick Riddell, 'Robert (Fleming) Gourlay,' Ontario Historical Society, *Papers and Records* 14 (1916): 5–13; S.R. Mealing, Introduction to Robert Gourlay, *Statistical Account of Upper Canada* (1822), abridged (Toronto 1974) 1–3

slavish consolation of the Poor Laws.[14] It was crusades of this kind that most often provided the proximate cause of his various disputes, his righteous indignation over a catalogue of human miseries inevitably chafing at obstruction, delay, and moderation.

Gourlay might have been more successful in spite of his character had his solutions been specific, practical, and consistent. In his search for perfectibility he could never quite make up his mind whether the nature of man or the nature of society was the source of vice. An ambiguous radical, he was uncertain as to means, now calling on government investigation and intervention, now on public mobilization and pressure. His target of the moment was usually determined by the avenue of most resistance. The one constant in his thought was land, and if for legal, political, or geographical reasons the poor of Britain could not find sufficient in their islands, then they must look elsewhere, and someone must look for them. Fortuitously, Gourlay had by 1817 pressing personal reasons for looking abroad, and his gaze was attracted by 866 acres his wife had inherited in Dereham Township, Upper Canada, close by her cousins Thomas Clark and William Dickson.[15] It must be constantly borne in mind that Gourlay's career in Upper Canada was, as Gerald Bloch warns, 'a logical extension of his activities in Britain' and was based upon 'a conceptual framework largely developed before he left for Upper Canada.'[16]

When Gourlay arrived in Upper Canada in June 1817, he had two objectives: the first was to observe and gather information relevant to the promotion of emigration and the production of his planned *Statistical Account of Upper Canada*; the second was to obtain for himself – perhaps in imitation of Clark and Dickson – a large grant of land, the populating of which he could personally oversee and control.[17] Thus the recovery of his personal fortune was nicely linked to the rehabilitation of the landless poor of Britain; and the thrust of his program was not unlike that of many other land agents. What Gourlay hoped would lift his description of Upper Canada out of the general run of topographical accounts was the superiority of his method.

14 Gourlay, *General Introduction*, lxxxiii–clxxxii; Gerald Bloch, 'Robert Gourlay's Vision of Agrarian Reform,' in Donald H. Akenson, ed., *Canadian Papers in Rural History*, vol. 3 (Gananoque, Ont., 1982) 110–28
15 Gourlay, *General Introduction*, clxxxiii; *Statistical Account*, vol. 2, 494–5; Bruce G. Wilson, *The Enterprises of Robert Hamilton: A Study of Wealth and Influence in Early Upper Canada, 1776–1812* (Ottawa 1983) 60–4
16 Bloch, 'Robert Gourlay's Vision,' 113
17 Gourlay, *General Introduction*, cccxv–cccxvi

Stanley Mealing drew attention to Gourlay's intellectual background in Scotland, where 'a flourishing tradition of practical scholarship,' of statistical reports and compilations, provided the basis for the political economy of the likes of Adam Smith. Sir John Sinclair's massive *Statistical Account of Scotland* was the most famous of these works, and it was compiled from the responses of parish ministers to a standardized questionnaire.[18] Gourlay proposed to apply this method – asking questions on the nature of the land, its resources, and man's improvements – to the New World and the practical problems of promoting emigration. He drew up a list of thirty-one questions during his voyage across the Atlantic, submitted them to the administrator of Upper Canada, Samuel Smith, and, after receiving Smith's sanction, published them on 30 October 1817 in the official newspaper, the *Upper Canada Gazette*, in the form of an address to the landowners of the province.[19] As first proposed, Gourlay's project was to be a comprehensive and objective quasi-governmental survey, one he had every intention of placing before the imperial authorities in London.[20]

Gourlay's method was not, however, as uncontroversial as it may first have appeared to Administrator Smith. The type of statistical account developed in Scotland was premised on the assumption 'that the systematic assemblage of information was of practical use, especially for the framing of government policy.'[21] Sinclair's work, for instance, contributed to a larger campaign in favour of enclosure. The Scottish statistical account lacked the inhibitions of such patriotic chorographies as T.C. Haliburton's *Historical and Statistical Account of Nova-Scotia*. Despite the similarity of their titles, Gourlay's and Haliburton's accounts issued from different traditions: the one political and economic, the other patriotic and geographic. A colonial patriot is unlikely to ask his informants, as Sir John Sinclair did, for the 'Means by which their situation could be meliorated' – at least not unless the responses were to be edited or censored. Yet this is precisely what Gourlay asked in his

18 Mealing, Introduction to Gourlay, *Statistical Account* (1974) 8–10; A. Skinner, 'Economics and History – The Scottish Enlightenment,' *Scottish Journal of Political Economy* 21 (1965): 1–22; Sir John Sinclair, *The Statistical Account of Scotland*, 21 vols (Edinburgh 1791–9)
19 Gourlay, *General Introduction*, clxxxv–cxcvi; *Statistical Accountl*, vol. 1, 70–4; vol. 2, cxxvi–cxxix
20 Gourlay, *Statistical Account* vol. 2, 459–61n; E.A. Cruikshank, 'The Government of Upper Canada and Robert Gourlay,' Ontario Historical Society, *Papers and Records* 23 (1926): 75–6
21 Mealing, Introduction to Gourlay, *Statistical Account* (1974) 8

thirty-first question: 'What, in your opinion, retards the improvement of your township in particular, or the province in general; and what would most contribute to the same?'[22] Furthermore, Gourlay did not attempt to place himself in a position to control the replies he received, for, not content to rely on the credibility of private communications from parish ministers or individual members of the gentry, he sought 'the authority of many,' and proposed that public meetings be held in every township to draft accurate and candid replies to his questionnaire.[23]

John Strachan, then Anglican rector of York and godfather to the provincial oligarchy, immediately saw the 'incendiary' potential of Gourlay's proposal and the means by which it was to be carried out. That very spring Lieutenant-Governor Francis Gore had been forced to prorogue the assembly when it threatened to pass resolutions favouring admission of American settlers and the sale of Crown and clergy reserves. These issues, and the administration's handling of them, were likely to come up at any public meeting held to answer Gourlay's interrogatory. Indeed, Gourlay's thirty-first question raised suspicions of his true motive and loyalty. The calling of extra-constitutional public meetings brought prevailing doctrines of virtual representation into question and evoked memories of similar meetings prior to the American and French revolutions, the rebellion in Ireland, and contemporary popular disturbances in England (shortly to culminate in the incident at Peterloo).[24] One did not have to be malevolent to draw these parallels, although there was certainly enough malevolence among the members of the governing élite toward agitators in any case. As the township meetings went forward through November and December, they smacked less of the methods of Sir John Sinclair than of the English militants Major John Cartwright, Henry Hunt, and Thomas Spence.

Gourlay might have survived Strachan's suspicions had he not acted in a way that seemed to confirm them. The first replies to the questionnaire had yet to arrive before Gourlay perceived political wrongs crying out to be righted. Under the influence of Clark and Dickson, who had a personal interest in attracting settlers to their lands on the Niagara frontier, in early

22 Gourlay, *Statistical Account*, vol. 1, 274
23 Gourlay, *General Introduction*, clxxxv–cxcvi
24 John Strachan to John Harvey, 22 June 1818, in *John Strachan: Documents and Opinions*, ed. J.L.H. Henderson (Toronto 1969) 66–8; [John Strachan,] *A Visit to the Province of Upper Canada in 1819*, by James Strachan (Aberdeen, Scotland, 1820) 186–92; T.M. Parssinen, 'Association, Convention and Anti-Parliament in British Radical Politics, 1771–1848,' *English Historical Review* 88 (1973): 504–17; cf, Bowsfield, 'Upper Canada in the 1820's,' 6–7, 143–5

November Gourlay began to advocate the lifting of restrictions on the entry of Americans. Using the pages of the *Niagara Spectator*, he went on to question the legal authority of the original exclusion and the motives of government officials – charges he escalated into a general conspiracy of oligarchic 'influences.' Deliberately ignoring the real worries officials had concerning American domination, Gourlay gave every appearance of fashioning a volatile alliance between certain land speculators and expatriate Americans already resident in Upper Canada. By the time his request for a grant of land was rejected in January 1818, Gourlay had already gone into full political opposition.[25] From this moment, although collection of information went on, Gourlay's plans for a statistical account became lost in his own personal campaign against the provincial élite.

Gourlay's subsequent career in Upper Canada may be briefly summarized. His second and third addresses to the landowners of Upper Canada, which appeared in February and April respectively, confirmed the political turn in his aims, now calling for a new series of township and district meetings, which were to culminate in a 'provincial convention.' His violence of address and the government reaction intensified in tandem. This conflict, which Gourlay could not hope to win, was one that could only damage the reputation of the colony: his allies, sensing this, deserted him. Clark and Dickson made their peace with the government and now actively sought Gourlay's prosecution.[26] Twice acquitted of libel, Gourlay was charged under the Sedition Act, denied bail, brought to trial after eight months in jail, and banished from the province in August 1819.[27] Upon his return to England, Gourlay hoped to renew the campaign for his own vindication and for the rights of Upper Canadians, only to find that the provincial assembly had denounced his recent actions. Gourlay washed his hands of a people unwilling to accept his plans for them: 'Now that silliness has prevailed, I must bid my political friends adieu, and think only of John Bull.'[28]

The publication in 1822 of Gourlay's two-volume *Statistical Account*, along with a third volume issued as a *General Introduction*, cannot be

25 Gourlay, *Statistical Account*, vol. 2, 421–4, 467–71, 556–64, cii–civ, cxxvi–cxxix; Wilson, *Enterprises of Robert Hamilton*, 102–3
26 Gourlay, *Statistical Account*, vol. 2, 471–83, 554–6, 581–7; Wilson, *Enterprises of Robert Hamilton*, 173–4
27 Gourlay's own version of these events is summarized in the *General Introduction*, v–xlvii. Both Cruikshank and Riddell provide heavily documented accounts of the court cases and the issues involved. S.F. Wise offers the best distillation of these by now overworked events.
28 Gourlay, *Statistical Account*, vol. 2, 630

separated from his tangled personal history in the province. What began as an officially sanctioned topographical description by an aspiring land agent ended as an outsider's violent political tract advocating 'radical change' in the provincial government. This shift in purpose made for a curious work, exhibiting the larger tension in Upper Canada between loyal patriotism and reform. Furthermore, the three volumes were composed while Gourlay was by his own admission 'in a state of distraction.'[29] Their consequent 'shrillness, irrelevancies, and disorder' are an obstacle the reader must overcome,[30] and it must be noted that the following outline of Gourlay's *General Introduction* and *Statistical Account* imposes an order only loosely obeyed in the works themselves.

The first volume of the *Statistical Account* generally represented Gourlay as loyal patriot and consisted of two parts: 'The Sketches of Upper Canada written by an Inhabitant' (1–268), and the text of the township reports as summarized by Gourlay (269–625). The former have been identified as the work of Barnabas Bidwell (1763–1833), an expatriate American and radical-reform politician. They were first written in 1811, revised in 1816, and had never before been printed.[31] Once again, in a short narrative history, the period of French rule was represented as 'extensive, but thin,' the result of an exploitive fur economy and aggressive military design. The arrival of the Loyalists was said to have ushered in a new era of solid agricultural settlement, secured by the establishment in 1791 of judicial and political forms in the 'epitome of the English government.'[32] The narrative was not continued; the battle sites of the War of 1812 were handled as part of the topography; no reference was made to subsequent political disputes. This being the case, the bulk of the 'Sketches' were thematic descriptions of the land, its potential, and the advances man had made since 1784. In the process of converting a wilderness into fruitful fields a new people was created, the 'predominant national character' of which was 'Anglo-American.' This was a hardy, sober, and industrious people, who produced 'no effervescence, personal or political.'[33] Bidwell concluded: 'Should population

29 Gourlay to Joseph Hume, 1 Apr. 1823, quoted in Riddell, 'Robert (Fleming) Gourlay,' 72

30 Wise, 'Robert Fleming Gourlay,' 335

31 Gourlay, *General Introduction*, clxxxv–clxxxvi; Mealing, introduction to Gourlay, *Statistical Account* (1974) 13; Graeme H. Patterson, 'Studies in Elections and Public Opinion in Upper Canada' (PH D Diss., University of Toronto 1969) 378n, and 'Barnabas Bidwell,' *DCB*, vol. 6 (Toronto 1987) 54–9

32 Gourlay, *Statistical Account*, vol. 1, 1–14, 204

33 Ibid., 247–56

continue to advance with its usual ratio of increase, the shores of these lakes all around, as well on the side of the United States, as that of Canada, will in a few years be an extensive range of villages and cultivated fields.'[34]

The text of the township reports did not, for the most part, challenge the optimistic picture drawn in the 'Sketches.' Contemporary anxiety over question thirty-one, reinforced by the preoccupation of modern historians, distorted the overall tenor of the reports. The first thirty questions did, after all, provide local residents with the opportunity to promote the resources of their township; and the second question, which asked the 'Date of the first settlement of your township, number of people and inhabited houses?' permitted settlers to measure their own historical progress. In light of the fact that in the fifty-seven township reports received the evil of absentee ownership was mentioned only twenty-four times, Crown and clergy reserves nineteen, want of people and capital fourteen, and the 'shutting out Americans' only five, answers to the thirty-first question did not undermine the optimism already expressed.[35] Responses were usually respectful, even when critical. Ancaster was the only township to send in what could be called an intemperate political reply, explicitly attacking as it did the 'gift and patronage' vested in the hands of the administrator and the executive council.[36]

It had been Gourlay's intention to present the evidence of the 'Sketches' and township reports in an unvarnished, convincing manner, without comment. In the event, his own developing political animosities, so clearly at odds with the optimistic tone of the reports he was receiving, compelled him to puncture the very credibility he had initially sought to establish. The first blow came in a footnote to the 'Sketches':

Here is the important question. How comes it that Upper Canada, with all these benefits, and whose settlement began ten years before that of the country running parallel with it, is now ten years behind that country in improvement, and its wild land selling in the market at a third of the price which similar lands fetch in the United States?[37]

Gourlay accused Bidwell of being too anxious to 'extol Upper Canada.' Indeed, 'from reading the "Sketches of Upper Canada," no one would suppose that any thing like discontent had ever existed among the

34 Ibid., 137
35 Ibid., 623–5
36 Ibid., 388–93
37 Ibid., 223n

people.'[38] The township reports gave the lie to such impressions, but not in a way that fully satisfied Gourlay. They too were frustratingly discreet. In particular, Gourlay could not understand why the exclusion of Americans did not figure more prominently among noted grievances. It did not occur to him either that colonists might not find this an important issue, or that some of them might actually share the oligarchy's fears of the United States. The only way he could account for this omission was to assume that the reports had been inhibited by fear of official retaliation.[39] This was the flaw in the township reports, the reason why one could not trust those that had been written, and, even more to the point, why so many had not been written at all.

The response to Gourlay's questionnaire had been gratifying in the districts of London, Western, Gore, and Niagara, but not in those districts lying to the east of the head of Lake Ontario. From the almost sixty surveyed townships of the Home district, for instance, he had received no replies at all.[40] Gourlay blamed the deficiency on 'the opposition of a monstrous little fool of a parson,' John Strachan. Actuated by his fear of losing control over the clergy reserves, Strachan was said to have mobilized his family of past students and present parishioners within the governing élite in an effort to frustrate Gourlay's design. The oligarchy silenced some individuals, inhibited others, but would not, Gourlay vowed, intimidate him. No scheme of emigration could work or even be promoted until this conspiracy was removed. This was the nub of the matter. As Gourlay self-righteously declared: 'It can never be right to hide weaknesses, if by exposure the cause can be removed.'[41] Strachan disagreed, as in time would many of Gourlay's allies.

Gourlay's accusations of conspiracy and corruption were not, then, based upon the township reports themselves; rather they provided a point of departure for his own history of affairs in Upper Canada.[42] The second, unexpurgated history was outlined in volume two of the *Statistical Account* and began in the usual documentary fashion, with excerpts from the British parliamentary debates on the Constitutional Act of 1791 (1–109), the *Travels* of François-Alexandre-Frédéric de La Roche-

38 Ibid., vol. 2, 313–16
39 Ibid., 424–6
40 Mealing, Introduction to Gourlay, *Statistical Account* (1974) 10–11
41 Gourlay, *Statistical Account*, vol. 1, 458–66, 552–70
42 Mealing, Introduction to Gourlay, *Statistical Account* (1974) 11

foucauld, Duc de La Rochefoucauld-Liancourt (127–202),[43] and summaries of Upper Canadian statutes to 1817 (203–91). Having placed this information before the reader 'without prejudice or bias,' Gourlay embarked on a 'Review' or gloss (292–538) in order to 'derive knowledge for decision and future transaction.'[44] This review was Gourlay's history of Upper Canada, and it exhibited him at his most disorderly and contradictory. It may be roughly summarized as follows:

In October 1792 Lieutenant-Governor John Graves Simcoe closed the first session of the Assembly of Upper Canada claiming that the province's constitution was the '*very image and transcript of that of Great Britain*.'[45] It was Gourlay's position that the constitution of Upper Canada was not, could not be, fashioned after that of the mother country. The 'circumstances' of time and place that had produced the British constitution could not be duplicated in Upper Canada, and it was a mistake to think that they could. Upper Canadian society was not identical to that of Great Britain. This was not necessarily a handicap, as the unreformed constitution, still 'suspended by the cobwebs of antiquity' and wedded to outdated notions of prerogative, was clearly in need of improvement. Upper Canadians in their American setting had an opportunity to become a new people, return to 'first principles,' and build a constitution based upon the sacred 'rights of man.'[46]

Unfortunately, in the process of transferring the British constitution to Upper Canada, basic rights of Englishmen were, if anything, further restricted. Responsible ministers in London, either because they were malevolent or because they were '*palpably ignorant of existing circumstances*,' had allowed control over Crown and wilderness lands to devolve upon the lieutenant-governor and his council. In Simcoe's honest and capable hands Upper Canada was safe from executive excesses. The fear was, as Liancourt had written, that subsequent men of mediocre powers would be

43 François-Alexandre-Frédéric de La Rochefoucauld, Duc de La Rochefoucauld-Liancourt (1747–1827), *Voyage dans les États-Unis d'Amérique, fait en 1795, 1796, et 1797,* 8 vols (Paris [1799]) translated by Henry Neuman as *Travels through the United States of North America, the Country of the Iroquois, and Upper Canada, in the Years 1795, 1796, and 1797; With an Authentic Account of Lower Canada,* 2 vols (London 1799); T.S. Webster, 'François-Alexandre-Frédéric de La Rochefoucauld, Duc de La Rochefoucauld-Liancourt, Duc d'Estissac,' *DCB* vol. 6, 388–9
44 Gourlay, *Statistical Account*, vol. 2, 292
45 Quoted in ibid., 112
46 Ibid., 294–5, 307–9

unable to resist temptation.[47] Once Simcoe was gone, Liancourt was proved correct, and a series of lieutenant-governors '*converted the trust reposed in them to purposes of selfishness*.' Land was the enticement by which governors corrupted their councillors (or vice versa – Gourlay was never entirely clear), and, even worse, suborned assemblymen. Imperial ministers initially may have been at fault, but ultimately 'the people must bear reproach' for their electoral decisions. 'I shall say the best I can for them,' wrote Gourlay, 'simplicity abounds in Canada.'[48]

In order to document the growth of oligarchy in Upper Canada, Gourlay gave a long extract from Jackson's *View of the Political Situation in ... Upper Canada* (318–27) – thereby symbolically marking his shift from the tradition of loyal patriotism to that of reform. If Jackson's appeal in 1809 for an imperial inquiry into provincial affairs had been heeded, it was Gourlay's belief that current problems would have been avoided, as might the War of 1812 itself – the latter being a result of the Americans' mistaking grievance for disloyalty.[49] The valiant militia proved the Americans deluded and the aspersions of the oligarchy mischievous. Incredibly, the British government, having seen clear evidence of the individual colonist's loyalty, acted now as if his disloyalty were proved. Against all common sense, and in defiance of the constitution, Lieutenant-Governor Gore shut off the influx of American settlers and prorogued an outraged assembly. As for the British government, it often acted as if the colony's leave-taking was only a matter of time. This could easily become a self-fulfilling prophecy.[50] Such was Gourlay's history of Upper Canada.

Having displayed past errors, Gourlay was in some confusion as to the conclusions to be drawn and remedies taken. He put forth a variety of palliatives: changes in personnel and of policy in the granting of land, a new system of taxation, and the abolition of almost all Upper Canadian statute law, among others.[51] In the end he always came back to the recommendation of his second and third addresses, calling on the landowners of Upper Canada to petition the Prince Regent, the British Parliament, and the lieutenant-governor for an inquiry into provincial affairs. This only served to highlight the ambiguous view Gourlay had of the British constitution and government. Was the source of Upper

47 Ibid., vol. 1, 575–6; vol. 2, 139–40
48 Ibid., vol. 1, 575; vol. 2, 296–9
49 Ibid., vol. 2, 328–34
50 Ibid., vol. 1, 571–7, 614–15; vol. 2, 416–18
51 Ibid., vol. 2, 305–6, 339, 404

Canada's ills now to become the source of its salvation? Was it 'the constitution in danger' or 'the dangerous constitution?'

Gourlay always denied he had any seditious or revolutionary intent, and admittedly he never explicitly did more than call upon the public to petition their government. On the other hand, he did hold what were for the time radical views on the rights of man and the constitutional role of public pressure. And what if the public were ignored? 'The most important and consolatory conclusion to be drawn from what has happened is this, that however arbitrary power may, for a time, have sway, it is by its acts, hastening to an end, especially in Canada.' This implied threat to the established order was rendered more ominous by Gourlay's sanctioning as necessary evils the excesses of the French Revolution. An even more appropriate example for Upper Canadian emulation was, in Gourlay's opinion, the American Revolution, which had created a state 'where things are as they should be.' It was the Americans who enjoyed a constitution founded on the rights of man rather than upon 'darkness and superstition'; it was to this nation that William Pitt should have looked for precedent when framing the constitution of Canada; and it was the 'enlightened' spirit of the new world that would eventually compel Upper Canadian yeomen to rise above their '*simplicity*' and rebuild the British constitution from within.[52] In the context of the times, Gourlay's radicalism and pro-American sentiment were untenable as public beliefs in Upper Canada.

When Gourlay returned to Great Britain, he continued to work for the rights of Upper Canadians and the promotion of their colony, relying on the support of his friends in the provincial assembly. Then in 1820 an election was held that saw the tenor of the assembly change against him; embittered, he for the third time redefined the direction of his work and his attitude toward Upper Canadian history.[53] Using the *General Introduction*, Gourlay set out to defend himself and prove to British legislators that, in spite of the Upper Canadians, Upper Canada could still play a vital, profitable role in the British interest if it accepted the nation's labouring poor. The imperial government was once more to be the engine of change; gone was Gourlay's faith in the Upper Canadian public, the enlightened yeomanry, and the influence of the environment. It was now his opinion that the Upper Canadians had 'degenerated from the date of

52 Gourlay, *General Introduction*, vi–vii, xlvii; *Statistical Account*, vol. 2, 300–9
53 Gourlay, *Statistical Account*, vol. 2, 628–32

their first settlement,' 'debased' by a corrupt provincial government and 'polluted by a mixture of bad fellows from all quarters.'[54] Far from being a history of progress, the story of Upper Canada was one of decline.

The precipitous alienation of Robert Gourlay from Upper Canadian society was in large part due to his being a British imperial, rather than an Upper Canadian, reformer.[55] He could not understand, actually could not tolerate, Upper Canadian sensitivity to criticism, especially to derogatory comparisons with the United States. Even more germane to his banishment was his failure to appreciate just how deeply animosities arising from the War of 1812 ran and how crucial the issue of loyalty had become to people in *and* outside the ranks of officialdom. Insensible to the pride and fears of Upper Canadians, Gourlay provided his enemies with the levers necessary to budge the basis of his initial support. An increasing number of addresses to Lieutenant-Governor Sir Peregrine Maitland and letters to the editors of Upper Canadian newspapers castigated Gourlay for tarnishing the image of loyal respectability so recently won in the war.[56] As early as October 1818 the people's representatives in the assembly as a body denounced 'the systematic attempts that have been made to excite discontent and organize sedition in this happy Colony,' and by thirteen to one voted to suppress the continuance of the township meetings organized by Gourlay.[57] In the end Gourlay had offended against both the colonists' code of loyalty and the patriotic conceit of their 'happy state.'

That said, Gourlay did manage to display in his *Statistical Account* Upper Canada's two nascent historical traditions. The first was that of loyal patriotism: a tradition that emphasized Upper Canada's role as an overseas extension of British civilization and tended to ignore or deny the inevitable dislocations imposed by distance and a new environment. The second was that of reform: a tradition built upon the realities of the local situation but weakened by signs of latent Americanism, charges of disloyalty, and the notion that Upper Canadians had departed radically from the norms of British constitutional propriety. Significantly, both traditions believed that Upper Canada was potentially an excellent environment in which to foster the virtues of the industrious yeoman; they simply had different preconceptions of the social and political role

54 Gourlay, *General Introduction*, xlviii, cccxi
55 Wise, 'Robert Fleming Gourlay,' 335
56 Errington, *The Lion, the Eagle, and Upper Canada*, 101–11; Bowsfield, 'Upper Canada in the 1820's,' 122–7
57 Cruikshank, 'Government of Upper Canada,' 92

the yeoman would fill. In time, as the British connection weakened and the American threat was isolated from proposals for local reform, there arose the possibility of building a common self-sufficient Upper Canadian patriotism. Gourlay did not advance this cause; he did not involve the two traditions in a dialectical interplay, much less in a reconciliation; given the times, however, it is doubtful he could have done so, even had he wanted to.

In the years following Gourlay's departure, the political environment in Upper Canada slowly changed. Memories of the War of 1812 faded and with them the poignancy of the loyalist issue. Settlers, once established, were less defensive, more self-confident, and increasingly articulate. The presumption that power could only be trusted to the hands of a few became, depending on one's taste, irritating or intolerable. By the end of the 1820s many felt comfortable saying what Gourlay earlier had been harassed for saying. Grievances of various sorts were aired, a variety of remedies proposed, and pent-up desire for reform released. As the power of reform rose, so did the respectability of reform historiography. Indeed, history was especially important to politicians seeking change. Locked out of executive and administrative positions and dependent on the assembly and public approval for political power, they were particularly innovative in restructuring popular perceptions of Upper Canadian political divisions and historical precedents. Reform politicians inadvertently became the most influential of historians.

The reformers' most important invention in this regard was the term 'Family Compact,' a general epithet that built on particular regional animosities against the provincial oligarchy and the local cliques of which it was in large measure composed.[58] In the hands of William Lyon Mackenzie (1795–1861), the arch-propagandist of the forces of radical reform, the general sentiment represented by the term 'Family Compact' came to mean not merely a collectivity of self-interested individuals whose rule was subversive of the rights of free-born Englishmen and dependent on monarchical prerogative, but also a party built into the social and economic structure of the province. To quote Mackenzie:

The family compact surround the Lieutenant-Governor, and mould him like wax, to their will; they fill every office with their relatives, dependents and partisans; by them justices of the peace are made and unmade; they have

58 Patterson, 'Elections and Public Opinion,' 498–516; see also his, 'An Enduring Canadian Myth: Responsible Government and the Family Compact,' *JCS* 12 (1977): 3–16

increased the number of the Legislative Council by recommending, through the Governor, half a dozen of nobodies and a few placemen, pensioners and individuals of well-known narrow and bigoted principles; the whole of the revenues of Upper Canada are in reality at their mercy; they are the paymasters, receivers, auditors, King, Lords, and Commons![59]

This accusation threw members of the oligarchy on the defensive; it questioned their conceit as the only true defenders of constitutional monarchy and the British connection; and it indirectly lessened the power of their retaliatory allegations of republicanism and sedition. Finally, in so far as it gave a wide variety of disaffected individuals a sense of joint outrage, it also united them in the face of a common foe.

The concept of the Family Compact was as historiographically dangerous as it was politically persuasive. By offsetting the oligarchy's indiscriminate charges of republicanism with their own absorbent definition of the Compact, advocates of reform polarized conceptions of Upper Canadian politics. The neat division between oligarchs and reformers (or, depending on one's point of view, between Loyalists and republicans) obscured such alternative sources of tension as regionalism, ethnicity, and religion. Furthermore, in their search for legitimacy opposition politicians annexed the past, placed all individuals and events into the mould of current categories, and made necessity of contingency, principle of expediency, and order of confusion. In the process they turned Upper Canadian history into a narrative of constitutional conflict rather than a description of material progress. The central figures in this conflict were Thorpe, Jackson, Willcocks, Weekes, and Gourlay, who, as alleged victims of Compact malevolence, formed a martyrology to the cause of reform into which Mackenzie insinuated himself as the most recent victim.[60] The more purpose history was credited with and the more meaningful it became, the more critical it was for reformers to ensure acceptance of their interpretation.

The nascent Reform party drew strength, then, from local events, each

59 William Lyon Mackenzie, *Sketches of Canada and the United States* (London 1833) 409. Patterson calls this oft-quoted passage the 'classic' definition of the Family Compact, 'Elections and Public Opinion,' 500.

60 Charles Lindsey, *The Life and Times of Wm. Lyon Mackenzie. With an Account of the Canadian Rebellion of 1837, and the Subsequent Frontier Disturbances, Chiefly from Unpublished Documents,* 2 vols (Toronto 1862) vol. 1, 238–9; Frederick H. Armstrong and Ronald J. Stagg, 'William Lyon Mackenzie,' *DCB,* vol. 9, 498

example of government unscrupulousness adding to a store of Compact outrages. According to Graeme Patterson this achievement ensured that 'strong positive value would be assigned to whatever sets of ideas were thereafter placed in opposition to notions of "compact government."'[61] If those advocating reform failed to take full advantage of their situation, it was largely because of their inability to turn common animosities into a collective agreement on specific remedies. Their reforms were too various and too often tainted by an American or republican provenance and thereby played directly to the strength of the governing élite and reinforced public concern over the incompatibility of loyalty and opposition.[62] Hidden among the welter of reform proposals there was, however, one suggestion that was shortly to achieve pre-eminence, namely, Robert Baldwin's call for the introduction of 'responsible government.'

In the tradition of the Anglo-Irish Whigs from whom he was directly descended, Robert Baldwin (1804–58) was a thorough believer in Britain's post-1688 constitutional monarchy, which preserved the Crown yet placed it under the lawful supremacy of Parliament.[63] In contrast to Mackenzie and many other reformers, Baldwin turned away from such American and republican remedies as an elective upper chamber or a written constitution. Instead he pinned his hopes on the idea of making the executive council responsible to the people's elected representatives after the fashion of the British cabinet. He asked for not a change in the British constitution, but the British constitution. It was this proposal that he put to Secretary of State for the Colonies Charles Grant, first Baron Glenelg, in a letter of 13 July 1836. In this letter Baldwin explained that the great principle for which Upper Canadian reformers were contending

consists of nothing more than having the provincial Government as far as regards the internal affairs of the Province, conducted by the Lieutenant-Governor (as Representative of the paramount Authority of the Mother-Country) with the advice and assistance of the Executive Council, acting as a

61 Patterson, 'Enduring Canadian Myth,' 10
62 G.M. Craig, 'The American Impact on the Upper Canadian Reform Movement before 1837,' *CHR* 29 (1948): 351–2; Errington, *The Lion, the Eagle, and Upper Canada*, 128
63 J.M.S. Careless, 'Robert Baldwin,' in J.M.S. Careless, ed., *The Pre-Confederation Premiers: Ontario Government Leaders, 1841–1867* (Toronto 1980) 96–7; Graeme Patterson, 'Whiggery, Nationality, and the Upper Canadian Reform Tradition,' *CHR* 56 (1975): 29–30; Michael S. Cross and Robert Lochiel Fraser, 'Robert Baldwin,' *DCB*, vol. 8 (Toronto 1985) 45–59

Provincial Cabinet, and composed of Men possessed of the public confidence, whose opinions and policy would be in harmony with the opinions and policy of the Representatives of the People.[64]

Baldwin did not back away from the notion of limiting the power of the lieutenant-governor (including that person's control over patronage), of cabinet solidarity, or of placing control over the internal affairs of the province in the hands of 'the most powerful Party in Parliament.' This was, he claimed, 'a remedy amounting merely to the application of an English principle to the [Upper Canadian] constitution as it stands.'[65]

Baldwin's formulation of responsible government was to become as historiographically influential as Mackenzie's definition of the Family Compact, and in many ways even more misleading. Baldwin's letter to Lord Glenelg conveyed the distinct impression that advocates of reform were united by the principle of responsible government, and also that responsible government – rather than a host of parochial matters – had been the point at issue between reformers and the Family Compact since at least 1820. In a brief historical note, Baldwin told Glenelg that responsible government was 'introduced into the address in reply to the speech from the throne' in 1828 or 1829, that it was the subject of an appeal by the assembly to London in 1835, and that it was the issue upon which reformers had clashed with Lieutenant-Governor Sir Francis Bond Head in the election of 1836. In none of these assertions was Baldwin factually correct.[66]

Despite its inaccuracies, Baldwin's interpretation of responsible government and his reading of Upper Canadian history had the advantage of bridging the gulf between reform and patriotism. He emphasized that the 'Yeomanry of Upper Canada' were not Americanized radicals but British citizens overseas, devoted to the constitutional monarchy and anxious to see the full rights and benefits of that system flourish in their province. He thought republicanism unnatural and unnecessary and the resort only of those driven to it in frustration by the corrupt and unconstitutional oligarchy. It was the common people of Upper Canada, not the members of the Family Compact, who were truly

64 Robert Baldwin to Lord Glenelg, 13 July 1836, NA, *Report, 1923* (Ottawa 1924) 332
65 Ibid., 331–5; cf, Patterson, 'Enduring Canadian Myth,' 10–13
66 Baldwin to Lord Glenelg, 336; [Chester New,] *Lord Durham's Mission to Canada. An Abridgement of 'Lord Durham: A Biography of John George Lambton, First Earl of Durham,' by Chester New* (1929), ed. H.W. McCready (Toronto 1963) 226

loyal to the British constitution and the British connection.[67] In short,
Baldwin's remedy claimed the title of patriot for the reform cause.

On the other side of the political divide, members of the governing élite
were at a historiographical disadvantage. They regarded loyalty to Great
Britain and the settlement of 1791 as final, denied the primacy of
constitutional conflict as the organizing principle of Upper Canadian
history, and questioned the motives of those who persisted in criticizing
the colony's 'happy state.' Real patriots should defend the colony, not
write narratives of political struggle. The fact that the oligarchs drew their
legitimacy from the imperial government, rather than from local events,
only provided a further disincentive to the development of a conservative
narrative of Upper Canadian history. Consequently, the actions of the
Loyalists in the American Revolution and the War of 1812, instead of
forming the basis for a historiography, were touchstones obviating the
need for one.[68] While the oligarchy's Loyalist message could still be
devastatingly effective in the tactical realm of contemporary politics, it did
suffer from at least two long-term strategic weaknesses: first, it denied the
existence of local grievances and the need for their amelioration; second,
it was blind to changing British perceptions of the role of the colonies in
the empire. According to Robert Fraser, it was the latter − the gentry's
faith in the imperial tie − that held the greatest potential for disruption: 'It
was the foundation of their political and economic beliefs which could not
be sustained if the imperial relationship was severed.'[69]

The Rebellion of 1837 released the political deadlock upon which
historiographical debate hinged. Initially the short outbreak of violence
disgraced advocates of reform, for it tarred all with the brush of sedition
in seeming fulfilment of the oligarchy's predictions. In the longer term
the exodus of those who took part in the rebellion made it easier to
distinguish between moderate and radical reformers. By fleeing the
country, Mackenzie and his allies took themselves off the spectrum of
legitimate political debate shared by those who stayed behind (much as
the Loyalists themselves had done when they left the United States in
1783). From presses in New York, Philadelphia, Cleveland, and Buffalo,
the 'Patriots' (as the exiles styled themselves) issued manifestos, broad-

67 Baldwin to Lord Glenelg, 329−31
68 In his study of the Upper Canadian gentry, 'Like Eden in Her Summer Dress,' Robert
   Fraser makes no reference to a conservative historiography of Upper Canadian
   events: one could not do the same if discussing the growth of the Upper Canadian
   reform movement. See also Bowsfield, 'Upper Canada in the 1820's,' 25.
69 Fraser, 'Like Eden in Her Summer Dress,' 137

sides, and accounts of the recent events in which they renounced the British connection, embraced republicanism, and called for American intervention in Upper Canada.[70] Their hyperbole, expected to motivate an American audience, alienated Upper Canadians.

Meanwhile, the victorious forces of the oligarchy were themselves being consumed in the moment of their success. They had won a battle the very fighting of which was proof of the reality and intensity of grievance in Upper Canada. Just as the persistence of the French fact confounded English-speaking patriots in Lower Canada, so did the rebellion prove that material progress must await the resolution of a political conflict. The era of uncritical patriotism was over, replaced by a contest for political direction. There followed two years of intense debate over the shape of the political resolution to Upper Canadian problems. It was not until Lord Durham's *Report* parted the sea in 1839 that the chosen theme of responsible government emerged on the far shore and the waters closed over all historiographic rivals.

John George Lambton, first earl of Durham (1792–1840), was the son of a north England landlord and colliery owner, from whom he inherited wealth and a commitment to the Foxite radical tradition.[71] The young Lambton was educated at Eton, served briefly in the British cavalry, and in 1813 was elected to the House of Commons for County Durham. He continued to represent this constituency until his elevation to the House of Lords in 1828 as Baron Durham. In 1830 he entered the Whig cabinet headed by his father-in-law, Charles Grey, Viscount Howick and second Earl Grey, and was instrumental in both the drafting and passage of the Reform Act of 1832 (2 William IV, c. 45). A mercurial and prickly colleague, whose friendship with the Radicals worried some moderate Whigs, Durham's resignation from the cabinet in 1833 on grounds of

70 Donald M'Leod (1799–1879), *A Brief Review of the Settlement of Upper Canada by the U.E. Loyalists and Scotch Highlanders, in 1783; And of the Grievances Which Compelled the Canadas to Have Recourse to Arms in Defence of Their Rights and Liberties, in the Years 1837 and 1838: Together with a Brief Sketch of the Campaigns of 1812, '13, '14: With an Account of the Military Executions, Burnings, and Sackings of Towns and Villages, by the British, in the Upper and Lower Provinces, during the Commotion of 1837 and '38* (Cleveland, Ohio, 1841) 6; Edward Alexander Theller (1804–59), *Canada in 1837–38, Showing, by Historical Facts, the Causes of the Late Attempted Revolution, and of Its Failure; The Present Condition of the People, and Their Future Prospects, together with the Personal Adventures of the Author, and Others Who Were Connected with the Revolution,* 2 vols (Philadelphia, Pa., 1841) vol. 1, 5–7; James Doyle, 'The Spirit of '38: American Literary Images of the Upper Canadian Rebellion,' *Journal of Canadian Culture* 1 (1984): 90–8
71 McCready, Introduction to [New,] *Lord Durham's Mission,* ix–xiv

ill-health was greeted with relief by the government, which promptly made him an earl and appointed him ambassador to Russia at St Petersburg. Durham's return to England in the summer of 1837 revived disquiet among the Whigs of the wobbly administration of William Lamb, second Viscount Melbourne. Under attack from the Radicals for their handling of Canadian affairs, the Whigs were uncertain as to how Durham might stir this pot. It must have seemed a stroke of genius therefore to appoint him governor-in-chief of British North America, with extraordinary powers as lord high commissioner and a mandate to make 'various and extensive inquiries into the institutions and administration of those Provinces; and to devise such reforms in the system of their government as might repair the mischief which had already been done, and lay the foundations of order, tranquillity, and improvement.'[72]

Lord Durham spent the months between his appointment as governor in January 1838 and his departure in April for Quebec City informing himself of the nature of the difficulties that had led to rebellion in the Canadas. He was especially worried by the severity of the revolt in the most populous colony, Lower Canada, and his reading and correspondence reflected this concern. His papers contain numerous letters, petitions, and memorials from the English-speaking minority of Lower Canada recommending the assimilation of French Canadians, different forms of union with Upper Canada, and varying degrees and kinds of constitutional change; a smaller portion of his papers are from sources sympathetic to French Canadians; very little was received from Upper Canada.[73] Among these many representations 'there is not,' Durham's biographer wrote, 'the slightest trace of Responsible Government or of an extensive measure of Self-Government.'[74] Nevertheless, already Durham imagined 'that the original and constant source of evil was to be found in the defects of the political institutions of the Provinces,' specifically 'from collision between the executive and the representatives of the people.' In drawing this conclusion, Durham relied on his own personal experience:

I looked on it as a dispute analogous to those with which history and experience have made us so familiar in Europe, – a dispute between a people demanding

72 *Lord Durham's Report: An Abridgement of 'Report on the Affairs of British North America'* by *Lord Durham* (1839), ed. Gerald M. Craig (Toronto 1963) 16–17. Unless otherwise stated, all references to Durham's *Report* are to this edition.
73 NA, Lord Durham Papers, MG 24, A 27, vols 25–9; Janet Ajzenstat, 'The Political Thought of Lord Durham' (PH D Diss., University of Toronto 1979) 17–20
74 [New,] *Lord Durham's Mission*, 51

an extension of popular privileges, on the one hand, and an executive, on the other, defending the powers which it conceived necessary for the maintenance of order.[75]

Durham may not have arrived in Canada convinced that responsible government was the answer: he did arrive convinced that the constitution was the problem.

Lord Durham resided in British North America for just over five months, during which period he and his staff – consisting most notably of Charles Buller and Edward Gibbon Wakefield – continued to collect information on the background to the rebellions as well as opinions regarding social and political remedies for the crisis. Almost all his stay was passed in Lower Canada, where the severity of the rebellion, the suspension of the constitution, and the problem of race demanded attention. Durham's personal examination of conditions in Upper Canada was limited to an eleven-day excursion, during which he met with Robert Baldwin, from whom he subsequently received a copy of the aforementioned letter to Lord Glenelg.[76] Durham had not had time to assimilate his scattered findings when he resigned in September over the failure of the Melbourne government to support his decision to banish a number of rebel leaders to Bermuda. In November Durham returned to England, and over the next two months he devoted himself to writing his famous *Report*. He presented it to the Colonial Office on 4 February 1839, and four days later it began to appear in *The Times*. It was subsequently printed in several Canadian newspapers, and before the year was out it had been published in pamphlet form by printers in London, Toronto, and Montreal.[77]

Lord Durham, like Gourlay before him, regarded the 'Canadian question' from a distinctly British point of view. He took for granted that 'no portion of the American Continent possesses greater natural resources for the maintenance of large and flourishing communities' than that occupied by the provinces of British North America. Great Britain, having 'founded and maintained these Colonies at vast expense of blood and treasure,' had a right to 'expect its compensation in turning their unappropriated resources to the account of its own redundant population.' Instead, these colonies had been a drain on the imperial treasury

75 *Lord Durham's Report*, 21–2
76 [New,] *Lord Durham's Mission*, 85–8; Robert Baldwin to the Earl of Durham, 23 Aug.
 1838, NA, *Report, 1923*, 326–8
77 [New,] *Lord Durham's Mission*, 164–7; Craig, Introduction to *Lord Durham's Report*, xi–xii

and had now in two instances rebelled against British rule. 'It is not necessary,' Durham wrote, 'that I should take any pains to prove that this is a state of things which should not, which cannot continue.'[78] If British North America was not to be lost or kept solely by military force, the colonists must be reconciled to the British connection and made useful to the empire. Believing that material prosperity was contingent upon a rearrangement in the affairs of men, Durham began at the point where loyal colonial patriots had for so long attempted to close debate. Durham accepted the basic premise of the tradition of grievance and reform in Upper Canada, yet could not be accused of disloyalty: he placed the defenders of the old order in the insoluble position their reliance on Britain had always threatened.

It is impossible now to reconstruct precisely how Lord Durham chose and selected his material for the Upper Canadian section of the *Report*, apart from comparison with interpretations circulating in the province itself. According to Chester New, such a comparison reveals 'a remarkably clear presentation of the Reformers' interpretation of the political situation in 1838 with its historical background.'[79] In an outline similar in spirit, and occasionally in wording, to Robert Baldwin's letter to Lord Glenclg, Durham found the cause of colonial strife in the failure to give British citizens abroad the constitution familiar to them at home. The institutions provided by the Constitutional Act of 1791 looked similar to the representative forms current in England, namely, an elected assembly, appointed council, and royal surrogate; but, 'in a deviation from sound constitutional principles,' the executive arm of the government was permitted to operate independently of the assembly, relying on the confidence of the Crown rather than that of the people. Not bothering with the usual courteous bow to the ideal of a balanced constitution, Durham declared it the glory of the Revolutionary Settlement of 1688 that the executive and legislative arms of the British government were brought into harmony by the pre-eminent role of the majority in Parliament:

> However partial the Monarch might be to particular ministers, or however he might have personally committed himself to their policy, he has invariably been constrained to abandon both, as soon as the opinion of the people has been irrevocably pronounced against them through the medium of the House of Commons.

78 *Lord Durham's Report*, 19–20, 125–7
79 [New,] *Lord Durham's Mission*, 168–9

The concession of representative institutions on any other principle seemed to Durham 'the rock on which the continental imitations of the British Constitution have invariably split.'[80]

The only reasonable excuse Durham could discover for the constitutional deformity imposed on British North America was the imperial government's belief that it was 'an incident of colonial dependence that the officers of government should be nominated by the Crown.' While he did not quarrel with the need to ensure the pre-eminence of British interests, it was Durham's argument that contemporary constitutional arrangements did not in fact retain direction of colonial affairs in the hands of either the Colonial Office or the local governor: the former was too distant and too indifferent to play an effective role; the latter was invariably ignorant of this charge when he arrived and was 'compelled to throw himself almost entirely upon those whom he [found] placed in the position of his official advisers.' It was the irresponsible body of office-holders who must, therefore, 'from the very nature of colonial government, acquire the entire direction of the affairs of the Province,' to the benefit of neither London nor the colonists.[81]

Of all the colonial oligarchies, none in Durham's opinion had 'exhibited itself for so long a period or to such an extent, as in Upper Canada.' Called the Family Compact – a label Durham did not take literally – this party consisted 'of native-born inhabitants of the Colony, or of emigrants who settled in it before the last war with the United States; the principal members of it belong to the Church of England, and the maintenance of the claims of that church has always been one of its distinguishing characteristics.' In terms which suggest a familiarity with Mackenzie's writings, Durham noted how the adherents of this party 'shared among themselves almost exclusively all offices of trust and profit,' whether in church, state, or justice, and how over time they had come to control nearly the whole of the province's waste lands. It was inconceivable to Durham that British yeomen would renounce the political principles of their birth or give up 'the spirit of Anglo-Saxon freedom' and submit to the irresponsible tyranny of the Compact. Inevitably an opposition grew in the assembly, 'which assailed the ruling party, by appealing to popular principles of government, by denouncing the alleged jobbing and profusion of the official body, and by instituting inquiries into abuses, for

80 *Lord Durham's Report*, 52–3, 56; cf, Ajzenstat, 'Political Thought of Lord Durham,' 136n
81 *Lord Durham's Report*, 55–6

the purpose of promoting reform.'[82] This dialectic was the motive force behind Upper Canadian history, and in accepting it, Durham sanctioned the historiography of reform.

As Lord Durham saw it, the solution to the political crisis in Upper Canada was simple: in 1791 the province had been given representative institutions; the British Crown must now be willing to 'submit to the necessary consequences of representative institutions'; and if the Crown had 'to carry on the Government in unison with a representative body, it must consent to carry it on by means of those in whom that representative body [had] confidence.' In the spirit of Baldwin's letter to Lord Glenelg, Durham called on the Melbourne government 'to follow out consistently the principles of the British constitution' and introduce into the government of all the colonies of British North America 'those wise provisions, by which alone the working of the representative system can in any country be rendered harmonious and efficient.' Chief among such provisions was the requirement that a ministry 'command a majority in the Parliament on great questions of policy.'[83]

Durham's only major adjustment to Baldwin's scheme was to define the extent to which a responsible executive council could apply its power. Durham retained for the British Parliament, and its responsible cabinet, control over the disposal of provincial Crown lands, foreign relations, external trade, and constitutional change.[84] He advocated these limits to ensure the pre-eminence of British interests, but in the Upper Canadian context his division of powers received a different emphasis: 'When Durham recommended a continuing political role for the imperial government, and when "responsible government" came to be understood within this context, the fact that it had once implied autonomy – or political separation from the mother country – became obscured.'[85] Henceforth responsible government could not be thrust aside as disloyal or alien; henceforth it was up to members of the Compact, not reformers, to justify their acts. Durham had sanctioned the Reform party and its, and more particularly Baldwin's, view of Upper Canadian history.

A month after the *Report* arrived in Upper Canada, a schoolmaster

---

82 *Lord Durham's Report on the Affairs of British North America* (1839), ed. C.P. Lucas, 3 vols (Oxford 1912) vol. 2, *The Text of the Report*, 79–81, 147–50
83 *Lord Durham's Report*, 138–9; R.M. Baldwin and J. Baldwin, *The Baldwins and the Great Experiment* (Don Mills, Ont., 1969) 162
84 *Lord Durham's Report*, 141–2
85 Patterson, 'Enduring Canadian Myth,' 10

residing at Whitby wrote to a friend in the United States that the old Compact hated Durham 'as the devil does holy water.'[86] The reason for this is clear enough: Durham's account of the unconstitutional and corrupt practices of the Compact rendered the official party as illegitimate as the rebellion had rendered the Mackenzie radicals. His history of Upper Canada stole from the oligarchy its claim to be the loyal party – its very *raison d'être* – and must not therefore go unchallenged. Certainly Durham left himself open to criticism by the brevity of his visit. Within days of the release of his *Report*, Chief Justice John Beverley Robinson (1791–1863), the Nestor of the old order, wrote to the new colonial secretary, Constantine Henry Phipps, first marquis of Normanby, to complain that the Upper Canadian section,

> in regard to its most numerous, and most important statements, either rests upon no evidence whatever, or, if it has indeed been founded on any evidence, it has been the ex parte evidence of an unknown number of unknown witnesses, of whom unknown questions have been asked by unknown parties, and possibly parties with unknown views, and full of unknown prejudices.[87]

Within weeks, select committees of both the assembly and the legislative council quickly issued reports enumerating Durham's errors of fact.[88]

It was one thing to find faults, quite another to provide a credible alternative to Durham's general interpretation of events. The oligarchs found the need to justify themselves a new and uncomfortable experience, not the least because, stripped of its Loyalist sentiment, their cause was difficult to defend. Their basic position was that, despite local difficulties, there existed no solution other than to stick by the constitution of 1791. Theirs was a pre-Reform Bill vision of the constitution, not of a monarch constrained by a majority in Parliament, but of power balanced equally among the monarchical, aristocratic, and democratic elements – a balance that depended for its stability on the hierarchical ordering of society. They accepted subordinate colonial status as an

---

86 Quoted in [New,] *Lord Durham's Mission*, 205–6
87 John Beverley Robinson to Lord Normanby, 23 Feb. 1839, quoted in ibid., 189; Patrick Brode, *Sir John Beverley Robinson: Bone and Sinew of the Family Compact* (Toronto 1984) ch. 14; Robert E. Saunders, 'John Beverley Robinson,' *DCB*, vol. 9, 668–79
88 Report of the Committee of the Legislative Council of Upper Canada on Lord Durham's Report [11 May 1839], in W.P.M. Kennedy, ed., *Statutes, Treaties and Documents of the Canadian Constitution, 1713–1929*, 2nd ed. (Toronto 1930) 374–82; [New,] *Lord Durham's Mission*, 201–5

essential, even desirable, and natural part of this order. In the Canadas the democratic, yeoman element, strengthened by 'the ease with which property [was] acquired,' and 'freed from the influence of great wealth, as well as from that of high station in the few,' would fly out of control if not counterbalanced by the steadying influence of appointed officials – the pseudo-aristocracy of the land. It was the disequilibrium of the young Upper Canadian society that made the proposal for responsible government so dangerous. With the executive council under democratic control, the lieutenant-governor would inevitably be moulded by the popular will. Durham's division of powers would break down and inadvertently 'lead to the overthrow of the great colonial empire of England.'[89]

This clarion call to subordination was not one that could be taken to the independent yeomen of Upper Canada. It was a measure of the oligarchy's dilemma that its Loyalist exhortation was directed not to fellow colonists but to the imperial government. It was the government in London that was now ready to cut its loyal colonial officials adrift. And why? Lord Durham himself denied the familial connection of the Compact; and, freed from allegations of nepotism, what else were the leaders of government, church, court, and business but the natural élite of the province? And what need this change? Had not the majority of the public voted for the governing party in 1836? Had not they rallied to defeat the rebel attempts to overturn the verdict of the polls? In short, where was this majority supposed by Durham to have been driven into despair of good government?

Unfortunately, all these questions, however valid, were based on what were, in the era between the Reform Act and the advent of free trade, increasingly outdated assumptions about the nature of society, the constitution, and the empire. Robinson wrote in his diary that when he pressed his views on Arthur Wellesley, first duke of Wellington – himself a pillar of the old order – the great Duke responded:

Your paper, my dear Sir, was written for a different Country – for a different state of things altogether. Your paper was written for 'Old England' – it was written for Old England Sir – but this is not 'Old England' – this is not Old England – not any thing like it. I speak of what I remember – but you see everything is totally changed.[90]

89 Report of the Committee of the Legislative Council, 376–8
90 NA, John Beverley Robinson Papers, MG 24, B 29, vol. 5, microfilm, reel M-204, Diary, 1838–40, 17, 1 May 1839; Brode, Sir John Beverley Robinson, 213–14

Durham's description of events in Upper Canada would serve its purpose none the worse for its defects.

Sir Francis Bond Head (1793–1875) was the one man who, theoretically at least, was in a position to discredit Durham and vindicate the cause of the oligarchs. In his *A Narrative*, published in 1839, Head did in fact unleash a flood of official dispatches, petitions, and other documents that were a devastating indictment of the inaccuracies of Durham's *Report*.[91] He went on to make a coherent case for his own impartiality as governor, for the basic loyalty and contentedness of the Upper Canadian people, and for the ephemeral nature of the rebellion. He made this case, however, primarily in order to defend himself from responsibility for the rebellion and only incidentally in order to justify and defend his supporters among the governing party, with whom his relations had in any event often been strained. He took pleasure not just in correcting Durham, but also in blasting the ungrateful Melbourne administration and an assorted cast of Upper Canadian politicians. He was, in the words of one biographer, 'utterly frank and utterly partisan, and thus inevitably damaging both to [himself] and to his cause.'[92] He even scandalously claimed to have purposely denuded the province of troops in order to lure Mackenzie into precipitate action.[93] Robinson wrote to his wife of Head: 'Any quiet Englishman will be apt to say, that man would make a rebellion any where.'[94] Ultimately the oligarchy had more to lose than gain through their association with Head. In time some would actually find solace in the belief that it was he rather than they who was responsible for the outbreak of violence in a basically contented province.

The lamentations of the oligarchy were in stark contrast to the rejuvenation Durham's *Report* imparted to the reform movement. Baldwin completely ignored the limitations Durham placed on the jurisdiction of colonial governments and instead seized on the positive recommendation of making the executive council responsible to the majority in the assembly as official approval of his program. Francis Hincks, the editor of the new reform newspaper, the *Examiner*, supported Baldwin's preten-

91 Francis Bond Head, *A Narrative* (1839), with notes by William Lyon Mackenzie, ed. S.F. Wise (Toronto 1969) 199–227
92 Wise, Introduction to ibid., xxv; see also his 'Francis Bond Head,' *DCB*, vol. 10 (Toronto 1972) 342–5
93 Head, *A Narrative*, 141–3. Head retracted this claim in a later work, *The Emigrant* (London 1846).
94 Quoted in Wise, Introduction to Head, *A Narrative*, xxvii; Brode, *Sir John Beverley Robinson*, 210

sions and dedicated that journal's pamphlet edition of the *Report* to Baldwin, the 'able advocate of those constitutional principles which have been at last recognized by a Governor-General of Canada.'[95] In order to cement the identification between Durham's *Report* and Baldwin's program, in the summer of 1839 Baldwin and Hincks promoted a series of 'Durham Meetings' at which reform agitation was successfully focused on the single issue of responsible government. By the time the first elections for seats in the new united legislature of Canada were held in 1841, Reform party candidates throughout Upper Canada (now Canada West) were appealing to electors primarily on the recommendations of Lord Durham's *Report*. 'It was the Report, the whole Report, and nothing but the Report.'[96]

Over the next decade politicians continued to argue over the exact nature of responsible government and the timing of its implementation, but for all their confusion they were now operating within the boundaries and traditions of moderate reform. That this should be so was largely due to the influence of Lord Durham's *Report*. Caught between the choice of a patriotism that denied reality and a tradition of reform that challenged loyalty to Great Britain, Upper Canadians sought reassurance that yearnings for a greater role in their own government were compatible with membership in the empire: 'Here Durham made an ideal contemporary hero. A man who in himself reconciled the opposites of aristocracy and democracy, who preached with such confident prophecy the reconciliation of self-government and colonial status – such a man was the ideal symbol of Canadian identity.'[97] Thus, no matter how great or small Durham's influence on the British government's decision to grant responsible government in 1848, he was for Upper Canadians a powerful and influential symbol of the victory of that principle and the historiography that stood behind it.

Durham did not write the *Report* for the people of Upper Canada alone. He did not regard responsible government as a solution for a problem peculiar to Upper Canada; he believed 'the tranquility of each of the North American Provinces was subject to constant disturbance from collision between the executive and representatives of the people'; and he assumed that the history of each province would exhibit the same salutary

95 Quoted in [New,] *Lord Durham's Mission*, 205
96 Ibid., 205–18; Careless, 'Robert Baldwin,' 114–16
97 Ged Martin, *The Durham Report and British Policy: A Critical Essay* (Cambridge 1972) 89–90

struggle by transplanted English yeomen to overcome an irresponsible oligarchy.[98] Therefore, the remedy forged in Upper Canada had a general application, and this in turn was an assumption of extraordinary significance for the writing of history in British North America. Up to this point the historiographies of Nova Scotia, Prince Edward Island, New Brunswick, Lower Canada, and Upper Canada had developed almost entirely in isolation one from the other – five distinct communities joined only by a common relationship with Great Britain. Durham was the first historian to declare that these provinces were joined not just by a common mother country but also by a common form of government and common institutions, interests, feelings, and habits.[99] Above all, he found that these five provinces were united by a history of beneficial struggle, which in the natural course of events must produce responsible government. It is not too strong to say that Durham made the historiography of Upper Canada that of all British North America. In short, Durham created a historiography that posited the problem of one colony as the problem of all.

Lord Durham could only assert that the struggle for responsible government was *the* theme of British North American history by distorting the history of individual provinces. One sees this most clearly in his lengthy discussion of Lower Canada. As Sir Charles Lucas noticed:

> Lord Durham set before himself, in regard to Canada, something like the problem which Aristotle propounded for solution in the *Politics*. He set himself to consider in the first place, what is the best constitution; and in the second place, what is the best constitution, given a particular set of conditions. He answered the second problem not so much by departing from his model constitution, as by proposing to alter the conditions so as to enable the model constitution to be brought into being.[100]

At its core, Durham's interpretation rested on the view that British North Americans were Englishmen overseas seeking the rights they were accustomed to at home. Unfortunately in Lower Canada, he held, the French race had appropriated the mantle of constitutional reform for their own reactionary purposes. Durham's method for dealing with such deviation from the natural state of colonial development was to recommend the elimination of the French through assimilation. Consequently, he suggested that 'in any plan, which may be adopted for the future

98 *Lord Durham's Report*, 21
99 Ibid., 17
100 C.P. Lucas, Introduction to *Lord Durham's Report*, ed. Lucas, vol. 1, *Introduction*, 125

management of Lower Canada, the first object ought to be that of making it an English Province.' His own recommendation for the union of Upper and Lower Canada was therefore an essential prerequisite for the granting of responsible government.[101]

In writing his account of events in Lower Canada, then, Lord Durham virtually adopted the anti-French attitude of the English-speaking minority in that province, along with the historiography on which it was based. Indeed, Durham's history of Lower Canada was almost indistinguishable from that of, for example, John Fleming. The French regime was represented as a quasi-feudal society ruled by military discipline and inhibited by the Roman Catholic Church. The conquest had offered Britain the opportunity to overturn this reactionary culture, but instead the government of the day had indulged the French Canadians in the hope of winning an ally in the struggle against the thirteen colonies – an indulgence that incredibly was extended in 1791 to the concession of representative institutions and a separate province. The result was to place 'an old and stationary society, in a new and progressive world.' The ignorant and subservient French-Canadian 'peasantry,' in contrast to the independent English-Canadian yeomen, were incapable of making democratic choices in their own best interests. They consequently fell prey to an élite of professional French-Canadian demagogues who were, for their part, jealous of the commercial acumen of the British settlers. In order to preserve their position in society, these demagogues rallied habitant voters and turned the liberal institutions of the assembly into a weapon for the reactionary obstruction of progressive legislation. This in turn 'cemented the singular alliance between the English population and the Colonial officials' in defence of royal prerogative.[102] It was, Durham believed, only through assimilation of the French Canadians that Lower Canadian constitutional development could be returned to its natural course. It was entirely in keeping with the tradition of the province's English-speaking historians that Durham should seek to deny rather than accommodate the reality of the racial situation.

Lord Durham's interpretation of British North American history was at its most imperious when dealing with the Maritime provinces and Newfoundland:

It is only necessary that I should state my impression of the general working of the Government in these Colonies, in order that if institutions similar to those

101 *Lord Durham's Report,* 22–3, 151; Ajzenstat, 'Political Thought of Lord Durham,' ch. 3
102 *Lord Durham's Report,* 26–9

of the disturbed Provinces should here appear to be tending to similar results, a common remedy may be devised for the impending as well as for the existing disorders.[103]

In brief communications with the respective lieutenant-governors of these colonies and during his meetings in early September 1838 with delegations of local politicians sent up to Quebec, Durham found the confirmation he wanted that constitutional problems did exist between the executive and popular branches of their governments, albeit in a benign form. No matter that Maritimers believed themselves to have other and more pressing concerns, Durham apparently knew better than they where their real problems lay.[104]

Lord Durham's universal solution to the difficulties confronting British North America had its roots in Upper Canada. In that colony the problem of colonial identity turned on the question of loyalty because it was in part the product of two empires, Great Britain and the United States. In order to serve partisan ends, politicians took the lead both in defining loyalty and in explaining the historical process by which it was fashioned. Competing for the label of patriot, they became Upper Canada's most influential historians. The intervention of Lord Durham, the Crown's official voice, was crucial. He decided not only that the history of Upper Canada was indeed a narrative of the hard-working, independent yeoman's struggle to obtain political power but that this struggle was legitimate. Conflict, which patriot historians traditionally sought to submerge, was now regarded as good, in fact essential.

The effect of Lord Durham's *Report* on the writing of history in English-speaking British North America went far beyond the simple sanctioning of reform historiography in Upper Canada. He declared that the salutary struggle for responsible government was – or should be – the motive force behind historical development in every colony. This conjunction of politics and history wrenched colonial historiography away from promotional chorographies and thematic descriptions and pushed it toward narratives of constitutional development. The foundation of a colony did not fix political and social arrangements, it merely inaugurated an era with its own forms of change. By making universal this process and the desire for responsible government, and by divorcing the

---

103 *Lord Durham's Report*, ed. Lucas, *Text of the Report*, 193
104 Ibid., 193–8, and William Young to Lord Durham, 20 Sept. 1838, vol. 3, *Appendixes*, appendix A, no. 5, 12–18

drive to control the executive from the particular circumstances in each colony, Durham made of British North American history a progressive battle on behalf of principle. This was a worthy theme and one that could be accommodated within the larger history of British constitutional growth. It was also the first attempt to fashion a truly national historiography.

5

A
National Consensus

The Durham *Report* recommended, and nine years later the British ministry granted, a large measure of responsible self-government to the united province of Canada. Synchronic imperial legislation emasculated the system of Navigation Acts that was mercantilism made manifest. The combined effect of the British government's proscription of certain of its own powers was to shift the locus of real authority over the future of domestic colonial affairs to the Canadas themselves. The need to influence British public opinion declined in direct proportion to the amplified prerogative of the provincial electorate. Governments, companies, and individuals continued to extol and defend the Canadas, but such boosterism no longer inhibited internal discussion of provincial matters, past, present, or future. Similarly, the establishment of limited colonial autonomy, without the repudiation of the imperial connection, legitimized and made loyal opposition. Freed from earlier restraints and buoyed by a new self-possession, historians in the Canadas restructured history for their new colonial audience.

The primary purpose of the new generation of Canadian historians was to narrate for their compatriots the story of how collectively they had struggled to raise the united province to its present stature, overcoming both the wilderness and an irresponsible élite. Indeed, argument and discord were elements of the past that historians no longer attempted to disguise, for, in contrast to patriot historians elsewhere in British North America, they saw conflict as a cause of, not an impediment to, improvement. A commitment to progress was universal; but, whereas others used narrative history to explain away the past and clear a path to the future, Canadian historians now demonstrated how struggle could be directed toward progress, and, if read aright, show the way to the future. History was for them a continuum, and their first task was to provide a credible line of descent. But they were also to bring open discord to a close, to end the partisan, racial, and other divisions of the past, and to fashion a new, unifying identity. From a history of struggle they would forge a national consensus.

The first and in many ways the most significant English-speaking historian to reorder Canadian history in the light of Durham's *Report* and the achievement of responsible government was John Mercier McMullen (1820–1907). Raised in a 'midland county' of Ireland, McMullen first surfaced in 1842 as a junior partner in a small mercantile firm located in Dublin. The business was not a success and, as junior, McMullen soon found himself on the street with nothing but an itch to see the world. Unfamiliar with the sea, he was reluctant to join the navy, and so (much to the chagrin of his relatives and friends) in the spring of 1843 he enlisted in the British army as a private. After a brief spell of training in an English depot, McMullen joined the Thirteenth Regiment of Light Infantry at Sukkar on the Indus River in what is today Pakistan. In 1845 the regiment's tour of overseas duty came to an end, and in October McMullen, now a staff sergeant, purchased his release from the army. He returned to Dublin and there wrote and published anonymously *Camp and Barrack-Room; Or, the British Army as It Is*, which revealed him as a self-possessed individual of intelligence, energy, and humour, unwilling to defer to men of lesser merit in superior position.[1] Unfortunately absence had not improved McMullen's prospects in Ireland, and in 1848 he emigrated to North America and settled at Brockville, Canada West. There, freed from the restraints of station, he dabbled in mercantile trade, book publishing, and journalism. And there too, in 1855, he published the first edition of his *History of Canada*.[2]

McMullen commenced work on his *History of Canada* only in 1853, snatching moments to research and write from the daily affairs of business. He had little personal experience of the country, and was further handicapped by the destruction by fire in 1849 of the parliamentary library. He therefore relied heavily on back issues of the Brockville weekly *Recorder* and on the private libraries of Brockville worthies, which, rather surprisingly, contained most of the major works and many of the minor pamphlets published to date relating to the Canadas.[3] These were to be his only sources, and if such research was hardly original, the

1 (London 1846) 5–8, 265–7
2 John McMullen, *The History of Canada, from Its First Discovery to the Present Time* (Brockville, Ont., 1855) 499–501
3 Ibid.; McMullen, *History of Canada*, 3rd ed., 2 vols (Brockville, Ont. 1891–2) vol. 1 (1891) iii–vii; vol. 2 (1892) 199

synthesis he produced certainly was. Here for the first time were the principles of Lord Durham applied to the histories of Upper and Lower Canada. Within the compass of a single volume McMullen told the story not of two colonies but of a single nation. The emphasis was deliberate. The historian's duty was, as McMullen perceived it, 'to infuse a spirit of Canadian nationality into the people generally – to mould the native born citizen, the Scotch, the English, and the Irish emigrant into a compact whole.' History was the background and substance of the economic and constitutional achievement that was Canada. 'To enable us to judge accurately the present – to regard our national future with confidence,' McMullen maintained, 'an acquaintance with the past is an absolute necessity.'[4] It was his assurance that the past was buttress for the future, that history was something to live up to, not down, that was novel to Canada. Written from pride in the present and faith in the future, McMullen's *History of Canada* was a search for the antecedents and determinants of progress.

Relative to the marathon of universal history, the Americans had developed in a sprint. In asserting that pre-Columbian America was a blank awaiting the imprint of 'civilized humanity,' McMullen was merely repeating a commonplace. To him the native people of the continent were irrelevant. Illiterate and without a written history, 'their social condition was in accordance with the rude status of mental culture, which this fact [bespoke].' They had no manufactures, no domesticated animals, little knowledge of agriculture, and were directed by superstitious and primitive religious notions. If this 'poor and thinly scattered community of improvident savages' had been succeeded by 'an orderly, industrious, and enterprising people,' whose genius and resources embodied 'all the germs of a mighty nation,' McMullen thought there could be 'little room for regret' that the possession of the country had been 'transferred to the Anglo-Saxon race, and that the rule of the fierce Indian' had forever passed away.[5]

McMullen expressed little more regret at the passing of the French regime. Relying primarily on the histories of George Heriot and William Smith, McMullen fashioned an account of New France that was their superior only in style. Once again imperious supervision by the home authorities was established as the central theme of the colony's history. The power vested in military governors, seigneurs, religious obscurantists, and economic monopolists effectively denied to colonists control

4 McMullen, *History of Canada*, 1st ed., Preface
5 Ibid., i–xiv

over their own destiny. Command of affairs did not lie in the hands of those having a personal stake in the colony. As a consequence, development was misdirected by imperial priorities, clerical arrogance, and individual corruption. The 'torpid repose' into which the internal political life of New France fell, 'repressed the energies of its inhabitants, and perpetuated their natural easy and indolent manners, which over three-quarters of a century of British freedom' had not, in McMullen's view, 'sufficed to remove.'[6]

McMullen did make some effort to be discriminating in his judgment of Frenchmen. Despite his strictures on the government and society of New France, he was eager to recognize valour and merit whenever he encountered it in an individual. Although defending a faulty cause, Jacques Cartier, the Comte de Frontenac, and Louis-Joseph de Montcalm, Marquis de Montcalm, had, in McMullen's opinion, exhibited certain laudable personal qualities. Still more exceptional were the compliments McMullen paid to Samuel de Champlain. Described as a brave, patient, and self-denying colonizer, who saw better than his superiors the potential of New France, Champlain was praised less for demonstrating bravery in, than for having the courage to see beyond, his time. McMullen saw – or at least portrayed – Champlain as a man who showed by his actions that he anticipated the future greatness not of a French colony but of a Canadian nation.[7] The founder of Quebec was transformed into the father of Canada, and in the process was the first of many to be assimilated into a pantheon of national heroes. To obtain a niche in this temple it was not enough to have a rare combination of admirable traits, one must have 'foresight.' Gazing into the past for the antecedents of the present, McMullen recognized those who stared back.

In summary, McMullen believed that the native people had done nothing and the French very little to develop the latent agricultural and manufacturing potential of North America. The failure of the French in particular was due to the metropolitan government's centralizing system of political and economic control, which denied colonists the opportunity to make their own decisions. Thus, with the largely ephemeral exception of the *coureurs de bois*, emigrants were drained of the vigour McMullen associated with self-reliance and the 'powerful incentive of individual profit.'[8] Not that McMullen advocated free play of self-interest (producing good in spite of itself); rather he sought a balance between submissive

6 Ibid., 1–121, but especially 95–6
7 Ibid., 3–8, 12–17, 80, 143–4, 170
8 Ibid., 30, 96, 106, 114

obedience and democratic anarchy. His *via media* was one that combined hard work and intelligence with responsible self-restraint. The ideal relationship between the mother country and its colonies was analogous: the former must trust its offspring to direct their own affairs judiciously; the latter must be dutiful in their observance of imperial obligations. Armed with this standard, McMullen knew what to look for and praise in the history of men and nations.

What McMullen posited as a universal model was, of course, simply an idealized vision of the Anglo-Saxon yeoman, albeit updated to accommodate commerce and a significant measure of political power. If one wished to know how New France should have been governed, one need only look south to the British American colonies, which 'presented the aspect of a free, self-governed people, grown rich and populous by their intelligence, their industry, and their love of justice.' There a trusting imperial government permitted colonists to create an American nationality that had room neither for a corrupt and parasitic élite nor for indolent settlers. Once these young colonies were aroused and turned their attention to the threat posed by New France, the eventual conquest of the latter was assured. McMullen could imagine no happier fate for the habitant than to be liberated from the heavy hand of the French state and the Roman Catholic Church and schooled in the free and independent laws of Great Britain. In common with so many of Lower Canada's English-speaking historians, McMullen could only regret that the conquest did not result in the immediate assimilation of the French in Quebec. If a new era was launched in 1760, it was one that brought its own problems into being.[9]

In keeping with his love of moderation, McMullen was quite specific as to how he thought the habitants ought to be absorbed. Their hearts and minds must be won by example and reason; force would achieve only superficial obedience. Thus, although the articles of capitulation signed in 1760 protected traditional French rights of persons, property, and religion, they won McMullen's praise for demonstrating the enlightened tolerance of British government. Similarly, the Proclamation of 1763, which sought to assimilate by royal fiat, earned his disapproval: 'The disorders it introduced produced a re-action, which has perpetuated the French civil law in Lower Canada to the present day, whereas, had changes been at first gradually and wisely introduced, as the altered condition of the people permitted, the laws of England ere now would

9 Ibid., 114–81

have been the rule of decision in that province.' Unfortunately the British government was incapable of adhering to a steady evolutionary program. Concerned by the presumption of the older British colonies, George III used French-Canadian anxiety over the Proclamation of 1763 as a pretext to pass the Quebec Act in 1774, and thereby returned the colony to many of its ancient, antidemocratic forms. Such extreme oscillations of government policy compromised British ideals, frustrated Quebec's English-speaking population, and removed all incentive for the habitant to reform. Even worse, American colonists rejected what they saw as George III's reactionary imitation of centralizing French policy and understandably, if regrettably, rebelled.[10]

The influx of Loyalists into Quebec in the wake of the American Revolution altered the balance of political power in the province in favour of the English-speaking residents and bolstered their demand that their full legal and political rights as British citizens be acknowledged. Acceding to the logic and strength of the case made by the English-speaking community of Quebec, the imperial government passed the Constitutional Act of 1791, which set constitutional forms in the province down to the Act of Union in 1840 (3–4 Vict., c. 35). The Constitutional Act provided neither the French- nor the English-speaking communities with a clear-cut victory, but it did mark a significant break with past fluctuations between extremes of policy: it sought to accommodate French civil law with English criminal law and granted an assembly only on condition that Roman Catholics be permitted to enter. Such a constitutional transformation created conditions potentially favourable to racial reconciliation and assimilation.[11]

Unhappily, in McMullen's opinion the Constitutional Act had at least two flaws fatal to its long-term successful operation. First, it constituted Upper Canada as a separate province, and thus removed the example and strength of an embryonic English-speaking majority and gave the ill-prepared habitant voter control over the Assembly of Lower Canada. Second, in neither the old nor the new province was full British constitutional government actually granted. Since 1688 it had been a parliamentary rule, according to McMullen, that 'when ministers could not command a majority they retired from office.'[12] In the Canadas the governor and his appointed councillors were effectively freed from the

10 Ibid., 173–95
11 Ibid., 206–11
12 Ibid., 234, 321–2

assembly's check. The combination of racial disharmony and constitutional imbalance inherent in the provisions of the act set off a new round of controversy centred on the legislatures themselves.

Had the Constitutional Act of 1791 preserved the integrity of Quebec's boundaries and of British political practices, the race problem in Lower Canada might have been resolved quietly. As it was, those difficulties that continued to exist in the province were, McMullen believed, pre-eminently constitutional. The grievance that ignited conflict was the control exerted over the colony's government by a corrupt and almost totally English-speaking oligarchy, formed under the cover of the authoritarian Quebec Act and now sheltered by appointed office. The mostly professional members of the French-Canadian élite, frustrated by their lack of access to positions of administrative power, roused the racial prejudice of uncomprehending habitant voters in order to capture a majority in the assembly, and from that body pushed their own self-interest under the guise of parliamentary right. While McMullen condemned the methods and hypocrisy of the French-speaking politicians, he nevertheless asserted that 'an irresponsible executive was at the root of most public disorders' in Lower as well as Upper Canada. In time, he continued, 'it became evident that Lower Canada had to pass through the same revolutionary ordeal as its western sister. In both provinces identical causes were producing precisely similar results, and at nearly the same time.'[13]

Starting with a clean racial slate – assuming one excluded the native people (which almost everybody did) – Upper Canada would appear to have been in a better position than its sister province to develop materially and coalesce as a community. McMullen agreed that the upper province started out well and praised Lieutenant-Governor John Graves Simcoe for his far-sighted and liberal approach to the distribution of land and his open policy toward late Loyalists. McMullen also admired the colony's first assemblymen, whom he described as plain farmers and merchants possessed of 'great common sense.' Unhappily, constitutional disharmony, not racial heterogeneity, lay at the root of disruption in the Canadas. McMullen perceived the formation of an oligarchy in Upper Canada as early as 1805, protected by appointed office and cohered by intermarriage. After the fashion of John Mills Jackson, Robert Gourlay, and William Lyon Mackenzie, McMullen recited the litany of martyred agitators, the call and response of Compact and reform. He was, however,

13 Ibid., 215–23, 316–22

more sanguine than his sources: first because he saw how economic development went speedily forward despite the defective constitution; and second because he knew from his post-union vantage point that constitutional struggle in the colony would be resolved successfully. Indeed, McMullen implied that just as material progress must be earned through hard work, so must constitutional responsibility if it was to be deserved.[14]

Hindsight also permitted McMullen to dismiss concern that political opposition was a symptom of a deeper disloyalty to Britain and monarchical institutions. He understood, though did not excuse, the Americans for their revolution during the momentary despotic list of George III. Britain had since righted itself, while the United States had, under Thomas Jefferson, tumbled into a democratic tyranny that found common cause with the likes of Napoleon. If Canadians were dissatisfied with the power accruing to the oligarchies, 'they were in no disposition to cure ills of this kind, by a recourse to the greater evil of unbridled republicanism.' The War of 1812 provided proof that Canadians of both races meant to keep their political opposition within the bounds of the empire. Comparatively few of them joined the American side, and large invading armies were 'repelled by a few regular troops, aided by the Canadian militia, whose patriotism and unflinching courage did them the greatest honor.' 'This circumstance,' McMullen added, 'goes far to establish the fact that the climate of Canada is more favourable to the growth of a hardy and military population, than the milder and more luxurious regions farther south.'[15]

The bitterness of the constitutional debate that McMullen subsequently chronicled was, in fact, deceptive. He assumed, but rarely mentioned, that the evolution of colonial political institutions went forward against a backdrop of significant economic growth and increasing social maturity. Outside the doors of the two legislatures, a 'rough, home-spun, generation' of colonists built a nation long before it was constitutionally recognized as such. In accepting the general reform interpretation of events in the Canadas, McMullen reversed its priorities: he did not believe progress in other fields to be contingent on political

14 Ibid., 225–6, 230–9, 328–34, 351, 357
15 Ibid., 241–8, 260, 265, 287. In his account of the War of 1812, McMullen contributed to the growth of two of the more popular myths of Canadian history: 'the Militia Legend of 1812' and 'the heritage of northern races.' See C.P. Stacey, 'The War of 1812 in Canadian History,' *Ontario History* 50 (1958): 153–9; and Carl Berger, 'The True North Strong and Free,' in Peter Russell, ed., *Nationalism in Canada* (Toronto 1966) 3–26.

change. His confidence in the settlers of Canada was such that he simply had no doubt that they would ultimately achieve a constitutional status commensurate with their worth as a people.[16]

McMullen's optimism made it difficult to account for rebellion, especially in Upper Canada. He made his task no easier by purposely minimizing the strength of what he called the 'ultras' of party conflict in the western province – that is, of republican annexationists on the one hand and die-hard oligarchs on the other. Building on an insight of Lord Durham's, McMullen suggested that the dramatic increase of immigrants from Britain following 1825 had 'completely restructured' the two great political parties of Upper Canada, for it reduced the republican element in the Reform party to 'a mere fractional proportion,' and created a moderate 'Conservative party' to replace the outworn Family Compact. Furthermore, under the moderating influence of British sentiment, *both* parties began to move, albeit at different rates, toward the understanding that responsible government – 'a ministry based on a Parliamentary majority' – was the natural path of constitutional reform and colonial self-government.[17] Upper Canadians were diverted from this moderate course only by the unhappy convergence of events that brought together the 'grievance-monger,' William Lyon Mackenzie, and 'another little man like himself,' Lieutenant-Governor Sir Francis Bond Head. Mackenzie led the radical 'refuse of the Reform Party,' and Head the remnants of the Family Compact, into a rebellious confrontation that generated more smoke than flame. In the end, what McMullen called 'Sir Francis Head's rebellion' had little to do with the vast majority of Upper Canadians, and its only lesson was to highlight the danger extremists and egotists presented to society as a whole.[18]

McMullen found it more difficult to maintain his optimism in the face of events in Lower Canada. Again following the lines of Lord Durham's interpretation, and relying on Robert Christie for information, McMullen expressed the concern of English-speaking Canadians that the unassimilated habitant was by nature opposed to improvement and innovation of any kind and was therefore unfit to wield the electoral power conceded by the Constitutional Act of 1791. Protected by their numerical superiority within Lower Canada, the majority of habitants 'were as illiterate, as unreflecting, and as little capable of judging for themselves in 1835, as they were when [Major General Jeffrey] Amherst descended the St

16 McMullen, *History of Canada*, 1st ed., 239–40, 381–4
17 Ibid., 347, 355–63, 413
18 Ibid., 345–6, 364

Lawrence for the final subjugation of Canada.' Indeed, goaded by an élite composed of 'briefless French lawyers and patientless young physicians' and led by an individual 'intoxicated' with 'visions of his prospective presidency of *La Nation Canadienne*,' the habitants lent their weight to a campaign for the creation of an independent country founded on the basis of race.[19] Unfortunately for all concerned, Louis-Joseph Papineau overestimated the strength of his own support and underestimated that of Britain and in a desperate gamble on rebellion met the defeat his cowardice and cause deserved. Having re-established its control, the Anglo-Saxon race must, in McMullen's opinion, move with more purpose and dedication toward the eventual assimilation of their French-speaking compatriots. In doing so they would have the assurance that time and history were on their side, but also the knowledge that their task would be much more difficult in the 1840s than it would have been in the 1760s.[20]

Rebellion in the Canadas was regrettable primarily because it was, in McMullen's view, unnecessary. From the outset he believed that those 'few political evils which existed must soon have disappeared before the pressure of constitutional agitation, the progress of national intelligence, and the increase of national population and wealth.' Those who thought the achievement of responsible government due to the efforts of Mackenzie and Papineau were doubly mistaken: first, because far from hastening the day of constitutional reform, the resort to violence aroused 'men's evil passions,' diverted energy and resources from useful pursuits, 'and checked the progress of the country.' Constitutional reform, when it came, was due to the legal measures taken by the large body of political moderates – led by Robert Baldwin and the Reform party, but followed closely by the Conservatives: 'to their efforts, when the storm had passed over, and not to the insane attempts at rebellion of Mackenzie and others, equally wicked and mischievous, may be ascribed the enviable political condition in which [the country] now finds itself.'[21]

McMullen had, perforce, to portray the subsequent mission and *Report* of Lord Durham not as a response to the immediate crisis of the rebellions, but as acknowledgment of the Canadas' coming of age. Put simply, settlers in the two provinces had reached that point in their progress and maturity at which it was no longer possible to govern without responsible institutions. Durham had the prescience to recognize this fact, and, 'short as his administration had been no individual ever benefitted

19 Ibid., 316–17, 374–5, 386–91, 460
20 Ibid., 386–94
21 Ibid., 421–50

Canada more.' McMullen described the 'celebrated Report,' on which he had relied so heavily, as 'a lasting monument of elaborate research, impartial scrutiny, and historical worth.' It led shortly both to the concession of responsible government and, just as significantly, to the beneficial imposition of a national union that commenced the long-delayed 'fusion of the two races.' Thus, McMullen concluded: 'The present prosperous condition of this country affords the best commentary on [Lord Durham's] wisdom and disinterested patriotism; and the almost total absence of political excitement, and the contented condition of the people at large, constitute the most durable monument to his memory.'[22]

It was McMullen's understanding that the actual grant of responsible government flowed from the October 1839 dispatch of John Russell, first Earl Russell, in which Russell instructed the new governor-general, Charles Edward Poulett Thomson (soon to be first Baron Sydenham), to ensure 'the harmony of the executive with the legislative authorities,' instructions given effective form by the Harrison-Baldwin resolutions of September 1841. McMullen assumed that in practice such harmony was to be obtained by rendering the principal members of the executive council dependent for their position, as in Britain, on the majority in the assembly. 'In this way the Canadian ministry would be directly responsible to the people' and the Compact system overthrown. Sydenham's problem, in the wake of the rebellions, was to find a party capable of obtaining a majority of public support: members of the Compact, radical Reformers, and most of the French-Canadian race were discredited; the Conservative party was dispirited; and the moderate Reform party was, if anything, too enthusiastic. In the short term, then, McMullen accepted that the governor-general must play a leading role in fashioning a political consensus among Canadians.[23]

Lord Sydenham earned high praise from McMullen for the selfless and far-sighted way in which he mediated among parties divided by race and political passion, reconciled doubters to the new forms, and restrained the exuberance of the Reform victors. If Sydenham had a weakness, it was that he was unwilling to admit French Canadians to his council. Fortunately his successor, Sir Charles Bagot, had no such qualms, and freely consulted with the disaffected race. For McMullen there was no question that this was the wisest policy for Bagot to adopt; differences between races must be removed if Canadians were ever to unite 'more

22 Ibid., 402–4
23 Ibid., 457–60, 477–8

cordially for the common weal.' Besides, 'the French-Canadian element was no longer in the ascendant – the English language had decidedly assumed the aggressive, and true wisdom consisted in forgetting the past, and opening the door of preferment to men of talent of French, as well as to those of British origin.' Indeed, 'a different policy would have nullified the principle of responsible government, and must have proved suicidal to any ministry seeking to carry it out.'[24]

It was McMullen's belief that under the ministrations of Sydenham and Bagot something approaching a national concord began to emerge in the Canadas. In fact, the underlying economic and social preconditions of nationalism had been in place for some time, and had it not been for the rebellions their political consequences would have emerged sooner. As it was, when Bagot's reactionary successor, Charles Theophilus Metcalfe, first Baron Metcalfe, 'sought to form a provisional, or irresponsible, cabinet,' his plans foundered on the intransigent opposition of the Canadian majority. The subsequent administration of James Bruce, eighth earl of Elgin and twelfth earl of Kincardine, was important not – as later historians would have it – for introducing responsible government, but because Elgin had the strength and self-confidence to turn over the reins of government to Canada's first unified ministry, that of Robert Baldwin and Louis-Hippolyte La Fontaine.[25]

McMullen charted Canada's growth 'in infancy, childhood, and youth,' and his tale had two important lessons for his fellow citizens. The first was that, for national unity to be achieved, the tendency to press 'for sweeping ultra measures,' for extremes of any kind, must be firmly resisted and guarded against. Baldwin had, to his detriment, briefly fallen into this trap in the heady days following the grant of responsible government, while on the other side the Conservative annexationist reaction to the Rebellion Losses Bill momentarily crippled that party's standing among the moderate majority of Canadians. The second lesson was that national unity was similarly imperilled by the continued existence of an aggressive and distinct French-speaking community. The antiprogressive traits of the French race, and its consequent isolationist and obstructionist political attitudes, must be transcended by modern Anglo-Saxon values, for the good of both the habitant and the nation of which he was now inextricably a part. If Canadians kept the practical lessons of their past in mind, McMullen was optimistic that they would avoid the pitfalls of radicalism

24 Ibid., 479–80
25 Ibid., 481–7; Graeme H. Patterson, 'An Enduring Canadian Myth: Responsible Government and the Family Compact,' *JCS* 12 (1977): 11–12

and race, and he observed with approval that the contemporary 'line of demarcation between Conservatives and Reformers [had] been so narrowed down as to render it difficult to be distinguished.'[26]

The historical line of descent traced by McMullen was, despite its reform provenance, an intensely conservative route. He thought change precarious if based on radical or abstract principles, more likely to induce a passionate reaction than attain a lasting improvement. He preferred slow and steady progress, built on the dignity and stability of the sequence of precedents that defined a nation's history. Those who accepted his *via media* must balance continuity with change and be wary of both the obstinacy of Tory attachments to the past and radical repudiations of it. That McMullen's conservatism was not meant to be purely theoretical is clear from the quietly partisan way in which he tracked the Conservative party back to pre-Rebellion roots and gave it a place in the ancestry of responsible government. At the same time he was quick to point out the extremist tendencies of the modern Reform party, in particular of George Brown's Clear Grits and Papineau's band of French-Canadian followers (shortly to become known as the *parti rouge*). One can in fact find in McMullen's *History of Canada* an incipient justification for the Hincksite reconciliation with moderate Conservatives and the formation of the new Liberal-Conservative party that was to govern Canada for so many years.[27]

'The present condition of Canada,' McMullen concluded, 'points to a future of national greatness of no ordinary magnitude.' The land held 'all the *desiderata* necessary to human happiness,' and past experience proved that when people joined in the exploitation of common economic resources, antagonisms of race and individuals eased. McMullen considered contemporary 'commercial and agricultural interests of all Canadian people ... alike: in every district they stand upon the same social basis, and produce similar political results.' Nor could the boundaries of the Canadas hold this sense of community, which must presently absorb 'all our North American provinces.' Such a development was both natural and good, for 'in ... union is strength, national influence, and national credit: while disunion must always lead to dissension, weakness, and the absence of national importance.' The remaining ties to Britain certainly

26 McMullen, *History of Canada*, 1st cd., 381–92, 478, 488–500
27 Ibid., 495–501. On McMullen's affinity for the Liberal-Conservative party, see NA, Henry James Morgan Papers, MG 21, D 61, vol. 28, McMullen to Henry James Morgan, Jan. 1896; and James MacPherson LeMoine, *Monographies et esquisses* ([Quebec 1885]) 53–4.

would not inhibit national growth, for while they secured the province from invasion, they involved 'no sacrifice of interests – no compromise injurious to Canadian welfare.' Indeed, the individual colonies were 'to all intents and purposes ... now practically as independent of the Mother Country, as the American Union.'[28] As was the case with Lord Durham's *Report*, in McMullen's *History of Canada* the history of British North America was but the history of the united Canadas – really Upper Canada – writ large.

What most clearly distinguished McMullen the historian from his predecessors was the way in which he drew sustenance from a narrative of his adopted country's past. He was able to do so because he was basically pleased with the outcome. Put another way, his confidence in the possession of the past was really confidence in the present. From the post-Union side of history, he could adopt historical interpretations put forward by Upper Canadian Reformers as remedies for constitutional problems without inheriting their sense of frustration and occasional pessimism. He now saw little to regret in a past that was by definition a success story. Ultimately, his history reflected a desire by Canadians to celebrate and consolidate achievement; the elaboration of potential was a secondary concern.

It should be clear by now that McMullen had a great deal in common with the Whig historians of Great Britain – the likes of Thomas Babington Macaulay, William Stubbs, Edward Augustus Freeman, and William Edward Hartpole Lecky. However, one should not mistake similarity for identity. The Whig interpretation of history was the product of a unique combination of, on the one hand, such universal historical concepts as change and continuity, and, on the other, a particular range of topics having contemporary relevance for nineteenth-century Britons.[29] There were portions of this tradition, such as the assumption that the Revolutionary Settlement of 1688 set the terms of the modern British constitution, that McMullen found useful, and others, such as the debate over the Norman Conquest, that he did not. The fact is that McMullen, like other

28 McMullen, *History of Canada*, 1st ed., Preface, 383, 391
29 The Whig interpretation of history was first identified and labelled by Herbert Butterfield in his *The Whig Interpretation of History* (London 1931) and his *The Englishman and His History* (Cambridge 1944). It has recently been more carefully analysed and defined in P.B.M. Blaas, *Continuity and Anachronism: Parliamentary and Constitutional Development in Whig Historiography and in the Anti-Whig Reaction between 1890 and 1930* (The Hague 1978); and in J.W. Burrow, *A Liberal Descent: Victorian Historians and the English Past* (Cambridge 1981). See also John Clive, 'Chosen People,' *New York Review of Books*, 24 June 1982, 41–4.

Canadian historians, had his own agenda, which included a vastly different set of challenges from those that interested British historians and dealt with a quite different conquest. True, his focus on constitutional development had a superficial resemblance to Whig historiography in Britain, but in Canada constitutional issues were tied much more closely to assumptions about material progress and geographic expansion and were intended to act as a centripetal force rather than as a justification for partisan traditions. In short, what was relevant in Britain was not necessarily relevant in Canada, and Canadian historiography was not simply an extension of its British counterpart.

On the whole it would seem best to leave the term Whig to the British and refer to the approach employed by McMullen, and the school of thought he represented, as 'the National interpretation' of Canadian history – National because it promoted the concept of Canada as a nation housing a common people who sought common goals and inhabited a common land, if not stretching from sea to sea, at least comprising all the British provinces of North America. The event that gave these historians their victorious hold over history was the passage of the Act of Union in 1840, the supposed corollaries of which – responsible government and assimilation of French Canadians – they wished to celebrate. Advocates of the National position used history to confirm their predispositions and were unapologetically anachronistic in their reading of the past. In their eyes ideologies were divisive, regionalism was parochial, and racial (that is, French-Canadian) distinctions were illegitimate. Conciliation, consolidation, and assimilation were the order of the day. The fact that subsequent events strained the reality of a unified and uniform country did not immediately undermine the confidence of National historians. Indeed their fervour increased in the face of adversity.

Canadians, in their quest for political order, social stability, and national identity, used history as a source of examples with which to implant in the minds of younger generations (and even mature politicians) an established pattern of acceptable conduct, to secure conformity by habit, not law. McMullen was the first Canadian historian successfully to articulate the spirit of this age, and there is no reason to doubt the judgment of Ken Windsor that *The History of Canada from Its First Discovery to the Present Time* 'was the standard guide to Canadian history in the second half of the nineteenth century.'[30] All 1,200 copies of the first

30 Kenneth N. Windsor, 'Historical Writing in Canada to 1920,' in Carl F. Klinck, gen. ed., *Literary History of Canada: Canadian Literature in English* (Toronto 1965) 216

edition were sold within three years, which, so far as one can tell, was another first for English-Canadian historians.[31]

Another sign that McMullen accurately reflected the sentiments of the time is the way his general approach was subsequently imitated and adopted by other historians. Those who followed, however, were not always convinced that narratives of past events were the only or even the best means historians had at their command to inculcate common values and inspire emotional bonds. Many historians, often quoting the ubiquitous Dr Samuel Smiles, high priest of the Victorian cult of self-help, to the effect that individual character was 'the only sure guarantee for social security and national progress,' turned to biography and the veneration of the nation's forefathers in the hope of uniting and rousing contemporary generations.[32] Consequent volumes of biographical sketches were intended to establish their subjects individually as personifications of Canadian political and social principles and character, as emotive examples for the present even more than as causative factors in the past. In truth, historians were not celebrating extraordinary men so much as the system that produced them.[33] Operating under this constraint, the resulting biographies were, not surprisingly, often bloodless.

The pre-eminent cataloguer of eminent Canadians was Henry James Morgan (1842–1913). Born at Quebec City, Morgan was the son of a veteran of the Napoleonic Wars who had come to the Canadas in 1838. His father died about 1847, and in 1853, at the age of eleven, Morgan entered the civil service as a page and then a sessional clerk. He continued in the government's employ, almost without interruption, until his

31 Morgan Papers, vol. 47, McMullen to Morgan, 5 Mar. 1861. McMullen's history proved far more influential than that of Charles Roger (1819–78?), who managed to publish only the first volume of a projected three-volume history entitled *The Rise of Canada, from Barbarism to Wealth and Civilisation* (Quebec 1856); Frederick H. Armstrong, 'Charles Roger,' *DCB*, vol. 10 (Toronto 1972) 627; M. Brook Taylor, 'The Writing of English-Canadian History in the Nineteenth Century' (PH D Diss., University of Toronto 1984) vol. 2, 285–7.

32 Quoted in Henry J. Morgan, *Sketches of Celebrated Canadians, and Persons Connected with Canada, from the Earliest Period in the History of the Province Down to the Present Time* (Quebec 1862), Motto. On Smiles see Timothy Travers, 'Samuel Smiles and the Pursuit of Success in Victorian Britain,' Canadian Historical Association, *Historical Papers* (1971): 154–68.

33 Henry J. Morgan, *The Place British North Americans Have Won in History. A Lecture Delivered at Aylmer, L.C., on Thursday Evening, 22nd February, 1866* (Ottawa 1866); Arthur H. Shaffer, *The Politics of History: Writing the History of the American Revolution, 1783–1815* (Chicago 1975) 135–6; cf, Windsor, 'Historical Writing in Canada,' 215

retirement on a pension in 1895.[34] This attachment to the Canadian government, in both its pre- and post-Confederation guises, influenced Morgan the historian in two important respects. First, his never-onerous duties gave him leisure to write. Indeed, there is some reason to believe that Morgan was actually assigned to offices as an 'extra' clerk in order that he might devote more time to his literary endeavours.[35] Second, a commitment to the central authority instilled in him a nationalism intolerant of competing identities.

Open and gregarious by nature, Morgan professed 'an intense love' for his native land, 'a just pride' in its achievements, and 'an ardent hope and desire for its future greatness.' Deeply concerned that the Union of 1840 was unravelling under regional, racial, and partisan pressures, in 1862 Morgan published his first important book, *Sketches of Celebrated Canadians*, in order to promote patriotism through the veneration and imitation of the founders of the United Province.[36] When similar problems threatened the young confederation in 1868, Morgan joined with such like-minded young patriots as Charles Mair, George Taylor Denison, III, and others to found Canada First, a semi-convivial and semi-political organization dedicated to the promotion of a common Canadian nationalism.[37] In short, few individuals could claim to have responded more readily to the challenge of a 'New Nationality' laid down by the martyred Thomas D'Arcy McGee.

Morgan's profession, for all its advantages, ultimately restrained and then subdued this activism. He was not a wealthy man and was sensitive about his position as a civil servant. In an era when almost all government jobs were to some extent patronage appointments, the career civil servant had to tack to the partisan wind of the times if he was to survive. Known as a Conservative (the *Sketches* were dedicated to sometime party leader Sir Allan Napier MacNab), Morgan received more than one object lesson in the realities of patronage, being dismissed briefly at least twice by

34 There is no biography of this biographer, and his life's story must be pieced together from John Charles Dent, *The Canadian Portrait Gallery*, 4 vols (Toronto 1880–1) vol. 4 (1881) 207–8; Norman Shrive, *Charles Mair: Literary Nationalist* (Toronto 1965) 26–31, 111, 162–3; and Carl Berger, *The Sense of Power: Studies in the Ideas of Canadian Imperialism, 1867–1914* (Toronto 1970) 49–50, 54, 70, 77.
35 NA, Isaac Buchanan Papers, MG 24, D 16, vol. 48, Henry James Morgan to Isaac Buchanan, 4 June 1862
36 Morgan, *Sketches of Celebrated Canadians*, vi–viii
37 Berger, *The Sense of Power*, ch. 2

unfriendly ministers.[38] He was therefore careful to disguise or suppress his partisan beliefs, and he dropped out of the Canada First movement when it began to take an active political role.

The implications for Morgan the historian were obvious. Intended as a work of exhortation, even the *Sketches of Celebrated Canadians* exhibited the reticence of a sessional clerk. Morgan thereafter concentrated on the compilation of such prosaic works as the *Canadian Parliamentary Companion*, the *Dominion Annual Register*, and one of the first bibliographies of publications relating to Canada, *Bibliotheca Canadiensis*.[39] According to drinking companion and fellow Canada Firster Charles Mair, Morgan became with age 'a mere collating machine.' 'Ye Gods!' Mair wrote in exasperation to their mutual friend George Taylor Denison, III, 'Think of a man's intellectual energies culminating in a pair of shears and a paste-pot.'[40] Sadly, only the product of his youth, the *Sketches of Celebrated Canadians*, made a lasting contribution to Canadian history.

Morgan presented his sketches in chronological order, which in methodological terms meant that the book was divided roughly in two, between biographies of those then dead and those still alive, practically between those active prior to, and those active after, the Rebellions of 1837–8. In the case of the former, Morgan relied on previously published accounts (in which he was widely read) for his information, and of the latter on the reminiscences of his subjects and personal observation. However, his cautious approach and interpretation transcended this division, for the pre- and post-Rebellion eras presented equally extensive minefields for the politically unwary historian. In any event Morgan was not writing to discuss divisions and problems, but to chronicle success. His aim was less to sort out good from bad than to fit all the deserving in.[41] The resulting text often fell short of the inspirational.

When Morgan came to write the *Sketches*, he could assume that his audience already had a stereotypical view of the French regime and the reasons for its collapse: the heavy hand of imperial, military, and religious hierarchies smothered individualism, enterprise, and freedom, and

38 Buchanan Papers, vol. 48, Morgan to Buchanan, 4 June 1862; 19 May, 27 June, 23 Sept., 6, 16 Oct., 2 Dec. 1864; Shrive, *Charles Mair*, 111
39 For a list of Morgan's publications see Norah Story, *The Oxford Companion to Canadian History and Literature* (Toronto 1967) 540.
40 Charles Mair to George Taylor Denison, III 6 Jan. 1884, quoted in Shrive, *Charles Mair*, 162–3. Berger refers to Morgan as 'a veritable Gradgrind,' *Sense of Power*, 49.
41 Morgan, *Sketches of Celebrated Canadians*, vii–viii

doomed the colony. Thus, Morgan was free to praise the 'resolve,' 'daring,' 'self-sacrifice,' and 'foresight' of individual Frenchmen – of Cartier, Champlain, and Montcalm – without having to provide a corresponding description of the defective society of which they were part.[42] Morgan gently implied the inevitability and desirability of the conquest of New France by Anglo-American forces, but had the luxury of not having to say so directly.

Similarly, when discussing the constitutional struggle of the 1820s and 1830s, Morgan paid lip-service to the common denunciation of the greedy Family Compact and the annexationist radicals, and then proceeded to exculpate their members as individuals. In his hands, for instance, Sir James Craig, John Beverley Robinson, and William Lyon Mackenzie were all honourable men of sincerely held, although mistaken, beliefs.[43] Morgan upheld criticism of extremism in general but avoided giving individual offence. The fact that he felt free to indulge in unrestrained criticism of Louis-Joseph Papineau and Wolfred Nelson said a great deal about the weakness of their contemporary legacy in English Canada.[44] The National interpretation still stood; Morgan did nothing to contradict it; he merely let it shoulder the burden of odium that inevitably accrues to the critic.

Morgan became more circumspect as he approached his own age. He wanted to promote unity and rise above the increasing acrimony of his time, and yet he had to deal with the individual parties to contemporary disputes. His solution to the problem was to solicit information from his subjects and then rely uncritically on their responses to construct a series of biographies that, when mixed with quotations from a few published sources, expressed individual and often contradictory points of view on the questions of the day.[45]

---

42 Ibid., 1–50
43 Ibid., 157–61, 283–6, 330–7
44 Ibid., 327–30, 337–40
45 Ibid., v–viii. Over the winter of 1860–1, Morgan sent out handwritten letters to his prospective subjects requesting biographical information; for example see NA, Louis-Hippolyte La Fontaine Papers, MG 24, B 14, vol. 17, 3020, [copy] Morgan to L.-H. La Fontaine, 5 Feb. 1861. He followed up these with a printed circular, which he sent off in May of 1861; for example see Buchanan Papers, vol. 48, Morgan to Buchanan, 28 May 1861. Morgan's requests were so vaguely worded that several of his respondents were confused as to his purpose. For instance J.M. McMullen wrote back: 'I do not understand clearly what you require. If you were to let me understand precisely what you want I might feel myself disposed to meet your views.' Morgan Papers, vol. 47, McMullen to Morgan, 5 Mar. 1861

This method flew directly in the face of advice given him in 1860 by Robert Phipps Dod (son of the late compiler of Britain's *Parliamentary Companion*, Charles Roger Phipps Dod):

> As you have asked for some advice on the subject, I will mention one or two points which I conceive to be important. First I have strongly to advise you to *begin* by aiming at perfect independence of the Members themselves in your supply of information – to collect your accounts of each man as complete as public records & journals will enable you – and then *when they are collected* to apply to every member without exception for information as if *you had collected nothing*. Next collate your two sets of accounts and you will not be trapped or humbugged by anyone ... Then furthermore let *no* member whatever *dictate* the account to be given of him.[46]

The whole point, as far as Morgan was concerned, was that he did not believe himself independent of the politicians he served, and his intuition was correct. His requests for information caused a flurry of letters among politicians anxious to divine his purpose and establish his *bona fides*.[47] In any event, he bent over backwards to include as many individuals as he could in his compilation, gave equal space to all regardless of merit, and permitted each to tell his own tale.[48]

The result, predictably enough, was that issues of historical detail were totally obscured by contradiction. One could, to give an example, piece together from the sketches of Robert Baldwin, John Sandfield Macdonald, and George-Étienne Cartier the common view: that Baldwin led the fight for responsible government – defined as a ministry dependent on a majority in the assembly; that Lord Durham accepted and promoted this solution, Lord John Russell instructed Lord Sydenham to institute it, and Sydenham did so by way of the Harrison-Baldwin resolutions of September 1841; and that the policy as pursued by Governor-General Sir Charles Metcalfe was reactionary and unconstitutional.[49] One could also find among other biographies several arguments to the contrary: in the

46 Morgan Papers, vol. 47, R.P. Dod to Morgan, 25 July 1860
47 For example, see La Fontaine Papers, vol. 17, 3029–30, Étienne Parent to La Fontaine, [copy] 29 Mar. 1861.
48 Isaac Buchanan embarrassed Morgan by inundating him with more information than he could use. In order to avoid offending his patron, Morgan subsequently helped Buchanan put his papers together in pamphlet form. Buchanan Papers, vol. 48, Morgan to Buchanan, 28 Sept., 13 Nov. 1861
49 Morgan, *Sketches of Celebrated Canadians*, 397–405, 537–41, 603–8

sketch of Lord Durham, R.M. Martin was quoted to the effect that the famed *Report* made only a 'vague declaration of responsible government, productive of no good result'; in the sketch of Sir Charles Metcalfe, Baldwin and La Fontaine were condemned for their advocacy of partisan government and the governor-general praised for his strong leadership and commitment to responsible government based on a coalition ministry of all the talents; in the sketch of John Alexander Macdonald it was admitted that the Harrison-Baldwin resolutions permitted more than one interpretation of responsible government; and, finally, in the sketch of Lord Elgin, the Lord Provost of Glasgow was quoted as giving Elgin the honour of introducing responsible government.[50] Ultimately Morgan left the reader to decide for himself when and by whom responsible government was introduced, and, for that matter, what it was.

This is not to say that Morgan made no points of his own. His purpose was, after all, not to give a coherent narrative of Canadian history, but to focus on those qualities of statesmanship that made certain individuals, and by extension the nation, great. The greatest of Canada's statesmen was, in Morgan's opinion, the man to whom the *Sketches of Celebrated Canadians* was dedicated, Sir Allan Napier MacNab. What made MacNab great was, according to Morgan, his talent for conciliation. In early life MacNab had been a devoted Tory, a supporter of the Family Compact; but, when he found that the country was averse to the continuance of his principles, 'he gracefully yielded to the wishes of the people.' Like Isaac Buchanan, John A. Macdonald, and Joseph-Édouard Cauchon, MacNab belonged 'to that modern school of practical politicians, who in all their acts and conduct, are aiming at success rather than the triumph of their personal opinions or principles; who think that circumstances alter cases.'[51]

Apply these criteria to the Metcalfe crisis, and it was clear to Morgan that Baldwin's and La Fontaine's stubborn adherence to an ultimately victorious principle was at the time politically maladroit because in advance of public opinion. Morgan implied that they and the like-minded George Brown were part of 'that small but obdurate class of politicians who refuse to compromise or modify their views, when success is likely to be the result of a few concessions.' Their stands, however honourable in principle, were inevitably divisive in practice. Morgan was not surprised that the great Reform ministry of 1848 fell apart, or that it was replaced by a coalition of moderate Reformers and Conservatives under McNab's

50 Ibid., 364, 370, 432–46, 500–9, 581–602
51 Ibid., 475, 611–12

leadership, which, despite 'much opposition and calumny,' had given the country 'seven years of wise government.'[52]

Thus by a more circuitous route did Morgan bring his readers to a position not far from McMullen's progressive conservatism. That Morgan had to be so circumspect was due, in the first instance, to his professional insecurity, in the second, to the general breakdown in the early 1860s of the Union of 1840, a breakdown characterized by the resurgence of Reform radicals, or Grits, and by the persistence of a self-determined French-Canadian community. Morgan was fearful of the centrifugal forces in his society, dedicated himself to limiting their effect, and sought to reassert the consensual values of the National tradition. Rigid adherence to principle, self-indulgence, and defence of region and race he labelled parochialism. In place of stern principle, he held up pragmatism and compromise as the tools of the true statesman, and the larger issues of the nation as the proper sphere for their exercise.

Morgan used an ancient trick of diplomats to teach contemporary politicians: he flattered his subjects into living up to an ideal he ascribed to them. There is, in fact, some evidence in the Confederation debates of the Canadian Parliament that politicians attempted, often in spite of themselves, to act in the image of a Morgan celebrity. Thomas D'Arcy McGee noticed this phenomenon and commented on it before his peers in the House of Commons:

We have, I believe, several hundred celebrities in Canada – my friend Mr. Morgan, I believe, has made out a list of them – (laughter) – but they are no longer now local celebrities; if celebrities at all they must be celebrities for British North America; for every one of the speeches made by them on this subject is watched in all the provinces, and in point of fact by the mere appearance of political union, we have made a mental union among the people of all these provinces.[53]

In short, just as McMullen provided an incipient justification for the Hincksite reconciliation with moderate Conservatives, so did Morgan provide the incipient justification for the Great Coalition of 1864.

When it came in 1867, Confederation rejuvenated nationalism in the two old Canadian provinces, especially among English-speaking citizens.

52 Ibid., 445, 558, 611–12
53 *Parliamentary Debates on the Subject of the Confederation of the British North American Provinces*, 3rd Session, 8th Provincial Parliament of Canada (Quebec 1865) 128

Not only did the new constitutional arrangement hold out the promise of political reconciliation and racial harmony, it also proffered a whole new range of national opportunities. It was politically, economically, and geographically liberating. In the eyes of many Canadians Confederation represented nothing less than a new era in the history of human progress in North America, perhaps even the happy ending historians had sought since the time of the promoters. Above all, it appeared, for a fleeting moment at least, that human nature too had changed and that the moral tone of society had taken a quantum leap forward, a leap symbolized by the Great Coalition, the death of partisanship, and the achievement of a national consensus.

It was during the heady years between 1865 and 1868 that John Fennings Taylor (1817–1882) wrote the biographical sketches for William Notman's three-volume *Portraits of British Americans*. Written in the confidence that Canada was on the threshold of national greatness, Taylor's sketches 'were pervaded by an exuberant sense of momentous achievement.'[54] In the introduction his excitement was palpable:

> The truth is, events of great national importance are hourly passing into history. Public opinion is visibly acquiring new animation. Political aspirations, moved by unseen influences, like the tide in spring, are rising to a purer level. Statesmen of different parties, appreciating the requirements of the hour, forgetting alike the rivalries and jealousies of the past, are agreed in declaring that the time is come when the power of these separated Provinces should be consolidated, when their individual strength should be knit together; when, as one great MONARCHICAL CONFEDERACY, they should practice in unison the graver duties of Government, should accept the burden of new obligations, and the administration of new trusts.[55]

Here was the real stuff of history, and Taylor, conscious of living in a time of great deeds and great actors, sought to record the careers of men who were truly inspirational and deserving of celebration.

It was largely accidental that it fell to Taylor to record the lives of Canada's statesmen of Confederation. Born in London, England, and educated at Radley in Oxfordshire, John Fennings Taylor came to Upper Canada in 1836 and settled in Toronto. Through the influence of his uncle, also John Fennings Taylor, the deputy clerk of the Legislative

54 Murray Barkley, 'John Fennings Taylor,' *DCB*, vol. 11 (Toronto 1982) 871–2
55 Fennings Taylor, ed., *Portraits of British Americans*, by William Notman, 3 vols (Montreal 1865–8) vol. 1 (1865) i–ii

Council of Upper Canada, Fennings Taylor, 'as the younger man was known to avoid confusion,' was appointed first office clerk of the council on 4 December 1836. In 1841, following the Act of Union, he was transferred to the office of the Legislative Council of the Province of Canada, and from there, following Confederation, to the office of the Senate of Canada, where he served until his death.[56] It was this non-partisan working proximity to the great and nearly great actors of the day that in 1864 recommended Taylor to Montreal photographer William Notman. What Notman required to complete the three volumes of studio portraits he was preparing for publication was a knowledgeable but uncontentious biographical sketch of each of the eighty-four eminent Canadian politicians, businessmen, and divines to be included. Taylor accepted Notman's request in the belief that accounts 'of courage, loyalty, devotion, high principle, and stainless honor, would not only promote innocent gratification and mental pleasure, but might, by exciting a sense of laudable emulation, tend to ... moral and national good.'[57]

Taylor's subject matter was predetermined by Notman's choice of portraits, which in turn had been selected on the basis of an individual's involvement with Confederation. As might be expected, the resultant collection was top-heavy with politicians from the two Canadian provinces, men who were both available to Notman and known to Taylor. However, in so far as Notman's portfolio and Taylor's familiarity permitted, the Portraits of British Americans also included businessmen, clerics, and politicians from the Maritimes and Newfoundland, provided also that their activities had buttressed Confederation. And because it was the purpose of Taylor and Notman to celebrate the union of British North America, Confederation not only established the criterion for inclusion in the Portraits, it also provided the sketches with a common interpretive bond: the achievement of Confederation, like the achievement of the lesser Union of 1840, sanctioned a retroactive reordering of history. Whereas Morgan, in professional insecurity and political uncertainty, had to pretend to a historical neutrality, Taylor knew which path had been taken and which side had emerged victorious. Thus, though a civil servant himself, Taylor had the confidence in the wake of Confederation to declare that the outcome of events should be so. He could, with Confederation in mind, weave a single narrative thread through his

---

56 *Ottawa Daily Free Press*, 5 May 1882; W. Stewart Wallace, 'The Two John Fennings Taylors,' *CHR* 28 (1947): 459; Barkley, 'John Fennings Taylor,' 871–2
57 Taylor, ed., *Portraits of British Americans*, vol. 1, v–vi. On William Notman see Stanley G. Triggs, *William Notman: The Stamp of a Studio* (Toronto 1985).

sketches, make all his biographies conform to it, and ensure that all his subjects were judged by it.

From the outset, Taylor had to face the fact that, for Confederation to be necessary, the Union of 1840 must be proved defective. In the event, his task was straightforward: rather than reorient the received interpretation of Canadian history, he continued it, assuming that McMullen had not mistaken the national direction of the country's past, just misjudged the moment of its resolution. What McMullen had ignored was the adverse effect the Act of Union's provision for the equal representation of the two old provinces in the new combined legislature had on subsequent political developments. Taylor argued that this measure, meant to protect English Canadians during a temporary period of numerical inferiority, had been seriously distorted by the great Reform ministry of 1848. According to Taylor, La Fontaine had, in 'dogmatic' defence of the French-Canadian race, induced Baldwin to match the dual representation in the legislature with dual administration in the cabinet, the 'involved consequence' of which was the adoption of the 'impracticable principle of ruling by sectional majorities in the same Legislature.' From the moment public men declined to recognize Canada as a whole, they ceased to think of it as a whole and failed to legislate for it as a whole. 'By creating two sections, their respective populations were provoked to compare those sections, and the comparison being followed by the discovery of important inequalities, a cry for adjustment inevitably followed.' Eventually the impolicy of the Reform ministry dwarfed 'the Government and the country by dividing them.'[58]

The revival of regional and racial parochialism was exacerbated by the extension to Canada of contemporary European ideological ferment. Taylor believed that the revolutionary upheavals of 1848 in Britain, Germany, and France were symptomatic of a rationalist trend in Western thought that was critical of divine right, the majesty of birth, and the pre-eminence of community. 'This curious passage in modern history possessed attractions for the visionary class all over the world,' and Canada, possessed of its own dreamers, was not immune to the contagion. Thus it was that just as the union came under stress, 'certain aspirants to human perfection, well meaning enthusiasts, set themselves to work to put everybody and everything in a state of moral and political repair.' Foremost among such enthusiasts was George Brown, whose crusade against the obscurantism of Roman Catholicism developed as its secular

58 Taylor, ed., *Portraits of British Americans*, vol. 1, 48, 129, 321–2; vol. 2 (1867) 195–6

counterpart the drive for representation by population. The mono-maniacal self-righteousness of these and other movements would brook no opposition, accept no compromise, and cumulatively threatened to rend the young nation.[59]

Fortunately for Canada there were countervailing tendencies. What-ever politicians might do, such men of commerce and industry as James Hodges, Charles John Brydges, and Isaac Buchanan were creating the economic infrastructure and the steel-rail backbone of a nation. Indeed, given Taylor's repeated reference to it, it is a wonder Notman did not include his photograph of the Victoria Bridge, completed in 1859 in order to span the St Lawrence River at Montreal for the Grand Trunk Railway.[60] Happily, these nation-builders did have political analogues in the person of such as John A. Macdonald, who, just as George Brown began to raise the antipopery and anti-Gallic cry in the Reform party, fashioned a span across the gulf of distrust that had separated the Conservative party from French Canadians. Still more significant from Taylor's point of view was the fact that there existed a French-Canadian leader, George-Étienne Cartier, who, unlike La Fontaine and Antoine-Amié Dorion, was not content simply to defend the preserve of his 'tribe,' but rather sought to reconcile his race to the reality of a greater Canadian nation. 'He fills,' Taylor wrote of Cartier,

a foremost place in the front ranks of Canadian statesmen – he has assiduously co-operated to secure equal rights to all parties, and having attained these blessings in a separated form, his desire now is, and it seems to be the aim of an increasing party in Canada, of which Mr. Cartier may be regarded as the type and representative, to fuse and conciliate all races as well as all sections in one perfect and harmonious whole.[61]

Taylor, like Morgan before him, distinguished clearly between politi-cians and statesmen: the former defended selfish ideological or parochial views, without a thought to practical long-term consequences; the latter set aside passions and old enmities, seized opportunity from changing circumstances, and willingly sacrificed personal to achieve national

59 Ibid., vol. 1, 409–10; vol. 2, 189–203
60 Ibid., vol. 1, 267–90, 347–70, 381–400; Triggs, *William Notman*, 38–9. For a provoca-tive discussion of the support science and technology provided for Confederation see Suzanne Zeller, *Inventing Canada: Early Victorian Science and the Idea of a Transcontinental Nation* (Toronto 1987) 5–9.
61 Taylor, ed., *Portraits of British Americans*, vol. 1, 27–8, 140

objectives. The one species was naturally reticent in the face of British North American union, the other enthusiastic at the prospect. However, in an elaboration of Morgan's dichotomy, Taylor held that the politician was as necessary as the statesman for the advancement of society, that without, for instance, the obstructive tactics of a Brown, a Dorion, or a John Sandfield Macdonald, the fulfilment of the Confederation strategy might have been impossible, its absolute indispensability obscured by lesser palliatives. Taylor revelled in the irony that the rationalists' actions achieved ends they never intended. That the ideologue George Brown should enter a coalition with his enemies in order to achieve representation by population and thereby inadvertently permit Confederation to usher in a 'new chapter in Canadian politics' illustrated once again to Taylor 'an old truth in English progress, namely, that history of constitutional government is, in part at least, the history of compromise and concession.'[62]

Taylor's was fundamentally a conservative view of man, history, and the constitution. It was his opinion that Britain was the only nation to have developed a mode of government in full recognition of man's limitations and essential irrationality. Constitutional monarchy protected human nature from itself by balancing property against persons, intelligence against ignorance, and community against individuals; it found safety in the variety as well as the number of councillors; and, above all, it understood that liberty was the gift of authority. Taylor celebrated Confederation, therefore, not as an act of union alone; he celebrated it also, perhaps principally, because it preserved the British constitution in North America. Confederation pre-empted annexationist and republican trends and protected Canadians from a democracy based exclusively on representation by population, a doctrine that history had rendered 'more conspicuous for its fallacy than its force.'[63] To be a Canadian nationalist was to be conservative.

In summary, it is possible to see in the work of John Mercier McMullen, Henry James Morgan, and John Fennings Taylor the emergence and formation of a historiographical consensus, namely, that the geographic, economic, and social imperatives of British North America dictated that its constituent parts composed, or should compose, one nation and one people, and furthermore that 'the process of transition to be accomplished wisely, must be accomplished without violence and especially without wrong.'[64] Theirs was a conservative interpretation of history,

62 Ibid., ii, 75–6, 137–9, 188
63 Ibid., vol. 2, 196–8
64 Ibid., 28

based on continuity with the past and satisfaction with the present, which rested warily beside their confident predictions of an ever-improving future. They sought to slacken the inherent tension between these positions by making future successes contingent on adherence to historical precedents. The future was only welcomed if it built on the past and did not seek to overturn it in despotism or revolutionize it in anarchic democracy. Such reservations suggest that Canada's National historians were not as confident of the future as they might appear at first blush. Indeed, it was their insecurity that in large measure drove them to educate the public and statesmen on how to build responsibly on the past displayed before them all in Canadian history.

One can see, for instance, just how fragile McMullen's faith in the nation's future was by reading the second edition of his *History of Canada*, which carried the narrative down to Confederation. In fact, Confederation's resolution to the problems of British North America never entirely overcame McMullen's disappointment at the failure of the Act of Union of 1840. Like Fennings Taylor, he blamed La Fontaine and the widespread persistence of French-Canadian particularism for the fatal provision of dual administration. Unlike Taylor, and indeed unlike the McMullen of the first edition, the McMullen of the second edition betrayed a real sense of bitterness toward the French-Canadian race and its Roman Catholic faith, a bitterness so strong that one suspects McMullen was drawing on his experience in Ireland. In any case, in the second edition McMullen displayed a greater tolerance for George Brown's religious and political crusades against the domination of the French Catholics than had hitherto been common in National historiography. In McMullen's hands Brown's actions appeared less as personal idiosyncrasy than as part of a general collapse of Canadian political life. By the early 1860s the 'factious spirit of the Assembly' had become, according to McMullen, 'wholly forgetful of the great public interests at stake,' and 'it appeared to be the sole aim of each of the rival parties to defeat their opponents, and secure themselves in power' – condemnation sweeping and inclusive.[65] McMullen obviously was distressed by the

---

65 McMullen, *History of Canada*, 2nd ed. (Brockville, Ont., 1868) 526–41, 569. The second edition was almost identical to the first for the period prior to 1850, the only significant changes being the insertion of a few paragraphs moderating previous criticisms of William Lyon Mackenzie (358–60, 377, 441, 468–70). This was apparently a response to Charles Lindsey's favourable handling of his father-in-law in *The Life and Times of Wm. Lyon Mackenzie. With an Account of the Canadian Rebellion of 1837, and the Subsequent Frontier Disturbances, Chiefly from Unpublished Documents*, 2 vols (Toronto 1862).

corruption, selfishness, and parochialism that laid the united province low.

Eventually faction 'literally exhausted itself.' With public affairs at a complete standstill, the leading political minds of the country applied themselves 'to discover some mode of escape.' 'One course, and one course only, promised relief; and that was the adoption of the "joint authority" scheme of Mr. Brown, so frequently voted down in Parliament, so long opposed, and so mercilessly ridiculed by friend and foe alike.' In McMullen's version of events, Confederation was not a clear and natural product of a historical dialectic: 'It would ... seem, as if a special Providence was controlling matters for its own wise purposes, and evoking results from the ambitions and passions of partisan leaders, directly tending to elevate this country to a position of greater eminence, and to increased usefulness among the nations.' If, like a majority of Canadians, McMullen 'gladly accepted the situation, and calmly and confidently awaited the progress of events,' he did so without the carefree enthusiasm of Taylor.[66] McMullen was by history made more wary, more embittered, more realistic.

In the second edition of McMullen's *History of Canada*, the National interpretation of the past began to unravel under the pressure of events. More than most men, the National historian required a consistently fair wind and could survive relatively little disappointment; a disillusioned National historian was a contradiction in terms. How convenient it would have been for their interpretation of the past to have found a point of stasis in the present and to have left the historical scene somewhere around the year 1867.

66 Ibid., 569–71

6
The Maritimes
Opt Out

The consensus of the Canadas' National school held few attractions for the patriot historians of the three Maritime provinces. They did not accept that responsible government was the principal theme of their respective histories; they did not believe that conflict was the engine of progress in their colonies; and they did not identify with the Canadian, particularly the French-Canadian, people. Maritime patriot historians instead focused on the moral and material progress of their colonies, believed that achievement came through the incremental efforts of generations of hard-working independent settlers, and saw in this process the basis of a distinctive identity. It was not, then, just that Canadian historians were high-handed and presumptuous; their interpretation did not fit the facts of the Maritime past.

The predicament was that the growing economic and political power of the Canadas seemed to prove the continentalist case made by its historians. The assumption that British North America was one land housing a common people seeking a common goal might appear ludicrous to Maritime historians but was difficult to contest in the face of Confederation. On the whole, Maritime patriots resisted the implications of the union, clung to their own interpretations, and sought to preserve distinct identities, only to discover themselves thereby rendered pejoratively provincial. With their future stolen from them, they slipped quietly into nostalgia for the past. History was their solace – and all the more inviolable for that.

Still, with Confederation well in the future, the initial reaction of most Maritime historians to events in the Canadas was one of smug superiority. This was certainly the case in Nova Scotia, where, on 8 June 1849, the people of Halifax turned out, with not a little satisfaction, to celebrate their city's one-hundredth anniversary. The official centrepiece of the day was an 'Oration' given by Beamish Murdoch, 'a descendant of one of the First settlers,' before a large audience gathered round a rostrum in the middle of the Common. Murdoch began by inviting his audience to imagine that day in 1749 when British settlers first cast eye on the desolate shores of Chebucto, on the primeval forest and fierce aborigines. Lacking not 'bold hearts and untiring spirits,' the original settlers set about their task of taming the wilderness with 'fortitude and firmness.' They first fashioned a town, then a city, and ultimately a province, another jewel in the Crown of the British empire. 'Should we not bless their memories,' Murdoch asked, 'when we survey the goodly inheritance they left us?' And should not those now gathered on the Common rededicate themselves to efforts on behalf of the province as strenuous as those of their forefathers? To these rhetorical questions Murdoch received rousing cheers in the affirmative. As one correspondent noted, 'all political and personal animosities were buried – all heartily united in the festivity, – and the celebration passed off without a single unpleasant occurrence to disturb the harmony.'[1]

Murdoch's 'Oration' – indeed the centenary celebration itself – was based on a formula of Nova Scotia patriotism established twenty years earlier in Thomas Chandler Haliburton's *An Historical and Statistical Account of Nova-Scotia*. The key to the formula was the founding of Halifax in 1749, an event that established the rule of British law and banished the chaos of native and Acadian custom, replacing an era of exciting romance with one of stolid achievement. Safe, peaceful, ordered, the land was ready to open its treasure to the hard work and thrift of arriving British yeomen. It was intended that this class of independent farmers, the backbone of Old England, provide the healthy economic, social, and political basis for New Scotland. The subsequent history of the province was little more than a catalogue of the accretion of human settlement. This formula, originally intended to defend and explain the colony before a British audience, gave Nova Scotians an image of themselves, an ideal to live up to. Moralistic, it taught lessons of behaviour in the belief that adherence to the yeoman ideal alone would assure that progress continued. It was a history of the past written with an eye to the future.

It was also a history written with a smug eye toward events in the Canadas. The congenial celebration held in Halifax contrasted sharply – and was intended to contrast sharply – with what A.R.M. Lower called

---

1 *Celebration of the Centenery [sic] Anniversary of the Settlement of the City of Halifax. June 8th, 1849* [Halifax 1850] 1, 8–11

'the sudden thunderstorm of spring riots' occasioned by the Rebellion Losses Bill earlier that same year in the Canadas, riots that culminated in the burning of the Parliament buildings at Montreal and the rotten-egging of Governor-General Lord Elgin. In Nova Scotia the transition to responsible government produced no comparable outburst of partisan or racial rage to mar the centennial year. Indeed during the celebrations in Halifax no one even thought to mention the achievement of responsible government. Murdoch drew a direct line of descent from 1749, a line unbroken by rebellion and free from the complications of a large French-speaking population. He concentrated instead on the incremental progress of colonization, of wilderness turned into farmland and small settlements turned into towns. The implication was that the evolution of Nova Scotia's constitutional position within the empire was a natural concomitant of responsible patriotism and material progress, not a solution to specific problems, and certainly not a response to immediate crises. Murdoch rejected the notion developed by Canadian historians that conflict generated progress and refused to accept Lord Durham's contention that the colonies of British North America were unwittingly united by their individual struggles for responsible government.

Nova Scotia historians went to some length to suppress internal conflict in order to maintain the image of a seamless web of steady progress dating back to 1749. For instance the Halifax Mechanics' Institute, which, since its inauguration in December 1831, had provided the principal forum in the province for lectures on historical topics, actively discouraged the introduction of fractious political questions. As early as 16 January 1831 the institute resolved 'that a lecture on the British Constitution proposed by Mr. Sutherland is inadmissable, on account of its tendency to lend to a political discussion.' When such politically active figures as Reform leader Joseph Howe and newspaper editor John Sparrow Thompson (1795–1867) subsequently lectured on historical topics before the body of the Mechanics, they were careful to keep to uncontentious subjects drawn from European and British history, or to the enumeration of Nova Scotia's material achievements and cultural growth.[2] In short, the conceit of the Nova Scotia patriot forbade the airing of internal disagreements, and, in contrast to the situation in the Canadas, there was no internal challenge of sufficient force to disturb it.

2 PANS, Journal of the Halifax Mechanics' Institute, MG 20, vol. 222A, 16 Jan., 9 May, 12 Dec. 1832; 8 Dec. 1835; 16 Mar. 1836; [John S. Thompson,] 'History, Being a Paper Read by John S. Thompson, Before the Halifax Mechanics' Institute, May 9, 1832,' Halifax Monthly Magazine, vol. 3, no. 23 (September 1832) 145–62

Beamish Murdoch (1800–76) had himself learned this lesson rather early on in his career as a historian. While Beamish was still a boy, his merchant father was placed in debtor's prison for seven years. Consequently raised by a maiden aunt, the youth worked hard to prove himself, being called to the provincial bar in 1822 and elected to a four-year term as assemblyman for Halifax Township in 1826. He was also determined to reform the system that had dealt so unjustly with his father. Murdoch ridiculed the presumptive power of the province's appointed legislative council from his seat in the House, and his first published work was *An Essay on the Mischievous Tendency of Imprisonment for Debt*.[3] At the same time he began to plan and research a series of 'Historical Memoirs' of the British North American colonies, covering the period 1819 to 1829. The purpose of these memoirs was to condemn the persistent attempts made by several governors and the various provincial councils to restrict the prerogative of assemblies over the expenditure of public money; this prerogative alone, in Murdoch's opinion, gave 'to the representatives of any people a weight and respectability in the management of public affairs.' Furthermore, with difficulties arising in every province from the same cause, he believed there must be 'some latent defects in the system.'[4] In this recognition that the otherwise disparate British colonies in America were united by a common constitutional problem, Murdoch foreshadowed the findings of Lord Durham.

Murdoch's 'Historical Memoirs' were never published. Defeated in the election of 1830, he withdrew from public affairs for a time to reconsider the rewards of iconoclasm. While his friend T.C. Haliburton received the acclaim of the assembly and a seat on the bench for writing the patriotic *Statistical Account*, Murdoch languished without office. Perhaps for this reason, Murdoch dropped his politically charged memoirs and turned instead to the compilation of a four-volume *Epitome of the Laws of Nova Scotia*, published in Halifax by Joseph Howe in 1832 and 1833. Written 'in humble imitation of the Commentaries of [William] Blackstone,' the *Epitome* was intended to provide provincial lawyers with a handbook of local laws and applicable imperial legislation, complete with discussions of

3 K.G. Pryke, 'Beamish Murdoch,' *DCB*, vol. 10 (Toronto 1972) 539–40; D.C. Harvey, 'Nova Scotia's Blackstone,' *Canadian Bar Review* 11 (1933): 339–44; Beamish Murdoch, *An Essay on the Mischievous Tendency of Imprisonment for Debt*, 2nd ed. (Halifax 1831)

4 PANS, Beamish Murdoch Papers, MG 1, vol. 726, Historical Memoirs of the British North American Provinces since His Present Majesty's Accession, book one, 26, 57

the modifications wrought by indigenous historical precedents.[5] Inevitably contentious constitutional issues arose, and when they did Murdoch retreated behind the bald statement of statute. The work was praised in the local press as impartial and comprehensive, and it established Murdoch as the foremost legal authority in Nova Scotia.[6] Once secure as a member of the local élite, Murdoch became more conservative – initially opposing the movement for responsible government – and less outspoken. By 1849, as a member of 'The Old Nova Scotia Society,' he was considered both an authoritative and a suitable person to speak of the history of Nova Scotia at the centennial day celebrations.[7]

Complacent and self-satisfied, the patriotic approach to Nova Scotia's history was also, in the absence of conflict, a trifle boring. Perhaps for this reason the successful centennial day celebrations did not inspire subsequent annual commemoration. In fact Haligonians did not assemble again in any number to mark the anniversary of their city and province until 1862. Emotions did not run so high on the second occasion, planning was not so elaborate, and the celebrations as a whole had – in this the era of the American Civil War – a more sombre, military character. Once more the avowed purpose of the day was to honour the work of earlier generations of Nova Scotians and to instil in contemporaries an imitative 'spirit of patriotism and enterprise.'[8] And once more an 'Oration' was given, this time by thirty-one-year-old Robert Grant Haliburton (1831–1901), a lawyer and son of 'the provincial historian.' However, in contrast to Beamish Murdoch, Haliburton announced that he had no intention 'of recalling minutely ... the dry details of the foundation of the city, which only possess an interest in the eyes of antiquarians.' Instead, he proposed to touch 'upon those topics which have a practical value, or which are

5 Beamish Murdoch, *Epitome of the Laws of Nova Scotia*, 4 vols (Halifax 1832–3) vol. 1 (1832) v–vi
6 Harvey, 'Nova Scotia's Blackstone,' 341–4
7 PANS, Thomas Beamish Akins Papers, MG 1, vol. 8, folder 4, 32, The Old Nova Scotia Society. The society was established at some point prior to 1838 and was at first officially known as the Nova Scotia Philanthropic or Charitable Society, later as the Nova Scotia Mutual Benefit Society, but was commonly referred to under the name given here. Members claimed to be descendants of the first generation of Haligonians and made it their self-appointed task to ensure that the anniversary of the city's establishment should never be forgotten.
8 'Object and Nature of the Anniversary Celebration, Held at Halifax, June 21st, 1862,' Preface to R.G. Haliburton, *The Past and the Future of Nova Scotia: An Address on the 113th Anniversary of the Settlement of the Capital of the Province* (Halifax 1862) np

deserving of inquiry by Nova Scotians.' Among such topics he listed the 'unfortunate Aborigines' and 'the advent of the Loyalists'; but pride of place went to a discussion of an issue R.G. Haliburton knew would be of immediate interest to his audience – the expulsion of the Acadians.[9]

Why the expulsion of the Acadians? Rather early on Nova Scotia's historians had reached a general consensus about the matter. First, through laziness and intermarriage with native people, the Acadians had squandered their opportunity to exploit the land; they were therefore fated to be superseded by a more energetic race of Anglo-Americans. Second, pressured by officials and Roman Catholic priests operating out of Louisbourg and Quebec, the Acadians had at the very least acquiesced in terrorizing assaults on peaceful British settlements; they were therefore expelled out of military, if admittedly cruel, necessity. The arrival of British settlers at Halifax was the central event of Nova Scotia history; the expulsion was a footnote; consciences need not be troubled.

On one occasion only had this consensus been challenged seriously. In the late 1780s a Halifax newspaper (since lost) published an excerpt from *A Philosophical and Political History of the Settlements and Trade of the Europeans in the East and West Indies* by Abbé Guillaume-Thomas-François Raynal, in which the Acadians were described as an inoffensive people living in an Arcadian idyll – a people whose removal was without justification. Nova Scotia patriots leapt to the defence of provincial honour. Two aging officials, Richard Bulkeley (1717–1800) and Isaac Deschamps (*c.*1722–1801), immediately condemned Raynal's account as philosophical fancy.[10] They were obliged to repeat their criticism of Raynal in 1790, when William Cochran, unaware of the earlier controversy, reprinted the same (presumably) offending passage in his *Nova-Scotia Magazine*.[11] Although T.C. Haliburton later made use of the extract from Raynal in the *Statistical Account,* he was careful to hedge it about with much less flattering views of the Acadians taken from the histories of

9 R.G. Haliburton, *The Past and the Future of Nova Scotia,* 7–8
10 The newspaper has not been located, but the Reverend Andrew Brown (1763–1834) made a note of the incident, as well as of the reactions of Deschamps and Bulkeley, and these observations were among those excerpts from the Brown papers published as 'The Acadian French,' Nova Scotia Historical Society, *Collections* 2 (1879–80): 149–50. See also B.C. Cuthbertson, 'Thomas Beamish Akins: British North America's Pioneer Archivist,' *Acadiensis* 7 (1977): 94–5.
11 [Guillaume-Thomas-François Raynal,] 'Historical Account of Nova Scotia,' *Nova-Scotia Magazine and Comprehensive Review of Literature, Politics, and News* (Feb. 1790) 82–7; [Richard Bulkeley and Isaac Deschamps,] 'The Case of the Acadians Stated,' ibid. (Apr. 1790) 287–9

Tobias Smollett and Thomas Hutchinson.[12] It was, in effect, permissible to regret the fate of the Acadians – especially if one were an assemblyman, like Haliburton, whose riding contained a significant French-speaking population – just so long as the reputation of the province was not brought into disrepute by the suggestion that the expulsion was anything other than fully justified by the military situation prevailing in the summer and autumn of 1755. The line was firm. By the time Murdoch rose to speak in 1849, the question was buried.

Though capable of handling internal dissent, Nova Scotia historians were about to be caught off guard by an external challenge to their patriotic complacency. Trouble began brewing on the evening of 5 April 1840 at a dinner given in the home of the American poet Henry Wadsworth Longfellow (1807–82). The novelist Nathaniel Hawthorne (1804–64) was one of the invited guests, and he arrived with the Reverend Lorenzo Conolly in tow. Conolly was rector of St Matthew's Episcopal Church in South Boston. Hawthorne had Conolly relate to Longfellow an Acadian tale that he, Conolly, had heard from one of his parishioners, Mrs George Mordaunt Haliburton, wife of a relative of Thomas Chandler Haliburton. Conolly told the story of a young Acadian maiden who at the dispersion was separated from her betrothed lover; they sought each other for years in their exile and at last were reunited in a hospital where the lover lay dying.[13] According to Conolly, when the tale was over Longfellow declared, 'It is the best illustration of faithfulness and the constancy of woman that I have ever heard of or read.'[14] Hawthorne, who had no immediate plans to use the story himself, gave Longfellow permission to use it as the basis for a poem. In the event, Longfellow did

12 Thomas C. Haliburton, *An Historical and Statistical Account of Nova-Scotia*, 2 vols (Halifax 1829) vol. 1, 135–98, 327–40
13 On 24 Oct. 1838, Hawthorne jotted down in his journal a brief summary of Mrs Haliburton's story as reported to him by Conolly. This is the first recorded version of the tale, and Hawthorne's wife, Sophia, included it when she edited and published *Passages from the American Note-Books of Nathaniel Hawthorne*, 2 vols (Boston 1868) vol. 1, 203. Unfortunately the manuscript of the relevant portion of Hawthorne's notebooks now cannot be found. Longfellow's undated memorandum of his conversation with the Reverend Conolly adds little to Hawthorne's account of the tale; see Manning Hawthorne and Henry Wadsworth Longfellow Dana, *The Origin and Development of Longfellow's 'Evangeline'* (Portland, Maine, 1947) 10–12. Years later Conolly himself recorded his memories of the tale but in a manner so elaborate and self-serving that it undermined his credibility; see ibid.
    See also Naomi Griffiths, 'Longfellow's *Evangeline*: The Birth and Acceptance of a Legend,' *Acadiensis* 11 (1982): 28–41.
14 Quoted in Hawthorne and Dana, *Development of Longfellow's 'Evangeline'*, 12

not commence writing until November of 1845, and publication of the finished poem, *Evangeline: A Tale of Acadia*, did not take place until October of 1847.[15]

Although Longfellow intended the poem to be primarily a morally uplifting example of the virtue of women, he was also determined to get the historical background correct. To this end he withdrew T.C. Haliburton's *Statistical Account* from the Harvard College Library on at least three occasions.[16] When composing *Evangeline*, Longfellow closely followed the *Statistical Account*, concentrated on Haliburton's long quotations from Raynal and the Journal of Colonel John Winslow (while ignoring the strictures of Smollett), and casually rendered lengthy passages of prose into hexameters. The result was that despite Longfellow's interest in the individual moral of the story, *Evangeline* was not dominated by the character of its heroine or any other individual. In the words of Naomi Griffiths: 'The essence of *Evangeline* is the history of the Acadians, whom Longfellow saw as a simple, devout and prosperous people, whose community was unwarrantedly and brutally destroyed by the English. This disaster was accepted by Longfellow's Acadians with stoic calm, Christian fortitude and resignation.' The Evangeline figure personified a general experience, 'an Eve from Paradise lost through no proven original sin.'[17] Despite the disclaimers of later life, Longfellow believed his picture to be historically accurate, writing in 1848 to one friend, 'you will be astonished at the tragedy enacted in the little Acadian village, not one feature of which have I darkened or deepened.'[18] In short, Longfellow blurred the line that traditionally separated fact from fiction.[19]

In twelve months *Evangeline* sold five editions of one thousand copies each. Its fame spread rapidly throughout North America, Great Britain, and (in several translations) Europe; and everywhere its picture of the pathetic suffering of the Acadians was accepted as historical fact.[20] Indeed

15 Samuel Longfellow, ed., *Life of Henry Wadsworth Longfellow, with Extracts from His Journals and Correspondence*, 2nd ed., 2 vols (Boston 1886) vol. 2, 5
16 The three occasions were 3 Mar. 1841, 19 Jan. 1846, and 9 Apr. 1847; see Hawthorne and Dana, *Development of Longfellow's 'Evangeline'*, 7n.
17 Griffiths, 'Longfellow's *Evangeline*,' 29
18 Longfellow to Jane Frances Chipman, 30 Mar. 1848, in *The Letters of Henry Wadsworth Longfellow*, ed. Andrew Hilen, 6 vols (Cambridge, Mass., 1966–82) vol. 3 (1972) 28
19 Maritime novelists and poets generally maintained the integrity of the line separating fact and fiction. See for example, Eugene [Samuel Douglas Smith Huyghue (1792–1877)], *Argimou: A Legend of the Micmac* (1847) ed. Gwendolyn Davies, Maritimes Literature Reprint Series No. 1 (Sackville, NB, 1977); or Maria Amelia Fytche (1844–1926), *The Rival Forts; Or, the Velvet Siege of Beauséjour* (Halifax 1907).
20 Griffiths, 'Longfellow's *Evangeline*,' 28

the way had been prepared by a variety of lesser works on the Acadian theme by other American authors who blamed the British Crown for the expulsion. In 1841 alone there appeared Mrs Catherine Read Williams's novel *The Neutral French*, Nathaniel Hawthorne's tale for children entitled 'The Acadian Exiles,' and historian George Bancroft's essay 'The Exiles of Acadia.'[21] None of these could compare, however, with *Evangeline*, which was, and perhaps remains, the most influential work of fact or fiction on the sad fate of the Acadians. By 1859 engravings of Evangeline by John Faed could be found in Halifax print shops, and in that same year Frederick Swartwout Cozzens published the first of many travelogues meant to introduce the armchair tourist to the homeland of the Acadian maiden.[22] In short, by the time R.G. Haliburton stood up to speak in June 1862, Nova Scotia's primary international reputation was as the site of an event that combined, in the words of one anonymous reviewer of Longfellow's poem, 'more of cruelty and suffering, more of perfidy and foul wrong, more of deliberate, premeditated atrocity, than any single act which we can call to mind.'[23]

In just a few years the pen of an American poet shattered the carefully cultivated conceit of Nova Scotia patriots. An event from an era traditionally exploited as a romantic foil against which to judge the later progress of the British regime was used to question the very legitimacy of that regime. The poem's evocative description of the cruel and unnecessary expulsion of the Acadians suggested that the province was built on an act of immorality that tainted all subsequent achievements. Longfellow's libel on the honour of the province could not go unchallenged, and Nova Scotia historians were duty bound to mount an effective counter-attack.

Although generated by defensive outrage, the Evangeline controversy made a positive contribution – at least in the short term. Interest in the past, deadened by years of complacency, was suddenly aroused; conflict was invigorating. The decided plan of campaign was to leave Longfellow

21 Catherine Read Williams (1790–1872), *The Neutral French; Or, the Exiles of Nova Scotia* (Providence, RI, 1841) vi–ix; Nathaniel Hawthorne, 'The Acadian Exiles,' in his *Famous Old People: Being the Second Epoch of Grandfather's Chair* (Boston 1841) 122–35; George Bancroft (1800–91), 'The Exiles of Acadia,' in *The Token and Atlantic Souvenir, an Offering for Christmas and the New Year* (Boston 1841) 279–89; see also Bancroft's *History of the United States from the Discovery of the American Continent*, 10 vols (Boston 1834–75) vol. 4 (1852) 206
22 Archibald MacMechan, 'Evangeline and the Real Acadians,' in his *The Life of a Little College and Other Papers* (Boston and New York 1914) 202; Frederick Swartwout Cozzens (1818–69), *Acadia; Or, a Month with the Bluenoses* (New York 1859). See also Griffiths, 'Longfellow's *Evangeline*,' 31.
23 Review of *Evangeline*, by Henry Wadsworth Longfellow, *North American Review* 66 (1848): 216

the high ground of poetry but breach his claim to credibility as a historian: the poet must be put back in his place. Determined to prove that the master of fiction was not a master of fact, Nova Scotia patriots turned to research and armed themselves with documents. As a result, the Evangeline controversy unexpectedly made English-speaking Nova Scotians more enthusiastic and better historians. Indeed, in 1857 antiquarian Thomas Beamish Akins (1809–91) exploited the spirit of the moment and successfully pressed the provincial government to establish a commission of public records, thereby creating the first public archives in British North America.[24]

T.B. Akins was born in Liverpool, Nova Scotia, the son of a descendant of those original Falmouth settlers who came to Nova Scotia from New England in 1761. Akins's mother, who died ten days after his birth, was the daughter of Thomas Beamish, port warden and merchant of Halifax. It was with the Beamish family that the young Akins grew up; in fact it was the same household that took in his stray cousin, Beamish Murdoch, the elder by nine years. Akins followed Murdoch to the Halifax Grammar School, studied law in Murdoch's office, and, after being called to the bar in 1831, continued to regard Murdoch as a patron or father figure.[25] Akins was retiring by nature and never married; he spent his winters in Halifax, his summers in Falmouth (he is known to have travelled outside the province on only one occasion – a trip to Prince Edward Island); and to the end of his days he dressed and comported himself after the fashion of the 1830s, wearing starched high collars and broadcloth ties and going clean-shaven.[26] Possessed of wealth sufficient for his needs (the exact source of which remains obscure), Akins increasingly turned his energies from his law practice to antiquarian studies. He was happiest working at home alone in his library, which contained not only a comprehensive collection of works relating to Nova Scotia but also such rarities as a first edition (1475) of Anton Koberger's Nuremberg Bible (the oldest Latin Bible then in Canada, possibly even in North America). At Akins's death, his collection was, according to Brian Cuthbertson, 'certainly the largest in private hands and in the rarity of some volumes the finest in the Dominion.'[27]

24 Cuthbertson, 'Thomas Beamish Akins,' 87–8. The creation of the archives of Nova Scotia preceded that of the Dominion archives by fifteen years, that of Ontario by forty-six.
25 Ibid., 86; B.C. Cuthbertson, 'Thomas Beamish Akins,' APLA [Atlantic Provinces Library Association] Bulletin, vol. 44, no. 5 (Mar. 1981) 49, 51
26 Archibald MacMechan, 'A Gentleman of the Old School,' Halifax Herald, 31 Dec. 1932; 'Death of Dr. Akins,' Morning Herald (Halifax), 7 May 1891
27 Cuthbertson, 'Akins,' APLA Bulletin, 49

No matter how broad Akins's interests, his first love remained the history of Nova Scotia. Drawn into the study of provincial history through work as an assistant for Haliburton's *Statistical Account*, Akins went on to produce a prize history of Halifax for the Mechanics' Institute in 1839 and then followed with histories of the Anglican Church in British North America and King's College, Windsor.[28] All three volumes were works of celebration and, in the best patriot spirit, avoided sectarian and partisan controversy. Both publications were nevertheless marked by extensive research and documentation and carefully charted the physical and organizational growth of their respective subjects. Through such writings Akins proved himself more an antiquarian than a historian, one interested in the who, what, and where of past events to the neglect of the how and why. Actually all Akins's histories should properly be regarded as by-products of his antiquarianism and bibliolatry. He was primarily concerned 'to preserve from oblivion the facts,' not to explain, and believed that 'the public documents of a country are its true history and nothing else.'[29]

It was this obsession with the collection of all known documents and books relating to Nova Scotia that led Akins in 1841 to press the Mechanics' Institute to establish a 'Depository of Colonial Records.' The proposal was accepted in principle and the decision reaffirmed in 1845 and 1846, but the sluggish response to the subscription list combined with Akins's ill-health to thwart the endeavour.[30] In light of this frustrating experience, Akins reconsidered his approach and thereafter attempted to interest the provincial government in a publicly funded archives. 'It was hard work,' as one member of the legislature later remembered, 'to indoctrinate the men of business with the ideas that belong rather to men of leisure.'[31] Nevertheless, Akins persisted, arguing that good government alone dictated that papers relating to, for instance, landholding and the financial affairs of the province should be put in order. Significantly,

28 Haliburton, *Statistical Account*, vol. 1, vii; Journal of the Halifax Mechanics' Institute, 6 Aug. 1838; 13 Apr., 13 May 1839; Thomas Beamish Akins, *Prize Essay on the History of the Settlement of Halifax, at the Mechanics' Institute, on 18th April, 1839* (Halifax 1847); *A Sketch of the Rise and Progress of the Church of England in the British North American Provinces* (Halifax 1849); *Brief Account of the Origin, Endowment and Progress of the University of King's College, Windsor, Nova Scotia* (Halifax 1865)

29 Akins, *A Brief Account ... of King's College*, i; T. B. Akins to Douglas Brymner, 4 June 1883, quoted in Cuthbertson, 'Thomas Beamish Akins,' 102

30 Journal of the Halifax Mechanics' Institute, 20 Feb. 1841; 13 Jan., 1 Mar., 30 June 1845; 6 May 1846

31 Adams George Archibald, 'Inaugural Address,' Nova Scotia Historical Society, *Collections* 1 (1878): 29

Akins also emphasized that there existed among the records preserved at Halifax evidence that would explain the reasons for the expulsion of the Acadians and in large measure exculpate the imperial and provincial administrators of the day. It was his belief that 'all papers that may in any way discover the motives, views and conduct of those engaged at that period in the settlement of the country, and which may tend to contradict or explain partial statements, or put in a new light, transactions hitherto considered harsh and cruel, should be given to the public.'[32] Akins quite simply used the Acadian controversy as a means to justify the creation of the archives as a whole. This was probably a decisive factor in the government's decision to create the Commission of Public Records and to appoint Akins the first commissioner of public records.

It was the shy Akins who supplied the gregarious R.G. Haliburton with documentary ammunition for the 1862 Oration. Indeed, the printed version of the speech was swollen by copious references to original sources, all of which were intended to illustrate the unneutral character of the Acadian community prior to the expulsion and to rebut more than a decade of adverse publicity for the province. It was particularly apposite that the junior Haliburton should deliver this message, for the son brought word that his father, when presented with the new information uncovered by Akins, disavowed certain passages in the *Statistical Account* as too sympathetic to the Acadians.[33] Longfellow's primary source thereby attempted to dissociate himself from the furor created by *Evangeline*.

R.G. Haliburton's essay was herald to Murdoch's monumental three-volume *History of Nova-Scotia, or Acadie*, published in instalments between 1865 and 1867. Murdoch, however, professed himself indifferent to the opinions of outsiders and claimed that his work was intended simply 'to preserve from oblivion the past occurrences in this province.' His stated goal was to collect and reduce into annals facts of interest, prefatory to the labours of some more ambitious historian. Many, he recognized, might regard this task 'as below the dignity of history,' but he believed that rendering the past 'in its own forms and colors and language' provided a 'more workmanlike foundation for true and abiding history' than 'floridity of style or most vivid declamation.'[34] Subsequent commentators

32 *Novascotian* (Halifax), 18 May 1857; Report of the Commissioner of Public Records, Nova Scotia, *Journal of the Legislative Assembly [JLA]* (1858) appendix 29, 234; ibid., (1859) appendix 8, 67

33 R.G. Haliburton, *The Past and the Future of Nova Scotia*, iii, 15n. There is no independent confirmation that T.C. Haliburton suffered such a change of heart.

34 Beamish Murdoch, *A History of Nova-Scotia, or Acadie*, 3 vols (Halifax 1865–7) vol. 1 (1865) v; vol. 2 (1866) iii–iv

took Murdoch at his word; they decried his method for its indiscriminate use of evidence, endless reproduction of documents, and failure to provide 'any sense of development through time'; but they also praised him for his 'indifference to what outside countries' might think of Nova Scotia, finding in this self-assurance signs of a new provincial maturity.[35]

Whatever the merits of Murdoch's method, the recent discovery of three letters written by him to John Edwards Godfrey (1809–84) of Bangor, Maine, clearly demonstrate that the Nova Scotia historian was far from immune to the Evangeline controversy and the perceptions of outsiders. In a letter dated 22 February 1869, Murdoch informed Godfrey:

> I was led into the labor & execution of my book, by a desire to throw the light of truth, if possible, upon the merits & demerits of the expulsion of the French Acadians from this country in 1755 – The abbe Raynal, – Bancroft, – Longfellow, &c had given popularity to a view of this transaction so disgraceful to the British name and nation, that we of Nova Scotia, who knew traditionally something of the truth, were annoyed at the reiteration of such severe charges against our nation. A friend [Akins?] urged me to undertake the task of vindication. I replied, that the only just course to pursue, would be to write the history of Acadie from its first discovery, in order to shew the true position of these Acadians at the time of their removal – and as our government had obtained at some expense authentic copies of all official correspondence connected with this province, both under the French & English rule: and I had ready access to all our archives, I set to work at the beginning viz – 1603 – not intending at first to bring my narration down much beyond 1756, the year of this exodus [sic].[36]

This private agenda provided the organizing principle for the first two volumes.

Murdoch, like the lawyer he was, placed before the jury of public opinion all the evidence he could discover relating to the Acadian question. Like Akins, another lawyer, he had an abiding faith in the

---

35 D.C. Harvey, 'History and Its Uses in Pre-Confederation Nova Scotia,' Canadian Historical Association, *Annual Report* (1938): 14–16; Kenneth N. Windsor, 'Historical Writing in Canada to 1920,' in Carl F. Klinck, gen. ed., *Literary History of Canada: Canadian Literature in English* (Toronto 1965) 222; Pryke, 'Beamish Murdoch,' 540

36 Beamish Murdoch to John E. Godfrey, 22 Feb. 1869. The other letters were dated 6 and 27 Feb. 1869. All three letters were recently published in Alice R. Stewart, James B. Vickery, and Edward S. Kellogg, eds, 'A Nova Scotia–Maine Historical Correspondence [Document],' *Acadiensis* 14 (1985): 108–20.

transparent meaning and incontrovertible truth of documents.[37] Thus Murdoch traced the events of the seventeenth century using unvarnished excerpts from the likes of Lescarbot, Champlain, and Charlevoix, adding little to Haliburton's similar summary of such sources twenty years before. When Murdoch hit the eighteenth century, however, he began to break new ground. With Akins at his elbow, Murdoch was able to deliver council minutes, governors' letterbooks, dispatches from the Board of Trade, and miscellaneous papers from Paris. While all these documents were, according to Akins, at Halifax 'in the office of the Provincial Secretary or in his custody at the time Mr. Haliburton published his "History of Nova Scotia,"' they had been largely ignored by that author.[38] That Murdoch succeeded where Haliburton failed was the result primarily of the organizational efforts of the record commissioner. Ordered, catalogued, and bound, the public papers of Nova Scotia were now accessible to any serious student willing to take the time to read them.

However discursive Murdoch's brief, the patient reader of the *History of Nova-Scotia* will find the author guiding him through its voluminous evidence by means of summaries interjected at random. To Murdoch the Acadians were not the simple pastoral people of Raynal's imagining; they were an ordinary people, a compound of good and evil, who, if left in peace, would eventually have reconciled themselves to the gentle hand of British rule. Unfortunately French officials resident in Paris, Louisbourg, and Quebec were determined to stimulate old loyalties within the Acadian community by means of agents, 'clerical and lay,' with a view to the eventual reconquest of Nova Scotia. While it was to the credit of the Acadian population generally that so few of their number heeded the French call to arms (even when placed under threat of native reprisal), it was also noted that a significant number of individuals participated in or assisted French incursions, most notably at Grand Pré in 1747 and Fort Beauséjour in 1755.[39] British officials on the scene, unsupported by the

37 Murdoch, *History of Nova-Scotia*, vol. 2, iv–v
38 T.B. Akins to Francis Parkman, nd, quoted in Francis Parkman, 'The Acadians Again,' *The Nation* (New York), 22 Jan. 1885, 73; T.B. Akins, letter to the editor, *Boston Evening Transcript*, 19 Mar. 1885. For independent confirmation that many of the documents in question were indeed available to researchers in the 1820s, see PANS, William Cochran Papers, MG 1, vol. 223, items 3–4, Memoranda ... with a View to a History of Nova Scotia. For an exhaustive reconstruction of Murdoch's research and use of sources see Patrick D. Clarke, 'The Makers of Acadian History in the Nineteenth-Century' (PH D Diss., Université Laval 1988) ch. 2.
39 Murdoch, *History of Nova-Scotia*, vol. 1, 477, 517–18; vol. 2, 40–3, 83–4, 104–5, 214–16, 286–7

home government, incapable of protecting the population or enforcing an unqualified oath of allegiance, temporized and granted that which they did not have the power or right to grant, namely, a conditional oath that exempted the Acadians from the necessity to bear arms. Although Murdoch, ever the lawyer, admitted that such indulgence of government 'might to some extent palliate [Acadian] errors, and partly account for their discontent and disaffection,' yet the fact remained, as the Acadians were told many times, an unconditional oath was the *sine qua non* of citizenship, and refusal to take such an oath was treason. 'It would be the acme of absurdity to go on thus,' Murdoch reasoned, 'with ... the chief part of the population feeling either a hostile sentiment, or at least indifferent to the success and progress of its rulers, and closely attached to a foreign power.' The establishment of the garrison and settlement at Halifax gave Britain the power to resolve this anomalous situation, and the threat of an imminent outbreak of war provided the proximate reason to act.[40] As Murdoch told Godfrey, 'I think impartial readers will conclude that the expulsion of the F. Acadians was not dictated by any low motives of gain, or mere malice, but from an honest belief entertained by the authorities at Halifax in 1755 of it's [sic] absolute necessity, as required to save Acadie from the French.'[41]

Murdoch accepted that in retrospect the expulsion of the Acadians was 'anything but agreeable,' and confessed 'it is not to be wondered at that the poet and the novelist have made capital of their sufferings.' Nevertheless, while 'all ... feelings of humanity are affected by the removal itself,' in Murdoch's opinion the historian should not permit himself to be carried away by sentimentality. The fact remained that 'in the disturbed state of the country' in 1755, 'military necessity produced measures that one may regard as cruel but unavoidable.' If there was any residual blame, it should be apportioned only to those responsible for the 'severity of the attendant circumstances' of the removal, specifically to Colonel John Winslow and the colonial troops he commanded.[42] In private correspondence Murdoch went even further and suggested to Godfrey that the deportation was initiated, executed, and justified by the likes of Governor William Shirley of Massachusetts, Colonel Winslow, and Chief Justice Jonathan Belcher − New Englanders all. In Murdoch's 'humble judgment,' the expulsion 'was a dismal affair altogether, but in reality one for

40 Ibid., vol. 1, 349–50, 465, 477, 517–18; vol. 2, 157–9, 286–7, 298–9. See also Murdoch, *Epitome*, vol. 2 (1832) 76–7.
41 Murdoch to Godfrey, 22 Feb. 1869, 115
42 Murdoch, *History of Nova-Scotia*, vol. 2, 287, 297–9

which New England was more responsible than Nova Scotia.' 'We Nova Scotians knew all these things,' he concluded, 'and we thought it hard that Bancroft & Longfellow should not only blame the act, but endeavor to fix the odium of it on the British government & people.'[43]

The case for the defence reached its apogee in 1869 with the publication of Akins's *Selections from the Public Documents of the Province of Nova Scotia*. In his reports as record commissioner, Akins had consistently recommended the publication of selected documents in order both to preserve and make accessible items in his care.[44] This was the custom in many American states, where local patriotism and legitimate concern for the perishable nature of so much of the nation's heritage allied in the mid-nineteenth century to produce a condition David D. Van Tassel labelled 'documania.'[45] In this spirit Akins envisaged the compilation of a series of volumes modelled on the four-volume *Documentary History of the State of New-York*, which was published at Albany in 1850–1.[46] In order to pry money loose from the provincial government for this project, Akins was wise enough to propose as his first 'specimen' volume a selection of papers relating primarily to the Anglo-French conflict in Acadia and the events surrounding the expulsion; and in 1865 the provincial legislature voted funds sufficient to publish one thousand copies of 'a single octavo volume of moderate size.'[47]

The resulting *Selections* – the only volume in the series that Akins was able to publish – contained virtually all documents in the possession of the record commission 'that could in any way throw light on the history and conduct of the French inhabitants of Nova Scotia, from their first coming under British rule, until their final removal from the country,' as well as a significant number of papers relating to the first establishment of a representative assembly in Nova Scotia.[48] Naturally the evidence pre-

43 Murdoch to Godfrey, 22 Feb. 1869, 115–16
44 Report of the Commissioner of Public Records, *JLA* (1858) appendix 29, 234; (1859) appendix 8, 66–7
45 David D. Van Tassel, *Recording America's Past: An Interpretation of the Development of Historical Studies in America, 1607–1884* (Chicago 1960) ch. 11
46 Report of the Commissioner of Public Records, *JLA* (1859) appendix 8, 66–7; (1864) appendix 25. *The Documentary History of the State of New-York* was compiled by Edmund Bailey O'Callaghan (1797–1880), an exiled *Patriote* from Lower Canada.
47 Report of the Committee on the Record Commission, *JLA* (1865) appendix 49, 1; Thomas B. Akins, ed., *Selections from the Public Documents of the Province of Nova Scotia. Published under a Resolution of the House of Assembly Passed March 15, 1865* (Halifax 1869) i–iii
48 Ibid., ii

sented in the *Selections* buttressed or reiterated the various points made by Murdoch. Furthermore, in one of the few editorial comments the retiring Akins permitted himself (typically it was in a footnote), he expressed agreement with Murdoch's conclusion that no blundering or temporizing on the part of subordinate officials could vary the position of the Acadians as subjects of the British Crown.[49] His conclusion: the French of Nova Scotia doomed themselves by their refusal to take an unqualified oath of allegiance.

The campaign launched by R.G. Haliburton, Murdoch, Akins, and others slowly re-established the credibility of the traditional Nova Scotia interpretation of the expulsion. In 1870 Dr William James Anderson (1812–73), president of the Literary and Historical Society of Quebec, published in the Society's *Transactions* a paper that compared the historical accuracy of Longfellow's *Evangeline* unfavourably with Akins's *Selections* in order to alert readers to the general danger of accepting as factual the history to be found in fiction, even when written by the likes of Sir Walter Scott, James Fenimore Cooper, or, for that matter, William Shakespeare.[50] Further sanction was obtained in 1887 from a still more prestigious source, namely, the *Narrative and Critical History of America*, edited by Justin Winsor (1831–97). In the fifth volume of that eight-volume compendium (which has rightly been described as 'a monumental summary and culmination of all previous work done in American historiography'), both the editor and the scholar assigned to the subject of Acadia, Charles C. Smith, praised Akins's *Selections* as the most important contribution to contemporary knowledge of the expulsion.[51]

But of all the endorsements earned by Akins and his confederates, the most important was the imprimatur of Francis Parkman (1823–93), the foremost American historian of the late nineteenth century. Parkman's multi-volume history, *France and England in North America*, begun in 1865, finally reached the Acadian deportation with the publication in 1884 of the instalment entitled *Montcalm and Wolfe*. In that volume Parkman made extensive use of the *Selections*, called it 'a Government publication of

49 Ibid., 267n
50 William J. Anderson, "Evangeline" and 'The Archives of Nova Scotia;" Or, the Poetry and Prose of History,' Literary and Historical Society of Quebec, *Transactions*, new ser., vol. 7 (1869–70) 5–36
51 Charles C. Smith, 'The Wars on the Seaboard: The Struggle in Acadia and Cape Breton,' in Justin Winsor, ed., *Narrative and Critical History of America*, 8 vols (Boston 1884–9) vol. 5 (1887) 418–9; Justin Winsor, 'Authorities on the French and Indian Wars of New England and Acadia, 1688–1763,' in ibid., 458–9. Van Tassel, *Recording America's Past*, vii, 169–70

great value,' and specifically cited Akins's footnote as an authority on the oath question.[52] Not content to rest there, Parkman expanded upon the Nova Scotia interpretation. He had done extensive research of his own in Paris among the little-explored papers of the archives of the Department of Marine and Colonies of France, and there he found additional evidence that the French government and Roman Catholic clergy had fomented rebellion within the Acadian communities of Nova Scotia. Furthermore, he believed that the agents of France had received a more sympathetic response from the Acadians than either Murdoch or Akins had suspected: 'In fact, the Acadians, while calling themselves neutrals, were an enemy encamped in the heart of the province.' In Parkman's opinion, New England humanitarianism had been unjust to its own and blind to the treachery of others. His famous conclusion was that 'the Government of Louis xv. began with making the Acadians its tools, and ended with making them its victims.'[53]

English-speaking Nova Scotians believed themselves vindicated. Their traditional view of the expulsion had been upheld by respected historical associations and by America's most authoritative historians. The *Selections* was suddenly in such demand from abroad that the government was compelled to ration distribution of copies.[54] Yet the success of Akins, Murdoch, and others was purchased only at the expense of contemporary Acadians, who, emerging from decades of obscurity and seclusion, had taken advantage of the popularity and evocative nature of Longfellow's poem to rally and begin the slow process of reconstructing some sense of collective identity.[55] They could no more let lie rationalization of the expulsion than English-speaking Nova Scotians could abide criticism of

---

52 Francis Parkman, 'Montcalm and Wolfe,' in his *France and England in North America* (1865–92), 2 vols, Library of America, ed. David Levin (New York 1983) vol. 2, 907n, 1027n

53 Ibid., 1022, 1039–40. See also Francis Parkman, letter to the editor, *Nation*, 6 Nov. 1884, 398; reprinted in *Letters of Francis Parkman*, ed. Wilbur R. Jacobs, 2 vols (Norman, Okla., 1960) vol. 2, 162–3.

54 PANS, Nova Scotia Historical Society Papers, MG 20, vol. 685, folder 7, 196, T.B. Akins to Colonel Clarke, 7 Sept. 1885

55 The first North American translation of *Evangeline* into French was published by Pamphile Le May at Quebec in 1865. On its expanding influence see Griffiths, 'Longfellow's *Evangeline*,' 35–41; and Jean-Paul Hautecoeur, *L'Acadie du discours: pour une sociologie de la culture acadienne* (Quebec 1975); Judith Elaine Cowan, 'Outcast from Paradise: The Myth of Acadia and Evangeline in Canadian Literature in English and French' (PH D Diss., Université de Sherbrooke 1983).

the measure. The first overt sign of this emerging confrontation was the strong Acadian reaction in 1886 to two popular lectures justifying the expulsion given at Halifax by Sir Adams George Archibald (1814–92) then the president of the Nova Scotia Historical Society (established in 1878).[56]

In their struggle to puncture the complacency of Nova Scotia's historians, the Acadian community found allies in Quebec. Certain influential French Canadians saw in Akins, and especially in Parkman (whom they could not ignore), a challenge to their conception of their own race as pastoral, simple, and God-fearing. Foremost among these critics was Abbé Henri-Raymond Casgrain (1831–1904), whose *Un Pèlerinage au pays d'Evangéline* was published in 1887 in an attempt to rebut the charges brought against France and the Acadians in *Montcalm and Wolfe*.[57] In private correspondence Parkman chided Casgrain, his erstwhile friend, for failing to bring any new facts to bear on the case. 'What you call "*La vraie histoire du Canada*" is,' Parkman objected, 'a legend evolved not from facts but from desires.' The reprimand continued in a later letter: 'We have had enough of poetry, imagination, and excited rhetoric touching the Acadian business. It is high time that it was considered dispassionately in the light of the evidence on both sides.' Before Casgrain 'could even pronounce an intelligent criticism' on *Montcalm and Wolfe*, Parkman insisted he must 'pursue a good deal more research in the archives of France and elsewhere.'[58] Piqued, this was just what Casgrain determined to do – with results damaging to Nova Scotia complacency.

The abbé spent the winter of 1887–8 in London examining the materials held by the Public Record Office and the British Museum and in Paris those held by the archives of the Department of Marine and Colonies. He returned to Canada in the spring and with some éclat

56 The lectures were given 7 Jan. and 4 Nov. 1886, and published as 'The Expulsion of the Acadians,' parts 1 and 2, Nova Scotia Historical Society, *Collections* 5 (1886–7): 11–95. For reaction to Archibald's lectures, see the *Morning Herald*, 6, 9, 13, 16, 17 Nov. 1886; 12 Jan. 1887.

57 (Quebec 1887); Hector Fabre, 'La fin de la domination française et l'historien Parkman,' Royal Society of Canada, *Proceedings and Transactions*, ser. 1, vol. 5 (1888) sec. i, 3–12; Serge Gagnon, *Le Québec et ses historiens de 1840 à 1920: La Nouvelle-France de Garneau à Groulx* (Quebec 1978) 171–2

58 Francis Parkman to Henri-Raymond Casgrain, 28 Nov. 1885; 23 Oct., 4 Nov. 1887, in *Letters of Francis Parkman*, vol. 2, 183–5, 211–14, 215–16. On the stormy relationship between Parkman and Casgrain see Howard Doughty, *Francis Parkman* (New York 1962) 303–13.

presented his findings on 24 May to the annual meeting of the Royal Society of Canada.[59] Although still unable convincingly to rebut charges of French-inspired Acadian treachery, Casgrain did discover evidence indicating that local British administrators had consistently and illegally prevented Acadians from exercising their right, guaranteed by the Treaty of Utrecht and the instruction of Queen Anne, to remove both themselves and their property to French-controlled territory. In Casgrain's opinion such official obstruction went far toward invalidating the British government's demand that the Acadians submit to an unconditional oath. However, this and other interpretive refinements were but a velvet glove covering the mailed fist. The real force of his attack was the stunning allegation that he had found proof of a conspiracy by the Nova Scotia government, or at least by certain of its officials, to destroy or suppress all evidence favourable to the Acadian case. According to Casgrain this cover-up had begun at the time of the expulsion and had continued under subsequent officials charged with the care of the province's papers, up to and including T.B. Akins.[60]

The origin of what Brian Cuthbertson calls the 'suppression of evidence syndrome' can be traced to T.C. Haliburton's footnoted explanation in the *Statistical Account* that his inability to discover at Halifax papers relating to the expulsion was probably due to a desire on the part of those involved in its execution to conceal particulars from a sense of shame.[61] Haliburton's charges were subsequently repeated by, among others, the novelist Mrs Williams and the American historian Philip Henry Smith.[62] The credibility of Haliburton's allegations – which related

59 Henri-Raymond Casgrain, 'Éclaircissements sur la question acadienne,' Royal Society of Canada, *Proceedings and Transactions*, ser. 1, vol. 6 (1888) sec. i, 23–75. Casgrain repeated his charges, with little variation, in the following: 'Coup d'oeil sur l'Acadie avant la dispersion de la colonie française,' *Le Canada-Français*, vol. 1 (1888) 114–34; 'Éclaircissements sur la question acadienne: le serment d'allégeance,' ibid., 404–43; *Un Pèlerinage au pays d'Evangéline*, 2nd ed. (Quebec 1888). Casgrain edited and published the most important of the documents he discovered in a series of appendices to *Le Canada-Français* entitled 'Collection de documents inédits sur le Canada et l'Amérique,' vol. 1 (1888) [Appendix] 5–211; vol. 2 (1889) [Appendix] 5–202; vol. 3 (1890) [Appendix] 5–227.

60 Casgrain, 'Éclaircissements,' *Proceedings and Transactions*, 24–42, 50n; Clarke, 'Makers of Acadian History,' 552–60, 682–91

61 Brian Cuthbertson, letter to the author, 1 Nov. 1983; Haliburton, *Statistical Account*, vol. 1, 196n

62 Williams, *The Neutral French*, vi–ix; Philip H. Smith (b. 1842), *Acadia: A Lost Chapter in American History* (Pawling, NY, 1884). Smith's history was a plagiarized version of James Hannay, *The History of Acadia, from Its First Discovery to Its Surrender to England by*

only to those officials directly involved in the expulsion, not to subsequent custodians of provincial papers —suffered a setback in 1885, when Smith engaged Parkman in a newspaper debate on the subject and came off second best. Parkman pointed out that papers of the sort Haliburton said didn't exist could be found published for all to see in the *Selections* and quoted Akins's assurance that they had been in the care of the provincial secretary at the time Haliburton was writing. The only conclusion to be drawn, according to both Parkman and Akins, was that Haliburton was not the diligent historian he might have been.[63]

Casgrain, for one, was not entirely convinced by the arguments of his New England friend. He was willing to admit that many documents relating to the expulsion might very well be preserved in Halifax, but suspected that there was a conspiracy to keep those among them damaging to the English cause hidden from all but friendly authors. The abbé cited as evidence the experience of French historian François-Edme Rameau de Saint-Père (1820—99), who, when researching at the offices of the Commission of Public Records of Nova Scotia in September of 1868, was refused permission to copy any material and was kept under constant supervision by hostile clerks.[64] Cuthbertson notes that 'Akins was away and the clerks may have been over zealous,' and, although suspicious, Rameau de Saint-Père himself did not explicitly charge the commission

---

the Treaty of Paris (Saint John 1879). Note that after 1862 those who drew attention to Haliburton's allegations apparently did not see, did not believe, or chose to ignore R.G. Haliburton's claim that his father had repudiated the charges made in the *Statistical Account*; see R.G. Haliburton, *The Past and the Future of Nova Scotia*, 15n.

63 Francis Parkman, 'The Acadian Tragedy,' *Harper's New Monthly Magazine*, vol. 69, no. 414 (November 1884) 877–86; Philip H. Smith, 'British Apologists,' *Nation*, 30 Oct. 1884, 374–5; Parkman, letter to the editor, ibid., 6 Nov. 1884, 398; Parkman, letter to the editor, *New York Evening Post*, 20 Jan. 1885; Parkman, 'Acadians Again'; Parkman, letter to the editor, *Boston Evening Transcript*, 22 Jan. 1885; Smith, letter to the editor, ibid., 11 Feb. 1885; Parkman, letter to the editor, ibid., 25 Feb. 1885; T.B. Akins, letter to the editor, ibid., 19 Mar. 1885; Smith, letter to the editor, ibid., 4 Apr. 1885; Smith, 'A New Study of the Acadian Question,' ibid., 26 June 1885. See Clarke, 'Makers of Acadian History,' 684–91.

64 Rameau de Saint-Père's purpose in coming to Halifax was to obtain information for his *Une Colonie Féodale en Amérique*. The first edition, covering the period 1604–1710, was published at Paris in 1877, and in 1889 a second, two-volume edition, covering the period 1604–1881, was issued. François-Edme Rameau de Saint-Père, *Colonie Féodale* (1877) xxxi; 'Voyages au Canada,' *Revue de l'Université Laval* 14 (1949–50): 76–8. For letters relating to Rameau's visit to the offices of the Commissioner of Public Records of Nova Scotia see PANS, MG 1, vol. 436, folder 5; and Casgrain, 'Éclaircissements,' *Proceedings and Transactions*, 23–4.

with suppression of evidence.[65] Nevertheless, Casgrain put the worst possible construction on the treatment Rameau de Saint-Père received, linked it with Haliburton's experience, and suggested that the two incidents formed a pattern – the only explanation for which was the selective suppression of evidence by Akins and his predecessors. Then, while in London, Casgrain discovered what he believed to be incontrovertible evidence of Akins's duplicity. Examining the original manuscripts from which Akins had had his copies made, Casgrain claimed to have found documents favourable to the Acadians that were omitted entirely from the *Selections* (he cited more than a dozen specific examples) and others that the record commissioner had included but edited to the advantage of the English cause.[66]

Akins was appalled. To one who had dedicated his life to the collection and preservation of documents and to the avoidance of publicity and controversy, Casgrain's charges were a nightmare. When Akins received full particulars of the abbé's paper in the autumn of 1889, his immediate reaction was to scour the archives of the record commission for the allegedly omitted documents; he found that almost all the items cited by Casgrain were 'enclosures in despatches' that had not originally been sent from Annapolis to Halifax at the time the government was transferred in 1749; these had not been copied subsequently by his scribe in England for the simple reason that, not knowing of their existence, Akins had not asked for them. As to Casgrain's charge that certain items in the *Selections* had been edited with a bias, Akins was at a disadvantage. The abbé gave no specific examples, and Akins, although he found no significant mistakes, could not be certain his copyist had not made errors.[67] On the other hand, Akins could cite several documents favourable to the Acadians which he *had* included in the *Selections* and could point to his

65 Cuthbertson, 'Thomas Beamish Akins,' 98n; Pierre Trépanier and Lise Trépanier, 'Rameau de Saint-Père et le métier d'historien,' *Revue d'histoire de l'amérique française* 33 (1979): 349; Clarke, 'Makers of Acadian History,' 237–8

66 Casgrain, 'Éclaircissements,' *Proceedings and Transactions*, 23–5, 50n

67 PANS, Ethnic Collections, MG 15, A., Acadians, vol. 1, folder 4, T.B. Akins to Henry Youle Hind, 18 Oct., 18, 19, 20 Dec. 1889; Akins Papers, vol. 1504, 72, Akins to Douglas Brymner, 24 Mar. 1890.

Casgrain never did substantiate the charge of significant deletions. Cuthbertson checked a large number of documents in the *Selections* against the originals and found no significant mistakes: 'When Akins did not include the whole document, he so noted and none of the deletions checked seem to me to substantiate the charges. The deletions are mostly of wordy instructions,' Cuthbertson, 'Thomas Beamish Akins,' 100n.

subsequent efforts to obtain for the record commission copies of other valuable papers sympathetic to the Acadians, some of which had recently been published.[68] Convinced in his own mind that Casgrain was operating under some grotesque misunderstanding, Akins took heart when, on 10 December 1889, the Nova Scotia Historical Society passed a unanimous resolution expressing its 'entire confidence in the integrity of Dr. Akins.'[69] With this expression of confidence, Akins hoped the matter would drop.[70]

Unfortunately the matter could not simply be dropped. Henry Youle Hind (1823–1908), a resident of Windsor, member of the Nova Scotia Historical Society, and no stranger to controversy, recognized that Casgrain's accusations were 'a matter of the highest importance in connection with the honor and credit of Nova Scotia and the record commission,' and he knew that until the matter was cleared up 'it was useless to talk of the history of this country as derived from Nova Scotia records.' Furthermore, Hind was one of many members of the society who also saw in the Acadian controversy an opportunity to revitalize waning popular interest in their organization. Thus, before the same December meeting of the society that had resolved itself in support of the record commissioner, Hind presented a paper in which he defended Akins but also thumped the abbé, suggesting that Casgrain himself had played fast and loose with the evidence and discovered nothing to alter the basic facts of the expulsion, namely, that the French government and Roman Catholic clergy were treacherous, the Acadians traitorous, and the British justified.[71] Akins requested of Hind that this be the last word on the subject and that Hind not use his name in the published version of the paper 'as the subject is anoying [sic] to me in my old age.' In contrast, the corresponding secretary of the historical society, Francis Blake

68 'The Acadian French [extracts from the papers of Andrew Brown],' Nova Scotia Historical Society, Collections; 'Journal of Colonel John Winslow ...,' part 1, ibid. 3 (1882–3): 71–196; part 2, ibid. 4 (1884): 113–246. The extracts from 'The Acadian French' include the following annotation by Brown: 'I know of no act equally reprehensible as the Acadian removal, that can be laid to the charge of the French nation. In their colonies nothing was ever done that approaches it in cruelty and atrociousness,' 150.

69 Nova Scotia Historical Society Papers, vol. 642, folder 1, 170–1, Minutes, 10 Dec. 1889; Morning Herald, 11 Dec. 1889. Note: Akins was awarded DCL honoris causa by King's College, Windsor, in 1865. Typically, he rarely used the title; see F. Blake Crofton, 'T.B. Akins, D.C.L.,' Dominion Illustrated, 30 May 1891, 507.

70 Ethnic Collections, A., Acadians, vol. 1, folder 4, Akins to Hind, 26, 31 Dec. 1889; PANS, MG 100, vol. 101, nos. 12 and 12a, Akins to Hind, 28 Jan. 1890

71 Morning Herald, 11 Dec. 1889

Crofton (1841–1912), excitedly informed Hind that Casgrain intended to respond in English in the *Morning Herald* to Hind's countercharges. A jubilant Crofton concluded: 'This controversy will be a godsend to the "Herald" and indeed to our Society too.'[72]

Akins was no longer in control of the controversy swirling around him, a predicament for which he was himself in part to blame. 'A Gentleman of the Old School,' he was wedded to the quiet and dispassionate collection and study of documents. The Evangeline controversy attracted him initially because the poem offended his sense of scholarly objectivity. Akins simply believed that Longfellow's account of the expulsion was inaccurate. What Akins failed to perceive was that *Evangeline* aroused controversy because of its symbolic importance to the contemporary French- and English-speaking communities of the Maritimes, not because of the scholastic merits of the picture it drew. He entered unexpectedly dangerous waters, then, when he used the passions aroused by the controversy to help justify the creation of a provincial archives and speed the publication of the *Selections*. Once in the controversy he could not get out, and he found himself both allied with and fighting people who did not play by his rules.

Many members of the Nova Scotia Historical Society did not, for instance, share Akins's disinterested antiquarianism and reverence for the sanctity of documents. Drawn almost exclusively from the Protestant élite of Halifax, their motives in joining the society were mixed. Some did so for no better reason than in anticipation of social intercourse among like-minded people, others to establish family pedigree and thereby lay claim to distinction. However, in common with local élites across North America in the closing decades of the century, many in the upper reaches of Halifax society adopted the vehicle of a historical organization to inculcate a respect for the order established by founding fathers and patriotism among all classes of people. This role took on particular importance in the wake of the Confederation-induced ambiguity of allegiance and in the face of the growing complexity of urban life.[73] It was a measure of Akins's success that the Nova Scotia Historical Society initially focused more on the collection of manuscripts and publication of articles than on the elsewhere more common fascination with the commemoration of notable anniversaries through parades, concerts,

72 PANS, MG 100, vol. 101, no. 12a, Akins to Hind, 28 Jan. 1890; Ethnic Collections, A., Acadians, vol. 1, folder 6, F. Blake Crofton to Hind, 25 Mar. 1890

73 Van Tassel, *Recording America's Past*, 186–90; Gerald Killan, *Preserving Ontario's Heritage: A History of the Ontario Historical Society* (Ottawa 1976) 4–15

historical tableaux, and so forth. It was a measure of his failure that he could not restrain the likes of Crofton and Hind, who regarded history as an arsenal from which to draw ammunition for contemporary battles.

The Abbé Casgrain too had no scruple about making personal charges or moulding historical evidence to fit his needs. As he confided to fellow French-Canadian historian Thomas Chapais (1858–1946):

> Je n'ai pas voulu faire de mon livre (*Un Pèlerinage...*) une oeuvre d'art (...) ce n'est pas une escarmouche qu'il s'agit d'engager, mais une bataille rangée. Derrière les Archibalds et les Parkman se cachent, vous le savez, des multitudes. Nous ne sommes que le petit nombre; il nous faut être les preux chevaliers d'autrefois chargeant à outrance ces nouveaux Sarrasins au cri de *Dieu le veut!* sans jamais demander merci.[74]

Not surprisingly the abbé took nothing back in his letter to the *Morning Herald* of 4 April 1890. Although Casgrain reiterated his charges in the mistaken belief that Akins had visited London (and could not therefore claim to be unaware of the documents omitted from the *Selections*), he did not persist simply because he was 'in *ignorance of the man*,' but rather because his cause was best served if the credibility of the record commission, and through the record commission those histories based on its holdings, was destroyed.[75]

Akins of course now had to respond. In a letter to the *Morning Herald* of 12 April he outlined his defence for the first time in public and took notice of Casgrain's erroneous belief that he had visited the Public Record Office and British Museum in London. However, Akins's objections were beside the point. When dealing with questions of national honour, historical accuracy is at best a luxury, occasionally a handicap, most often immaterial. There is no evidence that Casgrain ever repudiated, or even regretted, his allegations against Akins. Nor did anyone else pay much attention to the record commissioner. Five years later another French-Canadian historian, Édouard Richard (1844–1904), wrote that any serious student of Acadian affairs soon came 'face to face with systematic attempts, unmistakable and continually renewed, to falsify history,' of which Akins's *Selections* was a prime example.[76] Similarly, in 1899 the

74 Casgrain to Thomas Chapais, 18 Nov. 1887, quoted in Gagnon, *Québec et ses historiens*, 171–2
75 Crofton, 'T.B. Akins, D.C.L.'
76 Édouard Richard, *Acadia: Missing Links of a Lost Chapter in American History*, 2 vols (New York and Montreal 1895) vol. 1, 9–13

Honourable Pascal Poirier (1852–1933), an Acadian-born senator actively involved in the late-nineteenth-century renaissance of his people, wrote that Akins's suppression of evidence rendered him 'still more odious, perhaps, than [Charles] Lawrence,' the man most responsible for the original expulsion.[77] In August 1908 Poirier actually carried a resolution before the Acadian Convention held at St Basile, New Brunswick, demanding that the government of Nova Scotia set up a commission to examine the records of the provincial archives and expose all documents relevant to the expulsion previously suppressed.[78]

Francis Parkman, too, finally tired of the personal acrimony engendered by the Acadian controversy. In the last volume of his *France and England in North America*, published in 1892, he withdrew his previously unqualified support for Akins, and now preferred to pose as an objective arbiter standing in independent judgment over the biased assertions of Abbé Casgrain and the record commissioner.[79] Although Akins did not live to see this desertion, he certainly died fully aware of the power of poetry.

The Evangeline controversy had done its work on the writing of Nova Scotia history. Coming upon a scene of smug and tiresome self-satisfaction, Longfellow's poem renewed interest in the past and incited historians to undertake extensive research in long-neglected colonial documents. The creation of the record commission of Nova Scotia was a by-product of lasting significance. In time, however, contemporary passions overwhelmed attempts to deal with *Evangeline* in a scholarly way. As Naomi Griffiths emphasizes, the debate over the events of 1755 'was neither purely academic nor just the question of the historical reputation of Nova Scotia.' Once Acadians, and to a lesser extent French Canadians, had accepted *Evangeline* 'as an acceptable embodiment of their own myths,' the expulsion became the focal point of racial, religious, and political passions.[80] Eventually debate degenerated into unenlightening

77 Pascal Poirier, 'The Acadians Desolate,' *New Brunswick Magazine* (Saint John) vol. 2, no. 3 (Mar. 1899) 156. The comparison of enemies to Lawrence seems to have been a stock insult in Poirier's arsenal, one he also used, for instance, against Thomas Louis Connolly, Archbishop of Halifax; see K. Fay Trombley, *Thomas Louis Connolly (1815–1876): The Man and His Place in Secular and Ecclesiastical History* (np 1983) 287.
78 Nova Scotia History Society Papers, vol. 670, folder 2, Memorandum [of a paper read by Senator Pascal Poirier before the Acadian Convention at St Basile, NB, 15 Aug. 1908]
79 Francis Parkman, 'A Half Century of Conflict,' in his *France and England in North America*, vol. 2, 476n
80 Griffiths, 'Longfellow's *Evangeline*,' 35

polemic, as controversialists replaced historians, and pretence fact. In the process, the Evangeline controversy did almost irreparable damage to the reputation of two of the finest historians produced by Nova Scotia in the nineteenth century: Thomas Chandler Haliburton, because he had indirectly inspired Longfellow's poem, unwittingly provided grounds for allegations made against the record commission, and had been adopted by the Acadians as an 'honest' English-speaking historian;[81] and T.B. Akins, because he was unable convincingly to refute assertions that he was an archivist with prejudice.[82]

In retrospect, one can see how unlikely it was that the shell of patriot complacency should survive intact, with or without the hammer blows delivered by Longfellow's poem. The conceit of the likes of T.C. Haliburton, T.B. Akins, and Beamish Murdoch was based not so much on pride in past achievements as it was on faith in the future prospects of the province. Haliburton lost that faith rather early on, and turned to writing satires of his compatriots. Akins and Murdoch persisted, their optimism hardly dented by the Evangeline controversy. What finally dealt a mortal blow to the Nova Scotia patriots' smug interpretation of history was Confederation. An immediate blow to self-esteem and a long-term threat to material well-being, Confederation sapped the confidence upon which the patriot interpretation of history was based. Confederation also brought an end to independent provincial history, grafting, by fiat as it were, that of Nova Scotia onto the trunk of the new nation. It is little

81 There is an irony in the fact that the resurgence in late-nineteenth-century Nova Scotia of the popularity of T.C. Haliburton's fictional satires made it all the easier for his admirers to dismiss the *Statistical Account* as the fanciful work of a youth. See for instance F. Blake Crofton, 'Haliburton: The Man and the Writer,' in [A.B. DeMille, ed.,] *Haliburton: A Centenary Chaplet*, published for the Haliburton Club, King's College, Windsor, NS (Toronto 1897) 57–8. Note too that the first allegations of plagiarism against Haliburton date from this period: John G. Bourinot, 'Builders of Nova Scotia: A Historical Review; With an Appendix Containing Copies of Rare Documents Relating to the Early Days of the Province,' Royal Society of Canada, *Proceedings and Transactions*, ser. 2, vol. 5 (1899) sec. ii, 63.

82 Until Cuthbertson attempted in 1977 to rehabilitate Akins's reputation, virtually all those writing on the Acadian question subsequent to Casgrain accepted the abbé's charges without further investigation. See for example Arthur G. Doughty, *The Acadian Exiles: A Chronicle of the Land of Evangeline*, vol. 9, *Chronicles of Canada*, eds George M. Wrong and H.H. Langton (Toronto 1916), 167; John Bartlett Brebner, *New England's Outpost: Acadia before the Conquest of Canada* (New York 1927) 207n; *The Journals of Francis Parkman*, ed. Mason Wade, 2 vols (New York 1947), vol. 2, 547–8; H. Doughty, *Francis Parkman*, 303–13. Patrick Clarke still thinks the 'Akins caper unsolved'; 'Makers of Acadian History,' 558.

wonder, then, that the members of Nova Scotia's community of historians were, almost to a man, anti-Confederatesionists.

Complacency was replaced by nostalgia, confidence in the future with yearning for the past. It was typical, for instance, that Murdoch did not push his narrative past the days of his youth.[83] The third and final volume, which ends at 1827, has no interpretive coherence other than a desire to touch the events of a happier time. The chronologically arranged chapters are filled with scattered and random pieces of information – from storms at sea to murder in back alleys – held together only by the annual return of assemblymen to their duty in Halifax. Murdoch liked to reminisce about the qualities and merits of old political friends and enemies alike and was no longer entirely comfortable explaining the issues that had once divided them.[84] Although he made it clear that the irresponsibility of the councils was a long-term provocation to the assembly, he regarded the various crises in the relationship between the two branches of government as abnormal, the result of, as in the case of the 'Judges' affair,' a heavy influx of settlers, or, as in the case of the clash between Lieutenant-Governor Sir John Wentworth and Assemblyman William Cottnam Tonge, personal incompatibility.[85] The essential point was that Nova Scotians traditionally resolved their differences in relative calm and with relative civility, totally unlike their cousins in the Canadas. Nova Scotians were different.

Even more characteristic of the nostalgic flavour of post-Confederation historical writing in Nova Scotia was the burgeoning industry in local and county histories. These works were almost invariably produced by long-time residents, who, apart from a natural attraction to their past, were often prompted to put pen to paper by a unique prize offered annually from 1864 by King's College, Windsor, for the best history of a Nova Scotia county, a prize founded by and named after the ubiquitous T.B. Akins.[86] The initiation of the Akins Historical Prize Essay competition was a natural outgrowth of Akins's exhaustive approach to the collection of historical documents. By donating a sum sufficient to yield a

83 As early as 1866, Murdoch wrote to the Reverend Edward Ballard: 'I feel almost tired of work, it has been so heavy on me latterly to keep up with the press. I have to go over a mass of newspapers to get a few lines of fact.' Murdoch to Ballard, 17 Aug. 1866, quoted in Stewart, Vickery, and Kellogg, eds, 'Nova Scotia-Maine Historical Correspondence,' 115n
84 Murdoch, *History of Nova-Scotia*, vol. 3 (1867) 77
85 Ibid., 60–1, 98–9, 218–19, 249–50, 259–60, 273–4
86 M. Brook Taylor, 'Nova Scotia's Nineteenth-Century County Histories [Review Article],' *Acadiensis* 10 (1981): 159–67

prize of $30 per annum, Akins hoped to stimulate the young men and women of Nova Scotia to ransack county records and memories. As he wrote to the Governors of King's College: 'My attention has been frequently turned to the necessity of collecting and preserving local Records of the various Counties in the Province, as also those local traditions among the people relating to the commencement and progress of the settlements, which, as time rolls on, are becoming lost to posterity.'[87] To ensure the comprehensive nature of the project, a different county was named as the prize essay topic each year. In a little more than a decade Nova Scotia historians would inherit a complete source of local information to complement the provincial and imperial records of Halifax and London – at least such was the plan.

Before he died in 1891, Akins received twenty-two papers, covering fourteen counties, from twenty different authors, to whom sixteen awards were given.[88] Nine of the papers were subsequently published, among which may be noted that on Lunenburg County by Mather Byles DesBrisay (1828–1900),[89] on the County of Yarmouth by the Reverend John Roy Campbell (1841–?),[90] on the County of Annapolis by William Arthur Calnek (1822–92),[91] and on Pictou County by the Reverend George Patterson (1824–97).[92] Add to these such independent productions as James F. More's history of Queen's County,[93] and Akins had every right to be satisfied with the achievement of his compatriots in the field of local history.

Regrettably, few of these works met with Akins's whole-hearted approval. He had hoped to arouse a generation of young historians who would adhere to his own high standards of research. Instead, too often he read mediocre syntheses of previously published material or the products of credulous boosters, keen to pass on anecdotal tales, which, however

---

87 Quoted in *The Calender of King's College, Windsor, Nova Scotia, 1864* (Halifax 1864) 7
88 Winners and subjects are detailed in 'Akins Prize Essay,' Librarian's file, University of King's College, Halifax, Nova Scotia. The original manuscripts are held in the Treasure Room of the Library of King's College.
89 Mather Byles DesBrisay, *History of the County of Lunenburg* (Halifax 1870; 2nd ed., Toronto 1895)
90 John Roy Campbell, *A History of the County of Yarmouth, Nova Scotia* (Saint John 1876)
91 William Arthur Calneck, *History of the County of Annapolis, Including Old Port Royal and Acadia; With Memoirs of Its Representatives in the Provincial Parliament, and Biographical and Geneal. Sketches of Its Early Settlers and Their Families,* ed. Alfred William Savary (1831–1920) (Toronto 1897)
92 George Patterson, *A History of the County of Pictou, Nova Scotia* (Montreal 1877)
93 James F. More, *The History of Queen's County, N. S.* (Halifax 1873)

entertaining, were not the stuff of history. Once again Akins was faced with historical enthusiasts who refused to live by the code of the disinterested antiquarian. During an interview in the year before his death, Akins told the young Archibald McKellar MacMechan (1862–1933) that the motives and methods of the contestants had defeated 'his main intention in founding [the Prize].'[94]

The problem was that for the most part local historians were not interested in compiling masses of information as a cumulative monument to antiquarianism. Their purposes were parochial; they wanted to recall past achievements and reminisce about golden days; and even the best of them suffused their work with the warm glow of nostalgia. The Reverend J.R. Campbell, for instance, openly admitted at the outset of his admirable history of Yarmouth that his 'volume from the very nature of the case cannot be expected to be very interesting to many persons unconnected with the County.'[95] Accordingly, Campbell took as his priority the establishment of lists of first settlers, biographies of the eminent, and the dating of the foundation of early institutions. An oblation to early forefathers, this was not the place to look for critical evaluation of men and measures, or of sources. Nova Scotians wanted to be consoled.

Few if any Nova Scotia-born historians had the heart to discuss Confederation in their histories. Indeed, the only comprehensive political history of the province to appear in the nineteenth century was written by an outsider, the Scottish-born Duncan Campbell (1818–86). Campbell was a journalist by trade who had cut his professional teeth as an editorial writer for his country's first penny daily, the *Daily Bulletin*. For reasons unexplained, Campbell conducted a large group of Scottish emigrants to Halifax early in the summer of 1866 under the aegis of a provincial agency established in Glasgow by Charles Tupper's Conservative government. At Tupper's behest, Campbell stayed on in Nova Scotia to survey the colony as a potential home for immigrants and completed his report, 'a highly readable and informative document,' in time for the 1867 session of the legislature. Thereafter, he served briefly with the immigration service of the new federal Department of Agriculture, reported for the Halifax *Morning Chronicle* through 1869 and 1870, and then acted as secretary of the Halifax Industrial Commission. It was while holding the last-named position that he decided to undertake the writing of his *Nova Scotia, in Its Historical, Mercantile and Industrial Relations*, subsequently published at Montreal in 1873.[96]

94 MacMechan, 'A Gentleman of the Old School'
95 J.R. Campbell, *County of Yarmouth*, viii
96 Shirley B. Elliott, 'Duncan Campbell,' *DCB*, vol. 11 (Toronto 1982) 147–8

Campbell saw no good reason to avoid an examination of recent events in the history of the colony and declared his intention to fill the vacuum left by Haliburton, Akins, and Murdoch.[97] He brought to his work a touch of the old-fashioned promotional spirit, a newspaperman's eye for a story, and considerable expertise in the statistical background of recent industrial and mercantile developments in the province. He breezed through the years over which his predecessors had laboured, reaching the expulsion (in his volume of 519 pages) by page 132 – an event again described as a cruel necessity deplorably executed. Thereafter, his narrative was characterized by numerous and lengthy digressions on subjects as diverse as the Duke of Kent and the pathetic tale of the black Maroons, by sketches of 'many departed worthies,' and, as was the case with Murdoch's third volume, by the now familiar round of murders, natural disasters, and private scandals.

Campbell held his account together by returning at intervals to the course of the assembly's contest with the irresponsible executive. More determinedly anachronistic than Murdoch, he praised the foresight of Joseph Howe and the Reformers, condemned the obstructionism of the Tories, and related all disputes between the two branches of the provincial government to the central theme of the struggle for responsible government. Campbell also exhibited a democratic or populist bent unusual in Nova Scotia historiography: he lampooned the pretensions of British officials, expressed sympathy for the cause of the American rebels, ignored the Loyalists, and thought the War of 1812 a 'most unnatural contest.' Nevertheless, he was not himself a proponent of violent agitation; he was proud of the calm and reasonable way in which Nova Scotians moved toward responsible government; and he found in the method of its achievement more to distinguish them from, than to identify them with, Canadians.[98] Once responsible government was conceded in 1848, Campbell became less conciliatory and betrayed in his account of subsequent events the kind of partisanship and personal rancour he had previously condemned in others. He turned on Joseph Howe for opposing temperance and Confederation and praised his patron, Tupper, for championing the federal union and creating conditions of economic prosperity.[99]

Although a revised version of Campbell's history was adopted for use in provincial schools, it was first politically sanitized and remained

97 Duncan Campbell, *Nova Scotia in Its Historical, Mercantile and Industrial Relations*, (Montreal 1873) 3
98 Ibid., 157–65, 172–5, 208–9, 261–323
99 Ibid., 380–1, 394–5, 442–6, 465–72

atypical.[100] For the most part Nova Scotia historians rejected both responsible government as an organizing principle of their past and the corollary that their province had a heritage of constitutional struggle in common with the rest of British North America. They preferred to cling to their long-established identity based on peaceful development, defending it all the more vociferously as their province merged with the new nation. Longfellow's cut stung all the more to this heightened sensitivity. Ultimately the result was rather sad: Nova Scotia's historians refused to accept what they lacked the power to change.

Matters, as always, were less clear cut in the neighbouring province of New Brunswick, where the historiography of the late nineteenth century was characterized by great effort to little result. In large measure this was attributable to the absence in the province of a predominant cosmopolitan centre. Commercial Saint John, which had pretensions to the role, made a poor substitute. As late as 1873 the Mechanics' Institute possessed the only public library in the city, and, according to the institute's own account, it was 'in extent and character not at all adequate to the wants of a population so large.'[101] The following year several members of the municipal élite founded the New Brunswick Historical Society and started their own library, only to have it, along with that of the Mechanics' Institute, destroyed by the great fire that swept away much of the city in June 1877.[102]

The situation in Fredericton was, if anything, worse – although not from so calamitous a cause. As the seat of government and home to many public records, Fredericton should have offered advantages to prospective historians. Unhappily, no attempt was made during the nineteenth century to preserve, much less organize, government records. Writing in the 1860s, Lieutenant-Governor Sir Arthur Hamilton Gordon claimed that the documents then to be found in the office of the provincial secretary were threatened by 'dirt, neglect, and the curiosity of chance visitors,' and he declined to leave his sixty-two volumes of dispatches to the tender mercies of the provincial authorities.[103] Gordon's decision was

---

100 Duncan Campbell, *History of Nova Scotia, for Schools* (Montreal 1877). According to Shirley Elliott the school edition was included in the provincial curriculum for many years; 'Duncan Campbell,' 148.

101 *Mechanics' Institute of St. John, N.B. (1873–1874)* (np, nd); Gregory H. Theobald, 'George Foster and James Hannay: Studies of the Imperial Idea in New Brunswick, 1883–1900' (MA Diss., University of New Brunswick 1971) 17n

102 Clarence Ward, 'New Brunswick Historical Society,' New Brunswick Historical Society, *Collections* 1 (1894): 8

103 Quoted in Hugh A. Taylor, 'The Provincial Archives of New Brunswick,' *Acadiensis* 1 (1971): 73

probably wise. A fire in the Provincial Building in 1881 'made havoc with the old Catalogues,' and when the edifice was pulled down in 1888, workmen found 'bushels' of papers hidden in the walls and in the vaults beneath the roof: some of these 'were thrown to the winds,' and others were carried away by passing citizens.[104] In short, it required a special dedication to be a historian in New Brunswick.

Still, there was a great deal of activity despite such handicaps, especially in the larger and wealthier city of Saint John. It was there in 1874 that the New Brunswick Historical Society was formed by a group of individuals who have been recently and rather grandiloquently labelled the 'Saint John School.'[105] Members were drawn primarily from the ranks of the city's extensive professional and business community, many being evangelical Protestants active in Saint John civic life. Joseph Wilson Lawrence (1818–92), who spearheaded the organization of the society, was typical of its roster. Born in Saint John, he was both a lawyer and the inheritor of a prosperous family furniture manufactory. He was twice elected and four times defeated for a Saint John city seat in the provincial assembly and was a ubiquitous member on various civic commissions and boards. A vociferous anti-Confederationist, Lawrence was also actively involved in the temperance movement (taking a pledge of total abstinence along with Samuel Leonard Tilley in 1840), a founder in 1835 of the city's Young Men's Debating Society, and for twenty-five years a director of the Mechanics' Institute.[106] He was a man, in short, who took his and others' responsibilities seriously.

Why the likes of Lawrence should see it as part of their duty to establish a provincial historical society says much about their sense of themselves and about conditions then prevailing in Saint John. In laying claim to history, they were laying claim to a leading role in society. That they had to

104 Nova Scotia Historical Society Papers, vol. 684, 528, George Edward Fenety to the Corresponding Secretary, 19 Oct. 1881; *Gleaner* (Fredericton), 21 Apr. 1888, quoted in H.A. Taylor, 'Provincial Archives of New Brunswick,' 74

105 David Graham Bell, Introduction to Joseph Wilson Lawrence, *The Judges of New Brunswick and Their Times*, ed. Alfred Augustus Stockton, rev. William Odber Raymond (1907), Sources in the History of Atlantic Canada No. 4, ed. P.A. Buckner (Fredericton 1983 [i.e. 1985]) v

106 NBM, Joseph Wilson Lawrence Papers, Notebooks, A313, Some Reminiscences, 1835–1885, 1–6; A.A. Stockton, Introduction to J.W. Lawrence, *Foot-Prints; Or, Incidents in Early History of New Brunswick, 1783–1883* (Saint John 1883) v–vi; Bell, Introduction, viii–x.

   Others prominent in the early years of the New Brunswick Historical Society were: William Richard Mulharen Burtis (1818–82), George Upham Hay (1843–?), Jonas Howe (1840–1913), David Russell Jack (1864–1913), Isaac Allen Jack (1843–1903), A.A. Stockton (1842–1907), and Clarence Ward (1838–1915).

do so is a sign of the changes taking place in the city. The Saint John of the 1870s was undergoing an economic reorientation toward the new industrial era. This transformation was met with as much anxiety as exuberance. In a period of uncertainty, some civic leaders turned for encouragement or consolation to the legacy of the province's forefathers, the Loyalists, who had sacrificed individual material well-being for a deeper commitment to the principle of obedience to God and King. Indeed, the Loyalist symbol met two paradoxical concerns: one, that the Christian spirit was waning in an increasingly materialistic age; two, that New Brunswick in general, and Saint John in particular, had reaped little material benefit from Confederation. Loyalism – an ideal based on selfless patriotism – reaffirmed spiritual values and at the same time provided New Brunswickers with a special moral role within the new nation.[107]

Given this evocative purpose, it is hardly surprising that the New Brunswick Historical Society did not dedicate itself primarily to the publication of learned papers or even the systematic collection of documents. J.W. Lawrence was not T.B. Akins, and the crisis of confidence then being experienced in Saint John would not be met in the way the quite different Evangeline controversy was in Nova Scotia. The primary stimulus of the New Brunswick Historical Society was instead to organize for the centennial of the arrival of the Loyalist Spring Fleet at Saint John on 18 May 1783. Preparations under Lawrence's supervision began more than a full year before the event and included the raising of money through concerts for such purposes as the beautification of King Square and the Loyalist Burial Ground.[108] 'Loyalist Day' itself began with the re-enactment of the landing, followed by a parade, sermon, oration, speeches, and Centennial Prize Ode. More than 40,000 people were reported to have taken part in the day's events, and their only cause for disappointment was the abrupt cancellation of the fireworks finale when a spark inadvertently fell into an uncovered box and sent up the entire display.[109]

'The Loyalist Centennial of 1883 witnessed,' according to Murray Barkley, 'one of the most widespread, spontaneous, and sincere tributes

107 Theobald, 'George Foster and James Hannay,' 14–37; Murray Barkley, 'The Loyalist Tradition in New Brunswick,' *Acadiensis* 4 (1975): 21–9
108 NBM, New Brunswick Historical Society, Minute-Books, vol. 1, 19 Jan., 29 June, 11 Dec. 1882; 29 May, 2 June, 27 Nov. 1883
109 [J.W. Lawrence, ed.,] *Loyalists' Centennial Souvenir; New Brunswick Historical Society* (Saint John 1887); Barkley, 'Loyalist Tradition in New Brunswick,' 24–9

ever paid in New Brunswick to the memory of the Loyalists.'[110] Yet the concrete results were meagre. The occasion was not seized as a opportunity, for instance, to push for a provincial archives. Similarly, although productive of innumerable odes, songs, and epic poems, the day did not inspire any significant work of history. All that appeared were two commemorative publications, Lawrence's own *Foot-Prints; Or, Incidents in Early History of New Brunswick*, and David Russell Jack's *Centennial Prize Essay on the History of the County of St. John*. The latter was one of only two entries written in competition for a $200 award offered by the Mechanics' Institute,[111] and neither had permanent value. The celebration did not even spawn repetition in following years and, despite its success, it left Lawrence personally liable for a considerable debt.[112]

In fact debt, lack of support, and the demands of painstaking research all seemed to have conspired to keep Lawrence from the completion of his life's work, a history of the judges of New Brunswick in the form of biographical sketches. The book-length project grew from a simple paper presented before the inaugural meeting of the New Brunswick Historical Society and, following the centennial, he alternately revised and attempted to publish the manuscript down to within months of his death.[113] One suspects, however, that these were also convenient excuses for a man lacking the temperament and skill necessary to bring order to his papers.[114] In this, as in so much else, Lawrence was once again typical of his generation of provincial historians. Jonas Howe, another founding member of the New Brunswick Historical Society, put twenty years of research into compiling muster lists of various Loyalist regiments without

110 Barkley, 'Loyalist Tradition in New Brunswick,' 29
111 David Russell Jack, *Centennial Prize Essay on the History of the City and County of St. John* (Saint John 1883) iii–iv
112 New Brunswick Historical Society Papers, box 2, book 2, Jean M. Sweet, 'J.W. Lawrence – Some Personal Papers, Read before the New Brunswick Historical Society, 31 January 1956,' 5–6, Chief Justice John C. Allen to Lawrence, 26 Apr. 1884
113 J.W. Lawrence, 'The First Courts and Early Judges of New Brunswick, Read before the New Brunswick Historical Society, November 25, 1874,' *Maritime Monthly* (Saint John), vol. 5, no. 1 (Jan. 1875) 1–31; reprinted in New Brunswick Historical Society, *Collections* 20 (1971): 8–34; NA, Lawrence Collection: Chipman Papers, MG 23, D 1, vol. 80, 1–4, T.B. Akins to Lawrence, 10 Apr. 1880; NBM, William Francis Ganong Papers, Correspondence, box 8, packet 1, Lawrence to William Francis Ganong, 20 Oct. 1891
114 NBM, Ganong Library, 'New Brunswick History,' vol. 1, W.O. Raymond to William Francis Ganong, 18 May 1899, letter inserted in offprint of I.A. Jack, 'The Loyalists and Slavery in New Brunswick,' Royal Society of Canada, *Proceedings and Transactions*, ser. 2, vol. 4 (1898–9); Bell, Introduction, ix–x

any clear goal for publication. In the event, it was not until the society initiated its series of *Collections* in 1894 that Howe managed to get an article into print, and Lawrence had been dead fifteen years before his *Judges of New Brunswick* was finally published in 1907 (and even then it required the efforts of two editors to whip it into shape).[115]

Whatever the reason – financial, personal, the calamity of fire – Lawrence and his contemporaries were incapable of translating their enthusiasm into lasting form. In fact, the enthusiasm they generated may well be their major contribution to New Brunswick historiography, for it provided impetus to a second generation of Saint John historians, who were by temperament and training more committed to systematic research and publication and who found outlet in the historical society's *Collections*, the *New Brunswick Magazine* (1898–9), and *Acadiensis* (1901–8). Foremost among those to follow Lawrence were William Odber Raymond (1853–1923), rector in and later archdeacon of Saint John, and William Francis Ganong (1864–1941), professor of botany at Smith College, Massachusetts. Significantly, both men had received extensive postgraduate university training, Raymond in divinity at the University of New Brunswick (MA 1891, LL D 1901), and Ganong in the physical sciences at Munich (PH D 1894).[116] Although technically amateur historians, their approach was comprehensive, methodical, and exact. Ganong in particular insisted that historians 'must be trained rigidly in the modern scientific spirit of inquiry' and must 'guard against preconceived opinions.'[117] In short, they were comfortable in the environment of the professional historian, and their works were of an altogether different order.

There was in truth one other energetic historian writing and publishing in Saint John long before the advent of Raymond and Ganong, but not of the Lawrence circle. This was James Hannay (1842–1910).[118] Although

115 Jonas Howe, 'The King's New Brunswick Regiment 1793–1802,' New Brunswick Historical Society, *Collections* 1 (1894): 13–62. For the tangled history of Lawrence's manuscript see Bell, Introduction, ix–xiv.
116 On Raymond see Barkley, 'Loyalist Tradition in New Brunswick,' 35–42. On Ganong see Graeme Wynn, 'W.F. Ganong, A.H. Clark and the Historical Geography of Maritime Canada,' *Acadiensis* 10 (1981): 5–28; and John Bell and Gary Whiteford, 'Exploring New Brunswick with W.F. Ganong,' *Canadian Geographic*, vol. 99, no. 1 (Aug.–Sept. 1979) 38–43.
    Other members of this second generation were: William Godsoe MacFarlane (1870–1942), and John Clarence Webster (1863–1950).
117 Quoted in Wynn, 'W.F. Ganong,' 6
118 W.O. Raymond, 'James Hannay, D.C.L.,' Royal Society of Canada, *Proceedings and Transactions*, ser. 3, vol. 4 (1910) vii–viii; Theobald, 'George Foster and James Hannay,' 143–8

the son of a Presbyterian minister, trained as a lawyer, and first employed as official reporter of the Supreme Court of New Brunswick, he was not part of that self-conscious élite of evangelical civic leaders from which the early membership of the New Brunswick Historical Society was primarily drawn. Hannay was by inclination something of a radical, a self-appointed defender of civil and political liberties, and by 1872 he found a more congenial home in the hurly-burly of journalism as a member of the editorial staff of the Saint John *Daily Telegraph*. What attracted him first to history was the search for good stories, the kind of drama to which the likes of novelist Sir Walter Scott and historian Francis Parkman had opened many eyes. He wanted to excite and entertain people instead of teaching them sanctimonious lessons. If this were not enough to distinguish Hannay, he was an ardent supporter of Confederation who refused to indulge in nostalgia for a golden age of the pioneers.[119]

Hannay, not believing that New Brunswickers required either spiritual renewal or consolation, ignored the Loyalists in favour of the more promising adventures to be found in the history of Acadia. Although the toil of a court reporter and later that of the daily journalist was onerous, Hannay clearly worked very hard to read and research widely after the fashion established by Parkman. Unfortunately he wasted much of his initial effort on historical poetry, publishing odes and ballads in various newspapers and magazines, often under the pseudonym 'Saladin.'[120] More promising were a series of 'Sketches of Acadie,' which he published in *Stewart's Literary Quarterly* between 1867 and 1869. His first book was in the popular form of a captivity narrative, in this case of John Gyles, who was taken in 1689 as a child of nine by the Malecites of the Saint John River and held until 1698.[121] Hannay was also the author of the historical passages in Russell Herman Conwell's instant account of the great Saint John fire of 1877.[122]

119 There is, for instance, an upbeat, almost promotional tone, to [James Hannay,] *St. John and Its Business. A History of St. John, and a Statement in General Terms of Its Various Kinds of Business Successfully Prosecuted. The Dry Goods – Grocery – Insurance – Lumber – Manufacturing – The Press of St. John – The Shipping – A View of the Prospects and Possibilities of St. John as a Commercial Centre. Together with an Account of One Hundred Business Houses, Embracing the Leading or Representative Establishments in Each of the Different Lines* (Saint John 1875).

120 James Hannay, 'Latour: A Ballad of Acadie, A.D. 1643,' *Stewart's Literary Quarterly* (Saint John) vol. 3; no. 2 (July 1869) 113–15; Raymond, 'James Hannay'

121 James Hannay, ed., *Memoirs of Odd Adventures, Strange Deliverances, etc. (1736): Nine Years a Captive; Or, John Gyles' Experience among the Milicite Indians from 1689–1698* (Saint John 1875)

122 Russell Herman Conwell, *History of the Great Fire in Saint John, June 20 and 21, 1877* (Boston 1877) chs. 8–9

These early historical efforts were prefatory to and indicative of Hannay's first major work, *The History of Acadia, from Its First Discovery to Its Surrender to England by the Treaty of Paris*, published in Saint John in 1879. In particular, Hannay's first articles highlighted the ambiguous nature of his regard for the French regime: on one hand he was absolutely clear that it utterly failed to make any permanent imprint on what was to become New Brunswick; on the other he was attracted to the romantic futility that marked the career of the fur lords, to the heroic but vain defence against the English, and to the tragic expulsion of the Acadians. Although Hannay did his duty and collected and purchased 'all the books and publications bearing on the early history of New England and Acadia,' read Champlain, Lescarbot, and Akins's *Selections*, and had an indeterminate number of manuscript documents from Paris copied for his personal use, there was nothing unusual in his *History of Acadia* apart from the manner of its telling.[123] Gone were the copious quotations of T.C. Haliburton and Beamish Murdoch, and in their place was what one contemporary reviewer termed an 'interesting history, composed of so many consecutive stories, of a romantic, a chivalric, an amusing, an instructive, or sometimes, alas! of a bloody character.' The reviewer went on to say 'that owing to the author's style the work will be read by many who find it difficult to digest other historical works.'[124] This was precisely the affect Hannay desired to achieve.

Hannay's enthusiasm for historical research and writing naturally drew him on 29 September 1874 to the preliminary meeting of the New Brunswick Historical Society. Predictably his experience with the organization was not a happy one. Politically and ideologically at variance with the views of most members, Hannay did not share their aims, their methods, or their fascination with the Loyalists. Moreover, he did not like Lawrence and said so, thinking the elderly gentleman pompous and no historian. These sentiments were reciprocated. Lawrence disliked mavericks and accused Hannay (probably with justification) of hoarding research.[125] Under these conditions, it was just as well that Hannay

123 Hannay, *History of Acadia*, iii–iv. For an exhaustive reconstruction of Hannay's research and use of sources see Clarke, 'Makers of Acadian History,' ch. 4.
124 Isaac Allen Jack, review of *The History of Acadia*, by James Hannay, *Daily Telegraph* (Saint John) 1 Apr. 1879
125 Lawrence Collection: Chipman Papers, vol. 80, 5–8, T.B. Akins to Lawrence, 23 Nov. 1881; Nova Scotia Historical Society Papers, vol. 684, folder 7, 180, James Hannay to the Corresponding Secretary, 7 Apr. 1881; 261, Akins to the Recording Secretary, 3 Aug. 1881; NBM, Jonas Howe Papers, Letters Received, shelf 63, packet 1, I. DeLancey Robinson to Jonas Howe, 26 May 1883; New Brunswick Historical Society Papers, J.C. Allen to Lawrence, 26 Apr. 1884

departed just prior to the centennial celebrations in order to take up a position with the Montreal *Herald*.

Hannay was not gone for good. After a brief stint with the *Herald* and then a slightly longer one with the *Eagle* of Brooklyn, New York, he returned to Saint John in 1888, first with the *Gazette* and then back at the *Daily Telegraph*. To their evident surprise, the city's historical community found him a prodigal son and more congenial colleague. The waning influence of Lawrence was only partly responsible for this reconciliation. Whether through recent personal experience, a reaction to political events, or a newspaperman's instinctive reading of the public mood, Hannay had developed a visceral antipathy toward the United States and a consequent attraction to the Loyalists, the original anti-Americans. Between January and September of 1893 he published a thirty-seven-chapter 'History of the Loyalists' in the *Daily Telegraph*, claiming it would be, in his own modest words, 'the most important work ever issued from the Press of the Maritime Provinces.'[126] This was but herald to numerous other Hannay articles on the subject, all of which culminated in a full-length study of the War of 1812 in which the Loyalists this time won.[127] Hannay was, in short, now in tune with the general community of historians in New Brunswick, and was appointed historian of the New Brunswick Loyalist Society and later president of the New Brunswick Historical Society.[128]

The link with Hannay's earlier career was his continuing concern for civil and political liberties. He contended that the capacity for self-government was an innate characteristic of the Teutonic races, especially of the Anglo-Saxons. The history of the British people was for Hannay primarily a story of the precedent-by-precedent development of parliamentary institutions. The American Revolution was a major setback in the cause of human liberty, American demagogues having maliciously shattered the unity of race for their own low, personal motives of power and profit. The Loyalists stood firm and set an example in British North America of how reform could be achieved through such reasonable compromises as responsible government.[129] In order to prove the point, Hannay subsequently published biographies of Sir Samuel Leonard

---

126 *Daily Telegraph*, 3 Jan. 1893, quoted in Barkley, 'Loyalist Tradition in New Brunswick,' 31
127 James Hannay, *History of the War of 1812 between Great Britain and the United States of America* (Saint John 1901). It was republished in England under the more suggestive title of *How Canada Was Held for the Empire* (London 1905).
128 Barkley, 'Loyalist Tradition in New Brunswick,' 31–6; Theobald, 'George Foster and James Hannay,' 149–54
129 *Daily Telegraph*, 27 Jan. 1893; Theobald, 'George Foster and James Hannay,' 154–5

Tilley and Lemuel Allan Wilmot, as well as a two-volume account of New Brunswick, in which provincial history was poured into the mould of constitutional reform through responsible government and Confederation.[130]

Gone was the carefree interest in a good story that had earlier set Hannay apart. While hardly nostalgic or consolatory, Hannay's later writings were bent to crudely didactic ends of a kind Lawrence would have understood. The irony was that Hannay made this transition just as a new generation of historians came along espousing the virtues of scientific professionalism. To them Hannay's praise of Tilley and Wilmot was too partisan and his fixation with the development of responsible government in New Brunswick artificial. W.O. Raymond, for one, levelled criticism at Hannay's later work, especially the *History of New Brunswick*, which, he believed, did not live up to the promise of the *History of Acadia*.[131]

At least enthusiasts in late-nineteenth-century Saint John generated enthusiasm. Fredericton was apathetic. The only exception was George Edward Fenety (1812–99). Born in Halifax, at the age of seventeen Fenety entered the offices of Joseph Howe's *Novascotian* and there assimilated both the trade of journalism and the politics of reform. After six years with Howe, in 1835 Fenety went to the United States, where he established himself as the editor and proprietor of the *Planter's Advocate*, at Donaldsville on the Mississippi River. In 1839 he returned to the Maritimes and founded the *Commercial News* at Saint John, the first penny journal in the region. For almost twenty-five years Fenety used this editorial chair to champion reform causes, especially that of responsible government. It was his appointment in 1863 to the position of Queen's Printer and editor of the *Royal Gazette* that made the journalist a historian: it was necessary both that he move to Fredericton and that he moderate his partisanship; he had more time on his hands; and he was in a position to observe and interview the leading political characters of the day, examine the journals and debates of the legislature, and peruse the back files of his own and other newspapers.[132] Thus provided with the

130 James Hannay, *The Life and Times of Sir Leonard Tilley; Being a Political History of New Brunswick for the Past Seventy Years* (Saint John 1897); *Wilmot and Tilley*, Makers of Canada, ed. Duncan Campbell Scott and Pelham Edgar, vol. 17 (Toronto 1907); *History of New Brunswick*, 2 vols (Saint John 1909)
131 Ganong Papers, shelf 105, box 10, 14, W.O. Raymond to F. Bliss, 11 Feb. 1913; Theobald, 'George Foster and James Hannay,' 189–90
132 J.W. Lawrence, *Judges of New Brunswick*, 459–60; NBM, William Odber Raymond Papers, Scrapbooks, LDS 859586, no. 38, Reminiscences of George E. Fenety and the 'Morning News'

opportunity, the looming possibility of Confederation furnished a motive for a stocktaking of New Brunswick's development.

The historical development Fenety had in mind was that of responsible government, by which he meant rule by a party ministry commanding a majority in and responsible to the assembly. He was in complete accord with Lord Durham, writing that 'the absence of Ministerial responsibility to the Colonial Assemblies was, until a recent period, the primary cause of complaint, whether by the people of Canada, Nova Scotia, or New Brunswick.'[133] His purpose in compiling the two volumes of his *Political Notes and Observations* was to demonstrate the truth of this axiom by reference to events in New Brunswick. While Fenety admitted what he could not deny, that he had for many years spoken with 'the zeal of partizanship,' he promised to observe 'the most rigid impartiality' by reproducing 'in a compendious form "the sayings and doings" of honorable gentlemen who formerly figured in debate.' That is, following the example of Robert Christie, he intended to let participants speak for themselves. His major sources would be the newspapers of the day.[134]

The first volume, published in 1867, covered events more or less from the time of Fenety's arrival in the province down to 1854, that is to the close of the tenure of Lieutenant-Governor Sir Edmund Walker Head. Fenety assumed the familiarity of his audience with the recent past and did not provide a narrative so much as a running commentary on political developments, making the work at this date difficult to follow without considerable knowledge of the period. Still, the central problem of the volume is clear enough: New Brunswick voters and politicians did not conform to Fenety's expectations. Whereas in the Canadas and Nova Scotia the lines dividing reformers and defenders of the old order were clear and consistent, in New Brunswick the principle of responsible government was poorly understood, particularly its party aspect. For this Fenety blamed the weakness of reform leaders L.A. Wilmot and Charles Fisher and the quiescence of the press. 'There being no fixity of principles, no sufficient number of able, disinterested men, to take the lead, the practice for many years among our representatives was but a nibbling at Constitutional questions, and this too ... long after Responsible

133 George Edward Fenety, *Political Notes and Observations; A Glance at the Leading Measures that Have Been Introduced and Discussed in the House of Assembly of New Brunswick, under the Administrations of Sir William M.G. Colebrooke, Sir Edmund Walker Head, Hon. J.H.T. Manners-Sutton, and Hon. Arthur H. Gordon, Extending over a Period of Twenty-Five Years. Together with an Appendix to Each Chapter, Embracing a Notice of All Important Local Occurrences since 1840* (Fredericton 1867) vol. 1, vii
134 Ibid., iv–v

Government was established in Nova Scotia and Canada.' Fenety was particularly outraged when Wilmot and Fisher agreed to join a coalition government with their Conservative rivals in 1848, a decision he labelled 'treachery.'[135] As it was, Fenety did not believe responsible government was fully instituted until the election of 1854, following which Fisher formed 'the first Reform *Party* Government ever established in New Brunswick.'[136]

The real problem was not that New Brunswickers failed to live up to Fenety's expectations but rather that Fenety attempted to force them into a design of his own devising. He simply could not understand their reluctance to accept the principle of party government, when, as C.M. Wallace has recently written, 'Wilmot and Fisher were products of a system that achieved most of the features of responsible government without the necessity of political parties.'[137] The assembly controlled the raising and expenditure of funds and in large measure dictated the composition of each administration. Fenety's principled criticism and strong language therefore appeared churlish. Few readers of the *Political Notes* took his protestations of objectivity seriously, and the publication was 'criticized freely in the newspapers.'[138] Such criticism was likely to be even stronger as Fenety approached the subject of Confederation, and he continually put off completion of the second volume. Finally published in the pages of the Saint John *Progress* in 1894, it was never issued in book form. Instead Fenety was drawn back to the subject of responsible government and in 1896 published a biography of Joseph Howe, his mentor from years before.[139]

Fenety was exceptional, both as a historian in Fredericton and as a historian of constitutional development. Most historians of late-nineteenth-century New Brunswick, like their peers in Nova Scotia, preferred to eschew partisan discussion of recent political events and avoid the implication that responsible government represented a common historical bond with the rest of British North America. Instead they turned away from Confederation and sought consolation and renewal in provincial

135 Ibid., xv–xix, 283–7
136 Ibid., 475–6
137 C.M. Wallace, 'Lemuel Allan Wilmot,' *DCB*, vol. 10, 712
138 George Stewart, Review of *Political Notes and Observations*, by G.E. Fenety, *Stewart's Literary Quarterly*, vol. 1, no. 2 (July 1867) 77
139 G.E. Fenety, *Life and Times of the Hon. Joseph Howe, (The Great Nova Scotian and Ex-Lieut. Governor.) with Brief References to Some of His Prominent Contemporaries* (Saint John 1896)

history, finding in the Loyalists a particularly evocative symbol of spiritual strength in a time of adversity. If their nostalgia did not result in a renaissance of historical science, practical hurdles and personalities were largely responsible.

The last of the three Maritime provinces, Prince Edward Island, was, as always, an exceptional case. It was the one colony in the region where the old patriot verities had collapsed long before Confederation. Here the normal façade of colonial tranquillity and economic progress was breached by the divisiveness of the land question, which, like the issue of race in Lower Canada, simply would not go away.[140] Despite the best efforts of island patriots to inhibit criticism of the neo-feudal system of leasehold tenure, which vested ownership in the hands of a few, mostly absentee, magnates and operational supervision in the patriots' hands as agents, resident tenants demanded its abolition with increasing heat and radicalism. By the 1830s an informal 'Escheat party,' advocating the revocation of proprietorial title for nonfulfilment of the terms of the original grants of 1767, polarized island politics around the single issue of land tenure. This agitation contributed to a violent mood among the tenantry, many of whom refused to pay rents and occasionally banded together to threaten agents and sheriffs with physical violence. Indeed, apart from the French province, it is doubtful if any colony of British North America was so deeply divided as Prince Edward Island, and had it been geographically contiguous to Lower Canada its citizens might well have entered the Rebellions of 1837–8 with more gusto than William Lyon Mackenzie's radicals. As it was, troops were called out on more than one occasion to make a show of force in disaffected areas of the province.

The escheat movement, like the reform movement in Upper Canada, spawned a historical tradition of reform that challenged patriot notions that individuals rather than the system were to blame for any shortcomings in development. How, for instance, could a colonist live up to a yeoman ideal when the scheme of leasehold tenure denied him the independence essential to that ideal? The injustice of the system lay not merely in the failure of proprietors to fulfil the conditions of their grants

140 The best recent scholarship on the land question at mid-century is to be found in the *Dictionary of Canadian Biography*. See for example, Harry Baglole, 'William Cooper,' *DCB*, vol. 9 (Toronto 1976) 155–8; Ian Ross Robertson, 'George Coles,' ibid, vol. 10, 183–8; 'Edward Palmer,' ibid., vol. 11, 664–70. See also Ian Ross Robertson, 'Highlanders, Irishmen, and the Land Question in Nineteenth-Century Prince Edward Island,' in L.M. Cullen and T.C. Smout, eds, *Comparative Aspects of Scottish and Irish Economic and Social History* (Edinburgh [1977]) 227–40.

but in denying tenants complete possession of the fruits of their labour.[141] Both natural and legal justice were denied, therefore, when landlords availed themselves of backstairs influence in London to thwart the legitimate demands of the colonists. Such was the power of this influence that, following the 1838 electoral victory of the Escheat party, the then colonial secretary, Lord John Russell, refused to meet with an official delegate of the island legislature sent to present the colony's request for a court of escheat and other reform measures. Under these circumstances it was useless to talk of progress of any kind on Prince Edward Island.

What Lord John Russell refused, Lord Durham would have granted. A brief review of the evidence and an even briefer interview with island delegates sent to Quebec City was sufficient to convince Durham of the justice of the escheat cause, a cause he believed was blocked only by the influence of absentee proprietors resident in England. 'The only question,' wrote Durham, 'is whether that influence shall prevail against the deliberate acts of the colonial legislature and the universal complaints of the suffering colonists.' He, for one, had no doubt on the subject: 'My decided opinion is, that the royal assent should no longer be withheld from the [escheat] act of the colonial legislature.'[142] Although Durham's advice was not taken, his sanction was nonetheless important. While defenders of the *status quo* expressed outrage at his errors of fact, tenants rejoiced at his acceptance of their escheat tradition of grievance.[143] In time the old patriot position collapsed, and it simply became untenable for residents to defend the leasehold system.[144] If the land question itself was

141 Tenant ideology was expressed clearly in the thirty-four-clause petition of the Hay River Meeting, 20 Dec. 1836, printed in the *Royal Gazette* (Charlottetown) 10 Jan. 1837; reprinted in Harry Baglole, ed., *The Land Question: A Study of Primary Documents* (Charlottetown 1975) sec. B, doc. 3. See also the testimony of tenant farmer James Howatt before the Land Commission of 1860, in *Abstract of the Proceedings before the Land Commissioners' Court, Held during the Summer of 1860, to Inquire into the Differences Relative to the Rights of Landowners and Tenants in Prince Edward Island*, reporters J.D. Gordon and David Laird (Charlottetown 1862) 84–5.

142 Lord Durham to Lord Glenelg, 8 Oct. 1836 [i.e. 1838], quoted in Duncan Campbell, *History of Prince Edward Island* (Charlottetown 1875) 89–90; *Lord Durham's Report on the Affairs of British North America* (1839) ed. C.P. Lucas, 3 vols (Oxford 1912) vol. 2, *The Text of the Report*, 241–2

143 *Facts versus Lord Durham. Remarks upon that Portion of the Earl of Durham's Report, Relating to Prince Edward Island, Shewing the Fallacy of the Statements Contained Therein. To Which Is Added, a Tabular View of the British Provinces in North America, Shewing Their Territorial Extent, the Acres Under Cultivation, and Their Comparative Population*, by a Proprietor (London 1839)

144 Ian Ross Robertson, 'Political Realignment in Pre-Confederation Prince Edward Island,' *Acadiensis* 15 (1985): 56–7

not resolved immediately, at least a provincial consensus was re-established, this time based on a common heritage of political, economic, and social struggle rather than on calm development of island resources.

The escheat agitation and the persistence of the land question transformed the nature of provincial patriotism, yet surprisingly did not affect the reputation of John Stewart's *Account of Prince Edward Island.* That work remained the basis of provincial historiography because it was easy to ignore what Stewart did not make clear in the first place. With the outrage of a populist, Stewart had chronicled the persistent failure of the first generation of proprietors to live up to the conditions of their grants. The verve with which he did so implied that he wished to see resident tenants obtain title to the lands they worked. The radical tone of Stewart's rhetoric obscured the conservatism of his conclusions; namely, that individual proprietors and not the leasehold system were to blame for initial disappointments and that, through his own strenuous efforts as receiver-general of quit rents, an acceptable breed of landlords had been introduced to the island and had put an end to trouble.[145] Later historians, out of touch with the ins and outs of turn-of-the-century island politics, simply ignored or failed to perceive the fact that Stewart had whipped up public opinion in favour of escheat in order to extort title to land for the benefit of himself and his friends. Thus, when it came time to restructure the history of Prince Edward Island as a narrative of grievance rather than a description of achievement and potential, Stewart's *Account of Prince Edward Island* continued to serve as a standard text.

To the Reverend George Sutherland (1830–93), writing his own history of Prince Edward Island in 1861, the *Account* was 'valuable as a history, and creditable to [Stewart] as an author.'[146] A minister of the Free Church of Scotland, sectarian partisan, and temperance advocate, Sutherland was a man of strong opinions and little guile.[147] He read Stewart as a champion of the people who had identified the key element of the land question – the influence absentee proprietors exercised in London. Sutherland's self-imposed task was to chronicle the consequent

145 See above pages 36–8.
146 George Sutherland, *A Manual of the Geography and Natural and Civil History of Prince Edward Island, for the Use of Schools, Families, and Emigrants* (Charlottetown 1861) 114. Sutherland was also the author of the charming *The Magdalen Islands, Their Topography, Natural History, Social Condition, and Commercial Importance* (Charlottetown 1862).
147 There is no biography of George Sutherland, but see Henry J. Morgan, *Bibliotheca Canadiensis or a Manual of Canadian Literature* (Ottawa 1867); and Ian Ross Robertson, 'Party Politics and Religious Controversialism in Prince Edward Island from 1860 to 1863,' *Acadiensis* 7 (1978): 30–1.

failure of the assembly to obtain royal assent for such measures as a tax on wilderness lands, escheat, or compulsory land purchase. The beneficial corollary of this tale of woe was the unity of purpose and conscious identity it imparted to all islanders, thereby obscuring the many religious, ethnic, and political divisions that Sutherland had himself on occasion fostered. Indeed, writing in the mistaken belief that the provincial Land Commission Report of 1861 heralded the end of the leasehold tenure system, Sutherland thought Prince Edward Island on the threshold of a new era of moral and material progress.[148]

Sutherland was not alone in his belief that Prince Edward Island was on the verge of prosperity. Cornelius Birch Bagster (b. 1815) also wrote an account of the province during a visit to his birthplace in 1861 in order to highlight the progress made and the potential for future development. Bagster was unique, however, in his assumption that the leasehold system had little to do with the previously backward state of the island's development. 'While a poor excuse is better than none,' he wrote, 'out of this seeming evil, more lasting benefit will arise on the settlement question, than from any other cause.' Bagster's unusual reasoning was that colonies take time to develop and attempts at forced growth lead only to disappointment or worse. 'Refined in the fire' of the leasehold system, tenants emerged stronger and more capable settlers. Prince Edward Island was now ready for significant change and growth not because of the Land Commission Report but because natural growth had reached the appropriate stage.[149]

There was another reason Bagster was unique among nineteenth-century English-speaking historians of British North America – he had a sense of humour. What he called his history of Prince Edward Island was in fact an idiosyncratic tour through the legislative achievements of almost a century of island government. Lacking any motive for serious analysis of the land question or any other particular issue, Bagster simply poked fun at the pretension and pomposity of generations of politicians and officials. Bagster observed, for instance, that in 1825 'to diminish the use of rum and brandy there was a duty put on tea,' and 1843 saw 'another chapter on strong drink indited, followed by the diluting subject of pumps and wells.'[150] Nothing was safe from his ridicule, not even the

148 Sutherland, *Manual of the Geography*, 120, 135–6, 141–2, 147–54
149 C. Birch Bagster, *The Progress and Prospects of Prince Edward Island, Written during the Leisure of a Visit in 1861. A Sketch Intended to Supply Information upon Which Enquiring Emigrants May Rely, and Actual Settlers Adopt as the Basis of a Wider Knowledge of Their Beautiful Island Home* (Charlottetown 1861) 69–72, 137–8
150 Ibid., 21, 28

renaming of the province in 1797:

> Three hundred years after the first christening a second took place, and Saint John was, by legislative enactment, deprived of his *nominal* honors and possessions, which were then given to a live Prince. The excuses were two – 1st, the similarity of the names of distant places, all called 'St. John;' and 2ndly, to show loyalty to her sovereign lord by a sort of making friends with the head gardener.[151]

One only wishes more information were available on the life of the island-born Bagster, especially on his departure from the province in the 1840s after 'many hardships and much sorrow.'[152]

In the event, the optimism of Sutherland and Bagster, though differently based, proved equally mistaken. The proprietors refused to accept the, to them, unfavourable recommendations of the Land Commission Report; resident settlers subsequently organized the Tenant League bent on a campaign of occasionally violent civil disobedience; and the government consequently brought in troops from Halifax to restore order. By the summer of 1865 the outlook for a solution to the land question appeared distant and was seemingly rendered all the more remote by a revival of sectarian strife. Confederation, initially regarded as irrelevant and a needless complication, ultimately gained grudging acceptance largely because it offered access to the funds necessary to secure the purchase of land from absentee proprietors and to wipe out a large debt incurred in a wave of railway building mania.[153]

It was in the wake of the colony's entry into Confederation and on the verge of a final resolution of the land question that Nova Scotia historian Duncan Campbell issued a *History of Prince Edward Island*. In many ways this was not so much Campbell's history as that of the many islanders who supplied the visitor with information.[154] Foremost among these was William Henry Pope (1825–79), who as a politician and a journalist had been in the forefront of the push for Confederation. Pope, apparently with a history of his own in view, had done research among the colonial papers in London as well as made a thorough study of the relevant

151 Ibid., 12
152 Ibid., 138; PAPEI, St Paul's Anglican Church, Charlotte Parish, Prince Edward Island, Registry of Births and Baptisms, 14 Apr. 1843
153 Robertson, 'Political Realignment'
154 D. Campbell, *History of Prince Edward Island*, iii–iv. Many of these same individuals were prominent in the movement to create the Prince Edward Historical Society, which was incorporated in 1882; see *The Acts of the General Assembly of Prince Edward Island* (Charlottetown 1882) 85–6.

literature.[155] All of this and more was made available to Campbell, whose history is still worth consulting today.

The quality of the research aside, the most striking thing about Campbell's *History of Prince Edward Island* is the extent to which it mirrors the approach of John Stewart's *Account*. The basic issue of island history is the land question. On one side were resident settlers, hard-working tillers of the soil who aspired to the status of independent yeomen and sought redress through a popularly elected assembly. On the other side were absentee proprietors, members of an idle élite who lived off the avails of other men's toil and used corrupt influence in London to thwart just reform. It was a black-and-white conflict of outsider versus insider, them against us. All other issues, whether internal or external, paled before this: sectarian, racial, or class divisions must be submerged in the common struggle; without control over the land, what use was responsible government? Campbell's only innovation was to assume, now with more justification than Sutherland and Bagster, that the land question was, with Canadian help, as good as solved.[156]

The problem was – although neither Campbell nor Pope would admit it – that the province achieved its ostensible ambition of social and economic liberty at the cost of its hard-won political independence. Islanders gained a victory over one set of outsiders at the very moment they succumbed to another. Indeed, it was not long before the animus of generations was shifted from absentee proprietors in London to absentee bureaucrats in Ottawa. The neglect of the landlords was replaced by the neglect of the federal government, and the results were the same – economic stagnation.[157]

There was, as the ever-insightful J.M. Bumsted points out, an element of ambivalence in subsequent criticisms of Ottawa. Still locked into agrarian economic backwardness for which external forces were blamed, it was not at all clear how economic progress could occur on Prince Edward Island 'without a break with the past that, in effect, would repudiate the sense of history the historians had inculcated.'[158] Four

155 NA, William Henry Pope Papers, MG 27, I F 2, Duncan Campbell to William Henry Pope, 6 May 1874. I would like to thank Ian Ross Robertson for calling this letter to my attention. See also Ian Ross Robertson, 'William Henry Pope,' *DCB*, vol. 10, 597.
156 D. Campbell, *History of Prince Edward Island*, 53–4, 168–87
157 For a selection of contemporary criticisms see David Weale and Harry Baglole, *The Island and Confederation: The End of an Era* ([Summerside] 1973) 147–50.
158 J.M. Bumsted, '"The Only Island There Is:" The Writing of Prince Edward Island History,' in Verner Smitheram, David Milne, and Satadal Dasgupta, eds, *The Garden Transformed: Prince Edward Island, 1945–1980* (Charlottetown 1982) 14

generations of island historians had done their best to foster a sense of common identity that was insular, agrarian, and conservative. They had done so in order to fashion a resident political force capable of winning control of the island's economic destiny and ushering in an age of progress. Unfortunately, if by progress one meant the new age of cosmopolitan industrialization, the end was no longer compatible with the means. Did Canada withhold or threaten the fruits of the new capitalism? The people of Prince Edward Island were no longer sure.

Disoriented, island writers increasingly turned to the past for solace and regeneration. There the likes of Sir Andrew Macphail (1864–1938) found a common heritage of struggle leading not to the progress of materialism but to the self-sufficiency of traditional morality. 'The decay that set in immediately after the union' ushered in an era of unreasoning dissatisfaction and restiveness blind to the bucolic peace of the island.[159] However, this 'Golden Age' prior to Confederation was, more than most, a product of the imagination. Macphail admitted that as a boy he yearned only for escape from the insularity of the island and later as a professor of medicine found a happy niche far from home at Montreal's McGill University.[160] The vision was clear, the practice equivocal.

In summary, no other colonists of British North America had a greater sense of their own uniqueness than the colonists of Prince Edward Island. They were few in number, their land was small in size, and their island was isolated. But this was not the whole story, or even the beginning of the story. What imparted a special identity was the land question. It was the struggle to overturn the unusual lottery of 1767 that gave a peculiar twist to the social, economic, and political development of the province: it was a struggle without parallel in British North America; and it imposed a sense of unity on an otherwise disparate population. There was a historical gulf between Prince Edward Island and the rest of Canada wider than the Northumberland Strait, a gulf that prevented an easy accommodation both with modernization and with the new nation.

Prince Edward Island examples excepted, the complacency of provincial patriots in the Maritimes at mid-century was based on confidence in

159 Andrew Macphail, 'The History of Prince Edward Island,' in Adam Shortt and Arthur Doughty, eds, *Canada and Its Provinces: A History of the Canadian People and Their Institutions by One Hundred Associates*, vol. 13 (Toronto 1914). 305–75; *The Master's Wife* (1939), Introduction by Ian Ross Robertson, New Canadian Library No. 138 (Toronto 1977). On Macphail see Ian Ross Robertson, 'Sir Andrew Macphail as a Social Critic' (PH D Diss., University of Toronto 1974).
160 Bumsted, '"The Only Island There Is,"' 33

the future. Their optimism and pride were reflected in the smug tone of their histories and celebrations. It is a fragile vanity, however, which inhibits internal differences of opinion and brooks no external criticism – especially not from the likes of a New England poet. Ultimately their several conceits fell victim to Confederation and the challenge of a national history. Provincial historians, predisposed to reject assimilation by virtue of being *provincial* historians, by and large refused to accept the imposition of responsible government as an organizing principle of their pasts or as a fundamental link in the life of all British North American colonies. Certainly for most Maritime historians Confederation with continental Canada did not mark a new plateau from which to ascend to new peaks but rather a high-water mark from which to recede. Confidence wavered, complacency collapsed.

Maritime historians, whether in search of consolation or renewal, clung ever more closely to their particular provincial or even more local pasts. Their nostalgia for earlier times increased as the future darkened or simply became more complex. Of course in this they were part of a tendency common among late-nineteenth-century historians in North America, a tendency to meet the uncertainties of modern life through study of, even absorption in, a time when fewer questions were asked. This trend had special significance in a region that had difficulty accepting the nation into which it had been uncertainly drafted. If Maritime historians did not fall into arguing among themselves over this predicament, it was largely because the power to impose a solution did not lie in their hands. The lack of partisanship in their histories was a sign of their lack of control over the future. Indeed, there was a certain desperate delusion in the construction of their respective golden ages. As Harold Pinter would have it, 'there are some things one remembers even though they may never have happened.'

7

Partisans
and
Pessimists

A National historian is one who expects that his countrymen will do great things together in the future and therefore believes that they have done great things together in the past. When Confederation failed to live up to the expectation of its advocates, when optimism in the country's future waned, faith in the past as the buttress of progress diminished. The continuance of traditional regional, racial, religious, and political animosities, the inability to meet continental challenges, and the rise of new tensions in the western territories all combined to demoralize those who dreamed of a united and progressive nation state. Most disturbing was the collapse of the political vehicle of betterment, the Liberal-Conservative coalition. It was a central tenet of National historiography that lasting progress was achieved only by non-partisan conciliation and consolidation, that real statesmanship was the ability to harmonize, to accept a pragmatic compromise rather than indulge in rigid adherence to principle. In light of Confederation's failures, especially in light of the Pacific railway scandal, both the efficacy and the moral superiority of pragmatism were called seriously into question. How difficult it was, then, for the historian to maintain confidence in the inherent strength of Canada's institutions, or in its saving elements of national character, when faced with the many disruptive challenges of the late nineteenth century.

Those who stubbornly persevered with a conciliatory National point of view henceforth did so defensively or with a naïvety that defied contemporary circumstances. In truth, of course, National historians were essentially Upper Canadian historians in masquerade. Their conceit had never been accepted by French Canadians, and Maritimers had always been ambivalent about a historical interpretation that imposed a coherence foreign to their past and considered regional concerns parochial. Even within the English-speaking community of the United Canadas the National interpretation was only as strong as the Liberal-Conservative coalition on which it rode out of the 1850s. At no time was this coalition comprehensive: it refused to countenance die-hard Tories or radical Patriots, and it failed for many years to reach an accommodation with George Brown's Clear Grits. It was only a matter of time before a variety of political outcasts sought to challenge the hegemony of the ministry and the historical interpretation by which it was justified. The initial failures of Confederation released historians from the homogenizing restraint of National dogma and freed them to seek out justification for particularism. In the event, the first work to attempt a significant alteration of the consensual approach of the National school was published just prior to Confederation: it was, strangely enough, a biography of a radical written by a Conservative.

In 1862 Charles Lindsey (1820–1908), the English-born editor-in-chief of the Conservative Toronto *Leader*, published a two-volume account of the 'life and times' of his father-in-law, William Lyon Mackenzie.[1] Temperate in most things not touching Roman Catholics and French Canadians, Lindsey believed that 'the consolidation of the Canadian Commonwealth upon solid political and commercial foundations was a loftier aim than the gratification of sectional prejudice or any mere local ascendancy,' and he liked to think of the Liberal-Conservative coalition formed in 1854 as the effective proponent of sensible change as well as the natural descendant of Robert Baldwin's moderate party of Reform.[2] By disposition and conviction opposed to radical measures, Lindsey was nevertheless struck by the apparent energy, honesty, and fortitude of his rebel relation – character traits that did not accord with the popular image of Mackenzie as a power-hungry and slightly demented agitator. Compelled by filial duty and the demands of simple justice, Lindsey undertook to balance the exaggeration of caricature. With access to the enormous bulk of papers his father-in-law left behind upon his death in 1861, Lindsey proceeded to tell Mackenzie's tale not just with sympathy but through rebel eyes.

According to Lindsey, Mackenzie began his political career in Upper Canada as a mild reformer, even a conservative, whose first comments on

1 Charles Lindsey, *The Life and Times of Wm. Lyon Mackenzie. With an Account of the Canadian Rebellion of 1837, and the Subsequent Frontier Disturbances, Chiefly from Unpublished Documents*, 2 vols (Toronto 1862)
2 L.A.M. Lovekin, 'Charles Lindsey: An Ornament of Canadian Journalism,' *The Canadian Magazine* (Toronto) vol. 54 (Apr. 1920) 505

the provincial government in the public press were judicious if critical, and laudatory when deserved. Yet such was the overweening power of the unbridled governing élite – the notorious Family Compact – that any criticism, however inoffensive, was sufficient to incite a violent response, in Mackenzie's case the destruction of his *Colonial Advocate* press. In the subsequent tumble of action and reaction, Upper Canada swerved onto a path leading to rebellion; with each cycle Lindsey made it clear that Mackenzie and his friends were merely rebounding from the gross provocation of the unconstitutional and irresponsible proceedings of the government.[3] This was the rhythm of provincial history noticed by Lord Durham and John McMullen, and recognizing it was not in itself an innovation. What was novel was the role Lindsey awarded Mackenzie. As the rebel's son-in-law would have it, it was Mackenzie who fashioned a Reform party from disparate groups concerned with a variety of grievances, who first suggested and then focused attention on responsible government as the most effective cure for provincial ills, and who commanded the respect and support of a majority of Upper Canadians. Allegations that Mackenzie was a republican and an annexationist were put down to the systematic campaign of slander initiated by Lieutenant-Governor Sir Francis Bond Head or to a misunderstanding arising from the 'baneful domination' letter Mackenzie received from radical British parliamentarian Joseph Hume.[4] The rebellion itself failed only because of John Rolph's hesitancy on the day and the incompetence of the men selected to lead subsequent border raids.[5]

Unconventional as Lindsey's interpretation of Mackenzie's career was, it modified received opinion only in matters of detail. Indeed, by assigning Mackenzie a role as father of responsible government, Lindsey demonstrated that his own pre-Confederation faith in Durham's resolution of the constitutional impasse was essentially unshaken and his optimism for the future progress of the colony intact. Where Lindsey did part company in a fundamental way with National historians was over their conviction that responsible government had been carried by conciliatory men in spite of the rebellion. In Lindsey's scheme of things the Baldwinite Reformers were the (craven?) beneficiaries of Mackenzie's fierce determination to fight for a principle. Lindsey implied that constitutional progress was not always or solely the product of legitimate partisan conflict but at least occasionally proceeded from revolutionary

3 Lindsey, *Life and Times of Wm. Lyon Mackenzie*, vol. 1, 43–9, 80–93, 121
4 Ibid., 138–40, 179–80, 190–1, 202–3, 244–5, 300–3, 345–6, 361–78, 391
5 Ibid., vol. 2, 72–5, 165–84, 192–5

violence. The only way to tell whether the resort to arms was justified was by the crude yardstick of success. Thus, in so far as the Rebellion of 1837 failed in its short-term aim to overthrow the government, it was in Lindsey's opinion 'unfortunate and ill-advised'; in so far as it succeeded in its long-term object of reform, it was to be praised. It was Lindsey's final judgment that:

> Much of the liberty Canada has enjoyed, since 1840, and more of the wonderful progress she has made, are due to the changes which the insurrection was the chief agent in producing ... The amelioration which the political institutions of Canada have undergone would probably have come in time, if there had been no insurrection; but it would not have come so soon; and there is no reason to suppose that the Province would yet have reached its present stage of advancement.[6]

The ingratitude shown Mackenzie by those now administering the system he had been instrumental in creating was, in Lindsey's opinion, spiteful.[7]

Defiant in interpretation, Lindsey's biography was correspondingly unorthodox in method. Such advocates of national consensus as Fennings Taylor and Henry Morgan were gentle proponents: theirs being a cause ill-served by either exclusion or stark criticism, they made a sincere effort to present all points of view and showed bias primarily through praise. Lindsey, in contrast, demonstrated the impatience and intolerance of the self-righteous: Mackenzie had been wronged; his critics and opponents deserved censure; no effort was made to understand or present their attitudes. Convinced that Mackenzie was correct in his analysis of events, Lindsey presented only that perspective. Principle first divided, then selected, and ultimately restricted.

The partisan interpretive and methodological challenge to the National school had only just begun. Publication of *The Life and Times of Wm. Lyon Mackenzie* heralded a post-Confederation outburst of biographies written to justify individuals and parties.[8] In this less-confident age and in less-competent hands such studies provided a forum for the politically committed to refight old battles, apportion blame for defeats, and shift responsibility for national failures. Generally written by lieutenants of the

6 Ibid., vol. 1, 5
7 Ibid., vol. 2, 292–3
8 For a representative selection of relevant titles see Clara Thomas, 'Biography in Canada,' in Carl F. Klinck, gen. ed., *Literary History of Canada: Canadian Literature in English*, 2nd ed., 3 vols (Toronto 1976) vol. 3, 184–90.

men portrayed, based largely on memory and personal papers, these biographies were intended to secure and protect reputations, not establish historical truth. Few volumes did more than set out conflicting versions of the already intricate twists and turns of Canadian political life in the Union period. John George Hodgins's (1821–1912) edition of the papers of Egerton Ryerson, for instance, explained the latter's support for the constitutional position of Governor-General Metcalfe,[9] and Alexander Neil Bethune's (1800–79) life of John Strachan similarly undertook to defend the first Anglican bishop of Toronto's stand on such issues as the clergy reserves.[10] On the whole, historical enlightenment sank in direct proportion to the rising level of partisan vitriol.

Among this welter of biographies, the natural successor to Lindsey's Mackenzie was a work on the life of Clear Grit leader George Brown. *The Life and Speeches of Hon. George Brown* was written by Alexander Mackenzie (1822–92), long-time protégé of Brown and the first Liberal prime minister of Canada (1873–8).[11] Mackenzie undertook his literary task shortly after Brown's death from an assassin's bullet on 9 May 1880 and in the immediate aftermath of his own loss of the government to Sir John A. Macdonald's Conservatives and of the leadership of the Liberal party to Edward Blake. According to Dale Thomson, this conjunction of unfortunate events gave Mackenzie 'cause for doubt and perplexity.'[12] Mackenzie feared that the publisher of the *Globe* went to his grave a misunderstood and too-often maligned man whose role 'in securing constitutional changes which made Canada a home of civil and religious equality and liberty' had been ignored, and he was anxious lest his own accomplishments, as well as those of his party, suffer a similar fate. There was much to justify and much to explain, and while Mackenzie hoped his view of Brown's character and of recent events 'would be reasonably satisfactory to the public generally,' he freely admitted it would be especially so 'to those with whom [Brown] was politically popular.'[13]

9 [Egerton Ryerson,] *'The Story of My Life' by the Late Rev. Egerton Ryerson, D.D., LL.D., (Being Reminiscences of Sixty Years' Public Service in Canada.)*, ed. J. George Hodgins (Toronto 1883) 312–41. Hodgins served for many years under Ryerson before replacing him as chief administrator of education in Ontario.
10 A.N. Bethune, *Memoir of the Right Reverend John Strachan, D.D., LL.D., First Bishop of Toronto* (Toronto 1870) 87–95. Bethune succeeded his mentor Strachan as bishop, see Arthur N. Thompson, 'Alexander Neil Bethune,' *DCB*, vol. 10 (Toronto 1972) 53–7.
11 (Toronto 1882)
12 Dale Cairns Thomson, *Alexander Mackenzie: Clear Grit* (Toronto 1960) 364
13 A. Mackenzie, *Life and Speeches of Hon. George Brown*, iii–iv

However 'ill-advised' Alexander Mackenzie thought the rebellion, he accepted that it provoked the Durham *Report* and the recommendation of responsible government as a cure for the colony's ills. Unhappily, 'the fruits of victory were only partially realized by the victors,' for 'the principles of responsible government were not well understood by the people, nor much insisted upon by their leaders.' According to Mackenzie, 'leading men among reformers did not hesitate about accepting office with men belonging to the opposite party without any security that their responsibility to parliament should take precedence of their obligations to the representative of the Crown.' The 'timorousness,' ideological flabbiness, and occasional selfishness of Reform leaders permitted governors Sydenham, Bagot, and Metcalfe to retain an irresponsible residue of power within the command of their office. The arrival of George Brown in Upper Canada in 1843 rejuvenated Reformers. He clarified issues, raised 'fundamental principles of government,' and stressed that until such time as a unified party ministry was insisted upon by the majority in Parliament, governors would continue to interfere in the domestic affairs of the colony. Mackenzie maintained that Brown's 'action and advocacy very soon commanded an influence more powerful than had ever been evoked by any one man,' and that to his effort was due the greatest portion of credit for the introduction of full responsible government in 1848 during the regime of Governor-General Lord Elgin.[14]

Modern historians, fascinated by the development of responsible government as a practical constitutional arrangement and more recently as 'an enduring Canadian myth,' may be attracted to Alexander Mackenzie's account as one of the first to place the attainment of responsible government in 1848 rather than in the period 1839 to 1841.[15] Mackenzie and his contemporaries were themselves less concerned with when responsible government was achieved than with how and by whom. Mackenzie chose 1848 in order to give credit to idealism and Brown. It was his opinion that signal constitutional change was not brought about by the irenic Lord Sydenham or the conciliatory likes of Robert Baldwin and Francis Hincks, for their collective muddle served to obscure essentials and cause delay. It was only when Brown ended the conceptual confusion of the Reform party and instilled it with his own uncompromising tenacity

14 Ibid., 1–8, 147–54
15 For example, see Donald Swainson, Introduction to John Charles Dent, *The Last Forty Years: The Union of 1841 to Confederation* (1881) ed. Donald Swainson (Toronto 1972) v–xxix; and Graeme H. Patterson, 'An Enduring Canadian Myth: Responsible Government and the Family Compact,' *JCS* 12 (1977): 3–16.

of purpose that responsible government was finally achieved. The key to Brown's success was that 'he cared chiefly for a straight advocacy of essential principles, with the belief that every struggle brought them nearer to his reach.'[16] The lessons drawn by Mackenzie – lessons he tried to live up to and by which he judged the effectiveness of others – were that without strict adherence to principle nothing could be accomplished and that real progress was inevitably a product of struggle with the forces of reaction and the burden of inertia.

When applied to the subsequent political history of the United Canadas, Mackenzie's principled and confrontational approach, that it of course dealt with the opportunistic manoeuvres of Conservative leader John A. Macdonald, reserved its strongest criticism for Reformers who compromised. Brown, according to his approving biographer, 'saw no special benefit in having a government called by the name of reform, composed of men who called themselves reformers, if they were either unable or unwilling to give effect to reform measures and principles.'[17] This was precisely the unhappy defect displayed by the Reform ministry that took power in 1848. The new government failed to act on such crucial issues relating to the separation of church and state as the secularization of the clergy reserves and the abolition of seigneurial tenure, primarily because the 'timid' Baldwin buckled before 'the religious position of the French liberals,' who under Louis-Hippolyte La Fontaine repeatedly put national retrenchment before progressive reform. Brown controlled his frustration for a time out of loyalty to the party, but eventually (Mackenzie thought belatedly), he voiced his objections to the ministry's inaction and French-Canadian obstruction: by 1851 he had broken with the government, now under the leadership of Francis Hincks.[18]

Of Brown's break with the Reform party Mackenzie wrote:

It is of course a question for argument whether Mr. Brown's course was right or wrong; whether he was chiefly responsible for breaking up the reform party by the non-recognition of leaders who had been unfaithful, or whether Mr. Hincks, who avoided the introduction of promised and needful reforms rather than offend his opponents, and who coquetted with enemies, was the really responsible party.[19]

16 A. Mackenzie, Life and Speeches of Hon. George Brown, 19
17 Ibid.
18 Ibid., 22–42
19 Ibid., 41

The question was rhetorical. In light of Hincks's later acquiescence in a coalition with the Conservatives, Mackenzie believed that 'no one can be at a loss to discover upon whom the blame must be cast' for the dismemberment of Baldwin's party. Under the 'miserable pretence' of preserving the Union by maintaining a government with support in both the old provinces, Hincks declined to act: 'he lamentably failed at a critical time to show that he had the courage of his convictions,' and his subsequent 'treachery' proved he had none. Whereas Brown, 'in vigorously opposing his own political friends when recreant to their principles, undoubtedly secured the complete triumph of those principles at a much earlier day than if he had allowed them to neglect these interests with impunity.'[20] Throughout, Mackenzie assumed that had the Reform party rigidly adhered to principle, as Brown advocated, it could have acted regardless of the sentiments of French Canadians, Roman Catholics, and Conservatives; and he saw in Brown's campaign for representation by population a means by which the Liberal majority might yet enforce its program on a minority unconvinced of its beneficence.

From within Parliament and without, Brown led the purified remnant of the Reform party, the Clear Grits, in a decade-long struggle against a succession of do-nothing coalition governments. Once, after the cabinet led by Macdonald and George-Étienne Cartier resigned in July 1858, power was momentarily within Brown's grasp, but his ministry was aborted after a few days by the uncooperative refusal of Governor-General Sir Edmund Walker Head to grant a dissolution and was buried by means of the infamous 'Double Shuffle,' an unscrupulous parliamentary tactic of Macdonald's too-clever devising. Nevertheless, 'the ten years' conflict was about to end in a complete vindication of the policy pursued by Mr. Brown,' for the political deadlock caused by the conscientious stand of the Clear Grits eventually forced Macdonald 'to give effect to principles [the Conservatives] had steadily and vehemently opposed,' namely, representation by population and separation of church and state.[21] Unfortunately Macdonald made Brown pay a price for success: first, Brown had to accept reform within the context of a federal union of all British North America (on which Mackenzie's views were mixed); and, second, he had to agree to be part of a 'Grand Coalition' to ensure his measures would be carried (a compromise with which Mackenzie 'never concurred'). A bitter-sweet pill, 'the first day of July, 1867, saw the great

20 Ibid., 41–2, 150
21 Ibid., 59–76

reform accomplished for which Mr. Brown had toiled so many years, and saw also the Conservatives who opposed it to the last now reaping the fruit of their opponents' labour.' Brown's subsequent retirement from the coalition and later failure to obtain a reciprocity agreement with the United States during Mackenzie's Liberal interregnum were a frustrating conclusion to an illustrious career, and his assassination was in cruel harmony with Macdonald's dispatch of Mackenzie at the polls.[22]

Mackenzie admired Brown primarily because, 'let the consequences be what they might,' the Grit leader stuck by his principles. Mackenzie also professed to believe that Brown's approach to politics not only should be but was the most effective way to attain one's objectives. Unhappily, this presupposition was vitiated by the historical account provided: Brown did not achieve all his goals, achieved others only by compromise, and invariably suffered the humiliating experience of watching political rivals carry out and receive credit for his legislative and constitutional proposals. Angry at the injustice of it all, and further bewildered by the fickle nature of public opinion, Mackenzie concluded with the depressing observation that the National Policy of Macdonald's newly elected Conservative government would likely create a new élite, a new Family Compact more insidious and intractable than the pre-Rebellion original.[23] What began, then, as an attempt to show by what means political and religious liberty had been gained in Canada ended by questioning whether genuine progress had been made after all.

The atmosphere of doubt and perplexity in which Mackenzie wrote goes some way toward explaining the vehemence of the personal judgments he made, the denigration of Ryerson, Hincks, and La Fontaine, and the grudging compliments paid to Baldwin, William McDougall, and Michael Hamilton Foley. However, the basic problem with Mackenzie's historical vision was that, holding a specific set of rigid principles, he was unwilling to brook opposition or even, indeed especially, moderation. He sought to defeat rather than reconcile those with whom he disagreed. An Upper Canadian Grit who saw in Confederation a means – an imperfect means – of attaining party ends, Mackenzie proffered no vision of Canada as a new nation and remained intolerant of French Canadians, oblivious to the Maritimes, and ultimately parochial in outlook. As history, *The Life and Speeches of Hon. George Brown* had a strong interpretive framework fleshed out by the valuable papers of its subject

22 Ibid., 88–107, 138–9
23 Ibid., 138–9

and the memory of its author, but it was deformed by strident partisanship and ungenerosity of spirit.

The response to Mackenzie's volume was, not unexpectedly, partisan and vehement; his contemporaries strenuously challenged him on matters of detail and general interpretation; and within a year Joseph Edmund Collins (1855–92) furnished a Conservative rebuttal in the form of an indifferent biography of Sir John A. Macdonald.[24] But the Conservatives were not the only, or even the primary, target of partisan revision. Lindsey and Mackenzie saved their most stinging criticism for moderates within the reform camp, men who ostensibly held liberal ideals but were willing to compromise them for the sake of power. The personification of cynical accommodation was Francis Hincks (1807–85). It was Hincks, according to Mackenzie, who had supported the likes of Sydenham and Bagot in their attempt to withhold the full fruits of responsible government, who delayed the introduction of reform measures in order to appease French Canadians, and who in 1854 led moderate Reformers into a coalition under the direction of their long-time Tory rivals. Vilified by the Liberals and left to his own devices by the Conservatives, Hincks, in many ways the pivotal character of the Union period, was left on his own.

Two years after he surrendered power to the coalition led by MacNab, Hincks turned his back on Canada and for thirteen years served in the British colonial service, first as governor of Barbados and the Windward Islands, and then later of British Guiana (Guyana).[25] Knighted upon his retirement as a colonial administrator in 1869, Sir Francis returned to Canada and to the surprise of many was named minister of finance by

24 Joseph Edmund Collins, *Life and Times of the Right Honourable Sir John A. Macdonald, K.C.B., D.C.L., &c., Premier of the Dominion of Canada* (Toronto 1883). While the biography itself was forgettable, Collins's penultimate chapter on 'Thought and Literature' was one of the first significant attempts to draw attention to the country's new generation of poets and authors. Indeed, it was likely Collins who introduced Charles George Douglas Roberts to Archibald Lampman and thereby drew together the two central members of the group that was to be labelled the 'Confederation Poets.' John Coldwell Adams, 'Roberts, Lampman, and Edmund Collins,' in Glenn Clever, ed., *The Sir Charles G.D. Roberts Symposium*, Reappraisals: Canadian Writers, No. 10 (Ottawa 1984) 5–8; M. Brook Taylor, 'The Writing of English-Canadian History in the Nineteenth Century' (PH D Diss., University of Toronto 1984) vol. 2, 394–401; 'Joseph Edmund Collins,' *DCB*, vol. 12 (forthcoming)

25 For Hincks's career after 1854 see William G. Ormsby, 'Sir Francis Hincks,' in J.M.S. Careless, ed., *The Pre-Confederation Premiers: Ontario Government Leaders, 1841–1867*, Ontario Historical Studies Series (Toronto 1980) 186–9; and Ormsby's 'Sir Francis Hincks,' *DCB*, vol. 11 (Toronto 1982) 414–15.

Macdonald. This receipt of an important office from the hand of an ancient foe confirmed suspicions long-held by many Liberals regarding the integrity of the old Reformer. Hincks directed his department creditably for four years until, tired of the fray, he resigned office on the eve of the Pacific railway scandal. He did not run in the 1874 general election and thereafter withdrew from active political life. In 1875 Hincks assumed the presidency of the Consolidated Bank of Canada, 'but age and infirmity led him to neglect his duties and to sign documents without adequate scrutiny.' When the bank failed four years later, he was voted out of office by the shareholders and narrowly escaped a court conviction for making a 'wilfully false and deceptive return.'[26] It was in the midst of this crisis that Sir Francis began to write a series of extremely influential histories and memoirs intended to justify both himself and his methods.

As early as 1877 Hincks gave a short address, later published in pamphlet form, on the political history of Canada between 1840 and 1855, that is to say during the period of his deepest involvement.[27] In 1882 he wrote a series of articles in the Montreal *Herald* to review and rebut charges laid against him in Mackenzie's biography of Brown.[28] Two years later and in declining health, he published a volume of reminiscences of his public life.[29] In each case Hincks attempted to establish the wisdom of conciliation and the immaturity of rigid idealism. What unified his career was consistency of spirit not dogmatic adherence to detail, and the admitted series of compromises were justified by the fruits they brought forth. Although Hincks varied his accounts in matters of such significant detail as the occasion of the implementation of responsible government, he never wavered in his belief that timely moderation was the foundation of good government.

It was Hincks's proudest boast that he and Robert Baldwin were the fathers of responsible government. According to the version of events given in Hincks's *Political History*, the arguments of Baldwin and Hincks's *Examiner* convinced Lord Durham to recommend the extension of the 'existing system of Parliamentary government' to the Canadas; a step taken by Lord John Russell in his dispatch of 16 October 1839.

26 Ibid., 415
27 Francis Hincks, *The Political History of Canada between 1840 and 1855. A Lecture Delivered on the 17th of October, 1877, at the Request of the St. Patrick's National Association, with Copious Additions* (Montreal 1877)
28 Francis Hincks, review of *The Life and Speeches of Hon. George Brown*, by Alexander Mackenzie, *Herald* (Montreal) 13, 15, 19 Dec. 1882
29 Francis Hincks, *Reminiscences of His Public Life* (Montreal 1884)

Unfortunately, Durham's 'erroneous' impression that a 'national feud' existed between the French and English Canadians prompted him to recommend, and the British government to enforce, a union of the provinces in order first to control and then to absorb the French-speaking element of the population. This assimilating side to the Act of Union alienated French-Canadian Reformers at the very moment their English-speaking Upper Canadian brethren were engaged in political celebration. It was Hincks who realized that the Reform cause was doomed unless the racial breach was healed, and over the next few years he worked diligently to reconcile the followers of Baldwin and La Fontaine.

In the meantime, with the Tories similarly riven by the act's racial and political aspects, Lord Sydenham arrived to find no party capable of accepting his gift of responsible government. The governor-general was therefore forced to put himself at the head of a mixed ministry. Baldwin, holding out for government by a single party, withdrew his support from the ministry and sat with a minority in opposition. Hincks, recognizing the essential but temporary role Sydenham had to play, most often supported the ministerial majority and judged each measure on its merits, all the while trying to reconcile Sydenham to the biracial Reform party then forming. When the succeeding governor-general, Sir Charles Bagot, invited him to enter the ministry in the spring of 1842, Hincks leaped at the opportunity in order to create a beach-head for Baldwin and La Fontaine, both of whom joined him in the cabinet later in the year. 'The new coalition was one between men who held common views of public policy, and it was completely successful, having been approved by all but a unanimous vote in the House.'[30] In effect, party lines had finally hardened to the point where Canadians were capable of exercising the responsible form of government given them three years earlier. Playing a crucial role as middleman, Hincks had preserved the unity of the Reform party and then helped to make it acceptable to the likes of Sydenham and Bagot.

Responsible government was not, however, home free. According to Hincks, in Britain the Conservative government of Sir Robert Peel was determined to role back the constitutional concessions made by its more liberal predecessors, and it was given an opening to do so when Bagot died in 1843.[31] Sir Charles Metcalfe, the new governor-general, was provided with secret instructions to subvert the ministry he found in place and to

30 Hincks, *Political History*, 6–28
31 Ibid., 29

establish in its stead a mixed ministry with himself at its head. This conspiracy, including extracts from confidential dispatches, was laid out in the biography of Metcalfe written by John William Kaye in 1854. It was Kaye's contention that Metcalfe was correct in his belief that Durham never recommended, nor did Russell or Sydenham institute, responsible government by party, and that Canadian politicians had taken advantage of Bagot during his illness in order to presume to rule in place of the Crown's representative.[32] Hincks contradicted Metcalfe's interpretation of events by a judicious display of quotations from Lord Durham's *Report* and the pages of the *Examiner;* he also expressed shock at Kaye's approving revelation of Metcalfe's duplicitous conduct and outrage at the scurrilous abuse the biographer had heaped on Reform leaders, including Baldwin.[33]

Hincks's rebuttal of Metcalfe and Kaye was clear and convincing save in one particular: he was forced to concede that Metcalfe might reasonably conclude from a reading of Lord Sydenham's early dispatches that Sydenham did not believe in responsible government by party.[34] Sydenham's true opinion of responsible government, withheld from his constitutional advisers at the time, had first surfaced publicly in a collection of his papers edited by his brother and published in 1844.[35] Hincks, in some embarrassment, because he had tacitly supported the late governor-general's administration despite the reservation of the Baldwinite Reformers, declared himself 'bound to admit that Lord Sydenham appears to have modified his views very considerably during his residence in Canada,' but implied that Sydenham's initial reluctance to embrace the full implications of responsible government was in large measure a ploy meant to forestall local Tory opposition. It was 'quite immaterial' to Hincks 'whether Lord Sydenham yielded to conviction or

32 John William Kaye, *The Life and Correspondence of Charles, Lord Metcalfe; Late Governor-General of India, Governor of Jamaica, Governor-General of Canada; From Unpublished Letters and Journals Preserved by Himself, His Family, and His Friends,* 2 vols (London 1854) vol. 2, 476–85

33 Hincks, *Political History,* 12–16, 29–37. Kaye occupies a unique place in Canadian historiography by virtue of his characterization of Robert Baldwin as 'mischievous,' a 'fanatic,' and a man 'to delight in strife.' Kaye also thought Baldwin an American. See Kaye, *Life and Correspondence of ... Lord Metcalfe,* vol. 2, 490–1.

34 Hincks, *Political History,* 31–2

35 G. Poulett Scrope, *Memoir of the Life of the Right Honourable Charles Lord Sydenham, G.C.B., with a Narrative of His Administration in Canada* (London 1844) 256–68. The portion of the *Memoir* dealing with Sydenham's career in Canada was actually written by the governor-general's civil secretary, a Mr Murdoch.

to the fear of circumstances'; the fact remained that as governor-general he had formed a ministry that held itself responsible to the majority in the Canadian Parliament.[36] Hincks had nothing to apologize for: he had supported, perhaps even moulded, Sydenham's actions, not approved Sydenham's private reservations.

Hincks considered it fortunate for Anglo-Canadian relations that it was Lord John Russell who was called upon in July 1846 to form a new government in Britain, for he believed that the man who wrote the famous dispatch of October 1839 was determined to re-establish the constitutional harmony that had prevailed in Canada prior to the term of the retiring Metcalfe. Russell's chosen instrument of reconciliation was Lord Elgin, who 'from the period of his arrival ... manifested a fixed determination not to be embroiled in the personal controversies of his predecessors.' In the new governor-general's hands 'Government House became *once more* neutral ground, where no party distinctions were recognized.'[37] From the moment Baldwin and La Fontaine established the second Reform ministry in 1848, the system of government sanctioned in 1839 was never again in jeopardy. Firm moderation triumphed.

Hincks now had to explain why he led the party of Baldwin and La Fontaine into an alliance with the hated Conservatives in 1854. According to Hincks, in spite of the best efforts of Reform ministries, including his own, impatient splinter groups developed within the party in both the old provinces. Hincks was particularly disconcerted by criticism levelled at him by George Brown. He suspected that Brown's call for precipitate legislative reform in the face of the hesitancy of the French-Canadian wing of the party was a smoke-screen for bigotry. In an admirable if misleading passage, Hincks summarized his disagreement with Brown:

I complained of the 'systematic disregard of the feelings and wishes' of our allies in Lower Canada of the Roman Catholic faith, on the part of the *Globe* and those of the Reform party who supported its views. I never could be convinced that there was any tendency whatever towards aggression on the part of the Roman Catholics. I did not consider that the claims on the part of the Roman Catholics to have separate schools in Upper Canada, as the Protestants had always had in Lower Canada, or the claim to have educational or charitable institutions incorporated with a right to hold property, were acts of aggression. I considered, moreover, that, irrespective of the special merits of the questions at issue, great respect should be paid to the wishes of the great majority of the

36 Hincks, *Political History*, 31–2
37 Ibid., 37. Emphasis added.

population of Lower Canada, with whom the Liberals of Upper Canada were in cordial alliance, and on whose support they depended for procuring the settlement of questions in which they took an interest.[38]

Even if there was more to French-Canadian intransigence than Hincks was willing to admit, he nevertheless established that racial harmony and regional reconciliation were a prerequisite for meaningful progress. Means as well as ends were principles of the Reform party as he understood it. Brown's prejudice, masquerading as principle, disrupted the Reform party and turned it away from its moderate origins. Hincks, if he was to be true to himself and the tradition of Baldwin, had no choice but to search for allies closer in temperament as well as belief to himself, allies such as John A. Macdonald and the new moderate Conservative party.

The outline of events provided in the *Political History* was not out of harmony with either the facts or the sentiments of National historiography: responsible government was granted in 1839 (although not irrevocably secured until 1848), Brown and the Clear Grits induced the disruption of the great Reform party, and the cause of progress in Canada was best served by statesmen capable of reconciling races and regions to measures. It was to establish his claim to be such a statesman that Hincks authored the *Political History*, and for the most part he successfully defended the course his ministry had pursued from 1851 to 1854. Hincks was less convincing when he attempted to justify his early support of Sydenham's administration: it looked like simple expediency at the time, and the subsequent revelation that the governor-general's commitment to responsible government was suspect reflected poorly on Hincks's judgment. Thus, on this one issue Hincks subsequently shifted his ground. In his reminiscences Hincks conceded that Sydenham may have acted as his own prime minister because he wanted to, not simply because he lacked an alternative. Sydenham did disguise his true motives, however, and, unlike Metcalfe, did act with the consent of the majority in the Canadian Parliament. Sydenham's dissembling in effect minimized the harm he otherwise might have done, but it did lose him the right to be regarded as the father of responsible government. That honour now went more properly to Lord Elgin.[39]

It took some doing, but Hincks ultimately managed to construct an intelligible and consistent account of the twists and turns of his political

38 Ibid., 45
39 Hincks, *Reminiscences*, 41–7

career. He was able to do so primarily because he emphasized the conciliatory temperament of the Reform party. Indeed the Reform party was born out of a compromise between two racial groups. Moderate methods were as central a part of the Baldwin heritage as constitutional arrangements and specific measures. He had been true to the spirit of Reform, Brown to nothing more than its program.

Did adherence to principle equal tyranny? or did compromise equal cynical opportunism? Was loyalty to race, religion, and region admirable? or was the cause of national harmony pre-eminent? These were the questions around which partisan debate revolved, and they reflected the widespread ambiguity surrounding the focus of loyalty in the post-Confederation era. Such issues cried out for serious study and mature reflection by the country's historians. Unfortunately, for the most part historians reflected the ambivalent loyalty and partisan rancour of their compatriots generally. On the whole they failed the nation. One man who at least made the attempt to rise above the fray was John Charles Dent (1841–88).

Dent trained well for the role of a political historian. Born in England, he came to Canada with his parents as a child. He studied law and was called to the bar in 1865, but immediately returned to England to embark upon a career in journalism, or, more accurately, in the journalism of the new penny dailies. Over the course of the next decade Dent was employed in both England and the United States by a variety of highly competitive, popular (some would say sensational) newspapers. In 1876 Goldwin Smith lured Dent back to Toronto by offering him the editorship of John Ross Robertson's *Evening Telegram*, which Smith envisaged as a mass-market organ of the Liberal party. In the event, shortly after Dent's return publisher Robertson shifted sympathy to the Conservative cause, and Dent moved over to become editor of George Brown's *Weekly Globe*.[40] While working for the *Weekly Globe* Dent reacquainted himself with Canadian politics and soon demonstrated the peculiar historical bent of his inquiries by publishing in the pages of the paper a series of biographical sketches that attempted, as he later wrote, 'to place before the public an account of the lives of the leading personages who have figured in Canadian history, from the period of the first discovery of the country down to the present times.'[41] In these articles Dent exhibited not

40 Swainson, Introduction to Dent, *Last Forty Years*, v–vi; Graeme H. Patterson, 'John Charles Dent,' *DCB*, vol. 11, 246–7
41 John Charles Dent, *The Canadian Portrait Gallery*, 4 vols (Toronto 1880–1) vol. 4 (1881) v

only his 'penchant for the short, insightful character sketch' but also a determination to get his facts straight. Obviously pleased with the work and with the response it received, in 1880 Dent left the *Weekly Globe* and for the remaining eight years of his life attempted to survive as a free-lance writer of popular history.[42]

Dent's first major project was to collect, polish, and augment his sketches for publication in book form as *The Canadian Portrait Gallery* (1880–1). In common with his subsequent works, Dent published the *Canadian Portrait Gallery* by subscription in serial form over an approximately two-year period. As Donald Swainson explains this common nineteenth-century practice, a work would be issued monthly by indiscrete instalments in paper covers. When the set was complete, the publisher normally bound the parts for purchasers or issued a set of binding cases to produce hardcover volumes. The publisher thereby received revenue before the complete publication costs had to be met. An additional advantage to publisher and author alike was that, 'books published in parts brought higher prices than those published in the usual manner, and the selling of subscriptions enabled publishers to reach a larger market than was normally possible.' In the particular case of the *Canadian Portrait Gallery*, Dent, with his livelihood now riding on the outcome, took great care with the technical aspects of the four volumes: they were printed on high-quality paper, handsomely bound, profusely illustrated, and carefully indexed and proofread.[43] There is now no accurate record of how financially rewarding all this effort was to the author, but his surviving correspondence is noticeably lacking in those solicitations for support so common in the letters of other contemporary historians,[44] and according to Dent's obituary in the Toronto *Mail* the *Canadian Portrait Gallery* alone 'netted him upwards of $7,000.'[45]

The *Canadian Portrait Gallery* also had its intellectual rewards. In the process of revising his sketches for publication, Dent began an extensive examination of old newspapers from the Union period and before, as well as of the journals of the two old assemblies and the newer Canadian Parliament. He then proceeded to read virtually all the historical publications he could lay his hands on. Still not content, Dent solicited nineteen sketches from the likes of Charles Lindsey and hymnist

42 Swainson, Introduction to Dent, *Last Forty Years*, vii

43 Ibid., vi–vii, xx–xxi

44 For example, see the correspondence of Robert Christie, Charles Roger, Henry James Morgan, and especially the plaintive letters of William Kingsford.

45 *Mail* (Toronto) 29 Sept. 1888

Reverend Robert Murray (1832–1910),[46] and information from an even wider circle of historians of, and participants in, the events he was to describe.[47] In fact Dent's research and ambition quickly outstripped the format of the biographical sketch, and the publication of the *Canadian Portrait Gallery* was still incomplete when he decided to subsume much of it in a greater work, *The Last Forty Years: Canada since the Union of 1841*, which he began to issue in 1881. That Dent achieved so much so quickly was the result primarily of his own industry and application, but also in large measure of the advice and inspiration given him by one of the correspondents he contacted while researching the *Canadian Portrait Gallery* – none other than Sir Francis Hincks.

In search of material for a sketch of Robert Baldwin, Dent first wrote to Hincks in December of 1878 requesting a copy of the recently published *Political History*.[48] 'Dent's undertakings,' as Graeme Patterson observes, 'provided the old man with just the sort of opportunity for which he had long been waiting.'[49] Indeed, Hincks already had attempted to influence Canada's small community of historians through a collaboration with Louis-Philippe Turcotte (1842–78) on a second edition of the latter's *Le Canada sous l'Union*, until Turcotte's unexpected death put an end to the project.[50] Thus, along with a copy of the *Political History*, Hincks sent to Dent an offer: 'If you would like me to read either in the MSS or in proof your article before publication I shall have much pleasure in giving you my Candid opinion on matters of fact.'[51] Dent was only too glad to have the advice of the last leading politician of the 1840s still alive, and Hincks,

---

46 [Charles Lindsey,] 'Sir John A. Macdonald,' in Dent *Canadian Portrait Gallery*, vol. 2 (1880) 5–16; [Robert Murray,] 'Sir Samuel Cunard, Bart.,' in ibid., vol. 4, 182–4. Dent's own contributions to the *Canadian Portrait Gallery* amount to 185 sketches, or 888 of 959 pages; see Swainson, Introduction to Dent, *Last Forty Years*, vi–vii.

47 For example, Samuel James Watson (c.1842–81), Alpheus Todd (1821–84), Mrs Anne Brown (widow of George Brown), Henry James Morgan, and Benjamin Sulte (1841–1923). These letters were either bound or loosely inserted in the pages of Dent's working sheets for the *Canadian Portrait Gallery* and *The Last Forty Years: Canada since the Union of 1841*, 2 vols (Toronto 1881), now held by the Public Archives of Canada. For a physical description of the Dent collection see 'How History Is Written: The Hincks to Dent Letters,' ed. Elizabeth Nish, *Revue d'centre d'etude du Québec* (Montreal) 2 (1968): 31–4.

48 Only Hincks's return letter survives; Hincks to Dent, 17 Dec. 1878, in ibid., 38.

49 Patterson, 'John Charles Dent,' 247

50 Louis-Philippe Turcotte, *Le Canada sous l'Union, 1841–1867*, 2 vols (Quebec 1871–2); Hincks to Dent, nd, in 'How History Is Written,' ed. Nish, 41. On Turcotte see J.-C. Bonenfant, 'Louis-Philippe Turcotte,' *DCB*, vol. 10, 690.

51 Hincks to Dent, 17 Dec. 1878, in 'How History is Written,' ed. Nish, 38

as good as his word, checked facts, spotted sources overlooked, opened to Dent his invaluable memory of men and measures, and even contributed a sketch of Sir Dominick Daly to the *Canadian Portrait Gallery*.[52] Before long Dent was sending Hincks all his work in sheet form for comment and correction. This relationship lasted for four years and saw both the *Portrait Gallery* and the *Last Forty Years* through to publication.[53]

The question occurs, then, what influence did the old Reformer have on the shape and direction of the historian's work? First, not that Dent appeared to need it, Hincks provided encouragement and enthusiasm; second, he passed on a sense of time, place, and person that immeasurably enriched Dent's final narrative; and third, he corrected names, dates, and confusions in proofs received. On matters of general historical interpretation, however, Dent refused to be Hincks's tool. Despite the Reformer's constant urging, the historian did not, for instance, follow him toward the new 1848 date for the inauguration of full responsible government. Dent instead maintained the traditional mark of 1839 for many of the same reasons as Hincks had himself in the *Political History*.[54] Furthermore, the *Last Forty Years* displayed none of Hincks's empathy for French Canadians, whom Dent, trotting out all the old clichés, portrayed as rustic, ignorant, superstitious, and priest-ridden.[55] In fact, Dent did not think French Canadians were ever successfully reconciled to their English-speaking compatriots, either by Baldwin or Macdonald. In short, he rejected the very foundation on which Hincks's political career had been built.

Although Dent told at length and in great detail the by now conventional story of the coming of responsible government and Governor-General Metcalfe's subsequent attempt to turn back the constitutional clock, hints of the potential for racial and religious disruption in the Canadas were never banished entirely from the narrative. There was in Dent's account of the 1840s a residual sense of unease, even menace, which was not present in Hincks's *Political History*. Thus, while Dent has

52 [Francis Hincks,] 'The Hon. Sir Dominick Daly,' in Dent, *Canadian Portrait Gallery*, vol. 3 (1881) 69–71

53 Francis Hincks's letters to J.C. Dent have been extracted from Dent's workings sheets of the *Canadian Portrait Gallery* and the *Last Forty Years*, deposited in the NA, John Charles Dent Papers, MG 19, D 60, folders 1–4, transcribed (mercifully, given their frequent illegibility) by Elizabeth Nish, and published by her in 'How History Is Written,' 31–96.

54 Ibid., 54, Hincks to Dent, 14 Jan.; 59, 16 July; 60–1, 1 Aug.; 61, 29 Aug.; 66, 30 Sept. 1881. Dent, *Last Forty Years* (1881 edn) vol. 1, 38–41, 68, 125–36, 150, 159, 189–90

55 Ibid., ch. 3

been accused of being 'obsessed with the issue of responsible government'[56] (more than half the text of the *Last Forty Years* is devoted to the first decade), he always wrote with later difficulties in mind, always looked beyond 1839, 1848, or indeed 1854. To be sure, Brown is criticized yet again for exacerbating racial tensions and destroying the old Reform party, while Hincks and Macdonald are praised for valiant attempts to harmonize varying aspirations in pursuit of progressive legislation benefiting all, but Dent knew that the united provinces would ultimately find the French-Canadian community indigestible.[57] What is more, from the perspective of the 1880s Dent was in a position to know that Confederation did not resolve the problems of the nation. Regionalism and thoughtless partisanship persisted, and French Canada, now beyond hope of assimilation, remained distinct and ominously intransigent.[58] Unlike the partisans, Dent did not defend one party against another so much as lament the failure of both.

Dent had the spirit of a National historian and the instincts of a Liberal-Conservative partisan. He believed in a unified, progressive nation state in which all regional, racial, religious, and political animosities would be reconciled. What he did not have was present confidence that Canada was at or near this ideal. 'In the latter sections of *The Last Forty Years*,' Swainson observes, 'Dent displayed so much uncertainty about Canada's present that it is not strictly accurate to typify him as an historian bent on "the ratification if not the glorification of the present."' In short, Dent lacked the assurance to be resolutely anachronistic – it being difficult to draw a line of descent if one has lost direction. In place of purposeful continuity, Swainson argues that Dent utilized selected aspects of the past to stress relevant lessons, that his history, although episodic, was 'mission-oriented.'[59] If so, the mission was particularly ill-defined and the relevant lessons obscure. Dent himself quoted Justin McCarthy's question: 'What, then, have you, who call yourselves practical men, and despise the dreamers of dreams – what have you to suggest?'[60]

56 Swainson, Introduction to Dent, *Last Forty Years*, xiii
57 Dent, *Last Forty Years* (1881 edn) vol. 1, 17, 67, 229–30; vol. 2, 251, 263, 269–70, 300–12
58 Ibid., 488–90; [Henri-Raymond] Casgrain, 'Les Quarante dernières années: 'Le Canada depuis l'Union de 1841,'' par John Charles Dent. Étude critique,' Royal Society of Canada, *Proceedings and Transactions*, vol. 2 (1884) sec. 1, 51–61; Swainson, Introduction to Dent, *Last Forty Years*, xvi–xvii
59 Ibid., xviii
60 Dent, *Last Forty Years* (1881 edn) vol. 2, 524

The *Last Forty Years*, despite the best intentions of the author, provided no answers.

If Dent could not find the prescription for progress in history, J.C. Bourinot, the dean of Canadian critics, at least thought the *Last Forty Years* 'the best history of the period when responsible government was being firmly established in the two Canadas.'[61] Although Dent expressed firm opinions on men and measures, the extensive research his many footnotes displayed was his authority. While partisans were hurling invective and personalities at each other, he dispassionately chronicled their speeches, actions, and rationalizations. Collins, for one, thought Dent had 'fair ability, much prudence, and a mind and impulse under a state of rigid discipline.'[62] It is the depth and occasional uniqueness of Dent's research that gives what Elizabeth Nish calls his 'tedious and inexorable forced belly-crawl through four decades of our Canadian experience' its continuing value to subsequent generations of scholars. It is why, even as his interpretation of responsible government withers, the *Last Forty Years* continues to be 'rated high above all its contemporaries.'[63]

Oddly enough, Dent's strength as a historian told against him as an artist among his contemporaries. Collins, not admittedly an unbiased observer, declared that 'as a rule Mr. Dent's bones are marrowless, and his blood is cold.'[64] Macdonald's biographer clearly exaggerated – a little: Dent had not lost his touch at characterization or his ability to spot a dramatic moment, but by adhering to the schedule of a legislative calendar he lost control over the pacing and direction of his story, which, after wandering for forty years in the wilderness, he could lead to no promised land. This dispassionate and often plodding approach was altogether extraordinary in a man trained in the school of the penny daily. It did win for him the high ground in a bitterly partisan debate and the respect of a small group of peers. It did not, so far as one can tell, win for him popular acclaim or notoriety.

Whether it was the tedium or the predicament of legislative debate in post-Confederation Canada, Dent decided to move backward rather than

61 John George Bourinot, 'Canadian Studies in Comparative Politics: Parliamentary Compared with Congressional Government,' Royal Society of Canada, *Proceedings and Transactions*, vol. 11 (1893) ser. ii, Appendix: Bibliographical and Critical Notes, 98
62 Collins, *Life and Times of ... Sir John A. Macdonald*, 445–6; see also the review of *The Last Forty Years* in *Rose-Belford's Canadian Monthly and National Review*, vol. 7 (August 1881) 213–14
63 'How History Is Written,' ed. Nish, 31
64 Collins, *Life and Times of ... Sir John A. Macdonald*, 445

forward in search of a new subject. Eventually he settled on the rebellion in Upper Canada, which, while related to the achievement of responsible government, took place primarily outside the walls of the assembly. As a story, it had a well-defined beginning and satisfying conclusion, a variegated not to say eccentric cast of characters, moments of high drama and low comedy, and no complicating French Canadians. Above all, since the time of Lord Durham's *Report* the general lines of interpretation, in all their erroneous simplicity, had been set in the public imagination. The history of Upper Canada was a tale of struggle for political liberty, of good against evil. Its heroes and villains were known and recognized as such by all. On one side were the moderate reformers standing in the evolutionary tradition of responsible government; on the other side were reactionary British officials and local Tories, as well as a few radical republicans advocating violence in order to get their way. In short, Dent gave up trying to solve the problems of the nation in favour of telling a good story, and chose a subject that emphasized his skills as a writer over those as a researcher.

In *The Story of the Upper Canadian Rebellion*, published in two volumes in 1885, Dent gave a conventional account with the immediacy of a novelist. Although he once again drew his facts from 'long-forgotten newspapers, blue-books, pamphlets and unedited manuscripts,' he now used his research to colour rather than build his narrative.[65] Commencing with the courtroom drama of Robert Gourlay's trial, Dent embarked upon a recitation of the Reform martyrology that served not only as an indictment of rule by the Family Compact but also as a convenient means to display principle through personality. The remedy to Upper Canadian ills was as obvious as it was popular: 'On one cardinal point ... all [Reformers] were agreed: it was in the highest degree desirable that the Canadian constitution should be more closely assimilated to that of the mother-country, and that the Executive Council should be made responsible to the popular branch of the Legislature.'[66] It was the 'especial subject' of the *Story of the Upper Canadian Rebellion* to explain how the development of a small radical, republican element within the Reform party prevented overwhelmingly popular sentiment in favour of responsible government from working its peaceful way; how the radicals gave a

65 John Charles Dent, *The Story of the Upper Canadian Rebellion; Largely Derived from Original Sources and Documents*, 2 vols (Toronto 1885) vol. 1, 213–14
66 Ibid., 119–20

patina of legitimacy to Tory allegations of Reform disloyalty; and how the fear they engendered among moderate conservatives prevented the kind of centrist coalition that was achieved in 1854 from being formed in the 1830s. Partisan distinctions were thus maintained and exacerbated, and an unnecessary rebellion was the consequence. The outbreak of violence in 1837–8 did bring in its train Lord Durham and the concession of responsible government but at a price that need not have been paid.[67]

Dent's two-volume history of the rebellion in Upper Canada had no immediate application to the partisan controversies of his own day; it was simply a good tale well told. Yet, unlike the *Last Forty Years*, it called forth a storm of criticism. This was due in large measure to Dent's habit of presenting principle through personality: individuals were rarely permitted honest mistakes; aberrant political views were almost invariably taken as an outward sign of inward corruption. For the most part this effective and engaging literary device was safe enough, for few of Dent's contemporaries were likely to hold a brief for the likes of Sir Francis Bond Head or contest the heroic stature of Lord Durham. However, William Lyon Mackenzie still had his admirers, not the least of whom were his sons-in-law, Charles Lindsey and John King (1843–1916). They accepted neither the general proposition that the rebellion was unnecessary nor the specific allegation that Mackenzie's motives were 'malignant.' In press and pamphlet they and others leaped to the defence of Mackenzie both as a man and a politician and ridiculed Dent's attempt to make of Dr John Rolph a tragic hero of moderate reform.[68] The doctor was the weak link in Dent's story. Never entirely able to convince himself of Rolph's integrity, Dent failed to convince others. Although the controversy surrounding the *Story of the Upper Canadian Rebellion* eventually dissipated into a fruitless squabble over the respective roles of Mackenzie and Rolph in the

67 Ibid., 46–7, 231–2, 280; vol. 2, 282–300. In an otherwise excellent introduction to Dent's *Last Forty Years*, Donald Swainson argues that implicit in Dent's analysis of the rebellion 'was a revision of the widely accepted view that the rebellion was essential because it brought home to the British authorities the existence of a crisis in the affairs of British North America' (xi). As we have seen, in so far as there was a widely accepted view of the rebellion to be revised, it was Dent's.

68 For a few representative phrases indicating the fervour of Dent's detestation of Mackenzie, see Swainson's Introduction to the *Last Forty Years*, xii–xiii. A summary of the views of Mackenzie's defenders may be found in John King, *The Other Side of the 'Story,' Being Some Reviews of Mr. J.C. Dent's First Volume of 'The Story of the Upper Canadian Rebellion,' and the Letters in the Mackenzie-Rolph Controversy, also, a Critique, Hitherto Unpublished, on 'The New Story'* (Toronto 1886).

'Flag of Truce Incident,' it was not before Dent's credibility as an objective and detached historical observer had been compromised.[69]

Matters of detail aside, Dent's critics were undoubtedly justified in their suspicion that he had retreated from the 'moderation of tone, and, above all, perfect fairness and impartiality' that had been the hallmark of the *Last Forty Years*. Now, one anonymous reviewer objected, Dent had 'padded and extended and elongated, with fiction, hyperbole and exaggeration' to the point that 'speculative reconstruction' overwhelmed the facts.[70] But Dent had learned that pessimism and scholarly scruple do not sell; controversy does; and he apparently was willing to accept a loss of credibility as the price of successful notoriety. Unable to restructure the past in such a way as to give Canadians self-confidence in the future, unwilling to be confined to the limits and letter of his sources, Dent instead provided a good story. If this was an abrogation of his responsibilities as a historian, it was also an acceptance of his limitations as a conciliator or prophet.

With the publication of the *Story of the Upper Canadian Rebellion* and a subsequent turn toward pure fiction in *The Gerrard Street Mystery and Other Weird Tales*, John Charles Dent became simply another member, albeit a pre-eminent member, of the groups of historians regarded as 'popular,' even though a 'professional' opposite had yet to appear.[71] Like Dent, they were usually journalists, men like Charles Richard Tuttle (1848–c.1920)[72] and William Henry Withrow (1839–1908).[73] Unlike Dent, they usually

69 On the 'Flag of Truce Incident' see Dent, *Story of the Upper Canadian Rebellion*, vol. 2, 69–91; King, *Other Side of the 'Story', passim*; NA, John Rolph Papers, MG 24, B 24, vol. 1, 147–214, The Flag of Truce, 1837; G.M. Craig, 'John Rolph,' *DCB*, vol. 9 (Toronto 1976) 683–90.

70 Anonymous review of *Story of the Upper Canadian Rebellion*, by J.C. Dent, *Daily Mail* (Toronto) 19 Nov. 1885; reprinted in King, *Other Side of the 'Story'*, 15

71 John Charles Dent, *The Gerrard Street Mystery and Other Weird Tales* (Toronto 1888) was a posthumous collection of his purely imaginative work.

72 Charles R. Tuttle, *An Illustrated History of the Dominion of Canada, 1535–1876*, 2 vols, vol. 1 (Montreal and Boston 1877) vol. 2, *The Comprehensive History of the Dominion of Canada, with Art Engravings, from the Confederation of 1867 to the Close of 1878* (Montreal 1879); *Short History of the Dominion of Canada, from 1500 to 1878; With the Contemporaneous History of England and the United States* (Boston 1878). Tuttle also wrote histories of the states of Michigan, Iowa, Wisconsin, Indiana, Texas, and Alaska. For information on Tuttle see W. Stewart Wallace, *The Macmillan Dictionary of Canadian Biography*, 3rd ed. (Toronto 1963) 760–1.

73 William H. Withrow, *A History of Canada for the Use of Schools and General Readers* (Toronto 1876), subsequently reprinted in many different editions under a variety of titles; *Our Own Country Canada: Scenic and Descriptive. Being an Account of the Extent,*

did no research. As a group these popular historians were distinguished by their refusal to confront issues raised by partisans or to recognize concerns of pessimists. What, for instance, were contemporaries to make of Tuttle's claim that 'the ten years which have elapsed since [Confederation] was consummated are full of flattering testimonials to the wisdom of that union'?[74] Although such blind enthusiasm gave way in Withrow's *History of Canada* to a cautious reticence, the result was similarly unenlightening: 'there is,' Bourinot observed, 'no evidence in the work of original research or any attempt made to throw new light on controverted points.'[75] This judgment well could stand for the genre.

Upper Canada, since the days of Lord Durham the 'vanguard province' in matters of historiography as in much else, had by the 1880s lost its way. Historians operating at the national, that is to say central Canadian, level were no longer certain what to study, or why and how, and many of their number turned to an examination of the Dominion in its parts, much as their fellows in French Canada and the Maritimes had been doing all along – the only difference was that central Canadian historians professed to believe that the nation's parts made a homogeneous whole. As William Jordan Rattray (1835–83), author of *The Scot in British North America*, observed:

> There is an advantage in such a mode of treatment which cannot fail to suggest itself to the reader, after a moment's reflection. A subject complex and unwieldy in the mass, is much more readily dealt with, if it be taken up by instalments; and no division promises so much interest and instruction as that which marks off the various factors as they were, originally and before combination, and then to follow them down the stream of time where they will at last be lost in a homogeneous current of national life.[76]

Resources, Physical Aspect, Industries, Cities and Chief Towns of the Provinces of Nova Scotia, Prince Edward Island, Newfoundland, New Brunswick, Quebec, Ontario, Manitoba, the North-West Territory, and British Columbia. With Sketches of Travel and Adventure (Toronto 1889). For information on Withrow see Charles R. Steele, 'William Henry Withrow,' in William Toye, gen. ed., *The Oxford Companion to Canadian Literature* (Toronto 1983) 834–5.

74 Tuttle, *Illustrated History of the Dominion of Canada*, vol. 1, Preface

75 Bourinot, 'Canadian Studies in Comparative Politics,' 100. See also James MacPherson LeMoine (1825–1912), *Monographies et esquisses* ([Quebec 1885]) 51–2.

76 William Jordan Rattray, *The Scot in British North America*, 4 vols (Toronto 1880–4) vol. 1 (1880) 22. Similar sentiments were expressed in an anonymous review of *The Irishman in Canada*, by Nicholas Flood Davin, *Belford's Monthly Magazine: A Magazine of Literature and Art*, vol. 2, no. 6 (November 1877) 852. For information on Rattray see W. Stanford Reid, 'William Jordon Rattray,' *DCB*, vol. 11, 724–5.

The component or fragment might be, as in Rattray's case, an ethnic or racial group;[77] it might also be a religious denomination,[78] a region,[79] a county,[80] or a municipality;[81] the possibilities were endless, and the potential for fresh approaches and new research substantial. The assumption under which the authors of such works operated was that 'the nation is merely a widening of the circle of kin and acquaintance,' and for this reason the majority of them expressed a determination 'to avoid invidious comparisons':[82] in the event, some of them actually kept to their word.

These were, on the whole awkward works, for each author had to grapple with the fact that 'his history could not be written without, to some extent, writing the history of Canada.'[83] As can be imagined, the results varied widely. The journalists Rattray and Nicholas Flood Davin provided their respective races, the Scots and the Irish, with inspirational works, long on style and short on substance. For the most part they were content to cull from secondary sources the names of fellow countrymen who had played a role, however humble, in the creation of the new nation, Canada. At the other extreme, 'with a fine antiquarian instinct,' physician-educator William Canniff 'sought out and preserved masses of material

77 Nicholas Flood Davin (1843–1901), *The Irishman in Canada* (London and Toronto 1877) is the other major work in this group, although Egerton Ryerson, *The Loyalists of America and Their Times: From 1620 to 1816*, 2 vols, 2nd ed. (Toronto 1880), might almost be said to qualify.

78 For example see George Frederick Playter (c.1809–66), *The History of Methodism in Canada: With an Account of the Rise and Progress of the Work of God among the Canadian Indian Tribes, and Occasional Notices of the Civil Affairs of the Province* (Toronto 1862); John Saltkill Carroll (1809–84), *Case and His Contemporaries; Or, the Canadian Itinerants' Memorial: Constituting a Biographical History of Methodism in Canada, from Its Foundation into the Province till the Death of the Rev. Wm. Case*, 5 vols (Toronto 1867–77); William Gregg (1817–1909), *Short History of the Presbyterian Church in the Dominion of Canada, from the Earliest to the Present Time* (Toronto 1892).

79 For example, see William Canniff (1830–1910), *History of the Settlement of Upper Canada, (Ontario,) with Special Reference to the Bay of Quinte* (1869) ed. Donald Swainson (Belleville, Ont., 1971).

80 For example, see Thaddeus W.H. Leavitt (c.1844–1909), *History of Leeds and Grenville* (Brockville, Ont., 1879).

81 For example, see Charles Roger, *Ottawa Past and Present, or a Brief Account of the First Opening Up of the Ottawa Country, and Incidents in Connection with the Rise and Progress of Ottawa City and Parts Adjacent Thereto* ... (Ottawa 1871); Henry Scadding (1813–1901), *Toronto of Old* (Toronto 1873); with John Charles Dent, *Toronto, Past and Present: Historical and Descriptive; A Memorial Volume for the Semi-Centennial of 1884* (Toronto 1884).

82 Rattray, *Scot in British North America*, vol. 1, vi; Davin, *Irishman in Canada*, v–ix

83 Ibid., ix

that otherwise might have been lost.'[84] But the majority of these specialized works were, like William Gregg's *Short History of the Presbyterian Church in the Dominion of Canada*, plodding compendia of names and dates, with emphasis on the genealogy of families and institutions, on memorials to founding fathers, and not a little nostalgia.

Indeed, the most significant characteristic of local or specialized historians was the extent to which they preferred to look backward fondly rather than face up to tomorrow. While most authors proclaimed their faith in Canada's future, in harmony and prosperity, their works belied their affirmations. With some honesty, Davin confided: 'The time has not yet arrived when we can speak of a Canadian type, and until that day arrives, whether we are born on Canadian soil, or in the mother lands, we cannot safely forego the bracing and inspiring influences which come from country and race.'[85] Lacking the comfort of a well-defined nationality of their own, and uncertain of what shape it might take and when, a return to roots, of whatever sort, was a means for Canadians to orient themselves in the new political environment and more complex industrial age. As Carl Berger suggests:

It is in times of trial that the sense of nostalgia for a heroic history is heightened and in the midst of turbulence and change that traditions are most useful for maintaining the assurance of security. The mood of doubt, disillusionment, and uncertainty which culminated in the late 1880s provoked many of the appeals to the certainties of the past.[86]

English-Canadian roots did not of course extend back as far as the era of the French regime, nor indeed were they very deep in the history of the province of old Quebec. And if almost no significant research had been done into these two subject areas by English-speaking historians since the time of George Heriot and William Smith, this was because later historians were satisfied with the basic outline of events they inherited, with what Yves Zoltvany calls the 'liberal critique' of New France.[87] This critique began with the assumption that maladministration was responsi-

84 Swainson, Introduction to Canniff, *Settlement of Upper Canada*, iii
85 Davin, *Irishman in Canada*, 3
86 Carl Berger, *The Sense of Power: Studies in the Ideas of Canadian Imperialism, 1867–1914* (Toronto 1970) 95. See also Gerald Killan, *Preserving Ontario's Heritage: A History of the Ontario Historical Society* (Ottawa 1976) ch. 1.
87 Yves F. Zoltvany, *The Government of New France: Royal, Clerical, or Class Rule?* (Scarborough, Ont., 1971) ch. 2

ble for the slow development of New France, for the colony's hostile relations with the native people and its British neighbours, and for the enervation of its military capacity. The British conquest therefore came as a kind of liberation or salvation. In short, the liberal critique pitted reactionary French Roman Catholic absolutism against progressive Anglo-Protestant forces of liberty. Histories written from the French-Canadian point of view by the likes of François-Xavier Garneau (1809–66), Jean-Baptiste-Antoine Ferland (1805–65), and Benjamin Sulte (1841–1923) were occasionally read and referred to by, but made little impression upon, English Canadians.[88] It was typical that when journalist Andrew Bell (fl.1827–63) translated Garneau's *Histoire du Canada* in 1860, he did so, as he said, 'with such modifications as would make it acceptable to the entirety of our people,' which is to say he made changes to please English Canadians.[89]

Interest in the French regime picked up among English Canadians only as the successive volumes of American historian Francis Parkman's *France and England in North America* began to appear over the years 1865 to 1892.[90] Writing in 1877, Bourinot remarked:

It is safe to say that the English speaking people of Canada were, for the most part, entirely ignorant of the elements of interest that are to be found in the earlier annals of this country, until the American historian, Parkman, raised our history from that dull, prosaic level from which Canadian writers had been

---

88 Serge Gagnon, *Le Québec et ses historiens de 1840 à 1920: La Nouvelle-France de Garneau à Groulx* (Quebec 1978) 287–391

89 Quoted in William F.E. Morley, 'Andrew Bell,' *DCB*, vol. 9, 41–2. Bell published what Morley calls his 'creative translation' of François-Xavier Garneau, *Histoire du Canada depuis sa découverte jusqu'à nos jours*, 3 vols, 3rd ed. (Quebec 1859), under the title *History of Canada, from the Time of Its Discovery till the Union Year (1840–1)*, 3 vols (Montreal 1860).

90 These were, in order of appearance: *Pioneers of France in the New World* (1865; revised 1885); *The Jesuits in North America in the Seventeenth Century* (1867); *The Discovery of the Great West* (1869; revised 1879); *The Old Régime in Canada* (1874; revised 1893); *Count Frontenac and New France under Louis XIV.* (1877); *Montcalm and Wolfe*, 2 vols (1884); and *A Half-Century of Conflict*, 2 vols (1892). The seventh chronological part, *Montcalm and Wolfe*, was published eight years before part six, *A Half-Century of Conflict*, because Parkman's health, never good, seemed to be growing worse, and he feared he might not live to finish the part that had earlier given the inspiration for the entire project. See David Levin, 'Note on the Texts,' in Francis Parkman, *France and England in North America*, 2 vols, Library of America, ed. David Levin (New York 1983) vol. 1, 1435–8; vol. 2, 1511–13.

wont to view it, and revived the past in its most romantic and picturesque guise.[91]

This observation requires two of its own. First, the very quality of Parkman's work, at the same time as it attracted readers, discouraged would-be imitators. In effect, after Parkman what was there left to say?[92] Second, Parkman reinforced rather than altered received opinion in English Canada. He, like Heriot and Smith, saw the conflict between France and England in North America as 'a conflict between the forces of light and the forces of darkness, between the nation of Progress and the nation that stood opposed to it; between Anglo-Saxon Protestant liberty – which was the hallmark of Progress – and French Roman Catholic absolutism.'[93] What was remarkable was the reaction of French, not English, Canadians. The former, who could afford to ignore such a line of reasoning when it emanated from the lesser lights of English Canada, went into paroxysms when it was adopted by a foreign historian of international renown.[94] To English-speaking historians Parkman's interpretation was unexceptional, indeed gratifyingly so.

The Parkman-inspired rediscovery of New France by English-Canadian historians coincided with the revitalization of the long-dormant Literary and Historical Society of Quebec. The LHSQ was founded by Lord Dalhousie in 1824 with the primary intent, as the society's title and the preamble to its charter proclaimed, of promoting literary and historical study. In the event, the first three volumes of the LHSQ *Transactions*, published in 1829, 1830, and 1833, were almost exclusively devoted to natural science, travelogues, and anthropology.[95] Three volumes in a

91 John G. Bourinot, 'Forest Rangers and Voyageurs,' *Belford's Monthly Magazine*, vol. 1, no. 5 (Apr. 1877) 638n

92 For instance the otherwise worthy work of Henry Hopper Miles (1818–95) was completely obscured by Parkman's classic volumes. H.H. Miles, *The History of Canada under French Régime, 1535–1763* (Montreal 1872). For information on Miles see LeMoine, *Monographies et esquisses*, 49–50; and Geneviève Laloux-Jain, *Les Manuels d'histoire du Canada au Québec et en Ontario, de 1867 à 1914* (Quebec 1974) 107–8.

93 W.J. Eccles, 'The History of New France according to Francis Parkman,' *William and Mary Quarterly*, ser. 3, vol. 18 (1961) 163

94 Gagnon, *Québec et ses historiens*, 171–2

95 On the history of the LHSQ see John M. Harper, 'The Annals of an Old Society,' Royal Society of Canada, *Proceedings and Transactions*, vol. 3 (1885) sec. ii, 55–65; *The Centenary Volume of the Literary and Historical Society of Quebec, 1824–1924*, ed. Henry Ievers (Quebec 1924). For the society's publications see *List of Historical Documents and New Series of 'Transactions' Published by the Literary and Historical Society of Quebec* (Quebec 1927).

Historical Documents series appeared in 1838, 1840, and 1843 – which included the first publication of the 'Mémoires du S ... de C ... contenant l'histoire du Canada durant la guerre, et sous le gouvernement anglais' – but little else of historical significance was accomplished before the society lapsed into an extended period of inactivity.[96] In the early 1860s, Dr William James Anderson 'led a group of members who revived the society, reanimated its interest in securing and publishing documents on Quebec, and re-established its library and museum.' In 1866 Anderson began to write a series of articles for the *Transactions* of the LHSQ in which he reproduced and summarized interesting and curious documents relating to the French regime. In researching these essays Anderson made use of the Public Archives of Nova Scotia (which he visited in 1862), arranged for the transfer of some manuscripts from Halifax to Quebec, and later had other archival material brought from Britain to Canada. While on the executive of the LHSQ he was also instrumental in seeing two new volumes of *Historical Documents* through to publication.[97]

Renewed interest in the French regime had the happy consequence of diverting attention away from the fruitless disputes of partisans and the nostalgia of pessimists. Furthermore, the concern shown for documents by the LHSQ also showed a way out of the contemporary historiographical morass through a return to sources. Leading members of the LHSQ agitated for the creation of a national archives, and it was in answer to a petition from their organization that the Public Archives of Canada was established in 1872.[98] If this did not make an immediate difference to the state of most historical writing in Canada, it was in part because, as the reports of Dominion Archivist Douglas Brymner (1823–1902) make clear, the holdings of the NA were initially weighted toward the now-distant questions of the era prior to 1791. But it was also because effective use of an archives required new skills of organization and analysis.[99] Such skills were not easy to develop, as the career of William Kingsford

96 'Mémoires du S ... de C ... contenant l'histoire du Canada durant la guerre, et sous le gouvernement anglais,' Literary and Historical Society of Quebec, *Historical Documents* [ser. 1], vol. 1 (1838). For the importance of this document see above 92–4.
97 Elizabeth Waterston, 'William James Anderson,' *DCB*, vol. 10, 13–14
98 Henry H. Miles, 'On "Canadian Archives,"' Literary and Historical Society of Quebec, *Transactions*, new series, vol. 8 (1870–1) 53–71; W.J. Anderson, 'The Archives of Canada,' ibid., vol. 9 (1871–2) 117–31
99 Ian E. Wilson, 'Shortt and Doughty: The Cultural Role of the Public Archives of Canada, 1904–1935,' *Canadian Archivist* 2 (1973): 5–6

(1819–1898), the first English-Canadian historian to make extensive use of the NA, makes all too clear.[100]

Born in London, England, the son of an innkeeper, the young Kingsford enlisted in the First King's Dragoon Guards in March of 1838 on the eve of their departure for Lower Canada.[101] While stationed at Chambly in November of that same year, the regiment, under the command of Lieutenant Colonel Sir George Cathcart, helped to repress the second rebellion, and subsequently scourged the countryside round about. Unfortunately, Kingsford lacked the temperament and financial resources necessary to secure career advancement in the army, and in October 1841, apparently with the aid of friends in England, he purchased his release at the rank of corporal. He immediately thereafter embarked on a long career as a civil surveyor and engineer, which carried him from Canada to the United States, Panama, Sardinia, Britain, and Eastern Europe. During his travels Kingsford acquired several languages, including French, Italian, German, and Spanish, and at intervals produced pamphlets and books, generally of a technical nature, summarizing his experiences.[102] This migratory career suited Kingsford: happier in the field than in the office, never content with one employer for very long, he preferred to set his own standards and pace.[103]

Kingsford was periodically employed in Canada but did not return to stay until the late 1860s. In June 1873 Kingsford's Conservative sympathies won him the post of engineer in charge of federal harbour and river works on the St Lawrence and Great Lakes, and his professionalism ensured that he kept the appointment when the Liberal party of Alexander Mackenzie took power in November. In performing his duties 'faithfully and without sullenness' under Mackenzie, Kingsford unwit-

100 Ibid.; George M. Wrong, 'The Beginnings of Historical Criticism in Canada: A Retrospect, 1896–1936,' CHR 17 (1936): 6; J.K. McConica, 'Kingsford and Whiggery in Canadian History,' CHR 40 (1959): 108–10
101 For biographical information, see M. Brook Taylor, 'William Kingsford,' DCB, vol. 12 (forthcoming).
102 William Kingsford, History, Structure and Statistics of Plank Roads in the United States and Canada (Philadelphia, Pa., 1852); Impressions of the West and South during a Six Weeks' Holiday (Toronto 1858); The Canadian Canals: Their History and Cost, with an Inquiry into the Policy Necessary to Advance the Well-Being of the Province (Toronto 1865)
103 The pattern of Kingsford's career was not uncommon among nineteenth-century civil engineers who had yet to set their claims as a profession; see W.J. Reader, Professional Men: The Rise of the Professional Classes in Nineteenth-Century England (New York 1966) 69–71; and H.V. Nelles, Introduction to T.C. Keefer, Philosophy of Railroads and Other Essays (Toronto 1972) vii–lxiii.

tingly became the author of his own misfortune. Conservatives returning to power in October 1878 were suspicious of their appointee who had served the Liberals so well, and on the last day of 1879 Kingsford was dismissed by the same minister who had hired him, Hector-Louis Langevin. Kingsford's sense of professionalism was outraged by the partisan nature of his dismissal, and his long and ultimately futile campaign to gain reinstatement was the occasion of one of the first major debates in the House of Commons on the incompatibility of traditional patronage and new professionalism.[104]

Blocked by the government from further participation in major nation-building projects, too proud and perhaps too old to find the lesser assignments of private contracting rewarding, Kingsford turned, rather surprisingly, to the task of writing the history of Canada. Kingsford's motives are not entirely clear: he had been collecting Canadiana for twenty years or more and as a collector was attracted by the filling shelves of the Public Archives of Canada; he also drew a parallel between the engineer building the sinews and the historian building the spirit of the nation.[105] In any event, he dedicated the remainder of his life to writing a history of Canada through to the achievement of responsible government – which he dated from 1841 – based on original sources.[106] Indeed, 'there is,' he declared, 'but one mode of assuring historical truth, and that is by the collection of contemporary documents systematically arranged.' It was all so simple: one merely employed the objective and scientific criteria of the professional engineer to disinter what Kingsford called the 'Archaeology' of the past.[107] With all the dedication he could muster, and with perhaps just a touch of pomposity, Kingsford determined to set Canadian historiography aright. What began as a 'self imposed duty' would become in the completion 'a point of honour.'[108]

104 AO, William Kingsford Papers, MUS 1628, folder entitled Summary of Wm. Kingsford's career as a civil engineer, 1842–80. Compiled 1880, 4–7; letter to the editor, *Globe* (Toronto) 6 Apr. 1881, in ibid., MU 1630, Scrap Books, vol. 2, 37; William Kingsford, *Mr. Kingsford and Sir H. Langevin, C.B.: The Case Considered with the Official Correspondence. A Memoir for the Historian of the Future* (Toronto 1882)

105 Kingsford Papers, Correspondence, re an honorarium, Kingsford to Mackenzie Bowell, 5 Feb. 1895 [copy]

106 Ibid., Kingsford to Oliver Mowat, Aug. 1896 [copy]; William Kingsford, *The History of Canada*, 10 vols (Toronto 1887–98) vol. 1 (1887) 1–2

107 William Kingsford, *Canadian Archaeology: An Essay* (Montreal 1886) 5–6, 10; Kingsford, *History of Canada*, vol. 1, 1–2

108 Kingsford Papers, Correspondence, re an honorarium, Kingsford to Bowell, 5 Feb. 1895 [copy]; Kingsford to Richard Cartwright, 20 Aug. 1896 [copy]

The sixty-seven-year-old Kingsford did not shirk his duty. In the last twelve years of his life he produced the ten volumes of his *History of Canada*, at approximately five hundred pages each, as well as two volumes of bibliography. This required hard work and rigid adherence to the schedule he described to his friend William Buckingham: 'I rise at five and work until 9 – go to the Archives or Library – work until about 12. Home: dine at one – begin work at 3 – write letters I have to attend to or continue at MS until ¼ to 6. After tea I read or write & go to bed at eight such is my life – and so it must continue until I have ended my work.'[109] Kingsford, by keeping to this routine, was able to give his printers a new volume of the *History of Canada* on 30 November of every year. Nor was this an end to Kingsford's sacrifices: each volume cost him $1,200 to produce, which was, as he said, 'a great deal to father in Canada.' By 1896 he was in debt to his printer for nearly $900, to the Bank of Montreal for $425, and there was a mortgage on his furniture for a loan contracted to meet the cost of publication.[110] To relieve this financial burden Kingsford appealed repeatedly to the federal government for an honorarium of the kind previously given to French-Canadian historians François-Xavier Garneau, Henri-Raymond Casgrain, and Cyprien Tanguay (1819–1902), failing which he offered to sell his collection of Canadiana to the nation for $1,500.[111] When no aid was forthcoming, he was saved only by the intervention of three 'disinterested friends,' one of whom was Sir Sandford Fleming.[112]

Kingsford wrote as he built, quickly and efficiently, without qualification or meditation, under pressure of time and budget. Thus, while among the first historians to use the Public Archives extensively, his

109 AO, Alpheus Edward Byerly Papers, MU 455, folder entitled, 1892, Kingsford to William Buckingham, 5 Sept. 1892; see also University of Toronto Library, William Kingsford Papers, MS 106, Kingsford to James Bain, 14 June 1892
110 Byerly Papers, Kingsford to Buckingham, 12 Sept. 1892; Kingsford Papers, Correspondence, re an honorarium, Kingsford to Bowell, 5 Feb. 1895 [copy]; Kingsford to Mowat, Aug. 1896 [copy]
111 Kingsford Papers, Correspondence, re an honorarium, *passim*. It should be noted that Premier Mowat of Ontario subscribed for one hundred copies of Kingsford's *History of Canada*; see Byerly Papers, Kingsford to Buckingham, 12 Sept. 1892.
112 Kingsford Papers, Correspondence, re an honorarium, Kingsford to Bowell, 5 Feb. 1895 [copy]; Kingsford, *History of Canada*, vol. 10 (1898) iii; NA, Sandford Fleming Papers, MG 29, vol. 26, Kingsford to Sandford Fleming, 9 Mar. 1894 (brought to the author's attention by Carl Berger). In 1884–5 Kingsford was of some assistance to Fleming in the latter's campaign on behalf of 'Cosmic Time,' translating, for instance, the work of Otto Struve from the German; see NA, Edmund Allen Meredith Papers, MG 29, E 15, vol. 4, file entitled, Cosmic Time, 1884–1885, *passim*.

researches there were of necessity random and superficial and employed to flesh out rather than alter received opinion. Relying heavily on such precursors as Michel Bibaud (1782–1857), Robert Christie, and especially Lord Durham, Kingsford assumed that the British conquest of New France was a victory for constitutional liberty and material progress, that the assimilation of French Canadians was inevitable, that the road to responsible government was the unifying heritage of all British North American colonies, and that ultimately Canada was one nation composed of a single people inhabiting a common land. Although his conventional views were often expressed with the zeal of a revisionist, Kingsford's most arresting departures from historiographical norms – for instance his claim that Samuel de Champlain was a Huguenot -were products less of new scholarship than of personal eccentricity. The result was a generally uncoordinated recapitulation of commonplaces, interrupted by irrelevant digressions, and delivered in pedestrian prose at interminable length.[113]

The public applauded Kingsford's diligence and self-sacrifice: he was elected a member of the Royal Society of Canada in 1886 and was twice honoured with an LL D, from Queen's University in 1889 and from Dalhousie University in 1896.[114] Much to Kingsford's chagrin, however, it became increasingly clear that few individuals actually were reading the tedious volumes they felt duty bound to purchase.[115] Among those who did make the effort were the country's first generation of professional historians. In the pages of their new forum founded in 1896, the *Review of*

113 Kingsford, *History of Canada*, vol. 1, 15–22; vol. 10, 349; McConica, 'Kingsford and Whiggery,' 112–15. McConica picked out some of the crucial as well as bizarre turning points in Kingsford's *History of Canada*, but, unfamiliar with previous nineteenth-century English-Canadian historians, he greatly overestimated Kingsford's interpretive originality and influence.

114 'Decease of Fellows – The Historian Kingsford and the Poet Lampman,' Royal Society of Canada, *Proceedings and Transactions*, ser. 2, vol. 5 (1899) sec. ii, xxiv–xxxi; Queen's University Archives, Queen's University, Collection 207, vol. 1, Queen's Convocation Minutes, 24 Apr. 1889; Dalhousie University Library, Dalhousie University, Senate Minutes, 1895–6, 28 Apr. 1896; unidentified newspaper clippings, Kingsford Papers, Scrap Books, vol. 2, 91

115 It is clear from Kingsford's correspondence with them that Bowell, Cartwright, Mowat, Charles Tupper, Wilfrid Laurier, and William Stevens Fielding respected but had not read the *History of Canada*. Kingsford himself commented on this frustrating phenomenon in a letter to poet John Reade, 12 March 1892, quoted in Percy Parker Ghent, *John Reade and His Friends* (Toronto 1925) 44. My own copy of Kingsford's *History of Canada* came from the library of Dominion Archivist Douglas Brymner with the pages uncut.

Historical Publications Relating to Canada, they repeatedly took Kingsford to task for failing to meet their standards of comprehensive research and coherent argument.[116] Denied the opportunity to respond by the *Review*'s editor, George MacKinnon Wrong, Kingsford, always a good hater, struck back in the pages of *Queen's Quarterly.* While he often held his own in matters of detail, his reputation was hereafter that of an amateur.[117] Fortunately Kingsford did not live to endure this decline in his reputation, and he would have appreciated the gesture of tobacco magnate Sir William Christopher Macdonald, who in 1898 endowed the Dr William Kingsford Chair in history at McGill University. The endowment included provision for an annuity of $500 to be paid to Kingsford's widow, to which was added a civil list pension of £100 per annum from Queen Victoria.[118]

This rather sad end to William Kingsford's career as a historian stands as a symbol for his generation. By the turn of the century Canada's amateur historians – for such they now were – had lost their sense of purpose. No longer able to look forward, they had no reason to look back. The nationalism that had sustained them did not survive the buffeting events that followed on the heels of Confederation. While it was probably inevitable that partisan differences would resurface, their virulence and intractableness ultimately were enervating. More disturbing still was the complexity of the problems of change. Many historians actually began to retreat from the future and sought solace in loyalties predating that of the

116 Review of *History of Canada,* vol. 8, by William Kingsford, *RHPRC* 1 (1896): 10–19; Review of *History of Canada,* vol. 9, by William Kingsford, ibid. 2 (1897): 18–23; Review of *History of Canada,* vol. 10, by William Kingsford, ibid. 3 (1898): 18–20. The three anonymous reviews were rumoured to be the work of Ernest Alexander Cruikshank (1853–1939). On the beginnings of the critical history of professional historians in Canada see Carl Berger, *The Writing of Canadian History: Aspects of English-Canadian Historical Writing since 1900,* 2nd ed. (Toronto 1986) ch. 1.
117 [William Kingsford,] 'Reply of Dr. Kingsford to the Strictures on Volume VIII. of the "History of Canada" in the "Review of Historical Publications Relating to Canada,"' *Queen's Quarterly* (1897): 37–52. On Kingsford's reaction to criticism in general and of his *History of Canada* in particular, see his letters to James Bain found in the University of Toronto Library, William Kingsford Papers, MS 106, but especially Douglas Brymner to Bain, 8 Jan. 1889. On Wrong's rejection of Kingsford's attempts to respond within the pages of the *Review of Historical Publications Relating to Canada,* see NA, George Taylor Denison Papers, MG 29, E 29, vols 7–8, 3300–3, William Kingsford to George Taylor Denison, 15 Sept. 1897.
118 McGill University Archives, McGill University, Board of Governors, Minutes, 13 Dec. 1898; *Montreal Gazette,* 14, 19 Dec. 1898; undated clipping from the *Ottawa Free Press,* Kingsford Papers, MU 1631, Scrap Books, vol. 3, 207

young country. Initially resilient, then desperate, under pressure the morale of National historians finally snapped.

Alternatives to partisanship, however, were emerging. The nostalgia of pessimists opened new realms to study and implied love of the past for its own sake. New motives brought new methods in their train. A reverence for artifacts – the documents, publications, and articles of previous generations – manifested itself in a growing number of libraries, museums, and archives. But historians outside the universities were uncertain how to handle such new resources, and it was this uncertainty that, regardless of their efforts, permitted professionals to rank them as amateurs. The subject of this book is not, however, the rise of a new attitude, it is the elaboration, consideration, and enjoyment of an old one.

Conclusion

Throughout most of the nineteenth century English-Canadian historians primarily wanted to talk about the future. Indeed, initially there was little else to discuss. In the case of our first historians, the promoters, the future in question was their own. Rootless individuals on the make, they hid within the extensive effort being made to describe the New World to the Old. Their achievement, whatever their motives, was to explain away initial failure as that of men and measures, not the land, and then to civilize the wilderness by definition and illustration. Unfortunately, driven by hope of short-term gain, they overplayed their hand. The historical terrain between their present predictions and future development was filled with unaccountable obstacles. The reputation of the colonies they described sank along with their credibility as historians.

Promoters were replaced by patriots wedded to place as well as future. Loyalty to the colonial land of their birth imposed a long-term responsibility on patriots to describe their respective homes with greater accuracy and predict development with greater reliability. In the light of later achievements, early disappointments, too many now to be ignored, were regarded as the natural and unavoidable consequences of pioneer life. Patriots in fact turned the traditional formula of colonization on its head: men must live up to the land rather than the land to the men. The wilderness was a forge that fired a hardy and industrious society of independent yeomen, men and women who represented the best of the British heritage. The signal contribution of patriot writers was to fashion a colonial identity that was distinct yet compatible with continued loyalty to Great Britain.

Despite this common commitment to tame the land and shape a new people, British North American historiography was plural not singular:

progress was not so much a unifying principle of national existence as a pragmatic program for provincial development. Each colony had its own opportunities and problems to be chronicled in the exploiting and overcoming. Some situations were, like the racial division in Lower Canada, intractable; others, as in Upper Canada, amenable to resolution. Some provincial traditions – Prince Edward Island's, for example – developed in particular isolation; others, such as Nova Scotia's, in smug cosmopolitanism. In short, identical yeoman ideals fostered separate identities.

Inevitably there were obstacles to growth. In Prince Edward Island it was absentee proprietors, in Lower Canada the presence of French Canadians, and in Upper Canada an irresponsible, self-interested élite backed by the imperial government. Those seeking the power to shape their own destiny drew strength from local events and fashioned traditions of grievance to justify impatience. Flirting with rebellion, they were saved from final disloyalty by the settled solution of responsible government, which asked not for a change in the British constitution but for the British constitution itself. The sanction of Lord Durham was a crucial turning point. When he confirmed reform pretensions, he transformed the nature of colonial patriotism from a static ideal to a dynamic and comprehensive process. It was Lord Durham more than anyone else, furthermore, who established central Canada's conceit as arbiter of historical structure for all of British North America.

Canada's historians still had their eyes on the future, but the power to control the future now lay at home. Henceforth they wrote for Canadians, their purpose to motivate and direct an internal audience rather than influence an external authority. Pleased with present achievement, they were confident of future success if past habits of conciliation, consolidation, and assimilation were imitated and reinforced and remnants of radicalism, regionalism, and racism permitted to fade. From this set of convictions emerged a 'National school' of historians, National because they believed Canada to be one nation housing one people inhabiting a common land. This conception was broad enough to embrace all of British North America, and justified Confederation long before the event.

The expanding vision of Canadian historians ran up against conceits as strong as their own in the Maritime provinces. Maritime historians, confident in futures that did not include the Canadas, saw little reason to merge with the past of their continental brethren. They had their own agenda, their own lines of descent, lines that did not include French

Canadians and rebellion. Responsible government came to them in recognition of Maritime maturity, not as a solution to pressing problems or crises. If Canadian historians ultimately prevailed, it was not due to the persuasiveness of their case but rather to the brute strength of their government. Maritime historians, with their future suddenly stolen from them, were unenthusiastic nationalists and slow to reconcile to the new reality. Many retreated into nostalgia.

For Canadian historians, Confederation proved to be a Pyrrhic victory. The future that now was theirs suddenly darkened. It was not simply the failure of the new nation to assimilate French Canada and the Maritimes or to digest the new North West, it was also the loss of vision necessary to meet continental challenges. Failure, scandal, and corruption unleashed pent-up partisan rancour, which devoured pretensions to moral leadership. Historians themselves began to reflect the new partisanship and also, increasingly, pessimism. Like Maritime historians they too turned to the past for solace rather than inspiration. After a century of looking for a Golden Age in the future, Canadian historians now suddenly found it in the past.

How significant did contemporaries think these variously crude or elaborate reconstructions of the past? It is difficult to be precise. Historians were more influential in some periods than in others, and some historians were more influential than others. Consequences were also often incidental or unexpected. Promoters, for instance, had a momentary monopoly over the flow of information from the colonies that none of their successors could command, yet the patrons for whom they wrote were more influential than their writings in pressing cases and advancing careers. It was incidental that promoters left colonial reputations in shreds and unexpected that they provided the patriots who followed with the methodological tools to solve this problem.

The unintended consequences of patriot histories were even more important. Writing to defend their respective colonies before a British audience, the first generation of patriots provided credible descriptions of resources and narratives to explain difficulties encountered in their exploitation. While it seems unlikely that such works, many of which never reached the intended market, significantly altered opinions of the colonies abroad, by detailing hardships overcome and successes hard won, they provided colonists themselves with a sense of common achievement and identity. That this identity was almost invariably based on the ideal of the hard-working, independent yeoman farmer indicates that it was hardly the invention of patriot historians alone. Nevertheless, it was they who put it in a form directly relevant to a particular colony, thereby turning a universal ideal into a provincial model. This was an important turning point in every colony, and patriot historians played a perhaps vital role in the transition.

In the hands of those who benefited from the *status quo*, patriotism was a means both to inhibit criticism and to define loyalty in such a way as to exclude their adversaries. Politicians bent on change had therefore to recast history in a way that legitimized their opposition and made it loyal. Indeed, in the case of Upper Canada, reform politicians seized on conflict to fashion a history pregnant with purposive force to justify their actions. In the process, the likes of William Lyon Mackenzie, Robert Baldwin, and Francis Hincks became leading innovators of historical interpretation. Still, their version of history was never more than a useful weapon in the larger political conflict in which they were engaged: their history did not provide them with political victory; their political victory confirmed their history. Similarly, it was not the cogency of Lord Durham's *Report* but the growing power of the Canadas that substantiated his claim that the historiography of one colony was mirrored in all.

The National school of historians justified the pretensions of Canadians and the Liberal-Conservatives, although neither the united colony nor the party appeared to require it. In contrast, when the National interpretation also rendered the individual histories of the Maritime provinces parochial, it forced the historians and peoples of Nova Scotia, New Brunswick, and Prince Edward Island to cling all the more to their respective identities. The passing of their individual independence was the occasion of widespread and popular interest in and nostalgia for the early years. In defeat, Maritime historians found value. Paradoxically, in victory Canadian historians lost their way. When the nation and party to which they had fixed their interpretation faltered, they lost their sense of direction and purpose, and consequently their influence. It was into this breach that the professional historian, armed with independent justification for study, stepped.

In an effort to secure their own credentials, the first generation of professional historians disparaged the achievement of their dilettante predecessors. In doing so, they obscured, even from themselves, the extent to which they relied on assumptions and biases inherited from amateur historians of the eighteenth and nineteenth centuries. The basic premise, for instance, that the history of Canada was held together and co-ordinated by geographic expansion and constitutional growth still stood. Competing identities of region, race, and religion remained subordinated and in some ways illegitimate. The experience of central Canada continued to be imposed on the periphery. Such prejudices, stark at conception, were disguised by the elaboration and increasing sophistication of successive generations of historians. A search for the origin of our predispositions has the salutary effect of revealing their intolerance, bigotry, and chauvinism. At the same time one can recognize, behind both our predecessors' explicit involvement in contemporary affairs and our own professional commitment, a common fascination with the past that transcends rationalization.

Index

Acadia 94; Maritime promoters
on 20–3; J. Stewart on 33; T.C.
Haliburton on 50–2, 57–60,
182; New Brunswick patriots on 66,
72, 73, 77; Hannay on 217–18.
See also Acadians; Expulsion
controversy

Acadians: Maritime promoters on
22–3; J. Stewart on 33; T.C.
Haliburton on 49, 52, 57–9, 182,
186–7; P. Fisher on 68; Cooney
on 72, 74; Raynal on 186, 194;
Murdoch on 194; Parkman
on 198. *See also* Acadia; Expulsion
controversy

Acadiensis (1901–8) 216

*Account of the Present State of Nova-
Scotia, An* (1756): as a promotional pamphlet 12, 14

Agriculture, idealization of: J. Stewart
on 32, 39–40; T.C. Haliburton
on 48–9, 63, 182; P. Fisher on
67–8, 69–70; Baillie on 70–1;
Atkinson on 70–1; Cooney on 74;
Hatheway on 75; Gesner on 77,
78; Lewellin on 80; Maritime patriots on 82–3; Lower Canadian
patriots on 85, 100–1, 115; Heriot
on 89; W. Smith, Jr, on 94;
Fleming on 99; Upper Canadian
patriots on 118, 132–3; Gourlay
on 121–2; Prince Edward Island
patriots on 228–9. *See also* Yeomen, idealization of

Akins, Thomas Beamish 211, 214;
upbringing and early career
190–1; member of The Club 53;
nature of patriotism 207; antiquarianism of 191, 193–4, 196,
204, 208–10; and Nova Scotia
Commission of Public Records 56–
7, 190, 191–2, 194, 196, 200–7;
*Selections from the Public Documents
of the Province of Nova Scotia*
(1869) 196–9, 201–7, 202n, 218;
and the expulsion controversy
57n, 191–2, 194, 196–9, 200–7,
207n; charged with suppression
of evidence 200–7, 207n; critical of
T.C. Haliburton 56–7, 57n, 194,
200–1; influences R.G. Haliburton
192; influences Murdoch 193–4;
establishes Historical Prize Essay
208–10

American Revolution 124, 137; and Prince Edward Island 27, 28; and Quebec 95, 98, 116; Gourlay on 131; McMullen on 157, 159; Hannay on 219

Amherst, General Jeffrey 160

Anderson, Dr William James: and the expulsion controversy 197; and the Literary and Historical Society of Quebec 260

Anne, Queen of Great Britain and Ireland 200

Anonymity: of promoters 12–13

Antiquarianism 185; in Europe 23; of Akins 191, 193–4, 196, 204, 208–10

Archibald, Sir Adams George: and the expulsion controversy 199, 205

Arctic region 8

Aristotle 148

Articles of capitulation (1760): McMullen on 156

Atkinson, Rev. William Christopher: career 65, 70; author of emigrant guides to New Brunswick 70–2

Aumasson de Courville, Louis-Léonard: 'Mémoires du S ... du C ...' 92–3, 260

Bagot, Sir Charles: McMullen on 162–3; A. Mackenzie on 236, 240; Hincks on 242; Kaye on 243

Bagster, Cornelius Birch 228; *The Progress and Prospects of Prince Edward Island* (1861) 226–7

Baillie, Thomas 73; career 65, 70; *An Account of the Province of New Brunswick* (1832) 70–2

Baldwin, Robert: on responsible government 135–7, 270; letter to Glenelg, 13 July 1836 135–7, 140, 141, 143; influence on Durham 140, 141, 143; reaction to Durham's *Report* 146–7; McMullen on 161, 163; Morgan on 171–2; Taylor on 176; Lindsey on 232, 233; A. Mackenzie on 236–8, 239; Hincks on 241–6; Kaye on 243, 243n; Dent on 248, 249. *See also* Reform interpretation of Upper Canadian history

Bancroft, George: and the expulsion controversy 189; Murdoch criticizes 193, 196

Barkley, Murray: on the Loyalist centennial celebrations at Saint John, NB (1883) 214–15

Beamish, Thomas 190

Bédard, Pierre-Stanislas 106

Belcher, Jonathan: Murdoch on 195

Belknap, Jeremy: *American Biography* (1794–8) 54; *The History of New Hampshire* (1784–92) 55; T.C. Haliburton's reliance on 53, 54, 55

Bell, Andrew: *History of Canada* (1860), translation of Garneau's *Histoire du Canada*, 3rd ed. (1859) 258, 258n

Berger, Carl: on nostalgia 257

Bethune, Rev. Alexander Neil: biographer of Strachan 235

Bibaud, Michel: Kingsford's reliance on 264

Bidwell, Barnabas (Inhabitant): 'The Sketches of Upper Canada' (1816), Gourlay's use of 126–8

Biography: utility of 167, 234–5

Blackstone, William 184

Blake, Edward 235

Blanchet, Dr François-Xavier 105

Bloch, Gerald: on Gourlay 122

Bollan, William: career 13, 14–15; *The Importance and Advantage of Cape-Breton* (1746) 13, 14–15, 23

Bouchette, Joseph 103–4

Bougainville, Louis-Antoine de 87

Bourinot, John George: accuses T.C. Haliburton of plagiarism 53–4, 207n; on Dent 251; on Parkman 258

Bowen, Edward 104

Bromley, Walter: publisher of T.C. Haliburton's *General Description* 44; on the Micmacs 44n

Brown, Rev. Andrew: and the expulsion controversy 186n

Brown, George 232, 246; assassination of 235, 239; McMullen on 164, 179–80; Morgan on 172; Taylor on 176–7, 178; A. Mackenzie's biography of 235–40; Hincks on 244–6; Dent on 250

Brydges, Charles John: Taylor on 177

Brymner, Douglas: as Dominion archivist 260

Buchanan, Isaac: Morgan on 171n, 172; Taylor on 177

Buckingham, William 263

Bulkeley, Richard: and the expulsion controversy 186

Buller, Charles 140

Bulmer, Sir Fenwick 101

Bumsted, J.M.: on the Prince Edward Island land question 36–7, 38, 228

Burke, Edmund: on Nova Scotia 24

Calnek, William Arthur: and Akins Historical Prize Essay 209

Campbell, Duncan: early career 210; *Nova Scotia* (1873) 210–12; *History of Prince Edward Island* (1875) 227–8

Campbell, Rev. John Roy: and Akins Historical Prize Essay 209, 210

Canada, Dominion of: historians of 7–8, 267–71; McMullen on 179–80; partisan histories of 231–2, 234–5, 265–6; A. Mackenzie on 238–40; popular histories of 254–5; local, ethnic, and denominational histories of 255–7; national archives of 260–1, 262, 263–4. *See also* Confederation; National interpretation of Canadian history

Canada, Province of: established 147; advent of responsible government in 147, 152–3; historians of 7–8, 267–71; Christie on 114; McMullen on 153–4, 162–5, 179–80; Morgan on 170–3; Taylor on 175–8; reaction of Maritime patriots to events in 181, 182–3, 208, 211–12, 268–9, 270; Fenety on 221–2; Lindsey on 232; A. Mackenzie on 236–9, 240; Hincks on 241–6, 248–9; Dent on 248–51. *See also* Confederation; National interpretation of Canadian history

Canada First 168, 169

Canadian Historical Association 4

Canadian Historical Review (1920–) 4

Canniff, Dr William 256–7

Cape Breton Island 12n; Maritime promoters on 13, 14–15, 16, 21, 23, 26n

Carleton, Sir Guy: attitude toward French Canadians 86–7, 95

Cartier, George-Étienne: Morgan on 171; Taylor on 177; A. Mackenzie on 238

Cartier, Jacques: McMullen on 155; Morgan on 170

Cartwright, Major John 124

Casgrain, Abbé Henri-Raymond 263; *Un Pèlerinage au pays d'Evangéline* (1887) 199, 205; and expulsion controversy 199–206; charges Akins with suppression of evidence 200–6

Cathcart, Sir George 261

Cauchon, Joseph-Édouard: Morgan on 172

Champlain, Samuel de: Heriot on 90; W. Smith, Jr, on 92; McMullen on 155; Morgan on 170; Murdoch's reliance on 194; Hannay's reliance on 218; Kingsford on 264

Chapais, Thomas 205

Charlevoix, Pierre-François-Xavier de: career and writings 87–8; *Histoire et description générale de la Nouvelle France* (1744) 10, 23, 88–90, 92, 194; Maritime promoters' reliance on 10, 23; T.C. Haliburton's reliance on 53, 54; Heriot's reliance on 88–90; W. Smith, Jr's, reliance on 88, 92; Murdoch's reliance on 194

Château Clique 91

Chorography 45, 64, 86, 150

Christie, Robert: upbringing and career 104–7, 114; *Memoirs* 61, 105–6; *A Brief Review of the Political State of Lower Canada* (1818) 107–8; *Memoirs of the Administration of ... Sir Gordon Drummond* (1820) 108–9; *Memoirs of the Administration of ... the Right Honourable the Earl of Dalhousie* (1829) 109–10; *History of the Late Province of Lower Canada* (1848–55) 105–6, 110–14; purpose 106–7, 109, 110–11; method 61, 105–6, 113, 221; changing views on the nature of constitutional conflict in Lower Canada 106–13; influence 113–15; influences Murdoch 61; influences McMullen 160; influences Fenety 221; influences Kingsford 264

Civil War, American 185

Clark, Thomas: and Gourlay 122, 124, 125

Clear Grits 235; McMullen on 164; Morgan on 173; National interpretation and 232; A. Mackenzie on 237–8, 239; Hincks on 245. *See also* Brown, George

Club, The 53, 72

Cochran, Andrew 104

Cochran, Rev. William: 'Memoranda ... with a View to a History of Nova Scotia' 55, 56, 61; critical of T.C. Haliburton 55, 56; and expulsion controversy 186

Cogswell, Fred: on T.C. Haliburton 44

Colby, Charles William 3

Collins, Joseph Edmund: *Life and Times of ... Sir John A. Macdonald* (1883) 240, 240n; on Dent 251

Columbus, Christopher 9

Confederation: National interpretation and 7, 173–4, 231–2, 265–6, 268–9; Taylor on 174–8; McMullen on 179–80; Maritime patriots react to 181, 230; Nova Scotia patriots react to 181, 204,

207–12, 222–3; D. Campbell on 211, 227; New Brunswick patriots react to 213, 214, 222–3; Hannay on 217, 220; Fenety on 221–2; Prince Edward Island patriots react to 223, 227, 228–9; A. Mackenzie on 238–40; Dent on 250; Tuttle on 255

Conolly, Rev. Lorenzo: and the expulsion controversy 187, 187n

Conquest, Norman (1066) 165

Conquest of New France (1760) 73, 84; T.C. Haliburton on 59; Raynal on 87; W. Smith, Jr, on 93; salvation theory of 93–4, 100, 258; Durham on 149; McMullen on 156, 160–1; Morgan on 170; Kingsford on 264

Conservative Party
– of Canada 240, 246; McMullen on 161, 162, 163, 164; Morgan on 168, 172–3; Taylor on 177; A. Mackenzie on 235, 237–9, 240; Hincks on 244–5; Kingsford on 261, 262. See also Liberal-Conservative Party
– of New Brunswick: Fenety on 222

Constitutional Act (1791): English-speaking community of Lower Canada reacts to 85; W. Smith, Jr, on 95; Fleming on 98–9, 100; Christie on 110; cause of grievances in Upper Canada 118; Bidwell on 126; Gourlay on 128; Upper Canadian patriots on 137, 144; Durham on 141, 143, 149; McMullen on 157, 158, 160

Conwell, Russell Herman 217

Cooney, Robert: upbringing and career 65, 72–3; member of The Club 53, 72; A Compendious History of the Northern Part of ... New Brunswick (1832) 72–5

Cooper, Dr Astley Paston 101

Cooper, James Fenimore 197

Cornwallis, Edward: and the founding of Halifax 13, 24

Coureurs de bois: McMullen on 155

Cozzens, Frederick Swartwout 189

Craig, Sir James Henry 106; Fleming on 99; Christie on 107–8, 111; Morgan on 170

Crawley, Henry William 46

Crofton, Francis Blake: and the expulsion controversy 203–5

Cuthbertson, Brian: on Akins 190, 200, 201, 202n, 207n

Dalhousie, George Ramsay, ninth earl of: Christie and 104, 105, 106, 109; Christie on 109, 112; founder of the Literary and Historical Society of Quebec 259

Daly, Sir Dominick: Hincks on 249

Dartmouth, NS, native attack on (June 1750): Maritime promoters on 19, 21

Davin, Nicholas Flood 255n; The Irishman in Canada (1877) 256, 256n, 257

Day, John: An Essay on the Present State of ... Nova-Scotia (c. 1774) 25–6, 33

Denison, George Taylor, III 168, 169

Dent, John Charles: early career 246–7; avoids partisanship 246, 250–1, 254; The Canadian Portrait Gallery (1880–1) 247–9; The Last Forty Years (1881) 248–51, 253, 254; The Story of the Upper Canadian Rebel-

lion (1885) 251–4; *The Gerrard Street Mystery* (1888) 254; on the nature of constitutional conflict in Upper Canada 252–4; on the nature of political conflict in the province of Canada 248–51; on responsible government 249–50, 252–3; collaboration with Hincks 248–50; criticized by King 253–4

DesBarres, Joseph Frederick Wallet: *Letters to Lord ****** (1804) 26n; J. Stewart on 35–6, 37; MacGregor on 81

DesBrisay, Mather Byles: and Akins Historical Prize Essay 209

Deschamps, Isaac: and the expulsion controversy 186

Dickson, William: and Gourlay 122, 124, 125

Discourse: definition of 5; of nineteenth-century Canadian historians 5–8

Discovery, age of 9

Dod, Charles Roger Phipps: compiler of Britain's *Parliamentary Companion* 171

Dod, Robert Phipps: advises Morgan 171

Dorion, Antoine-Amié: Taylor on 177, 178

Double shuffle, the (1858): A. Mackenzie on 238

Douglass, William: T.C. Haliburton's reliance on 53, 54, 55, 59

Du Gua de Monts, Pierre 51

Durham, John George Lambton, first earl of: upbringing and career 138–40; *Report* (1839) 138–51, 152–3, 154, 160–2, 165, 171–2,
183, 184, 221, 224–5, 233, 236, 241–2, 243, 252, 253, 255, 264, 268, 270; purpose 139–41; influenced by Baldwin 140, 141, 143; on the nature of constitutional conflict in Upper Canada 139–40, 141–8; on the nature of constitutional conflict in Lower Canada 139–40, 148–9; on Newfoundland 149–50; on the Maritime colonies 148, 149–50; on the Prince Edward Island land question 224–5; on responsible government 139–40, 141–3, 147–51; sanctions reform interpretation of Upper Canadian history 138–51, 268; inspires National interpretation of Canadian history 152–3, 255, 268, 270; Robinson's reaction to 144, 145; F.B. Head's reaction to 146; Baldwin's reaction to 146–7; influences McMullen 153, 154, 160–1, 165; McMullen on 161–2; Morgan on 171–2; Murdoch on 183, 184; Fenety on 221; influences Lindsey 233; A. Mackenzie on 236; Hincks on 241–2, 243; Kaye on 243; Dent on 252, 253; influences Kingsford 264. *See also* National interpretation of Canadian history; Reform interpretation of Upper Canadian history

Egmont, John Perceval, second earl of 26, 33–4

Elgin, James Bruce, eighth earl of 183; McMullen on 163; Morgan on 172; A. Mackenzie on 236; Hincks on 244, 245

Encyclopaedists 87

English Canadians: French-Canadian stereotype of 96; Laterrière on 101–2

Enlightenment historians 87–8

Escheat movement on Prince Edward Island 223–5

Evangeline: A Tale of Acadie (1847). *See* Longfellow, William Wadsworth

Expulsion controversy, Acadian: T.C. Haliburton on 55, 57n, 58–9, 186–7, 188, 192, 192n, 194, 200–1, 200n, 202, 207; Akins on 57n, 191–2, 194, 196–9, 200–7, 207n; disrupts Nova Scotia patriots 185–207, 212, 229–30; R.G. Haliburton on 186, 189, 192, 192n, 197, 200n; Longfellow's *Evangeline* and 187–90, 187n, 192, 193, 196, 197, 198, 198n, 204, 206–7, 212, 214, 230; Nova Scotia Commission of Public Records and 191–2, 194, 196–9, 200–7; Murdoch on 193, 194–6, 197–8; Parkman on 197–8, 199–201, 205, 206; Acadian/French-Canadian reaction to 198–207, 198n; Casgrain on 199–206; D. Campbell on 211; Hannay on 218

Faed, John: engravings of Evangeline 189

Family Compact 144; political utility of the term 133–5; W.L. Mackenzie on 133–4, 136; Durham on 142–3, 145; McMullen on 158, 160, 162; Morgan on 170, 172; Lindsey on 233; Dent on 252

Fanning, Edmund: J. Stewart on 34–5, 36–7, 79, 81; MacGregor on 81

Fenety, George Edward: early career 220–1; *Political Notes and Observations* (1867) 221–2; on the nature of political conflict in New Brunswick 221–2; *Life and Times of ... Joseph Howe* (1896) 222

Ferland, Jean-Baptiste-Antoine 258

Fisher, Charles: Fenety on 221–2

Fisher, Peter 71, 72, 73; upbringing and career 65–6; *Sketches of New-Brunswick* (1825) 65–70; *Notitia of New-Brunswick* (1838) 68; nature of patriotism 67–8, 69–70, 82; on the timber trade 68–70

Fisheries: J. Stewart on 32; T.C. Haliburton on 49, 60; Maritime patriots on 83; Heriot on 89

Flag of Truce Incident, the (1837): Dent on 253–4

Fleming, John: career 96–7; *Some Considerations* (1810) 85, 97–8, 100; *Political Annals of Lower Canada* (1828) 97–100, 101; on the nature of constitutional conflict in Lower Canada 85, 97–100, 115; influence 100–1; Laterrière reacts to 101, 103, 105; influences Durham 149

Fleming, Sir Sandford: supports Kingsford 263, 263n

Foley, Michael Hamilton: A. Mackenzie on 239

Fraser, Robert 120, 137

Fredericton, NB: Gesner on 78; historical writing in 212–13, 220, 222

Free trade 7, 64, 113, 119, 145

Freeman, Edward Augustus 165

French Canadians 84–5; W. Smith, Jr, on 94–5; Fleming on 97–8; Laterrière on 101–2; Christie on

110–12; Durham on 148–9; McMullen on 154–5, 163–4, 179–80; National interpretation and 166, 231–2; A. Mackenzie on 237, 239; Hincks on 242–6, 249–50; Dent on 249–50; Kingsford on 264. *See also* Acadians

French Revolution 124; Gourlay on 131

Frontenac, Louis de Buade de: Heriot on 90; W. Smith, Jr, on 92; McMullen on 155

Fur trade: Heriot on 89–91; W. Smith, Jr, on 92

Ganong, William Francis 216

Garneau, François-Xavier 263; *Histoire du Canada*, 3rd ed. (1859) translated by Bell as the *History of Canada* (1860) 258

Gaspé: Cooney on 72–5; Christie and 105, 114

Geographical History of Nova Scotia, A (1749): claim to be the first history in English relating to Canada 10; as a promotional pamphlet 10, 12, 17, 19, 21–2; significance of 21–2

George III, King of Great Britain and Ireland: McMullen on 157, 159

George, Sir Rupert: provides T.C. Haliburton with access to public documents 53, 56, 194

Germans: T.C. Haliburton on 49

Gesner, Abraham: career 65, 76; *Remarks on the Geology and Mineralogy of Nova Scotia* (1836) 76; *New Brunswick* (1847) 76–8; nature of patriotism 77–8; on the timber trade 77–8; influence 78, 82

Glenelg, Charles Grant, first baron: Baldwin's letter to, 13 July 1836 135–7, 140–1, 143

Godfrey, John Edwards: Murdoch's correspondence with 193, 195

Goldsmith, Oliver: on the nature of history 56

Gordon, Sir Arthur Hamilton 212

Gore, Francis 118, 124; Gourlay on 130

Gourlay, Robert Fleming 140; upbringing and early career 120–2; mental instability of 121, 126; political role in Upper Canada 122–5, 131–2; *Statistical Account of Upper Canada* (1822) 122, 125–31, 132; *General Introduction* (1822) 125–6, 131–2; agrarian radicalism of 121–3, 130–1, 132–3; changing views on the nature of constitutional conflict in Upper Canada 125–33; McMullen on 158; Dent on 252

Great Coalition of 1864: Morgan and 173; Taylor on 178; A. Mackenzie on 238

Gregg, Rev. William: *Short History of the Presbyterian Church in ... Canada* (1892) 257

Grey, Charles Grey, viscount Howick and second earl 138

Griffiths, Naomi: on Longfellow's *Evangeline* 188, 198n, 206

Gyles, John: Hannay on 217

Haliburton, Mrs George Mordaunt: and the origins of Longfellow's *Evangeline* 187

Haliburton, Robert Grant: Halifax anniversary 'Oration' (1862) 185–6, 189, 192, 192n, 200n; and the expulsion controversy 186, 189, 192, 192n, 197, 200n

Haliburton, Thomas Chandler 67, 187, 211; upbringing and early career 42–4; member of The Club 53; *The Clockmaker* (1836) 42, 43, 62, 63; *A General Description of Nova Scotia* (1823) 42, 43, 44, 44n, 50, 63, 69; *An Historical and Statistical Account of Nova-Scotia* (1829) 42–63, 69–70, 73, 76–7, 123, 182, 184, 186–7, 188, 191, 192, 194, 200–1, 200n, 207n; *Rule and Misrule of the English in America* (1851) 62, 62n; correspondence with Wiswall 42, 44, 45, 46, 47–8, 50, 51, 53; historical method 45–8, 50–7, 60–1, 76–7, 186–7, 194, 218; charged with plagiarism 46n, 53–6, 62, 62n, 207n; nature of patriotism 42–4, 48–50, 60–1, 63, 69–70, 82–3, 182; and the expulsion controversy 55, 57n, 58–9, 186–7, 188, 192, 192n, 194, 200–1, 200n, 202, 207; P. Fisher and 69–70; Gesner and 76–7; Cooney's reliance on 73; Gourlay and 123; influences R.G. Haliburton 182; Longfellow's reliance on 188, 207

Halifax, NS, founding of (1749) 13–14, 15–16; historiographic significance of 19, 21–2, 24, 33, 66, 85; T.C. Haliburton on 52, 58–9, 182; Murdoch on 182; centennial celebration of 181–3, 185; anniversary celebration of 1862 185–6

Halifax Mechanics' Institute 183, 191

Hannay, James (Saladin): early career 216–17, 218–19; 'Sketches of Acadie' (1867–9) 217; *The History of Acadia* (1879) 218, 220; 'History of the Loyalists' (1893) 219; *History of the War of 1812* (1901) 219; *History of New Brunswick* (1909) 220; and the New Brunswick Historical Society 217, 218, 219; and J.W. Lawrence 218–19; nature of patriotism 219–220

Harris, R. Cole 116

Harrison, Samuel Bealey. *See* Harrison-Baldwin Resolutions

Harrison-Baldwin Resolutions (1841): McMullen on 162; Morgan on 171–2

Harvey, Daniel Cobb: on the intellectual awakening of Nova Scotia 41

Hatheway, Calvin Luther: career 65, 75; *The History of New Brunswick* (1846) 75

Hawthorne, Nathaniel: and the origins of Longfellow's *Evangeline* 187, 187n; and the expulsion controversy 189

Head, Sir Edmund Walker: Fenety on 221; A. Mackenzie on 238

Head, Sir Francis Bond 136; *A Narrative* (1839) 146; critical of Durham 146; Robinson on 146; McMullen on 160; Lindsey on 233; Dent on 253

Heriot, George 257, 259; early career 88–9; *The History of Canada* (1804) 89–91; *Travels through the Canadas* (1807) 89–91; on New France 89–91; and W. Smith, Jr 88, 92, 93; and Fleming 97; McMullen's reliance on 154

Hincks, Francis 270; career 240–1;

The Political History of Canada
(1877) 241–5, 248–9; *Reminiscences*
(1884) 241, 245–6; reaction to
Durham's *Report* 146–7; on the
nature of political conflict in
the province of Canada 242–6; on
responsible government 241–6,
249–50; collaboration with Dent
248–50; critical of Kaye 243;
McMullen on 164, 173; A. Mackenzie on 236–8, 239, 240
Hind, Henry Youle: and the expulsion
controversy 203–5
Hodges, James: Taylor on 177
Hodgins, John George: biographer of
Ryerson 235
Holland, Samuel Johannes: survey of
Prince Edward Island 26–7, 31,
85
Hollinger, David A. 5
Howe, Jonas: on Loyalist regiments
215–16
Howe, Joseph 183; nature of patriotism 41, 49; on T.C. Halibur-
ton 50, 62, 82; on Acadia 51–2;
member of The Club 53; as pub-
lisher 62, 72, 184, 220; D. Campbell
on 211; Fenety's biography of
222
Hume, Joseph 233
Hunt, Henry 124
Hurons 90. *See also* Native peoples
Huskisson, William 49
Hutchinson, Thomas: T.C. Halibur-
ton's reliance on 53, 54, 186–7

Île Royale. *See* Cape Breton Island
Île Saint-Jean. *See* Prince Edward
Island
Importance of Settling and Fortifying
Nova Scotia, The (1751): as a pro-
motional pamphlet 12, 14, 19, 20,
21–2, 24
Irish, the: Lewellin on 80; McMullen
on 154; Davin's history of in
Canada 256
Iroquois 90. *See also* Native peoples
Island of St John. *See* Prince Edward
Island

Jack, David Russell: *Centennial Prize*
Essay (1883) 215
Jackson, John Mills 134; *A View of the*
Political Situation of the Province of
Upper Canada (1809) 119; Gourlay's
reliance on 130; McMullen's reli-
ance on 158
Jacobins 102
Jefferson, Thomas: McMullen on 159
Johnson, Samuel 17, 44–5
Judges' Affair, the, in NS: Murdoch
on 208

Kaye, John William: biographer of
Metcalfe 243, 243n
Kellie, Thomas Erskine, ninth earl
of 121
Kempt, Sir James: Christie on 112
Kent, Edward Augustus, Duke of 211
King, John: critical of Dent 253–4
Kingsford, William: upbringing and
career 260–2; sense of professionalism 262; *The History of Canada*
(1887–98) 262–5; purpose 262;
use of the National Archives 262,
263–4; criticized by professional
historians 264–5
Koberger, Anton 190

La Fontaine, Louis-Hippolyte:

McMullen on 163, 179; Morgan on 172; Taylor on 176, 177; A. Mackenzie on 237, 239; Hincks on 242, 244

Lahontan, Louis-Armand de Lom d'Arce de 87

La Jonquière, Jacques-Pierre de Taffanel de 93

Langevin, Hector-Louis 262

La Rochefoucauld-Liancourt, François-Alexandre-Frédéric de La Rochefoucauld, Duc de: *Travels through the United States* (1799), Gourlay's reliance on 128–9, 129–30

La Salle, René-Robert, cavelier de: Heriot on 90

Laterrière, Pierre-Jean de Sales: career 101; *A Political and Historical Account of Lower Canada* (1830) 101–3; on the nature of constitutional conflict in Lower Canada 101–3; reacts to Fleming 101, 103, 105; and Christie 105, 107

La Tour, Charles de Saint-Étienne de: Maritime promoters on 22; Gesner on 77

Lawrence, Charles: Poirier on 206, 206n

Lawrence, Joseph Wilson: career 213; and the New Brunswick Historical Society 213–16; and the Loyalist centennial celebrations at Saint John, NB (1883) 214–15; *Foot-Prints* (1883) 215; *The Judges of New Brunswick* (1907) 215–16; and James Hannay 218–19

Le Canadien (Québec): Christie on 108, 111

Lecky, William Edward Hartpole 165

Le Loutre, Abbé Jean-Louis 93

Le Roy de La Potherie, Claude-Charles 87

Lescarbot, Marc: T.C. Haliburton's reliance on 53, 54; Murdoch's reliance on 194; Hannay's reliance on 218

Lewellin, John Lewellin 81; career 79–80; *Emigration. Prince Edward Island* (1832) 79–80

Liberal Party 246, 261; A. Mackenzie on 235, 238–9, 240; and Hincks 241. *See also* Clear Grits; Liberal-Conservative Party; Reform Party

Liberal-Conservative Party: McMullen on 164; Morgan on 172–3; and National interpretation of Canadian history 231–2, 270; Lindsey on 232; A. Mackenzie on 237–8, 240; Hincks on 244–5; Dent on 250. *See also* Conservative Party; Liberal Party; Reform Party

Lindsey, Charles: career 232; *The Life and Times of Wm. Lyon Mackenzie* (1862) 179n, 232–4, 235; on the nature of constitutional conflict in Upper Canada 232–4, 240; challenges the National interpretation of Canadian history 232, 233–4; partisan nature of 232, 233–4; contributor to Dent's *The Canadian Portrait Gallery* 247–8; critical of Dent 253

Linnaeus 32

Literary and Historical Society of Quebec: *Transactions* of 197, 259–60; *Historical Documents* of 260; agitates

for a national archives 260. *See
also* National Archives of Canada
Little, Otis: background and career
13–14, 15, 24; *The State of Trade
in the Northern Colonies Considered*
(1748) 12, 13–14, 15, 16, 17, 20,
21; as promoter 13–14, 15
Longfellow, William Wadsworth:
Evangeline: A Tale of Acadie (1847)
and the expulsion controversy
187–190, 187n, 192, 193, 196,
197, 198, 198n, 204, 206–7, 212,
214, 230
Louisbourg 13, 26, 186, 194; T.C.
Haliburton on 54, 58
Lower, A.R.M. 182–3
Lower Canada 223, 267; established
85; W. Smith, Jr, on 95–6; Fleming on 85, 97–100, 115, 138,
149; Laterrière on 101–3; Christie on 106–15; union with Upper
Canada 114, 115, 116; Durham
on 139–40, 148–9; McMullen
on 154, 156–62; Morgan on
170
Loyalists
– New Brunswick 63, 85; P. Fisher
on 66, 68, 72; Baillie on 72;
Cooney on 73, 74–5; Hatheway
on 75; Gesner on 77; Loyalist
centennial celebrations at Saint
John, NB (1883) 214–15, 219,
222–3; Jonas Howe on 215–16;
Hannay on 217, 218, 219
– Nova Scotia: T.C. Haliburton on
48–9; R.G. Haliburton on 186;
D. Campbell on 211
– Quebec (Lower Canada): Fleming
on 98; Christie on 107; McMullen on 157

– Quebec (Upper Canada) 116;
Bidwell on 126; Upper Canadian
patriots on 137; McMullen on 158
Lucas, Sir Charles: on Durham 148

Macaulay, Thomas Babington 165
McCarthy, Justin 250
McCulloch, Thomas 49
MacDonald, Capt. John, of Glenala-
dale 28, 36
Macdonald, Sir John Alexander: Mor-
gan on 172; Taylor on 177; A.
Mackenzie on 235, 237–9; Collins's
biography of 240, 251; Hincks
on 240–1, 245; Dent on 249, 250
Macdonald, John Sandfield: Morgan
on 171; Taylor on 178
Macdonald, Sir William Christopher:
endows Kingsford Chair of History at McGill University (1898) 265
McDougall, William: A. Mackenzie
on 239
McGee, D'Arcy 168, 173
MacGregor, John: career 80; *Historical and Descriptive Sketches of the
Maritime Colonies* (1829) 80–1
Mackenzie, Alexander 261; career
235; *The Life and Speeches of Hon.
George Brown* (1882) 235–40; on
the nature of political conflict in
the province of Canada 236–9,
240; partisan nature of 235,
239–40; pessimism 235, 239–40;
Hincks 241
Mackenzie, William Lyon 223, 270;
on Christie 113; provides classic
definition of the 'Family Compact'
133–4, 136, 142; martyr to the
reform cause 134; radicalism of discredited 137, 144; McMullen

on 158, 160, 161, 179n; Morgan on 170; Lindsey's biography of 179n, 232–4, 235, 253; Dent on 253–4; King on 253–4

MacMechan, Archibald McKellar 210

McMullen, John Mercier: early career 153; *Camp and Barrack-Room* (1846) 153; *History of Canada* 1st ed. (1855) 153–67; 2nd ed. (1868) 179–80; influenced by Durham 153, 154, 160–1, 165; on the nature of constitutional conflict in Upper Canada 154, 157–62, 165; on the nature of constitutional conflict in Lower Canada 154, 156–62; on the nature of political conflict in the province of Canada 154, 158, 162–5; on responsible government 160–4; and the reform interpretation of Upper Canadian history 159–60, 165; on the nature of Canadian nationalism 154, 155–6, 163–5; and the National interpretation of Canadian history 165–7; Morgan and 170n, 173; Taylor and 176, 179, 180; Lindsey and 233. *See also* National interpretation of Canadian history

MacNab, Sir Allan Napier 240; Morgan dedicates the *Sketches of Celebrated Canadians* to 168; Morgan on 172–3

Macphail, Sir Andrew 229

Maguire, Abbé Thomas: critical of W. Smith, Jr 95–6

Mair, Charles 168; on Morgan 169

Maitland, Sir Peregrine 132

Malecites 217. *See also* Native peoples

Maroons, the black 211

Martin, Robert Montgomery: on Durham 172

Maseres, Francis 86

Massachusetts: relationship to Nova Scotia 13, 14, 15

Massachusetts Historical Society: and T.C. Haliburton 53, 59, 62n

Maugerville settlement: P. Fisher on 66

Mealing, Stanley: on Gourlay 123

Melbourne, William Lamb, second viscount 139, 140, 143, 146

Menou d'Aulnay, Charles de: Maritime promoters on 22; Gesner on 77

Mercantilism 152; Maritime promoters and 16–17; T.C. Haliburton on 49–50

Metcalfe, Charles Theophilus Metcalfe, first baron: McMullen on 163; Morgan on 171–2; Ryerson on 235; A. Mackenzie on 236; Hincks on 242–4, 245; Kaye's biography of 243; Dent on 249

Micmacs 44n. *See also* Native peoples

Miles, Henry Hopper 259n

Milnes, Sir Robert Shore: Fleming on 99

Minot, George Richards: T.C. Haliburton's reliance on 53, 54, 55, 59

Miramichi fire (1825) 72; Cooney on 74–5

Montcalm, Louis-Joseph de Montcalm, Marquis de: McMullen on 155; Morgan on 170

Montgomery, Sir James William 35, 37

More, James F.: and Akins Historical Prize Essay 209

Morgan, Henry James: upbringing and career 167–8; *Sketches of Cel-*

ebrated Canadians (1862) 168–73;
Canadian Parliamentary Compan-
ion (1862–76) 169; *Dominion Annual*
Register (1878–86) 169; *Bibliotheca*
Canadiensis (1867) 169; method
168–9, 170–1, 170n; on the nature
of political conflict in the province
of Canada 170–3; on the nature
of Canadian nationalism 168–9,
172–3; and Taylor 175, 177–8;
and the National interpretation of
Canadian history 178–9, 234.
See also National interpretation of
Canadian history
Morris, Charles, III 46
Murdoch, Beamish 211; upbringing
and career 182, 184–5; member
of The Club 53; 'Historical Memoirs' 61, 184; *An Essay on ... Im-*
prisonment for Debt, 2nd ed. (1831)
184; *Epitome of the Laws of Nova*
Scotia (1832–3) 184–5; Halifax
centennial 'Oration' (1849) 182–3,
185; *A History of Nova-Scotia*
(1865–7) 192–6, 208; purpose
192–3; correspondence with
Godfrey 193, 195; and Akins
190, 193–4; method 192–4,
218; exploits the Nova Scotia
Commission of Public Records
192–4; nature of patriotism
182–3, 207; rejects the National
interpretation of Canadian
history 182–3, 208; on responsible government 182–3, 184–5,
208; and the expulsion controversy 193, 194–6, 197–8
Murray, James 84; attitude toward
French Canadians 86–7; W.
Smith, Jr, on 95

Murray, Rev. Robert: contributor to
Dent's *The Canadian Portrait*
Gallery 247–8

Napoleon I, Emperor of France:
McMullen on 159
National Archives of Canada (Ottawa):
founding 260; Kingsford and 260–
1, 262, 263–4
National interpretation of Canadian
history: origins and characteristics 152–3, 165–7, 178–80,
268–9, 270–1; McMullen on
153–67, 179–80; Morgan on 168–
73; Taylor on 174–78; links to
the Liberal-Conservative party
164, 172–3, 231–2, 270; Nova
Scotia patriots react to 181–5, 207–
12, 229–30, 231–2, 268–9, 270;
New Brunswick patriots react to
181, 222–3, 229–30, 231–2,
268–9, 270; Prince Edward Island
patriots react to 181, 228–9,
229–30, 231–2, 268–9, 270; undermined by partisans 231–2, 234–5,
265–6, 269, 270–1; Fenety and
220–2; Lindsey and 232–4; A.
Mackenzie and 239–40; Hincks
and 245–6; Dent and 250–1;
Kingsford and 264. *See also* Partisans; Patriots; Reform interpretation of Upper Canadian history
National Policy, the: A. Mackenzie
on 239
Native peoples 9, 116, 258; Maritime
promoters on 10, 21–4, 39;
T.C. Haliburton on 49, 50, 58, 60,
182; P. Fisher on 68; Cooney
on 72, 73, 74; Maritime patriots on
83; missionaries to 87; Heriot

on 89–90; W. Smith, Jr, on 92; McMullen on 154, 155; Murdoch on 182; R.G. Haliburton on 186. *See also* Hurons; Iroquois; Malecites; Micmacs

Navigation Laws 49, 152

Neilson, John 92n, 105

Nelson, Dr Wolfred: Morgan on 170

New, Chester: on Durham 139, 141

New Brunswick 7–8, 12n, 15; T.C. Haliburton on 44; early character of 63–4; patriot history of 64–78, 82–3, 212–23, 229–30, 267–9, 270; Christie calls for the annexation of the Gaspé to 105; Durham on 148, 149–50

New Brunswick Historical Society: founding 212, 213, 213n, 215, 217, 218, 219; purpose 214; *Collections* 216; and the Loyalist centennial celebrations at Saint John (1883) 214–15

New England: relationship to Nova Scotia 13, 14–15, 21, 42; T.C. Haliburton on 57, 58, 60, 60n

Newfoundland 8, 175; Durham on 149

New France: conquest of 84–7; French historians on 87; Charlevoix on 87–8; Heriot on 89–91; W. Smith, Jr, on 92–3; Fleming on 97; liberal critique of 100, 257–9; Durham on 149; McMullen on 154–5, 156; Morgan on 169–70; English-Canadian historians on 257–60; Parkman on 258–9

Nish, Elizabeth: on Dent 251

Normanby, Constantine Henry Phipps, first marquis of 144

Northwest Territories 8, 231, 269

Nostalgia 7; of Maritime patriots 181, 229–30, 269, 270; of Nova Scotia patriots 208–12; of New Brunswick patriots 217, 222–3; of Prince Edward Island patriots 229; of local historians 257; of Canadian historians 265–6, 269, 270

Notman, William: *Portraits of British Americans* (1865–8) 174–5; photograph of Victoria Bridge 177

Nova Scotia 7–8, 12n; promoters of 10–26; intellectual awakening of 41–3; patriot history of 44–63, 82–3, 181–212, 229–30, 267–9, 270; Durham on 148, 149–50; Fenety on 221, 222

Nova Scotia Central Board of Agriculture 46

Nova Scotia Commission of Public Records: origins 56–7, 190, 191–2; and the expulsion controversy 191–2, 194, 196–9, 200–7. *See also* Akins, Thomas Beamish

Nova Scotia Historical Society: and the expulsion controversy 199, 203–5

Nova Scotia Provincial Agricultural Society 52

O'Callaghan, Edmund Bailey: *Documentary History of the State of New-York* (1850–1) 196, 196n

Old Nova Scotia Society 185, 185n

Ouellet, Fernand 96n, 109

Pacific railway scandal 231, 241

Papineau, Louis-Joseph 107; Christie introduces to Parkman 114; McMullen on 161, 164; Morgan on 170

Parkman, Francis: and the expulsion

controversy 197–8, 199–201,
205, 206; influence as a stylist 217;
revives Canadian interest in the history of New France 258–9
Parti canadien (Canadian party) 91;
Fleming on 99; Christie on
106–7, 107–9, 110–13
Parti rouge: McMullen on 164
Partisans 6; characteristics of 7–8,
269, 270–1; Maritime patriots
shun 61, 83, 182, 183, 191, 222–3,
230; Prince Edward Island patriots as 223–5; Lower Canadian
patriots as 84–6, 93–5, 97–100,
100–1, 101–3, 103–4, 113, 115,
138, 139, 149; Upper Canadian
patriots as 118–51, 270; National
interpretation of Canadian history
undermined by 231–2, 234–5,
246, 255, 260, 269, 270–1; Lindsey as 232–4; A. Mackenzie as 235,
239–40; Hincks as 245–6; Dent
shuns 246, 250–1, 254. *See also*
National interpretation of Canadian
history; Patriots
Patriotes: Christie on 114
Patriots 8; characteristics of 6–7,
82–3, 267–9, 269–70; react to
promoters 6–7, 38, 41–3, 64–5,
82–3
– of Nova Scotia 41–63, 82–3, 181–
212, 229–30, 267–8, 268–9, 270;
and the intellectual awakening 41–
3; nature of patriotism 41–4,
48–50, 61, 63, 82–3, 181, 182, 207–
8, 212, 229–30, 267–8, 270; react
to the National interpretation of
Canadian history 181–5, 207–12,
229–30, 231–2, 268–9, 270;
and the expulsion controversy
185–207

– of New Brunswick 63–78, 82–3,
212–23, 229–30, 267–8, 268–9,
270; nature of patriotism 67–8, 69–
70, 71, 74, 77–8, 82–3, 214, 219–
20, 229–30, 267–8, 270; react to the
National interpretation of Canadian history 181, 222–3, 229–30,
231–2, 268–9, 270
– of Prince Edward Island 78–82,
82–3, 223–9, 229–30, 267–8,
268–9, 270; nature of patriotism
78–9, 81–2, 82–3, 224–5, 228–
9, 229–30, 267–8, 270; react to the
National interpretation of Canadian history 181, 228–9, 229–30,
231–2, 268–9, 270; transformed
by the land question 223–5, 228–9
– of Lower Canada 84–115, 268,
270; dilemma of 84–6, 93–5,
97–100, 100–1, 101–3, 103–4, 113,
115, 138, 139, 149
– of Upper Canada 117–51, 268,
270; partisan nature of 118–37,
270; significance of the Rebellions
of 1837–8 for 137–8; significance of the Durham *Report* for
138–46, 270; Reformers' claim to
title of 147, 150–1, 270
– of Canada 152–80, 268–9, 270–1;
patriotism as nationalism 152–3,
165–7, 178–80, 268–9, 270–1; undermined by partisans 231–2,
234–5, 246, 265–6, 269, 270–1.
See also National interpretation of
Canadian history; Partisans; Reform interpretation of Upper Canadian history
Patterson, Rev. George: and Akins
Historical Prize Essay 209
Patterson, Graeme: on the Family
Compact 135

Patterson, Walter: J. Stewart on 34–5, 36

Peel, Sir Robert: Hincks on 242

Perley, Moses Henry 65

Pessimism 165; of Canadian historians 7, 231, 255, 260, 266, 269, 270; of A. Mackenzie 235, 239–40; of Dent 250–1, 254

Peterloo 124

Pichon, Thomas 15n, 26, 31

Pinter, Harold 230

Pitt, William 88; Gourlay on 131

Poirier, Pascal: and the expulsion controversy 206, 206n

Pope, William Henry 227–8

Prevost, Sir George 104; Christie on 108, 111

Prince, Rev. Thomas: T.C. Haliburton's reliance on 54

Prince Edward Island 7–8, 12n; Pichon on 15; conquest of 26; origins of land question on 26–9; J. Stewart on 29–38, 39–40, 48, 78–9, 81, 82, 225, 228; T.C. Haliburton on 44; patriot historians of 78–83, 225–30, 267–9, 270; Durham on 148, 149–50, 224–5. See also Escheat movement; Prince Edward Island land question

Prince Edward Island Land Commission (1860) 227; Sutherland on 226; Bagster on 226

Prince Edward Island land question: origins of 26–9; J. Stewart on 30–8, 78–9, 81, 225, 228; Lewellin on 79–80; MacGregor on 80–1; transforms the nature of island patriotism 223–5, 229; Durham on 224–5; Sutherland on 225–6, 227; Bagster on 226; D. Campbell on 228

Professionalization of history 3–4, 7–8, 216, 220, 262, 264–5, 266, 270–1

Promoters 8, 117, 150; characteristics of 6–7, 9–15, 38–40, 267, 269; credibility of 15–20, 24–6, 38–40, 267; as historians 20–4, 38–40; of the Maritimes 10–26, 38–40; J. Stewart as 29–33, 38, 39; patriots react to 6–7, 38, 41–3, 64–5, 82–3; T.C. Haliburton reacts to 41–7, 50, 51, 60; dilemma of, in Quebec 84–5. See also Patriots

Public Archives of Canada. See National Archives of Canada

Quebec 84–5; Heriot on 91; W. Smith, Jr, on 93–5; Fleming on 97–8; Laterrière on 101–2; Christie on 107, 110; Durham on 149; McMullen on 156–8

Quebec Act (1774) 85; W. Smith, Jr, on 95; Fleming on 98, 100; Christie on 110; Durham on 149; McMullen on 157, 158

Rameau de Saint-Père, François-Edme: and the expulsion controversy 201–2

Rattray, William Jordon: The Scot in British North America (1880–4) 255–6

Raymond, Rev. William Odber 216; on Hannay 220

Raynal, Abbé Guillaume-Thomas-François: A Philosophical and Political History, 3rd ed. (1777) 55, 59, 87, 186; on New France 87; T.C. Haliburton's reliance on 53, 55, 59, 188; Longfellow's reliance on 188; and the expulsion controversy

55, 59, 186, 188, 193; Murdoch criticizes 193

Rebellions of 1837–8 91, 110, 223; Christie on 113, 114; historiographic significance in Upper Canada 137–8; Durham on 139, 140–1; Robinson on 145; F.B. Head on 146; McMullen on 160–1, 162; Morgan on 169; Lindsey on 233–4; A. Mackenzie on 236; Dent on 252–4, 253, 253n; Kingsford and 261

Rebellion Losses Bill (1849) 183; McMullen on 163

Reform Act (1832) 144, 145; Durham and 138

Reform interpretation of Upper Canadian history 223; origins and characteristics 118–20; Gourlay and 122–33; political utility of 133–7, 268, 270; Rebellions of 1837–8 and 137–8; Durham's *Report* and 138–46, 268, 270; as foundation for the National interpretation of Canadian history 147–51, 268, 270; McMullen adopts 159–60, 165. *See also* National interpretation of Canadian history; Patriots; Responsible government

Reform Party of
– Upper Canada 147; McMullen on 160–4; Morgan on 172; Taylor on 176, 177; Lindsey on 232–4; A. Mackenzie on 236–8, 240; Hincks on 241–6; Dent on 249–50. *See also* Clear Grits; Liberal Party; Liberal-Conservative Party
– New Brunswick: Fenety on 222

Responsible government: historiographic significance of in Lower

Canada 113, 115; Christie on 114; political utility of the term 135–7, 270; Baldwin on 135–7, 270; Durham on 139–40, 141–3, 147–51, 268, 270; agitation for in Upper Canada 143–7; key to the National interpretation of Canadian history 147–51, 152–3, 166, 268, 270; McMullen on 160–4; Morgan on 171–2; Maritime patriots and 181–3, 184–5, 212, 230, 269; Murdoch on 182–3, 184–5, 208; D. Campbell on 211; Hannay on 220; Fenety on 220–2; Lindsey on 232–4; A. Mackenzie on 236–7; Hincks on 241–6, 249–50; Dent on 249–50, 252–3; Kingsford on 262, 264. *See also* National interpretation of Canadian history; Reform interpretation of Upper Canadian history

Review of Historical Publicatons Relating to Canada (1896–1918): and the professionalization of historians 4, 264–5; Kingsford criticized in 264–5

Revolutionary Settlement of 1688: Baldwin on 135; Durham on 141; McMullen on 157, 165

Richard, Édouard: and the expulsion controversy 205

Richardson, John Frederick 117, 117n

Richmond, Charles Gordon Lennox, fourth duke of, and Lennox: Christie on 108

Rimmington, Gerald T.: on T.C. Haliburton 46

Robertson, John Ross 246

Robinson, John Beverley: critical of Durham's *Report* 144–5; conversation with Wellington 145; critical of F.B. Head 146; Morgan on 170

Rollo, Andrew Rollo, fifth baron 26

Rolph, Dr John: Lindsey on 233; Dent on 253–4

Royal Proclamation of 1763 84; W. Smith, Jr, on 95; Fleming on 97; McMullen on 156–7

Royal Society of Canada 200, 264

Russell, John Russell, first earl of: October 1839 dispatch of, McMullen on 162; Morgan on 171; Hincks on 241, 244; Kaye on 243; refuses escheat on Prince Edward Island 224

Ryerson, Rev. Egerton: Hodgins's biography of 235; A. Mackenzie on 239

St Basile, NB, Acadian convention at (1908) 206

Saint John, NB: P. Fisher on 69; Gesner on 78; historical writing in 212, 213–20

Saint John Mechanics' Institute 212, 213, 215

Saint John School of historians 213

Sandby, Paul 88

Scots, the: T.C. Haliburton on 49; Rattray's history of in Canada 255–6

Scott, Sir Walter 41, 217

Scrope, G. Poulett: biographer of Sydenham 243, 243n

Selkirk, Thomas Douglas, fifth earl of 35, 37

Seven Years' War: T.C. Haliburton on 54

Shakespeare, William 197

Sherbrooke, Sir John Coape: Christie on 108, 111

Shiels, Andrew: member of The Club 53

Shirley, William: patron of Little and Bollan 13–15; Murdoch critical of 195

Simcoe, John Graves 117–18; Gourlay on 129–30; McMullen on 158

Sinclair, Sir John: *The Statistical Account of Scotland* (1791–9), influence on Gourlay 123, 124

Smiles, Dr Samuel 167

Smith, Adam 25, 123

Smith, Charles C: on Akins 197

Smith, Charles Douglass: MacGregor on 80, 81

Smith, David William 117–18

Smith, Goldwin 246

Smith, Philip Henry: and the expulsion controversy 200–1

Smith, Samuel 123

Smith, Titus 46

Smith, William, Sr 91, 91n; as historian of New York State 92; originator of the salvation theory of the conquest of New France 93; recommends the assimilation of French Canadians 94

Smith, William, Jr 257, 259; career 91; *History of Canada* (1815) 91–6; on New France 92–3; on the nature of constitutional conflict in Quebec (Lower Canada) 93–5; and Heriot 88, 92, 93; and Fleming 97; McMullen's reliance on 154

Smollett, Tobias George: *Continuation of the Complete History of England* (1760–1) 53, 54, 55, 56, 59, 186–7,

188; Goldsmith's review of 56; T.C. Haliburton's reliance on 53, 54, 55, 59, 186–7, 188

Somerset, Edward Adolphus Seymour, eleventh duke of 121

Spence, Thomas 124

Stewart, John: upbringing and career 29–30, 36–8; receiver-general of quit rents 29, 31, 35, 37, 225; *An Account of Prince Edward Island* (1806) 29–38, 48, 78–9, 81, 82, 225, 228; purpose 30, 36–8, 81, 225; on the Prince Edward Island land question 30–8, 78–9, 81, 225, 228; key to historical interpretation 32–3, 38, 39, 48; influence 37–8, 39, 78–9, 82, 225, 228; Sutherland on 225

Stewart, Peter 29, 36

Strachan, Rev. John: and Gourlay 124, 128; Bethune's biography of 235

Stuart, James 104, 106–7

Stubbs, William 165

Sulte, Benjamin 258

Sutherland, Rev. George 228; *A Manual of ... Prince Edward Island* (1861) 225–6; on the Prince Edward Island land question 225–6, 227

Swainson, Donald: on Dent 247, 250, 253n

Sydenham, Charles Edward Poulett Thomson, first baron: McMullen on 162, 163; Morgan on 171; A. Mackenzie on 236, 240; Hincks on 242–4, 245; Kaye on 243; Scrope's biography of 243, 243n

Tanguay, Cyprien 263

Taylor, John Fennings: upbringing and career 174–5; biographical sketches 174–8; on the nature of political conflict in the province of Canada 176–8; on the nature of Canadian nationalism 174–8; and the National interpretation of Canadian history 178–80, 234; and Morgan 175, 177–8; and McMullen 176, 178–80. *See also* National interpretation of Canadian history

Tenant League, the 227

Thompson, John Sparrow 183

Thomson, Dale: on A. Mackenzie 235

Thorpe, Robert 119, 134

Tilley, Sir Samuel Leonard 213; Hannay's biography of 219–20

Timber trade: J. Stewart on 32; T.C. Haliburton on 49, 60; advent in New Brunswick 64; P. Fisher on 68–70; Baillie on 70–1; Atkinson on 70–1; Cooney on 74; Gesner on 77–8; Maritime patriots' suspicion of 83

Tonge, William Cottnam: Murdoch on 208

Treaty of Paris (1763) 26, 84: T.C. Haliburton on 52, 59

Treaty of Utrecht (1713) 12n, 73; T.C. Haliburton on 57; Casgrain on 200

Tupper, Sir Charles 210: D. Campbell on 211

Turcotte, Louis-Philippe: *Le Canada sous l'Union* (1871–2) 248

Tuttle, Charles Richard 254–5

Union, Act of (1840) 114, 115, 116,

175; Durham recommends 148–9; McMullen on 157, 162, 165, 179; and the National interpretation of Canadian history 166; Morgan on 168, 173; Taylor on 176; Hincks on 242

Union Bill (1822): Fleming on 99–100; Laterrière on 103; Christie on 109

United Province of Canada. *See* Canada, Province of

Upper Canada: established 116–17; proposals for union with Lower Canada 99–100, 103, 109; union with Lower Canada 114, 115, 116; origins of constitutional conflict in 117–20, 268; Gourlay on 122–33; Reform interpretation of 117–20, 133–8, 147–51, 223, 270; Durham on 138–51, 154; McMullen on 154, 157–62, 165; Morgan on 170; Lindsey on 232–4; A. Mackenzie on 236; Hincks on 241–2; Dent on 252–4. *See also* Reform interpretation of Upper Canadian history

Van Tassel, David D. 196

Victoria, Queen of Great Britain and Ireland: grants an annuity to Kingsford's widow 265

Wakefield, Edward Gibbon 140

Wallace, Carl Murray 222

War of 1812 42, 104, 116, 119, 133, 137; Laterrière on 102–3; Christie on 107, 108, 111; Bidwell on 126; Gourlay on 130, 132; McMullen on 159; D. Campbell on 211; Hannay on 219

Warkentin, Germaine 18

Wedderburn, Alexander: career 65, 70; *Statistical and Practical Observations, Relative to ... New-Brunswick* (1835) 70–2

Weekes, William 119, 134

Wellington, Arthur Wellesley, first duke of: conversation with Robinson 145

Wentworth, Sir John: Murdoch on 208

Whig interpretation of history 165–6, 165n

Willcocks, Joseph 119, 134

Williams, Mrs Catherine Read: and the expulsion controversy 189, 200

Wilmot, Lemuel Allan: Hannay's biography of 220; Fenety on 221–2

Wilson, John: career 13, 14; *A Genuine Narrative of ... Transactions in Nova Scotia* (c. 1751) 14, 20–1, 25

Windsor, Kenenth N.: on McMullen 166

Winslow, Colonel John: journal of, T.C. Haliburton's reliance on 59, 188; Murdoch critical of 195

Winsor, Justin: *Narrative and Critical History of America* (1884–9) 197

Wiswall, Peleg: on patriotism 42, 82; 'Notes for a History of Nova Scotia' 51, 61; correspondence with T.C. Haliburton 42, 44, 45, 46, 47–8, 50, 51, 53

Withrow, Rev. William Henry 254–5

Wrong, George MacKinnon 3–4; and Kingsford 265

Wyatt, Charles Burton 119

Wynne, John Huddlestone 53

Yeomen, idealization of 267, 268, 269–70; J. Stewart on 39–40; T.C. Haliburton on 48–9, 63, 182; P. Fisher on 67–8, 69–70; Gesner on 78; Maritime patriots on 82–3; W. Smith, Jr, on 94; Fleming on 99; Christie on 107; Upper Canadian patriots on 118, 132–3, 145; Gourlay on 121–2, 131; Baldwin on 136; Durham on 142, 147–8, 150; McMullen on 155–6; Prince Edward Island patriots on 223–4, 228–9. *See also* Agriculture, idealization of

Young, Arthur 121
Young, John (Agricola) 49

Zoltvany, Yves: on the liberal critique of New France 100, 257–8